CHILD ABUSE AND DOMESTIC VIOLENCE

ISSN 1935-1216

CHILD ABUSE AND DOMESTIC VIOLENCE

Melissa J. Doak

INFORMATION PLUS® REFERENCE SERIES
Formerly Published by Information Plus, Wylie, Texas

Detroit • New York • San Francisco • New Haven, Conn • Waterville, Maine • London

Child Abuse and Domestic Violence

Melissa J. Doak
Paula Kepos, Series Editor

Project Editors: Elizabeth Manar, Kathleen
  J. Edgar

Rights Acquisition and Management: Barb
  McNeil, Aja Perales

Composition: Evi Abou-El-Seoud, Mary Beth
  Trimper

Manufacturing: Cynde Bishop

Product Management: Carol Nagel

For product information and technology assistance, contact us at
Gale Customer Support, 1-800-877-4253.
For permission to use material from this text or product,
submit all requests online at **www.cengage.com/permissions.**
Further permissions questions can be e-mailed to
permissionrequest@cengage.com

Cover photograph: Image copyright Oleg Kozlov, Sophy Kozlova, 2008. Used under license from Shutterstock.com.

Gale
27500 Drake Rd.
Farmington Hills, MI 48331-3535

ISBN-13: 978-0-7876-5103-9 (set)   ISBN-10: 0-7876-5103-6 (set)
ISBN-13: 978-1-4144-3371-4   ISBN-10: 1-4144-3371-9

ISSN 1935-1216

This title is also available as an e-book.
ISBN-13: 978-1-4144-5756-7 (set)
ISBN-10: 1-4144-5756-1 (set)
Contact your Gale sales representative for ordering information.

Printed in the United States of America
1 2 3 4 5 6 7 13 12 11 10 09

TABLE OF CONTENTS

PREFACE

Child Abuse and Domestic Violence is part of the *Information Plus Reference Series*. It updates and replaces two earlier titles in the series: *Child Abuse: Betraying a Trust* and *Violent Relationships: Battering and Abuse among Adults*. The purpose of each volume of the series is to present the latest facts on a topic of pressing concern in modern American life. These topics include today's most controversial and studied social issues: abortion, capital punishment, care for the elderly, crime, energy, the environment, health care, immigration, minorities, national security, social welfare, women, youth, and many more. Even though this series is written especially for high school and undergraduate students, it is an excellent resource for anyone in need of factual information on current affairs.

By presenting the facts, it is the intention of Gale, a part of Cengage Learning, to provide its readers with everything they need to reach an informed opinion on current issues. To that end, there is a particular emphasis in this series on the presentation of scientific studies, surveys, and statistics. These data are generally presented in the form of tables, charts, and other graphics placed within the text of each book. Every graphic is directly referred to and carefully explained in the text. The source of each graphic is presented within the graphic itself. The data used in these graphics are drawn from the most reputable and reliable sources, in particular from the various branches of the U.S. government and from recognized organizations. Every effort was made to secure the most recent information available. Readers should bear in mind that many major studies take years to conduct, and that additional years often pass before the data from these studies are made available to the public. Therefore, in many cases the most recent information available in 2009 is dated from 2006 or 2007. Older statistics are sometimes presented as well, if they are of particular interest and no more-recent information exists.

Even though statistics are a major focus of the *Information Plus Reference Series*, they are by no means its only content. Each book also presents the widely held positions and important ideas that shape how the book's subject is discussed in the United States. These positions are explained in detail and, where possible, in the words of those who support them. Some of the other material to be found in these books includes historical background, descriptions of major events related to the subject, relevant laws and court cases, and examples of how these issues play out in American life. Some books also feature primary documents, or have pro and con debate sections giving the words and opinions of prominent Americans on both sides of a controversial topic. All material is presented in an even-handed and unbiased manner; readers will never be encouraged to accept one view of an issue over another.

HOW TO USE THIS BOOK

Every year millions of American adults are subjected to physical, sexual, verbal, or emotional abuse by their intimate partners. Perhaps even more disturbingly, millions of children suffer from such abuse at the hands of the people who are supposed to care for them. Many more have their basic needs neglected. This volume provides the best information available on the prevalence, causes, and devastating consequences of this intimate violence. The challenges that domestic violence and child abuse pose to the legal system are also covered in detail.

Child Abuse and Domestic Violence consists of nine chapters and three appendixes. Each chapter covers an aspect of the problems of child abuse and domestic violence in the United States. For a summary of the information covered in each chapter, please see the synopses provided in the Table of Contents at the front of the book. Chapters generally begin with an overview of the basic facts and background information on the chapter's topic, then proceed to examine subtopics of particular interest. For example, Chapter 8: Rape and Stalking begins by providing the statistics of rape in the United States. Then marital rape is examined in detail, such as the attitudes of this type of rape, its occurrence, and its effects on the victims. Next, acquaintance rape is looked at. This discussion focuses on college rape, the influence of alcohol on sexual assault, sexual coercion, fraternities and athletics, and date rape drugs. Rape among lesbians and gay men is also addressed. The focus then shifts to stalking. This examination looks at who these stalkers are, when the stalking begins, the legal response to stalking, and the legislation that protects against stalking. The chapter concludes by noting the most recent type of stalking: cyberstalking—online harassment and threats that can escalate to frightening and even life-threatening offline violence. Readers can find their way through a chapter by looking for the section and sub-section headings, which are clearly set off from the text. Or, they can refer to the book's extensive index, if they already know what they are looking for.

Statistical Information

The tables and figures featured throughout *Child Abuse and Domestic Violence* will be of particular use to readers in learning about these issues. These tables and figures represent an extensive collection of the most recent and important statistics on child abuse and domestic violence. For example, graphics include statistics on the prevalence of child maltreatment and on the relationship between childhood victimization and later criminality. They also cover the link between alcohol usage and domestic violence and the effectiveness of mandatory arrest policies in preventing additional domestic violence. Gale, a part of Cengage Learning, believes that making this information available to readers is the most important way to fulfill the goal of this book: to help readers understand the issues and controversies surrounding child abuse and domestic violence in the United States and reach their own conclusions about them.

Each table or figure has a unique identifier appearing above it, for ease of identification and reference. Titles for the tables and figures explain their purpose. At the end of each table or figure, the original source of the data is provided.

To help readers understand these often complicated statistics, all tables and figures are explained in the text. References in the text direct readers to the relevant statistics. Furthermore, the contents of all tables and figures are fully indexed. Please see the opening section of the index at the back of this volume for a description of how to find tables and figures within it.

Appendixes

Besides the main body text and images, *Child Abuse and Domestic Violence* has three appendixes. The first is the Important Names and Addresses directory. Here, readers will find contact information for a number of organizations that study child abuse and domestic violence, fight these crimes, or advocate influential positions on these issues. The second appendix is the Resources section, which is provided to assist readers in conducting their own research. In this section, the author and editors of *Child Abuse and Domestic Violence* describe some of the sources that were most useful during the compilation of this book. The final appendix is the detailed index.

ADVISORY BOARD CONTRIBUTIONS

The staff of Information Plus would like to extend its heartfelt appreciation to the Information Plus Advisory Board. This dedicated group of media professionals provides feedback on the series on an ongoing basis. Their comments allow the editorial staff who work on the project to make the series better and more user-friendly. Our top priorities are to produce the highest-quality and most useful books possible, and the Advisory Board's contributions to this process are invaluable.

The members of the Information Plus Advisory Board are:

- Kathleen R. Bonn, Librarian, Newbury Park High School, Newbury Park, California

- Madelyn Garner, Librarian, San Jacinto College–North Campus, Houston, Texas

- Anne Oxenrider, Media Specialist, Dundee High School, Dundee, Michigan

- Charles R. Rodgers, Director of Libraries, Pasco-Hernando Community College, Dade City, Florida

- James N. Zitzelsberger, Library Media Department Chairman, Oshkosh West High School, Oshkosh, Wisconsin

COMMENTS AND SUGGESTIONS

The editors of the *Information Plus Reference Series* welcome your feedback on *Child Abuse and Domestic Violence*. Please direct all correspondence to:

Editors
Information Plus Reference Series
27500 Drake Rd.
Farmington Hills, MI 48331-3535

CHAPTER 1

DEFINING CHILD ABUSE AND DOMESTIC VIOLENCE

DOMESTIC VIOLENCE

"Violence against women" means any act of gender-based violence that results in, or is likely to result in, physical, sexual or psychological harm or suffering to women, including threats of such acts, coercion or arbitrary deprivation of liberty, whether occurring in public or in private life.

—United Nations Declaration on the Elimination of Violence against Women (December 20, 1993)

The United Nations Populations Fund (UNFPA) states in *State of the World Population 2005: The Promise of Equality—Gender Equity, Reproductive Health, and the Millennium Development Goals* (2005, http://www.unfpa .org/swp/2005/pdf/en_swp05.pdf) that "violence against women has long been shrouded in a culture of silence." Sometimes, women as well as men accept gender violence as a normal aspect of relationships between men and women. For these reasons, reliable statistics about violence against women of all kinds, including domestic violence, are hard to come by. However, the UNFPA states that "worldwide, one in three women has been beaten, coerced into unwanted sexual relations, or abused—often by a family member or acquaintance." Clearly, many women suffer as a result of ongoing domestic violence.

So what is domestic abuse? Early definitions focused exclusively on physical assault and bodily injury. For example, the Colorado Advisory Committee to the U.S. Commission on Civil Rights offered this definition of a battered wife in *The Silent Victims: Denver's (CO) Battered Women* (1977): "A woman who has received deliberate, severe and repeated physical injury from her husband, the minimal injury being severe bruising." This definition excluded acts such as pushing, slapping, pinching, or other violent acts perpetrated by husbands on their wives that produced no or minimal bruising, as well as threats of violence.

In their groundbreaking work based on their 1975 National Family Violence Survey and 1985 National Family Violence Resurvey, Murray A. Straus and Richard J. Gelles define spousal violence in specific actions, known as the Conflict Tactics Scale. This scale is now the measure most widely used to estimate the extent of spousal abuse. According to the scale, a spouse can be considered abusive if he or she:

- Throws something at a partner

- Pushes, grabs, or shoves

- Slaps

- Kicks, bites, or hits the partner with a fist

- Hits or tries to hit the partner with an object

- Beats up the partner

- Threatens the partner with a knife or a gun

- Uses a knife or fires a gun at the partner

In the twenty-first century, a broader interpretation is accepted, and abuse is understood to include sexual and psychological actions and harm, such as marital rape and forced isolation. Gelles of the University of Pennsylvania notes in "Estimating the Incidence and Prevalence of Violence against Women: National Data Systems and Sources" (*Violence against Women*, vol. 6, no. 7, July 2000) that feminist scholars and advocates have expanded the definition to encompass issues of intent, control, and power, and conceptualize the problem of violence against women as "coercive control." In "Mission Statement and Purpose" (2005, http://www.ncadv.org/aboutus.php/), the National Coalition against Domestic Violence (NCADV) defines battering as a pattern of behavior through which a person establishes power and control over another person by means of fear and intimidation. The incorrect belief that abusers are entitled to control their partners is a primary cause of aggression and abuse, according to the NCADV.

The NCADV also describes battering as emotional, economic, and sexual abuse, as well as using threats, male privilege, isolation, and various other strategies, including the involvement of the children of those being battered, to maintain power through fear and intimidation. The organization argues it is important to view all these behaviors as battering to understand how verbal threats, a single slap, or an insult can escalate to a life-threatening situation.

In *Multi-country Study on Women's Health and Domestic Violence against Women* (2005, http://www.who.int/gender/ violence/who_multicountry_study/summary_report/summary _report_English2.pdf), an international examination of violence, the World Health Organization (WHO) also defines domestic abuse in terms broad enough to include the wide variety of abuses that occur throughout the world. The WHO's focus is on domestic violence against women by their intimate partners. It includes physically aggressive acts such as slapping, pushing, shoving, hitting with a fist or object, beating, kicking, choking, burning, and threatening with a weapon. It also includes sexually violent acts such as forced sexual intercourse or sexual humiliation.

Historical Recognition of the Problem

Societal recognition of domestic violence as a problem is a recent historical development. Domestic violence has existed in almost all societies throughout history. Vivian C. Fox of Worcester State College notes in "Historical Perspectives on Violence against Women" (*Journal of International Women's Studies*, vol. 4, no. 1, November 2002) that its origin can be traced back centuries to the development of patriarchal and hierarchical systems of authority in which males controlled all property. In such systems women and children were often considered to be the property of men. The growth of male-oriented societies promoted the widely accepted belief in male superiority that in turn formed the basis for women's subordination. This belief in men's domination over women, which was often supported by economic, social, cultural, and religious institutions, made it acceptable for men to use violence as a way to control women.

In fact, U.S. law supported a man's right to control his wife by force until the end of the late nineteenth century. In a landmark Alabama case in 1871, a court found that a husband did not have the right to physically abuse his wife, even "moderately" or with "restraint." In the case, *Fulgham v. State* (46 Ala. 143, 145–146), the court ruled that a married woman deserved protection under the law. The ruling stated:

> A rod which may be drawn through the wedding ring is not now deemed necessary to teach the wife her duty and subjection to the husband. The husband is therefore not justified or allowed by law to use such a weapon, or any other, for her moderate correction. The wife is not to be considered as the husband's slave. And the privilege, ancient though it be, to beat her with a stick, to pull her hair, choke her, spit in her face or kick her about the floor, or to inflict upon her like indignities, is not now acknowledged by our law.

Also in 1871 the Massachusetts Supreme Court rejected a husband's manslaughter defense that he had a right to chastise his wife for drunkenness. He had hit his inebriated wife several times on the cheek and temple; she had fallen as a result, hit her head, and died. In this case, *Commonwealth v. McAfee* (108 Mass. 458, 461), the Massachusetts Supreme Court announced that "beating or striking a wife violently with the open hand is not one of the rights conferred on a husband by the marriage, even if the wife be drunk or insolent."

Even though the Alabama and Massachusetts cases declared that husbands did not have the right to physically chastise their wives, no criminal penalties were yet attached to physical abuse. In fact, in a case three years earlier, *State v. Rhodes* (61 N.C. 453 [1868]), the North Carolina Supreme Court declared that even though a husband's whipping of his wife "would without question have constituted a battery if the subject of it had not been the defendant's wife," it refused to convict him of assault and battery, ruling that if domestic assaults were prosecuted, "the evil of publicity would be greater than the evil involved in the trifles complained of." In 1910 the U.S. Supreme Court ruled in *Thompson v. Thompson* (218 U.S. 611) that a wife had no cause for action on an assault and battery charge against her husband because it "would . . . open the doors of the courts to accusations of all sorts of one spouse against the other, and bring into public notice complaints for assault, slander, and libel." Thus, even though court decisions affirmed that a husband could no longer legally beat his wife, in almost all cases a battered wife in the early twentieth century still had no legal recourse against her husband.

The ruling of a 1962 landmark case changed the legal consequences of physical abuse of a spouse. In *Self v. Self* (58 Cal. 2d 683), the California Supreme Court agreed with earlier rulings, stating that a spouse's right to sue would "destroy the peace and harmony of the house." Despite this finding, the court observed that this outdated assumption was based "on the bald theory that after a husband has beaten his wife there is a state of peace and harmony left to be disturbed." Therefore, "one spouse may maintain an action against the other" for physical abuse. However, despite this ruling, by 1965 there had been little change. Jurisdictions throughout the United States continued to ignore the needs of battered women.

Social and Legal Recognition of Domestic Violence

Public perception and handling of domestic violence began to change significantly in the 1970s. The consciousness-raising groups that emerged during the rise of U.S. feminism in the 1960s and 1970s provided small groups of women a place to discuss their problems. Their analysis of personal problems—including domestic violence—allowed them to understand women's collective oppression. This became the basis for feminist collective action.

Efforts to aid battered women arose out of this feminist consciousness. The first battered women's shelter was founded in 1971 by Erin Pizzey in London, England. Pizzey, the recognized founder of the modern women's shelter movement, wrote the first book to be published on domestic violence, *Scream Quietly or the Neighbours Will Hear*, in 1974. Authors in the United States followed suit. In 1975 Susan Brownmiller's *Against Our Will: Men, Women, and Rape*, a book about the politics and sociology of rape, was published, and in 1976 Del Martin's book *Battered Wives* appeared, focusing specifically on violence within marriage functioning as part of male dominance of women.

In 1973 the first battered women's shelter in the United States opened in St. Paul, Minnesota. By 1976 there were four hundred programs for battered women operating in the United States. EMERGE, the first treatment program for male offenders, opened in Boston, Massachusetts, in 1977, and the following year many states enacted laws to protect victims of domestic violence. More than a decade later, in 1988, the U.S. surgeon general declared domestic abuse the leading health hazard to women in the United States. According to the National Network to End Domestic Violence, in *Domestic Violence Counts: 07—A 24-Hour Census of Domestic Violence Shelters and Services across the United States* (January 30, 2008, http://nnedv.org/docs/Census/DVCounts2007/DVCounts07_Report_Color.pdf), in 2007, 1,949 battered women's shelters were operating around the nation. On September 25, 2007, 25,321 domestic violence victims were living in those emergency shelters; another 27,882 adults and children received non-residential services during that twenty-four-hour period. However, the annual $175 million federal budget for shelter services was eliminated in the reauthorization of the Violence against Women Act in 2005.

LEGISLATION AGAINST VIOLENCE. In 1994 the Violence against Women Act granted female victims of violence, including battered women, federal civil rights protection. The civil rights section of the act was tested in 1999, when Christy Brzonkala filed a civil suit after being raped by two football players from Virginia Polytechnic Institute. In a five-to-four decision in *United States v. Morrison et al.* (529 U.S. 598 [2000]), the U.S. Supreme Court ruled that Congress could not enact a federal civil remedy "for victims of gender-motivated violence." Individuals who committed crimes motivated by a gender bias, the Court ruled, could not be held accountable at the federal level.

Congress passed a revised act in October 2000—Victims of Trafficking and Violence Protection Act—which included the sections Strengthening Law Enforcement to Reduce Violence against Women, Strengthening Services to Victims of Violence, Limiting the Effects of Violence on Children, and Strengthening Education and Training to Combat Violence against Women. As a result of the Supreme Court ruling, the new legislation made no mention of women's civil rights. The Violence against Women Act was renewed again in 2005. Even though spouse abuse is illegal in the United States and women may now sue their abusers for damages at the state level, battering continues. Many women still feel helpless and trapped in abusive relationships, unable to tell others about their problems and unsure of where to seek and obtain help.

EMOTIONAL AND PSYCHOLOGICAL ABUSE

Most definitions of abuse focus on situations where physical violence was either threatened or used. Official definitions used by the courts and police do not include emotional or psychological abuse, although domestic violence activists believe that such abuse can cause as much long-term damage as acts of physical violence.

Emotional and psychological abuse is usually harder to define than physical abuse, where bruises and scars are clearly evident. Almost all couples scream and shout at one another at some point. However, abuse is distinguished from the heated arguments that may follow in the course of otherwise healthy relationships because the abuser uses words to project power over a mate in a demeaning way. This can produce serious and often debilitating emotional or psychological consequences.

Some domestic violence researchers and counselors equate emotional abuse with the Amnesty International definition of psychological torture, which includes verbal degradation, denial of power, isolation, monopolizing perceptions, and threats to kill. Health and social service workers who counsel victims cite emotional violence as one of several factors that may paralyze women, preventing them from fleeing dangerous and abusive relationships. Furthermore, they believe that early identification of and effective intervention to end emotional abuse may prevent this emotional violence from escalating to physical abuse.

Verbal Aggression

Murray A. Straus and Stephen Sweet examine in "Verbal/Symbolic Aggression in Couples: Incidence Rates and Relationships to Personal Characteristics" (*Journal of Marriage and the Family*, vol. 54, no. 2, May 1992) verbal aggression as it was measured in the 1985 National Family Violence Resurvey data. The researchers find no significant differences between man-to-woman and woman-to-man verbal aggression. They also find that when one partner engages in verbal aggression, the other responds in similar fashion. Women report more abuse regardless of who initiated the aggression, but Straus and Sweet are unable to determine whether men minimize the incidence of verbal abuse or women exaggerate it.

Straus and Sweet do not find any correlation between race or socioeconomic status and verbal aggression. They do find, however, a link between age and levels of abuse, indicating that verbal aggression declines with age regardless of how much conflict there is in a relationship. Their analysis also reveals a direct connection between alcohol consumption and verbal aggression—the more often men drink excessively, the more likely they are to be verbally abusive. Similarly, the more women use drugs, the greater the probability of verbal abuse. For men, however, drug use does not significantly affect the use of verbal abuse. Straus and Sweet caution that their research reveals a correlation between alcohol use and abuse, but not causation—in other words, it demonstrates a relationship between alcohol consumption and abuse, but it does not show whether men and women drink to provide themselves with excuses for abusive behavior or whether drinking causes their aggression.

Several studies find that verbal aggression is a precursor to physical violence. For example, Margareta Hydén of Stockholm University notes in "Verbal Aggression as a Prehistory of Woman Battering" (*Journal of Family Violence*, vol. 10, no. 1, March 1995) that in most cases a "verbal fight," with the aim of making one's partner feel worthless, precedes battering. Another study finds that verbal aggression is correlated with physical violence during pregnancy. Lynda M. Sagrestano et al. find in "Demographic, Psychological, and Relationship Factors in Domestic Violence during Pregnancy in a Sample of Low-Income Women of Color" (*Psychology of Women Quarterly*, vol. 28, no. 4, December 2004) that pregnant women who report verbal aggression in their relationship are more likely to report physical abuse than their nonpregnant peers. In addition, those who report verbal aggression experience more frequent physical abuse than women who do not experience verbal aggression.

ABUSE OF IMMIGRANT WOMEN

The U.S. Census Bureau (February 2005, http://www .census.gov/population/socdemo/foreign/ppl-176/tab01-1.pdf) reports that in 2004 the total foreign-born population was 34.2 million people, or 11.9% of the U.S. population. Over seventeen million were female. In "Immigrant Victims of Domestic Violence" (2007, http://www.ncadv .org/files/immigrantvictims.pdf), the NCADV explains that abuse of immigrant women remains a problem in the United States. Immigrant women may be at increased risk for various reasons, including a cultural background that teaches them to defer to their husband. Many foreign-born women cannot speak English and do not know their rights in the United States. Others fear they will be deported or have no resources or support systems to turn to for help.

Many immigrants come from cultures that are radically different from the predominant American society.

FIGURE 1.1

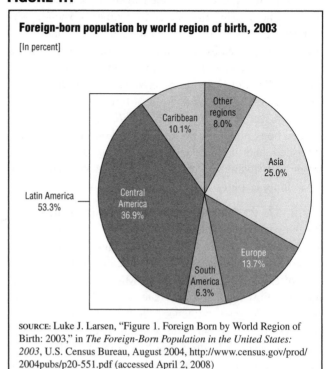

Foreign-born population by world region of birth, 2003

[In percent]

SOURCE: Luke J. Larsen, "Figure 1. Foreign Born by World Region of Birth: 2003," in *The Foreign-Born Population in the United States: 2003*, U.S. Census Bureau, August 2004, http://www.census.gov/prod/ 2004pubs/p20-551.pdf (accessed April 2, 2008)

Among the Asian-American community, including Chinese, Vietnamese, Indians, Koreans, Thais, and Cambodians, there is widespread acceptance of male dominance and a belief that the community and the family take priority over the individual. The NCADV finds high levels of battering among some Asian groups; up to 60% of Korean women have been battered by their husbands. Asian women are generally raised to accept their husband's dominance and are more reluctant to complain or to leave than their native-born counterparts. Complicating the problem of domestic abuse in this community are strong family ties, economic dependency, the stigma of divorce, and the fear of bringing shame to the family.

In March 2003 Asian immigrants accounted for 25% of all immigrants in the United States. (See Figure 1.1.) By 2007 Asian immigrants made up 36.4% of all legal permanent residents, more than any other group. (See Table 1.1.) Some Asian women have been sent to the United States as the result of arranged marriages to live with men they barely know. In some cases the husband takes his immigrant bride's money, jewelry, and passport, leaving her completely dependent on him. The abusive husband often tells his immigrant wife that if she leaves him, she will be deported. For some abused immigrant women, it would be worse to return home and bring shame on their family than to stay with the abusive partner.

The NCADV provides in "Immigrant Victims of Domestic Violence" the "Power and Control Wheel," which shows some of the distinctive ways that battered

TABLE 1.1

Legal permanent residents by region and country of birth, fiscal years 2005–07

Region/country of birth	2007 Number	2007 Percent	2006 Number	2006 Percent	2005 Number	2005 Percent
Total	**1,052,415**	**100.0**	**1,266,129**	**100.0**	**1,122,257**	**100.0**
Region:						
Africa	94,711	9.0	117,422	9.3	85,098	7.6
Asia	383,508	36.4	422,284	33.4	400,098	35.7
Europe	120,821	11.5	164,244	13.0	176,516	15.7
North America	339,355	32.2	414,075	32.7	345,561	30.8
Caribbean	119,123	11.3	146,768	11.6	108,591	9.7
Central America	55,926	5.3	75,016	5.9	53,463	4.8
Other North America	164,306	15.6	192,291	15.2	183,507	16.4
Oceania	6,101	0.6	7,384	0.6	6,546	0.6
South America	106,525	10.1	137,986	10.9	103,135	9.2
Unknown	1,394	0.1	2,734	0.2	5,303	0.5
Country:						
Mexico	148,640	14.1	173,749	13.7	161,445	14.4
China, People's Republic	76,655	7.3	87,307	6.9	69,933	6.2
Philippines	72,596	6.9	74,606	5.9	60,746	5.4
India	65,353	6.2	61,369	4.8	84,680	7.5
Colombia	33,187	3.2	43,144	3.4	25,566	2.3
Haiti	30,405	2.9	22,226	1.8	14,524	1.3
Cuba	29,104	2.8	45,614	3.6	36,261	3.2
Vietnam	28,691	2.7	30,691	2.4	32,784	2.9
Dominican Republic	28,024	2.7	38,068	3.0	27,503	2.5
Korea	22,405	2.1	24,386	1.9	26,562	2.4
El Salvador	21,127	2.0	31,782	2.5	21,359	1.9
Jamaica	19,375	1.8	24,976	2.0	18,345	1.6
Guatemala	17,908	1.7	24,133	1.9	16,818	1.5
Peru	17,699	1.7	21,718	1.7	15,676	1.4
Canada	15,495	1.5	18,207	1.4	21,878	1.9
United Kingdom	14,545	1.4	17,207	1.4	19,800	1.8
Brazil	14,295	1.4	17,903	1.4	16,662	1.5
Pakistan	13,492	1.3	17,418	1.4	14,926	1.3
Ethiopia	12,786	1.2	16,152	1.3	10,571	0.9
Nigeria	12,448	1.2	13,459	1.1	10,597	0.9
All other countries	358,185	34.0	462,014	36.5	415,621	37.0

SOURCE: Kelly Jefferys and Randall Monger, "Table 3. Legal Permanent Resident Flow by Region and Country of Birth: Fiscal Years 2005 to 2007," in *U.S. Legal Permanent Residents: 2007*, U.S. Department of Homeland Security, Office of Immigration Statistics, March 2008, http://www.dhs.gov/xlibrary/assets/ statistics/publications/LPR_FR_2007.pdf (accessed April 2, 2008).

immigrant women are abused. These include threatening to report a woman to the U.S. Citizenship and Immigration Service, to have her deported, to report her for working "under the table," or to withdraw her petition to legalize her immigration status—these are just a few of the many actions an abusive husband may take to control his immigrant wife.

U.S. immigration laws have unintentionally contributed to the problem of abuse among immigrant women. The Immigration Marriage Fraud Amendment was passed in 1986 in an attempt to prevent immigrants from illegally obtaining resident status through a sham marriage to a U.S. citizen. The amendment requires that spouses, usually husbands, petition for conditional resident status for an undocumented mate. Conditional status lasts a minimum of two years, during which time the couple must remain married. If the marriage dissolves, the immigrant loses conditional status and may be deported. As a result, some wives become prisoners of abusive husbands for as long as the husbands control their conditional resident

status. Even though the law was amended under the Immigration Act of 1990 to permit a waiver of conditional status if the immigrant could prove battery or extreme cruelty, the initial filing for conditional status was still in the hands of the husband; if the abuse began before he filed the petition, the woman had no legal recourse.

The reauthorization of the Violence against Women Act in 2005 provides some added supports for battered immigrant women. First, the act provides a way for women to petition for residency status for themselves and for their children. A woman's spouse will not be informed she is applying. In addition, the act provides a way for deportation proceedings against a battered woman to be canceled, waiving deportation and granting legal permanent residency.

New policies and programs for recent immigrant victims have emerged across the country, especially in cities with large immigrant populations. To improve the communication between immigrants and the criminal justice system, authorities have made special efforts to reach immigrant victims by hiring multicultural criminal justice staffs and providing informational materials in a variety of languages. Police representatives also attend meetings of immigrant groups, and members of the immigrant community are encouraged to serve as representatives on citizen police committees.

The most effective programs to assist immigrant women acknowledge the multiple pressures these women face during their efforts to become oriented and to assimilate themselves into American culture and society. Along with cultural shock and language barriers, many immigrant women confront racism, class prejudice, and sexism. Fear of authority and the absence of social networks and support services compound the problem. Finally, recognizing that many women are brought to the United States in circumstances that increase the likelihood of victimization—as mail-order brides, child care workers, or prostitutes—is an important step in stemming the crisis and addressing the crime of domestic violence. According to Marianne Sullivan et al., in "Participatory Action Research in Practice: A Case Study in Addressing Domestic Violence in Nine Cultural Communities" (*Journal of Interpersonal Violence*, vol. 20, no. 8, August 2005), promising experimental programs include battered immigrant women in the development of programs to address battering in their communities.

DOMESTIC ABUSE AMONG SAME-SEX COUPLES

One aspect of domestic abuse that has often been overlooked is violence between men or women in same-sex relationships. There are few published studies about this subject, but Vernon R. Wiehe finds in *Understanding Family Violence: Treating and Preventing Partner, Child, Sibling, and Elder Abuse* (1998) that comparable forms of physical, emotional, and sexual abuse occur between partners in same-sex relationships as in heterosexual relationships, with one difference: emotional abuse may also include threats to disclose a partner's homosexuality. In "Domestic Violence and Lesbian, Gay, Bisexual and Transgender Relationships" (2008, http://www.ncadv.org/files/lgbt.pdf), the NCADV concurs, emphasizing as well that lesbian, gay, bisexual, and transsexual individuals face an additional barrier to getting help: fear of discrimination or bias from police or other helping professionals.

Researchers have difficulty comparing the prevalence of partner abuse in same-sex relationships with abuse rates in heterosexual relationships because they must rely on nonrandom, self-selected samples. These studies consider people who identify themselves as homosexuals and agree to participate in a research study as opposed to randomly selected people representative of the population to be studied. As with other forms of abuse, same-sex partners may underreport violence in their relationships. Most of the published studies examining same-sex domestic violence indicate that abuse rates for same-sex couples are about the same as for heterosexual couples, such as Michelle Aulivola's "Outing Domestic Violence: Affording Appropriate Protections to Gay and Lesbian Victims" (*Family Court Review*, vol. 42, no. 1, January 2004) and Stephen S. Owen and Tod W. Burke's "An Exploration of the Prevalence of Domestic Violence in Same Sex Relationships" (*Psychological Reports*, vol. 95, no. 1, August 2004). Even though violence rates against heterosexual and homosexual women are comparable, violence against homosexual men is higher than against heterosexual men.

How Abusive Are Women in Same-Sex Relationships?

Some survey data about women in same-sex relationships indicate that lesbians endure considerable levels of physical and sexual violence. In "Physical and Sexual Violence Experienced by Lesbian and Heterosexual Women" (*Violence against Women*, vol. 6, no. 1, 2000), Linda A. Bernhard of Ohio State University observes that even though lesbians, like other women, are at risk of abuse from past and present male partners, they also risk being victimized by their female partners. In addition, because lesbians are also at greater risk for hate crimes than their heterosexual counterparts, they may experience more violence than heterosexual women.

Based on the limited research done on lesbian violence, it appears the risk factors for abuse are similar to those of heterosexual women. Dependency and jealousy, both of which may precipitate abuse in heterosexual relationships, have been identified as the main contributors of lesbian battering. The literature about this subject also contains clinical case studies and anecdotal reports indicating that lesbian batterers may also abuse alcohol or drugs, feel powerless, and suffer from low self-esteem. Kimberly F. Balsam and Dawn M. Szymanski state in "Relationship Quality and Domestic Violence in Women's Same-Sex Relationships: The Role of Minority Stress" (*Psychology of Women Quarterly*, vol. 29, no. 3, September 2005) that the stress specific to living as a lesbian correlates with both domestic violence perpetration and victimization.

Battered lesbians are among the most underserved population of battered women, often facing denial from other lesbians and homophobia from health and social service providers. Many states have narrow definitions of family that deny gay and lesbian victims of domestic violence the possibility of seeking family court orders of protection or other civil redress. Complicating the issue are the myths that same-sex violence is mutual and the abuse is not as dangerous or destructive as heterosexual abuse. In fact, according to health care providers, the abuse is rarely mutual and can be just as harmful as abuse in heterosexual relationships.

WHAT IS CHILD ABUSE?

Child abuse is often a secret. Since the 1960s, however, Americans have become increasingly aware of the problems of child abuse and neglect (together referred to as child maltreatment). In *Juvenile Court Statistics* (1966), the Children's Bureau of the U.S. Department of Health, Education, and Welfare (and later of the U.S. Department of Health and Human Services [HHS]) reports that in 1963 some 150,000 young victims of maltreatment were reported to authorities. The HHS notes in *Child Maltreatment 2006* (2008, http://www.acf.hhs.gov/programs/cb/pubs/cm06/cm06.pdf) that in 2006 state child protective services (CPS) agencies received about 3.3 million reports of child maltreatment involving about 6 million children.

Official Definitions of Child Abuse

Official definitions of child abuse and neglect differ among institutions, government agencies, and experts. The Child Abuse Prevention and Treatment Act (CAPTA) Amendments of 1996, which amended the 1974 CAPTA and was reauthorized by the Keeping Children and Families Safe Act of 2003, defines child maltreatment in this way: "The term 'child abuse and neglect' means, at a minimum, any recent act or failure to act, on the part of a parent or caretaker [including any employee of a residential facility or any staff person providing out-of-home care who is responsible for the child's welfare], which results in death, serious physical or emotional harm, sexual abuse or exploitation, or an act or failure to act which presents an imminent risk of serious harm."

It should be noted that this definition of child abuse and neglect specifies that only parents and caregivers can be considered perpetrators of child maltreatment. Abusive or negligent behavior by other people—strangers or people known to the child—is considered child assault.

Based on a concern that severely disabled newborns may be denied medical care, CAPTA also considers as child abuse and neglect the "withholding of medically indicated treatment," including appropriate nutrition, hydration, and medication, which in the treating physician's medical judgment would most likely help, improve, or correct an infant's life-threatening conditions. However, this definition does not refer to situations where treatment of an infant, in the physician's medical judgment, would prolong dying, would be ineffective in improving or correcting all the infant's life-threatening conditions, or would be futile in helping the infant to survive. In addition, this definition does not include circumstances where the infant is chronically or irreversibly comatose.

CAPTA Defines Four Main Types of Child Maltreatment

PHYSICAL ABUSE. Physical abuse is the infliction of physical injury through punching, beating, kicking, biting, burning, shaking, or otherwise harming a child. Physical abuse is generally a willful act. There are cases, however, in which the parent or caretaker may not have intended to hurt the child. In such cases, the injury may have resulted from overdiscipline or corporal (physical) punishment. Nonetheless, if the child is injured, the act is considered abusive.

SEXUAL ABUSE. Sexual abuse includes fondling a child's genitals, intercourse, incest, rape, sodomy, exhibitionism, and commercial exploitation through prostitution or the production of pornographic materials.

PSYCHOLOGICAL ABUSE. Psychological abuse includes acts or omissions by the parents or by other caregivers that have caused, or could cause, serious behavioral, cognitive, emotional, or mental disorders. In some cases of emotional abuse, the abuser's action alone, without any harm evident in the child's behavior or condition, is enough cause for intervention by CPS agencies. For example, the parent or caregiver may use extreme or bizarre forms of punishment, such as locking a child in a dark room or closet.

Other forms of psychological abuse may involve more subtle acts, such as habitual scapegoating (erroneously blaming the child for things that go wrong), belittling, or rejection of the child. For CPS to intervene, demonstrable harm to the child is often required. Even though any of the types of child maltreatment may be found separately, different types of abuse often occur in combination with one another. Emotional abuse is almost always present when other types are identified.

CHILD NEGLECT. Child neglect is an act of omission characterized by failure to provide for the child's basic needs. Neglect can be physical, educational, or emotional. Physical neglect includes failure to provide food, clothing, and shelter; refusal of or delay in seeking health care (medical neglect); abandonment; inadequate supervision; and expulsion from the home or refusal to allow a runaway to return home. Educational neglect includes permitting chronic truancy, failure to enroll a child of mandatory school age in school, and failure to take care of a child's special educational needs. Emotional neglect includes substantial inattention to the child's need for affection, failure to provide needed psychological care, spousal abuse in the child's presence, and allowing drug or alcohol use by the child. It is important to distinguish between willful neglect and a parent's or a caretaker's failure to provide the necessities of life because of poverty or cultural factors.

State Definitions

CAPTA provides a foundation for states by identifying a minimum set of acts or behaviors that characterize child abuse and neglect. Each state, based on CAPTA guidelines, has formulated its own definitions of the different types of child maltreatment. State definitions, however, such as of neglect, may be unclear. For example, states typically define neglect as the failure to provide adequate food, clothing, shelter, or medical care. About one-fifth of states do not have a separate definition for neglect. Moreover, most CPS agencies consider recent incidence of neglect instead of patterns of behavior that may constitute chronic, or continuing, neglect.

States define child abuse and neglect in three areas in state statutes: reporting laws for child maltreatment, criminal codes, and juvenile court laws. Most state laws also include exceptions, such as religious exemptions, corporal punishment, cultural practices, and poverty.

A DESCRIPTION OF MALTREATED CHILDREN

Perhaps better than a definition of child abuse is a description of the characteristics likely to be exhibited by abused and/or neglected children. The Child Welfare Information Gateway indicates in the fact sheet "Recognizing Child Abuse and Neglect: Signs and Symptoms" (2007, http://www.childwelfare.gov/pubs/factsheets/signs.cfm) that, in general, abused or neglected children are likely to have at least several of the following characteristics:

- Their behavior or school performance suddenly changes

- They do not get medical attention for problems brought to their parents' attention

- They seem always watchful for something bad to happen

- They are passive and withdrawn

- They do not want to go home

  Physically abused children may:

- Have unexplained burns, bruises, or broken bones

- Have fading bruises still visible after a school absence

- Seem frightened of parents

- Shrink away from adults

- Report injury at the hands of a parent or other caregiver

  Sexually abused children may:

- Exhibit difficulty walking or sitting

- Suddenly refuse to change for gym

- Begin having nightmares or wetting the bed

- Show sudden appetite changes

- Demonstrate bizarre or precocious sexual knowledge or behavior

- Contract a venereal disease, especially before age fourteen

- Run away from home

- Report sexual abuse at the hands of a parent or other caregiver

Victims of Physical Abuse

Victims of physical abuse often display bruises, welts, cuts, burns, fractures, lacerations, strap marks, swellings, and/or lost teeth. Even though internal injuries are seldom detectable without a hospital examination, anyone in close contact with children should be alert to multiple injuries, a history of repeated injuries, new injuries added to old ones, and untreated injuries, especially in young children. Older children may attribute an injury to an improbable cause, lying for fear of parental retaliation. Younger children, however, may be unaware that a severe beating is unacceptable and may admit to having been abused.

Physically abused children frequently have behavior problems. Especially among adolescents, chronic and unexplainable misbehavior should be investigated as possible evidence of abuse. Some children come to expect abusive behavior as the only kind of attention they can receive and so act in a way that invites abuse. Others break the law deliberately to come under the jurisdiction of the courts to obtain protection from their parents. Children who have been abused may display a wide array of behavioral problems including being aggressive or disruptive, displaying intense anger or rage, being self-abusive or self-destructive, feeling suicidal or depressed, using drugs or alcohol, fearing certain adults, and avoiding being at home.

Parents who inflict physical abuse generally provide necessities, such as adequate food and clean clothes. Nevertheless, they get angry quickly, have unrealistic expectations of their children, and are overly critical and rejecting of their children. According to the Child Welfare Information Gateway, parents who physically abuse their children may offer unconvincing explanations for injuries to their children, describe their children in negative ways (e.g., as evil), or use harsh physical discipline with their children. Abusive parents may avoid other parents in the neighborhood and school activities. Even though many abusive parents have been mistreated as children themselves and are following a learned behavior, an increasing number who physically abuse their own children do so under the influence of alcohol and drugs.

Victims of Physical Neglect

Physically neglected children are often hungry. They may go without breakfast and have neither food nor money for lunch. Some take the lunch money or food of other children and hoard whatever they obtain. They show signs of malnutrition, such as paleness, low weight relative to height, lack of body tone, fatigue, inability to participate in physical activities, and lack of normal strength and endurance.

These children are usually irritable. They show evidence of inadequate home management and are unclean and unkempt. Their clothes are often torn and dirty. They may lack proper clothing for different weather conditions, and their school attendance may be irregular. In addition, these children may frequently be ill and may exhibit a generally repressed personality, inattentiveness, and withdrawal. They are in obvious need of medical attention for correctable conditions such as poor eyesight, poor dental care, and lack of immunizations.

A child who suffers physical neglect also generally lacks parental supervision at home. For example, the child may frequently return from school to an empty house. Even though the need for adult supervision is, of course, relative to both the situation and the maturity of the child, it is generally held that a child younger than age twelve should always be supervised by an adult or at least have immediate access to a concerned adult when necessary.

Parents of neglected children are either unable or unwilling to provide appropriate care. Some neglectful parents are mentally deficient. Most lack knowledge of parenting skills and tend to be discouraged, depressed, and frustrated with their role as parents. Alcohol or drug abuse may also be involved.

Medical neglect refers to the parents' failure to provide medical treatment for their children, including immunizations, prescribed medications, recommended surgery, and other intervention in cases of serious disease or injury. Some situations involve a parent's inability to care for a child or lack of access to health care. Other situations involve a parent's refusal to seek professional medical care, particularly because of a belief in spiritual healing.

Victims of Emotional Abuse and Neglect

Emotional abuse and neglect are as serious as physical abuse and neglect, although this condition is far more difficult to describe or identify. Emotional maltreatment often involves a parent's lack of love or failure to give direction and encouragement. The parent may either demand far too much from the child in the area of academic, social, or athletic activity or withhold physical or verbal contact, indicating no concern for the child's successes and failures and giving no guidance or praise.

Emotional maltreatment can be hard to determine. Is the child's abnormal behavior the result of maltreatment on the part of the parents, or is it a result of inborn or internal factors? Stuart N. Hart et al. list in "Psychological Maltreatment" (John E. B. Myers et al., eds., *The APSAC Handbook on Child Maltreatment*, 2002) problems associated with emotional abuse and neglect, including poor appetite, lying, stealing, enuresis (bed-wetting), encopresis (passing of feces in unacceptable places after bowel control has been achieved), low self-esteem, low emotional responsiveness, failure to thrive, inability to be independent, withdrawal, suicide, and homicide.

GOVERNMENT SERVICES FOR CHILDREN

The federal government first provided child welfare services with the passage of the Social Security Act of 1935. Under Title IV-B (Child Welfare Services Program) of the act, the Children's Bureau received funding for grants to states for "the protection and care of homeless, dependent, and neglected children and children in danger of becoming delinquent." Before 1961 Title IV-B was the only source of federal funding for child welfare services.

The 1961 Social Security Amendment Act required each state to make child welfare services available to all children. The law further required states to provide coordination between child welfare services (under Title IV-B) and social services (under Title IV-A, or the Social Services program), which served families on welfare. The law also revised the definition of child welfare services to include the prevention and remedy of child abuse. In 1980 Congress created a separate Foster Care program under Title IV-E.

Title IV-A became Title XX (Social Services Block Grant) in 1981, giving states more options regarding the types of social services to fund. As of 2008, child abuse prevention and treatment services remained an eligible category of service.

State Programs That Help Children at Risk

Under Title IV-B Child Welfare Services (Subpart 1) and Promoting Safe and Stable Families (Subpart 2) programs, families in crisis receive preventive intervention so that children will not have to be removed from their home. If this cannot be achieved, children are placed in foster care until they can be reunited with their family. If reunification is not possible, parents' rights are terminated and the children are made available for adoption.

States use the Foster Care (Title IV-E) program funds for the care of foster children and for the training of foster parents, program personnel, and private-agency staff. Title XX funds provide services such as child day care, CPS, information and referral, counseling, and employment.

The Child Abuse Reporting Network

In 1961 C. Henry Kempe, a pediatric radiologist, and his associates proposed the term *battered child syndrome* at a symposium on the problem of child abuse held under the auspices of the American Academy of Pediatrics. The term refers to the collection of injuries sustained by a child as a result of repeated mistreatment or beatings. The following year, Kempe et al. published the landmark article "The Battered Child Syndrome" (*Journal of the American Medical Association*, vol. 181, July 7, 1962). The term *battered child syndrome* developed into the word *maltreatment*, encompassing not only physical assault but also other forms of abuse, such as malnourishment, failure to thrive, medical neglect, and sexual and emotional abuse.

Kempe et al. proposed that physicians be required to report child abuse. According to the National Association of Counsel for Children, by 1967, after Kempe et al.'s findings had gained general acceptance among health and welfare workers and the public, forty-four states had passed legislation that required the reporting of child abuse to official agencies, and the remaining six states had voluntary reporting laws. This was one of the most rapidly accepted pieces of legislation in U.S. history. Initially, only doctors were required to report and then only in cases of "serious physical injury" or "nonaccidental injury." In the twenty-first century, all the states have laws that require not only doctors but also most professionals who serve children to report all forms of suspected abuse and either require or permit any citizen to report child abuse.

One of the reasons for the lack of prosecution of early child abuse cases was the difficulty in determining whether a physical injury was a case of deliberate assault or an accident. In the latter part of the twentieth century, however, doctors of pediatric radiology were able to determine the incidence of repeated child abuse through sophisticated developments in x-ray technology. These advances allowed radiologists to see more clearly things such as subdural hematomas (blood clots around the brain resulting from blows to the head) and abnormal fractures. As a result, these advances brought about more recognition in the medical community of the widespread incidence of child abuse, along with growing public condemnation of abuse.

FEDERAL CHILD ABUSE LEGISLATION

The passage of CAPTA in 1974 created the National Center on Child Abuse and Neglect (NCCAN), which developed standards for handling reports of child maltreatment. NCCAN also established a nationwide network of CPS and served as a clearinghouse for information and research on child abuse and neglect.

Since 1974 CAPTA has been amended a number of times. (See Figure 1.2.) In 1978 the Child Abuse Prevention and Treatment and Adoption Reform Act promoted the passage of state laws providing comprehensive adoption assistance. The act provided grants to encourage the adoption of children with special needs and broadened the definition of abuse, adding a specific reference to sexual abuse and exploitation to the basic definition. That same year the Indian Child Welfare Act was also enacted to reestablish tribal jurisdiction over the adoption of Native American children.

In response to the public outcry about the placement of an increasing number of children in foster care, Congress passed the Adoption Assistance and Child Welfare Act of 1980, with the goal of promoting family reunification. In 1988 the Child Abuse Prevention, Adoption, and Family Services Act replaced the original 1974 CAPTA, mandating, among other things, the establishment of a system to collect national data on child maltreatment.

In 1994 Congress passed the Multiethnic Placement Act, directing states to actively recruit adoptive and foster families, especially for minority children waiting a long time for placement in a home. Pursuant to the Child Abuse Prevention and Treatment Act Amendments of 1996, NCCAN was abolished. Its functions have subsequently been consolidated within the Children's Bureau.

By 1997 the federal government had realized that reuniting abused children with their families did not always work in the best interests of the children. Congress revisited the "reasonable efforts" for family reunification originally mandated by the 1980 Adoption Assistance and Child Welfare Act. Under the 1997 Adoption and Safe Families Act, "reasonable efforts" was clarified to mean the safety of the child comes first. States were directed to indicate circumstances under which an abused child should not be returned to the parents or caretakers.

According to the U.S. General Accounting Office (now the U.S. Government Accountability Office [GAO]), in *Foster Care: Recent Legislation Helps States Focus on Finding Permanent Homes for Children, but Long-Standing Barriers Remain* (June 2002, http://www.gao.gov/new.items/d02585.pdf), despite the legislation's intention to increase adoptions of children from foster care, many barriers to obtaining permanent families for foster children remain. In *African American Children in Foster Care: Additional HHS Assistance Needed to Reduce the Proportion in Care* (July 2007, http://www.gao.gov/new.items/d07816.pdf), the GAO explains that these barriers can be especially difficult for African-American children to surmount. The lack of flexibility in state use of funding means that services to support the extended families of children in kinship care or legal guardians contribute to longer stays of African-American children in foster care.

The Promoting Safe and Stable Families Amendments of 2001 was enacted partly to address the rising number of children with incarcerated parents. The law provided a grant program for creating mentoring services for these children. The law also created a new program to assist youth aging out of foster care, helping them pursue an education or vocational training.

In 2003 CAPTA received reauthorization through 2008 under the Keeping Children and Families Safe Act. The law, among other things, directs more comprehensive training of CPS personnel, including a mandate that they inform alleged abusers, during the first contact, of the nature of complaints against them. The law calls

FIGURE 1.2

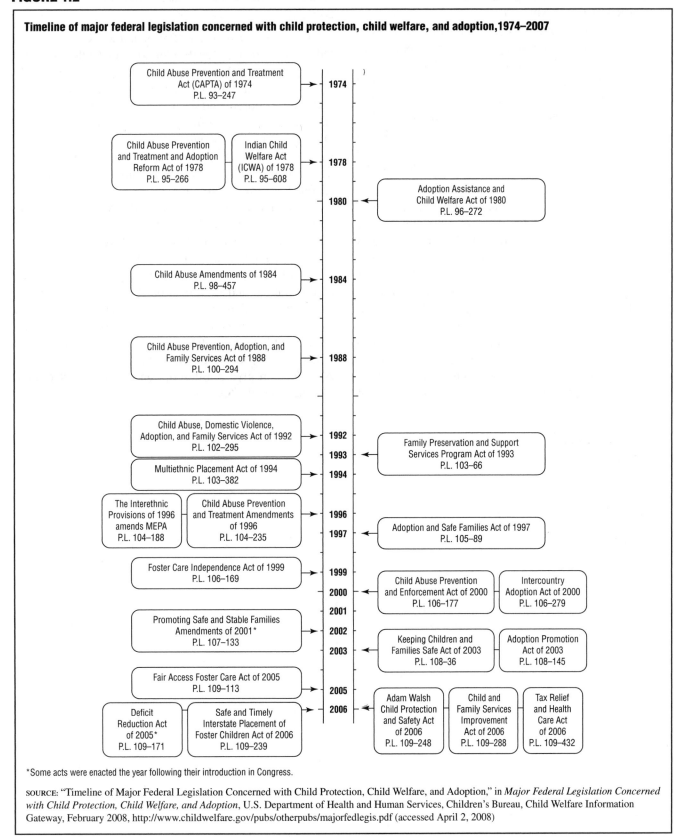

Timeline of major federal legislation concerned with child protection, child welfare, and adoption,1974–2007

Child Abuse Prevention and Treatment Act (CAPTA) of 1974 P.L. 93–247	→ 1974
Child Abuse Prevention and Treatment and Adoption Reform Act of 1978 P.L. 95–266 / Indian Child Welfare Act (ICWA) of 1978 P.L. 95–608	1978
	1980 ← Adoption Assistance and Child Welfare Act of 1980 P.L. 96–272
Child Abuse Amendments of 1984 P.L. 98–457	→ 1984
Child Abuse Prevention, Adoption, and Family Services Act of 1988 P.L. 100–294	→ 1988
Child Abuse, Domestic Violence, Adoption, and Family Services Act of 1992 P.L. 102–295	→ 1992
	1993 ← Family Preservation and Support Services Program Act of 1993 P.L. 103–66
Multiethnic Placement Act of 1994 P.L. 103–382	→ 1994
The Interethnic Provisions of 1996 amends MEPA P.L. 104–188 / Child Abuse Prevention and Treatment Amendments of 1996 P.L. 104–235	1996
	1997 ← Adoption and Safe Families Act of 1997 P.L. 105–89
Foster Care Independence Act of 1999 P.L. 106–169	→ 1999
	2000 ← Child Abuse Prevention and Enforcement Act of 2000 P.L. 106–177 / Intercountry Adoption Act of 2000 P.L. 106–279
	2001
Promoting Safe and Stable Families Amendments of 2001* P.L. 107–133	→ 2002
	2003 ← Keeping Children and Families Safe Act of 2003 P.L. 108–36 / Adoption Promotion Act of 2003 P.L. 108–145
Fair Access Foster Care Act of 2005 P.L. 109–113	→ 2005
Deficit Reduction Act of 2005* P.L. 109–171 / Safe and Timely Interstate Placement of Foster Children Act of 2006 P.L. 109–239	→ 2006 ← Adam Walsh Child Protection and Safety Act of 2006 P.L. 109–248 / Child and Family Services Improvement Act of 2006 P.L. 109–288 / Tax Relief and Health Care Act of 2006 P.L. 109–432

*Some acts were enacted the year following their introduction in Congress.

SOURCE: "Timeline of Major Federal Legislation Concerned with Child Protection, Child Welfare, and Adoption," in *Major Federal Legislation Concerned with Child Protection, Child Welfare, and Adoption*, U.S. Department of Health and Human Services, Children's Bureau, Child Welfare Information Gateway, February 2008, http://www.childwelfare.gov/pubs/otherpubs/majorfedlegis.pdf (accessed April 2, 2008).

for child welfare agencies to coordinate services with other agencies, including public health, mental health, and developmental disabilities agencies. The law also directs the collection of data for the Fourth National Incidence Study of Child Abuse and Neglect, which was completed in February 2008. Congressional hearings to reauthorize CAPTA were begun in June 2008, which was set to expire by the end of the year.

Federal Legislation Dealing with the Prosecution of Child Abusers

Until 1995 none of the federal child abuse legislation dealt specifically with punishing sex offenders. In December of that year, with growing acknowledgment of and concern about sex crimes against minors, Congress passed the Sex Crimes against Children Prevention Act of 1995. The act increased penalties for those who sexually exploit children by engaging in illegal conduct, or for exploitation conducted via the Internet, as well as for those who transport children with the intent to engage in criminal sexual activity.

Three years later Congress enacted the Protection of Children from Sexual Predators Act of 1998 that, among other things, established the Morgan P. Hardiman Child Abduction and Serial Murder Investigative Resources Center (CASMIRC) as part of the National Center for the Analysis of Violent Crime. The purpose of CASMIRC (2008, http://www.fbi.gov/hq/isd/cirg/ncavc.htm) is "to provide investigative support through the coordination and provision of federal law enforcement resources, training, and application of other multidisciplinary expertise, and to assist federal, state, and local authorities in matters involving child abductions, mysterious disappearances of children, child homicide, and serial murder across the country."

Congress passed the Prosecutorial Remedies and Other Tools to End the Exploitation of Children Today Act in April 2003. Among other things, the act establishes a national Amber Alert Program for recovering abducted children and provides that there will be no statute of limitations for sex crimes and abduction of children. (Under previous laws, the statute of limitations expired when the child turned twenty-five years old.) The law also provides for severe penalties for sex tourism (defined as travel with the intent to engage in illicit sexual conduct) and the denial of pretrial release for suspects in federal child rape or kidnap cases. The Amber Alert Program is named after Amber Hagerman of Texas, who was abducted and murdered in 1996. She was nine years old. A witness notified police, giving a description of the vehicle and the direction it had gone, but police had no way of alerting the public. Amber Alert allows for a voluntary partnership between law enforcement, broadcasters, and transportation agencies, whereby an urgent bulletin is broadcast to the public via the Emergency Alert System giving a description of the abducted child and the alleged abductor.

CHAPTER 2
DETECTING, MEASURING, AND PREVENTING CHILD ABUSE

INCIDENCE AND PREVALENCE OF CHILD MALTREATMENT

Statistics on child abuse are difficult to interpret and compare because there is little consistency in how information is collected. The definitions of abuse vary from study to study, as do the methods of counting incidents of abuse. Some methods count only reported cases of abuse. Some statistics are based on estimates projected from a small study, whereas others are based on interviews.

Researchers use two terms—*incidence* and *prevalence*—to describe the estimates of the number of victims of child abuse and neglect. Andrea J. Sedlak and Diane D. Broadhurst, in the *Third National Incidence Study of Child Abuse and Neglect* (*NIS-3*; 1993, http://www.childwelfare.gov/systemwide/statistics/nis.cfm#n3), define incidence as the number of new cases occurring in the population during a given period. The incidence of child maltreatment is measured in terms of incidence rate: the number of children per one thousand children in the U.S. population who are maltreated annually. Surveys based on official reports by child protective services (CPS) agencies and community professionals are a major source of incidence data. (The term *child protective services* refers to the services provided by an agency authorized to act on behalf of a child when his or her parents are unable or unwilling to do so. This term is also often used to refer to the agency itself.)

Prevalence, as defined by Sedlak and Broadhurst, refers to the total number of child maltreatment cases in the population at a given time. Some researchers use lifetime prevalence to denote the number of people who have experienced child maltreatment at least once in their life. To measure the prevalence of child maltreatment, researchers use self-reported surveys of parents and child victims. Examples of self-reported surveys are the landmark 1975 National Family Violence Survey and the 1985 National Family Violence Resurvey conducted by Murray A. Straus and Richard J. Gelles.

Studies based on official reports depend on a number of things happening before an incident of abuse is recorded. The victim must be seen by people outside the home, and these people must recognize that the child has been abused. Once they have recognized this fact, they must then decide to report the abuse and find out where to report it. Once CPS receives and screens the report for appropriateness, it can then take action.

For the data to become publicly available, CPS must keep records of its cases and then pass them on to a national group that collects these statistics. Consequently, final reported statistics are understated estimates—they are valuable as indicators but not definitive findings. Because of the hidden nature of child abuse, it is unlikely that statistics that accurately reflect the true scope of maltreatment will ever be available.

COLLECTING CHILD MALTREATMENT DATA

The 1974 Child Abuse Prevention and Treatment Act (CAPTA) created the National Center on Child Abuse and Neglect (NCCAN) to coordinate nationwide efforts to protect children from maltreatment. As part of the former U.S. Department of Health, Education, and Welfare, NCCAN commissioned the American Humane Association to collect data from the states.

In 1985 the federal government stopped funding data collection on child maltreatment. In 1986 the National Committee to Prevent Child Abuse (NCPCA; now called Prevent Child Abuse America) picked up where the government left off. The NCPCA started collecting detailed information from the states on the number of children abused, the characteristics of child abuse, the number of child abuse deaths, and the changes in the funding and extent of child welfare services.

In 1988 the Child Abuse Prevention, Adoption, and Family Services Act replaced the 1974 CAPTA. The new law mandated that NCCAN, as part of the U.S. Department of Health and Human Services (HHS), establish a national data collection program on child maltreatment. In 1990 the National Child Abuse and Neglect Data System (NCANDS), which was designed to fulfill this mandate, began collecting and analyzing child maltreatment data from CPS agencies in the fifty states and the District of Columbia. NCANDS has since conducted the Child Maltreatment survey annually. The most recent survey as of August 2008 was *Child Maltreatment 2006* (2008, http://www.acf.hhs.gov/programs/cb/pubs/cm06/cm06.pdf), which was published by the Administration for Children, Youth, and Families (ACYF).

The data collected from states are not completely reliable because each state has its own method of gathering and classifying the information. Most states collect data on an incident basis; that is, they count each time a child is reported for abuse or neglect. If the same child is reported several times in one year, each incident is counted. Consequently, the reported number of incidents of child maltreatment may be greater than the reported number of maltreated children that CPS is aware of.

As part of the 1974 CAPTA, Congress also mandated NCCAN to conduct a periodic National Incidence Study of Child Abuse and Neglect (NIS). Data on maltreated children are collected not only from CPS agencies but also from professionals in community agencies, such as law enforcement, public health, juvenile probation, mental health, and voluntary social services, as well as from hospitals, schools, and day care centers. The NIS is the single most comprehensive source of information about the incidence of child maltreatment in the United States, because it analyzes the characteristics of child abuse and neglect that are known to community-based professionals, including those characteristics not reported to CPS. The most recent study is *NIS-3*. This report is based on a nationally representative sample of more than 5,600 professionals in 842 agencies serving 42 counties. *NIS-3* includes not only child victims investigated by CPS agencies but also children seen by community institutions (such as day care centers, schools, and hospitals) and other investigating agencies (such as public health departments, police, and courts). In addition, victim counts were unduplicated, which means that each child was counted only once. Data collection for *NIS-4* began in 2004; reports were scheduled to be published beginning in late 2008.

Definition Standards

NIS-3 uses two standardized definitions of abuse and neglect:

- Harm Standard—requires that an act or omission must have resulted in demonstrable harm to be considered as abuse or neglect

- Endangerment Standard—allows children who had not yet been harmed by maltreatment to be counted in the estimates of maltreated children if a non-CPS professional considered them to be at risk of harm or if their maltreatment was substantiated or indicated in a CPS investigation

VICTIMS OF MALTREATMENT
Rates of Victimization

CPS DATA. According to the ACYF, in *Child Maltreatment 2006*, in 2006 CPS agencies received an estimated 3.3 million referrals, or reports, alleging the maltreatment of about 6 million children, which may include some children who were reported and counted more than once. States may differ in the rates of child maltreatment reported. States differ not only in definitions of maltreatment but also in the methods of counting reports of abuse. Some states count reports based on the number of incidents or the number of families involved, rather than on the number of children allegedly abused. Other states count all reports to CPS, whereas others count only investigated reports.

NCANDS explains that in 2006 forty states, Puerto Rico, and the District of Columbia submitted child-level data for each report of alleged maltreatment. Child-level data include, among other things, the demographics about the children and the perpetrators, types of maltreatment, and dispositions (findings after investigation or assessment of the case). Another nine states reported more general maltreatment data. CPS agencies screened in (accepted for further assessment or investigation) 2 million (61.7%) referrals out of a total of 3.3 million referrals. Overall, the rate of maltreatment referrals (whether accepted for further investigation or not) ranged from 20.9 per 1,000 children in Arizona to 128 per 1,000 children in West Virginia. (See Table 2.1.)

In 2006 an estimated 885,245 children were victims of maltreatment in the United States. (See Table 2.2.) Even though the rate of investigations (dispositions) per 1,000 children rose from 43.8 in 2002 to 47.8 in 2006, the rate of victimization actually fell from 12.3 per 1,000 children in 2002 to 12.1 in 2006. (See Figure 2.1.)

Table 2.2 shows the types of maltreatment children suffered in 2006. In that year, 567,787 of the 885,245 children found maltreated by CPS agencies had suffered neglect. Another 19,180 suffered medical neglect. In other words, 66.3% of all children found to be maltreated by CPS agencies in 2006 were victims of neglect or medical neglect. Another 142,041 (16%) children were victims of physical abuse, 78,120 (8.8%) children were victims of sexual abuse, 58,577 (6.6%) children were victims of emotional, or psychological, maltreatment, and another 133,978 (15.1%) children experienced other types of maltreatment,

TABLE 2.1

Screened-in and screened-out referrals, by state, 2006

State	Child population	Screened-in referrals		Screened-out referrals		Total referrals	
		Number	%	Number	%	Number	Rate
Alabama	1,114,301	18,651	61.0	11,923	39.0	30,574	27.4
Alaska	181,434	5,755	57.3	4,283	42.7	10,038	55.3
Arizona	1,628,198	33,743	98.9	359	1.1	34,102	20.9
Arkansas	691,186	25,524	66.0	13,163	34.0	38,687	56.0
California	9,532,614	225,911	67.1	110,684	32.9	336,595	35.3
Colorado	1,169,301	30,940	48.1	33,437	51.9	64,377	55.1
Connecticut	818,286	28,500	64.3	15,798	35.7	44,298	54.1
Delaware	203,366	5,781	80.1	1,434	19.9	7,215	35.5
District of Columbia	114,881	5,077	90.0	567	10.0	5,644	49.1
Florida	4,021,555	151,822	59.4	103,957	40.6	255,779	63.6
Georgia	2,455,020	60,277	80.1	14,938	19.9	75,215	30.6
Hawaii							
Idaho	394,280	6,662	43.5	8,639	56.5	15,301	38.8
Illinois							
Indiana	1,577,629	44,051	65.5	23,239	34.5	67,290	42.7
Iowa	710,194	25,029	59.0	17,428	41.0	42,457	59.8
Kansas	695,837	15,164	49.9	15,206	50.1	30,370	43.6
Kentucky	999,531	48,649	76.0	15,404	24.0	64,053	64.1
Louisiana							
Maine	280,994	5,949	32.3	12,485	67.7	18,434	65.6
Maryland							
Massachusetts	1,448,884	38,918	59.7	26,274	40.3	65,192	45.0
Michigan							
Minnesota	1,257,264	19,846	34.9	36,956	65.1	56,802	45.2
Mississippi	759,405	16,888	71.5	6,733	28.5	23,621	31.1
Missouri	1,416,592	47,491	51.0	45,563	49.0	93,054	65.7
Montana	217,848	8,737	69.2	3,883	30.8	12,620	57.9
Nebraska	445,033	13,109	53.3	11,507	46.7	24,616	55.3
Nevada	634,520	14,982	73.7	5,339	26.3	20,321	32.0
New Hampshire	297,625	6,640	41.5	9,359	58.5	15,999	53.8
New Jersey							
New Mexico	508,930	16,565	52.7	14,888	47.3	31,453	61.8
New York							
North Carolina							
North Dakota	144,934	3,791	50.2	3,763	49.8	7,554	52.1
Ohio							
Oklahoma	894,034	36,673	57.5	27,092	42.5	63,765	71.3
Oregon	856,259	25,598	42.1	35,140	57.9	60,738	70.9
Pennsylvania							
Puerto Rico	1,018,651	13,797	48.0	14,964	52.0	28,761	28.2
Rhode Island	237,451	8,441	66.3	4,298	33.7	12,739	53.6
South Carolina	1,039,653	16,712	67.2	8,143	32.8	24,855	23.9
South Dakota	194,681	3,908	27.4	10,352	72.6	14,260	73.2
Tennessee	1,442,593	61,886	67.5	29,734	32.5	91,620	63.5
Texas	6,493,965	166,728	82.9	34,382	17.1	201,110	31.0
Utah	791,198	20,206	65.3	10,734	34.7	30,940	39.1
Vermont	133,389	2,315	18.9	9,916	81.1	12,231	91.7
Virginia	1,806,847	29,141	51.7	27,219	48.3	56,360	31.2
Washington	1,526,267	35,698	46.8	40,578	53.2	76,276	50.0
West Virginia	389,071	23,210	46.6	26,575	53.4	49,785	128.0
Wisconsin	1,312,530	29,029	57.2	21,751	42.8	50,780	38.7
Wyoming	121,794	2,437	46.2	2,842	53.8	5,279	43.3
Total	**51,978,025**	**1,400,231**		**870,929**		**2,271,160**	
Percent			61.7		38.3		
Weighted rate							43.7
Number reporting	42	42	42	42	42	42	42

SOURCE: "Table 2–1. Screened-in and Screened-out Referrals, 2006," in *Child Maltreatment 2006*, U.S. Department of Health and Human Services, Administration on Children, Youth, and Families, 2008, http://www.acf.hhs.gov/programs/cb/pubs/cm06/cm06.pdf (accessed May 20, 2008)

including abandonment, congenital drug addiction, and threats to harm them. Some children were victims of more than one type of maltreatment.

CPS statistics indicate that child physical and sexual abuse declined in the 1990s. In "Child Maltreatment Trends in the 1990s: Why Does Neglect Differ from Sexual and Physical Abuse?" (*Child Maltreatment*, vol. 11, no. 2,

2006), Lisa M. Jones, David Finkelhor, and Stephanie Halter of the University of New Hampshire use corroborating evidence to argue that there is evidence for a real decline in child abuse, not only a decline in reported cases. For example, the National Crime Victimization Survey shows a large decline in sexual assaults against teenagers; the Minnesota Student Survey of Children shows a 22% decline in sexual abuse between 1992 and

TABLE 2.2

Types of maltreatment sustained by victims, by state, 2006

State	Victims	Neglect		Physical abuse		Medical neglect		Sexual abuse	
		Number	%	Number	%	Number	%	Number	%
Alabama	9,378	3,911	41.7	3,666	39.1	2,448	26.1		
Alaska	3,481	2,007	57.7	496	14.2	152	4.4	158	4.5
Arizona	4,469	3,156	70.6	1,063	23.8	319	7.1		
Arkansas	9,180	5,194	56.6	1,729	18.8	526	5.7	2,400	26.1
California	89,500	64,206	71.7	11,076	12.4	6,584	7.4		
Colorado	10,862	7,585	69.8	1,715	15.8	168	1.5	1,024	9.4
Connecticut	10,174	9,285	91.3	633	6.2	389	3.8	452	4.4
Delaware	1,933	842	43.6	372	19.2	49	2.5	165	8.5
District of Columbia	2,759	1,595	57.8	405	14.7	165	6.0	152	5.5
Florida	134,567	43,542	32.4	15,182	11.3	2,195	1.6	4,621	3.4
Georgia	39,802	28,365	71.3	4,124	10.4	1,998	5.0	1,642	4.1
Hawaii	2,045	323	15.8	233	11.4	27	1.3	93	4.5
Idaho	1,651	1,249	75.7	264	16.0	11	0.7	78	4.7
Illinois	27,756	18,876	68.0	6,857	24.7	746	2.7	4,974	17.9
Indiana	20,925	15,247	72.9	2,609	12.5	519	2.5	4,346	20.8
Iowa	14,589	11,581	79.4	1,888	12.9	146	1.0	789	5.4
Kansas	2,630	586	22.3	524	19.9	69	2.6	670	25.5
Kentucky	19,833	17,299	87.2	2,186	11.0			801	4.0
Louisiana	12,472	9,845	78.9	3,179	25.5			903	7.2
Maine	3,548	2,428	68.4	631	17.8			376	10.6
Maryland									
Massachusetts	36,151	33,096	91.5	4,677	12.9	981	2.7		
Michigan	27,148	20,637	76.0	4,728	17.4	463	1.7	1,227	4.5
Minnesota	7,623	5,779	75.8	1,194	15.7	112	1.5	920	12.1
Mississippi	6,272	3,725	59.4	1,249	19.9	196	3.1	934	14.9
Missouri	7,108	3,674	51.7	2,220	31.2	2,039	28.7		
Montana	1,775	1,248	70.3	214	12.1	30	1.7	149	8.4
Nebraska	6,160	5,239	85.0	799	13.0	5	0.1	607	9.9
Nevada	5,345	4,535	84.8	954	17.8	113	2.1	198	3.7
New Hampshire	822	565	68.7	138	16.8	23	2.8	161	19.6
New Jersey	11,680	6,759	57.9	3,392	29.0	717	6.1	1,026	8.8
New Mexico	5,926	4,404	74.3	791	13.3	144	2.4	269	4.5
New York	80,077	73,269	91.5	8,484	10.6	3,519	4.4	2,710	3.4
North Carolina	28,422	14,814	52.1	1,817	6.4	373	1.3	1,378	4.8
North Dakota	1,438	913	63.5	158	11.0	24	1.7	77	5.4
Ohio	41,449	22,507	54.3	9,214	22.2	8	0.0	7,283	17.6
Oklahoma	13,414	11,146	83.1	2,407	17.9	465	3.5	885	6.6
Oregon	12,927	4,770	36.9	983	7.6	260	2.0	1,230	9.5
Pennsylvania	4,177	146	3.5	1,420	34.0	102	2.4	2,525	60.5
Puerto Rico	15,066	8,539	56.7	3,529	23.4	1,553	10.3	584	3.9
Rhode Island	4,400	3,771	85.7	552	12.5	64	1.5	249	5.7
South Carolina	10,795	7,790	72.2	3,270	30.3	420	3.9	772	7.2
South Dakota	1,529	1,349	88.2	187	12.2	65	4.3		
Tennessee	19,182	10,187	53.1	6,549	34.1	416	2.2	3,914	20.4
Texas	69,065	51,073	73.9	15,409	22.3	2,649	3.8	7,406	10.7
Utah	13,043	2,754	21.1	1,949	14.9	43	0.3	2,322	17.8
Vermont	861	42	4.9	442	51.3	20	2.3	372	43.2
Virginia	6,828	4,204	61.6	1,904	27.9	170	2.5	950	13.9
Washington	7,294	5,971	81.9	1,264	17.3	441	6.0		
West Virginia	8,345	4,635	55.5	2,047	24.5	124	1.5	382	4.6
Wisconsin	8,583	2,567	29.9	1,218	14.2	3,007	35.0		
Wyoming	786	557	70.9	50	6.4	7	0.9	62	7.9
Total	885,245	567,787		142,041		19,180		78,120	
Percent			64.1		16.0		2.2		8.8
Number reporting	51	51	51	51	51	40	40	51	51

2001 and a 12% decline in physical abuse during the same period; and many social problems with recognized connections to child maltreatment have declined, including runaways, teen pregnancy, and adolescent suicide. Jones, Finkelhor, and Halter state that all these declines indicate a "general improvement in the well-being of children across the United States." Rates of child neglect, however, did not decline over the period. Figure 2.1 shows that rates of child maltreatment fluctuated somewhat from year to year in the early 2000s, but remained fairly steady between 2002 and 2006.

NIS DATA. The NIS, while providing older data, gives a clearer picture of the incidence of child maltreatment because it collects data not just from CPS agencies but also from other community professionals. In 1996, under the Harm Standard, nearly 1.6 million children were victims of maltreatment, a 67% increase from the Second National Incidence Study of Child Abuse and Neglect (*NIS-2*; 1986) estimate (931,000 children) and a 149% increase from the First National Incidence Study of Child Abuse and Neglect (1980) estimate (625,100 children). (See Table 2.3.) Significant increases occurred for all types

TABLE 2.2

Types of maltreatment sustained by victims, by state, 2006 [CONTINUED]

State	Psychological maltreatment		Other		Unknown or missing		Total maltreatments	
	Number	%	Number	%	Number	%	Number	%
Alabama	80	0.9					10,105	107.8
Alaska	1,157	33.2					3,970	114.0
Arizona	34	0.8					4,572	102.3
Arkansas	109	1.2	6	0.1			9,964	108.5
California	15,774	17.6	150	0.2			97,790	109.3
Colorado	487	4.5			44.3	4.1	11,422	105.2
Connecticut	309	3.0					11,068	108.8
Delaware	529	27.4	160	8.3			2,117	109.5
District of Columbia	52	1.9	898	32.5			3,267	118.4
Florida	2,416	1.8	91,884	68.3			159,840	118.8
Georgia	8,727	21.9	183	0.5			45,039	113.2
Hawaii	26	1.3	1,860	91.0			2,562	125.3
Idaho	2	0.1	120	7.3			1,724	104.4
Illinois	56	0.2					31,509	113.5
Indiana							22,721	108.6
Iowa	97	0.7	1,524	10.4			16,025	109.8
Kansas	453	17.2	623	23.7	39	1.5	2,964	112.7
Kentucky	115	0.6					20,401	102.9
Louisiana	320	2.6	29	0.2			14,276	114.5
Maine	1,379	38.9					4,814	135.7
Maryland								
Massachusetts	70	0.2	6	0.0			38,830	107.4
Michigan	561	2.1	707	2.6			28,323	104.3
Minnesota	55	0.7					8,060	105.7
Mississippi	582	9.3	22	0.4			6,708	107.0
Missouri	478	6.7					8,411	118.3
Montana	352	19.8	4	0.2			1,997	112.5
Nebraska	387	6.3					7,037	114.2
Nevada	451	8.4					6,251	117.0
New Hampshire	15	1.8					902	109.7
New Jersey	96	0.8			14	0.1	12,004	102.8
New Mexico	1,100	18.6					6,708	113.2
New York	576	0.7	20,470	25.6			109,028	136.2
North Carolina	87	0.3	229	0.8	9,724	34.2	28,422	100.0
North Dakota	779	54.2					1,951	135.7
Ohio	4,136	10.0					43,148	104.1
Oklahoma	3,073	22.9				10.0	17,977	134.0
Oregon	317	2.5	7,666	59.3			15,226	117.8
Pennsylvania	56	1.3					4,249	101.7
Puerto Rico	4,076	27.1	1,846	12.3			20,127	133.6
Rhode Island	3	0.1	42	1.0			4,681	106.4
South Carolina	137	1.3	18	0.2			12,407	114.9
South Dakota	46	3.0					1,647	107.8
Tennessee	73	0.4					21,139	110.2
Texas	1,021	1.5					77,558	112.3
Utah	5,664	43.4	2,629	20.2			15,361	117.8
Vermont	8	0.9					884	102.7
Virginia	75	1.1	1	0.0			7,304	107.0
Washington							7,676	105.2
West Virginia	2,046	24.5	668	8.0			9,902	118.7
Wisconsin	41	0.5	2,176	25.4			9,009	105.0
Wyoming	94	12.0	57	7.3			827	105.2
Total	**58,577**		**133,978**		**10,221**		**1,009,904**	
Percent		**6.6**		**15.1**		**1.2**		**114.1**
Number reporting	**49**	**49**	**26**	**26**	**5**	**5**	**51**	**51**

SOURCE: "Table 3–6. Maltreatment Types of Victims, 2006," in *Child Maltreatment 2006*, U.S. Department of Health and Human Services, Administration on Children, Youth, and Families, 2008, http://www.acf.hhs.gov/programs/cb/pubs/cm06/cm06.pdf (accessed May 20, 2008)

of abuse and neglect, as compared to the two earlier NIS surveys. The 1.6 million child victims of maltreatment in 1993 reflected a yearly incidence rate of 23.1 per 1,000 children under age eighteen.

In 1993, under the Endangerment Standard, more than 2.8 million children experienced some type of maltreatment. (See Table 2.4.) This figure doubled the *NIS-2* estimate of 1.4 million. As with the Harm Standard, marked increases occurred for all types of abuse and neglect. The incidence rate was 41.9 per 1,000 children under age eighteen.

Gender of Victims

CPS DATA. In 2006 CPS agencies found a higher rate of child maltreatment among girls (12.7 cases per 1,000 children) than among boys (11.4 cases per 1,000 children).

(See Table 2.5.) About 48.2% of maltreated children were boys and 51.5% were girls.

NIS DATA. NIS data allow comparisons of types of maltreatment suffered by boys and girls. Under both the Harm and Endangerment Standards of *NIS-3*, more females were subjected to maltreatment than males. Females were sexually abused about three times more often than males.

Males, however, were more likely to experience physical and emotional neglect under the Endangerment Standard. Under both standards, males suffered more physical and emotional neglect, whereas females suffered more educational neglect. (See Table 2.6 and Table 2.7.) Males were at a somewhat greater risk of serious injury and death than females.

Age of Victims

CPS DATA. Younger children represented most of the maltreated victims among CPS agencies in 2006. Older children are less likely to be victimized than younger children. The victimization rate for infants was 24.4 per 1,000 children. (See Figure 2.2.) The rate then dropped to 14.2 per 1,000 toddlers aged one to three and 13.5 per 1,000 children aged four to seven. The rate then dropped again to 10.8 per 1,000 children aged eight to eleven and 10.2 per 1,000 children aged twelve to fifteen. Teens aged sixteen and seventeen had the lowest rate, at 6.3 per 1,000.

Children of different ages suffered different types of maltreatment in 2006. Nearly three-quarters of the youngest children under age three suffered from neglect (72.2% of infants and 72.9% of children aged one to three), whereas only a little more than half (55%) of those aged sixteen and older did. (See Table 2.8.) By contrast, 14.3% of infants under age one and 10.8% of toddlers aged one to three suffered physical abuse and 0.4% of infants and 2.6% of toddlers suffered sexual abuse, whereas 22% of maltreated children aged sixteen and older suffered physical abuse and 16.1% suffered sexual abuse.

FIGURE 2.1

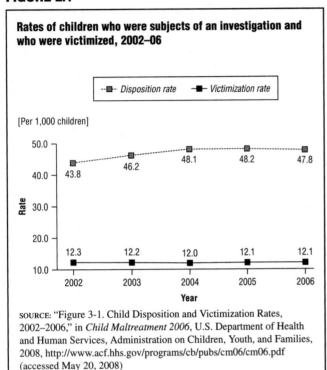

Rates of children who were subjects of an investigation and who were victimized, 2002–06

SOURCE: "Figure 3-1. Child Disposition and Victimization Rates, 2002–2006," in *Child Maltreatment 2006*, U.S. Department of Health and Human Services, Administration on Children, Youth, and Families, 2008, http://www.acf.hhs.gov/programs/cb/pubs/cm06/cm06.pdf (accessed May 20, 2008)

TABLE 2.3

Comparison of actual maltreatment incidence rates to estimates of maltreatment incidence rates, by Harm Standard guidelines, selected years 1980–93

| | NIS-3 estimates 1993 | | Comparisons with earlier studies | | | |
| | | | NIS-2: 1986 | | NIS-1: 1980 | |
Harm Standard maltreatment category	Total number of children	Rate per 1,000 children	Total number of children	Rate per 1,000 children	Total number of children	Rate per 1,000 children
All maltreatment	1,553,800	23.1	931,000	14.8	625,100	9.8
Abuse:						
All abuse	743,200	11.1	507,700	8.1	336,600	5.3
Physical abuse	381,700	5.7	269,700	4.3	199,100	3.1
Sexual abuse	217,700	3.2	119,200	1.9	42,900	0.7
Emotional abuse	204,500	3.0	155,200	2.5	132,700	2.1
Neglect:						
All neglect	879,000	13.1	474,800	7.5	315,400	4.9
Physical neglect	338,900	5.0	167,800	2.7	103,600	1.6
Emotional neglect	212,800	3.2	49,200	0.8	56,900	0.9
Educational neglect	397,300	5.9	284,800	4.5	174,000	2.7

Note: Estimated totals are rounded to the nearest 100. NIS = National Incidence Study of Child Abuse and Neglect.

SOURCE: Andrea J. Sedlak and Diane E. Broadhurst, "National Incidence of Maltreatment under the Harm Standard in the NIS-3 (1993) and Comparison with the NIS-2 (1986) and the NIS-1 (1980) Harm Standard Estimates," in *The Third National Incidence Study of Child Abuse and Neglect*, U.S. Department of Health and Human Services, National Center on Child Abuse and Neglect, 1996

TABLE 2.4

Comparison of actual maltreatment incidence rates to estimates of maltreatment incidence rates, by Endangerment Standard guidelines, 1986 and 1993

Endangerment Standard maltreatment category	NIS-3 estimates 1993		Comparison with NIS-2 1986	
	Total no. of children	Rate per 1,000 children	Total no. of children	Rate per 1,000 children
All maltreatment	2,815,600	41.9	1,424,400	22.6
Abuse:				
All abuse	1,221,800	18.2	590,800	9.4
Physical abuse	614,100	9.1	311,500	4.9
Sexual abuse	300,200	4.5	133,600	2.1
Emotional abuse	532,200	7.9	188,100	3.0
Neglect:				
All neglect	1,961,300	29.2	917,200	14.6
Physical neglect	1,335,100	19.9	507,700	8.1
Emotional neglect	584,100	8.7	203,000	3.2
Educational neglect	397,300	5.9	284,800	4.5

Note: Estimated totals are rounded to the nearest 100. NIS = National Incidence Study of Child Abuse and Neglect.

SOURCE: Andrea J. Sedlak and Diane E. Broadhurst, "National Incidence of Maltreatment under the Endangerment Standard in the NIS–3 (1993) and Comparison with the NIS–2 (1986) Endangerment Standard Estimates," in *The Third National Incidence Study of Child Abuse and Neglect*, U.S. Department of Health and Human Services, National Center on Child Abuse and Neglect, 1996

NIS DATA. Sedlak and Broadhurst find in *NIS-3* a low incidence of maltreatment in younger children, particularly among those under age five. This may be because, before reaching school age, children are less observable to community professionals, especially educators—the group most likely to report suspected maltreatment. The researchers explain that there was a disproportionate increase in the incidence of maltreatment among children as they reached ages six through fourteen. (See Figure 2.3 and Figure 2.4.) Sedlak and Broadhurst note that the incidence of maltreatment among children older than age fourteen decreased. Older children are more likely to escape if the abuse becomes more prevalent or severe. They are also more able to defend themselves and/or fight back.

Under the Harm Standard only ten per one thousand children in the zero-to-two age group experienced overall maltreatment. (See Figure 2.3.) The numbers were significantly higher for children aged six to seventeen. Under the Endangerment Standard twenty-six per one thousand children aged zero to two were subjected to overall maltreatment.(See Figure 2.4.) A slightly higher number of children (thirty-three per one thousand children) in the oldest age group (fifteen- to seventeen-years-old) suffered maltreatment of some type. As with the Harm Standard, children between the ages of six and fourteen had a higher incidence of maltreatment.

TABLE 2.5

Sex of child abuse victims, by state, 2006

State	Boys			
	Population	Number	Rate	Percent
Alabama	569,693	3,868	6.8	41.2
Alaska	93,616	1,654	17.7	47.5
Arizona	833,054	2,114	2.5	47.3
Arkansas	353,375	3,990	11.3	43.5
California	4,881,203	42,760	8.8	47.8
Colorado	599,328	5,384	9.0	49.6
Connecticut	418,647	4,944	11.8	48.6
Delaware	103,967	931	9.0	48.2
District of Columbia	57,989	1,383	23.8	50.1
Florida	2,059,269	66,923	32.5	49.7
Georgia	1,253,307	19,863	15.8	49.9
Hawaii	154,398	978	6.3	47.8
Idaho	202,396	820	4.1	49.7
Illinois	1,644,077	13,522	8.2	48.7
Indiana	808,588	9,536	11.8	45.6
Iowa	364,353	7,280	20.0	49.9
Kansas	356,861	1,139	3.2	43.3
Kentucky	51 2,879	9,795	19.1	49.4
Louisiana	557,078	6,123	11.0	49.1
Maine	144,333	1,761	12.2	49.6
Maryland				
Massachusetts	740,637	17,534	23.7	48.5
Michigan	1,269,277	13,360	10.5	49.2
Minnesota	643,382	3,601	5.6	47.2
Mississippi	387,296	2,817	7.3	44.9
Missouri	724,624	3,033	4.2	42.7
Montana	111,707	844	7.6	47.5
Nebraska	227,697	2,998	13.2	48.7
Nevada	324,811	2,698	8.3	50.5
New Hampshire	152,152	381	2.5	46.4
New Jersey	1,068,295	5,610	5.3	48.0
New Mexico	259,161	2,946	11.4	49.7
New York	2,309,646	39,488	17.1	49.3
North Carolina	1,105,822	14,335	13.0	50.4
North Dakota	74,357	748	10.1	52.0
Ohio	1,415,611	19,419	13.7	46.9
Oklahoma	458,280	6,570	14.3	49.0
Oregon	438,459	6,173	14.1	47.8
Pennsylvania	1,435,343	1,475	1.0	35.3
Puerto Rico	520,558	7,140	13.7	47.4
Rhode Island	121,649	2,142	17.6	48.7
South Carolina	532,135	5,251	9.9	48.6
South Dakota	99,992	701	7.0	45.8
Tennessee	738,005	8,819	11.9	46.0
Texas	3,318,089	33,033	10.0	47.8
Utah	406,285	6,099	15.0	46.8
Vermont	68,396	351	5.1	40.8
Virginia	923,740	3,272	3.5	47.9
Washington	783,021	3,551	4.5	48.7
West Virginia	199,354	4,047	20.3	48.5
Wisconsin	671,960	3,436	5.1	40.0
Wyoming	62,559	387	6.2	49.2
Total	**37,560,711**	**427,027**		
Rate			11.4	
Percent				48.2
Number reporting	51	51	51	51

Race and Ethnicity of Victims

CPS DATA. In 2006 rates of child maltreatment as recorded by CPS agencies were highest among African-American children (19.8 per 1,000 children) and lowest among Asian-American children (2.5 per 1,000 children). (See Figure 2.5.) Pacific Islanders had a rate of 14.3 per 1,000 children, Native American and Alaskan Native children had a rate of 15.9 per 1,000 children, Hispanics had a rate of 10.8 per 1,000 children, and whites had a rate of 10.7 per 1,000 children.

TABLE 2.5

Sex of child abuse victims, by state, 2006 [CONTINUED]

State	Girls Population	Girls Number	Girls Rate	Girls %	Unknown or missing Number	Unknown or missing %
Alabama	544,608	5,486	10.1	58.5	24	0.3
Alaska	87,818	1,775	20.2	51.0	52	1.5
Arizona	795,144	2,349	3.0	52.6	6	0.1
Arkansas	337,811	5,185	15.3	56.5	5	0.1
California	4,651,411	46,657	10.0	52.1	83	0.1
Colorado	569,973	5,478	9.6	50.4	0	0.0
Connecticut	399,639	5,204	13.0	51.1	26	0.3
Delaware	99,399	1,000	10.1	51.7	2	0.1
District of Columbia	56,892	1,374	24.2	49.8	2	0.1
Florida	1,962,286	67,512	34.4	50.2	132	0.1
Georgia	1,201,713	19,939	16.6	50.1	0	0.0
Hawaii	143,683	1,060	7.4	51.8	7	0.3
Idaho	191,884	831	4.3	50.3	0	0.0
Illinois	1,571,167	14,035	8.9	50.6	199	0.7
Indiana	769,041	11,338	14.7	54.2	51	0.2
Iowa	345,841	7,307	21.1	50.1	2	0.0
Kansas	338,976	1,491	4.4	56.7	0	0.0
Kentucky	486,652	9,917	20.4	50.0	121	0.6
Louisiana	532,923	6,349	11.9	50.9	0	0.0
Maine	136,661	1,779	13.0	50.1	8	0.2
Maryland						
Massachusetts	708,247	17,850	25.2	49.4	767	2.1
Michigan	1,209,079	13,788	11.4	50.8	0	0.0
Minnesota	613,882	4,022	6.6	52.8	0	0.0
Mississippi	372,109	3,451	9.3	55.0	4	0.1
Missouri	691,968	4,075	5.9	57.3	0	0.0
Montana	106,141	867	8.2	48.8	64	3.6
Nebraska	217,336	3,160	14.5	51.3	2	0.0
Nevada	309,709	2,635	8.5	49.3	12	0.2
New Hampshire	145,473	441	3.0	53.6	0	0.0
New Jersey	1,021,043	6,031	5.9	51.6	39	0.3
New Mexico	249,769	2,912	11.7	49.1	68	1.1
New York	2,204,696	40,330	18.3	50.4	259	0.3
North Carolina	1,049,565	14,087	13.4	49.6	0	0.0
North Dakota	70,577	688	9.7	47.8	2	0.1
Ohio	1,354,424	21,980	16.2	53.0	50	0.1
Oklahoma	435,754	6,842	15.7	51.0	2	0.0
Oregon	417,800	6,754	16.2	52.2	0	0.0
Pennsylvania	1,369,530	2,702	2.0	64.7	0	0.0
Puerto Rico	498,093	7,685	15.4	51.0	241	1.6
Rhode Island	115,802	2,253	19.5	51.2	5	0.1
South Carolina	507,518	5,403	10.6	50.1	141	1.3
South Dakota	94,689	813	8.6	53.2	15	1.0
Tennessee	704,588	10,354	14.7	54.0	9	0.0
Texas	3,175,876	35,879	11.3	51.9	153	0.2
Utah	384,913	6,879	17.9	52.7	65	0.5
Vermont	64,993	510	7.8	59.2	0	0.0
Virginia	883,107	3,555	4.0	52.1	1	0.0
Washington	74,246	3,741	5.0	51.3	2	0.0
West Virginia	189,717	4,266	22.5	51.1	32	0.4
Wisconsin	640,570	5,093	8.0	59.3	54	0.6
Wyoming	59,235	398	6.7	50.6	1	0.1
Total	**35,832,971**	**455,510**			**2,708**	
Rate				**12.7**		
Percent					**51.5**	**0.3**
Number reporting	**51**	**51**	**51**	**51**	**51**	**51**

SOURCE: "Table 3–8. Sex of Victims, 2006," in *Child Maltreatment 2006*, U.S. Department of Health and Human Services, Administration on Children, Youth, and Families, 2008, http://www.acf.hhs.gov/programs/cb/pubs/cm06/cm06.pdf (accessed May 20, 2008)

TABLE 2.6

Maltreatment rates under the Harm Standard by gender, 1993

[Per 1,000 children]

Harm Standard maltreatment category	Males	Females
All maltreatment	21.7	24.5
Abuse:		
All abuse	9.5	12.6
Physical abuse	5.8	5.6
Sexual abuse	1.6	4.9
Emotional abuse	2.9	3.1
Neglect:		
All neglect	13.3	12.9
Physical neglect	5.5	4.5
Emotional neglect	3.5	2.8
Educational neglect	5.5	6.4
Severity of injury:		
Fatal	0.04	0.01
Serious	9.3	7.5
Moderate	11.3	13.3
Inferred	1.1	3.8

SOURCE: Adapted from Andrea J. Sedlak and Diane D. Broadhurst, "Sex Differences in Incidence Rates per 1,000 Children for Maltreatment under the Harm Standard in the NIS-3 (1993)," in *The Third National Incidence Study of Child Abuse and Neglect*, U.S. Department of Health and Human Services, National Center on Child Abuse and Neglect, 1996

TABLE 2.7

Maltreatment rates under the Endangerment Standard by gender, 1993

Endangerment Standard maltreatment category	Males	Females
All maltreatment	40.0	42.3
Abuse:		
All abuse	16.1	20.2
Physical abuse	9.3	9.0
Sexual abuse	2.3	6.8
Emotional abuse	8.0	7.7
Neglect:		
All neglect	29.2	27.6
Physical neglect	19.7	18.6
Emotional neglect	9.2	7.8
Educational neglect	5.5	6.4
Severity of injury:		
Fatal	0.04	0.01
Serious	9.4	7.6
Moderate	14.1	15.3
Inferred	2.1	4.6
Endangered	14.5	14.8

SOURCE: Adapted from Andrea J. Sedlak and Diane D. Broadhurst, "Sex Differences in Incidence Rates per 1,000 Children for Maltreatment under the Endangerment Standard in the NIS-3 (1993)," in *The Third National Incidence Study of Child Abuse and Neglect*, U.S. Department of Health and Human Services, National Center on Child Abuse and Neglect, 1996

WHY ARE MINORITY CHILDREN OVERREPRESENTED IN CPS DATA? In *Children of Color in the Child Welfare System: Perspectives from the Child Welfare Community* (2003, http://www.childwelfare.gov/pubs/otherpubs/children/index.cfm), Susan Chibnall et al. explore the attitudes and perceptions of CPS personnel regarding the overrepresentation of minority children, particularly African-American children, in the child welfare system. According to the researchers, even though African-American children make up 15% of all children in the United States, they represent 25% of substantiated maltreatment victims. In addition, these children account for 45% of all children in foster care.

Chibnall et al. studied nine child welfare agencies across the country. They interviewed agency administrators, supervisors, and caseworkers. The child welfare personnel gave a variety of reasons minority children are overrepresented in the child welfare system, including:

- Poverty and poverty-related issues—child welfare personnel thought that African-American families are more likely than other ethnic and racial groups to be poor, leaving them more vulnerable to social problems such as child maltreatment, domestic violence, and substance abuse. Moreover, these families typically live in areas lacking resources where they can go for assistance.

- Visibility—poor families are more likely to use public services, such as public health care, making them more visible to mandated reporters when they are experiencing problems, including child abuse and neglect.

- Overreporting—many study participants proposed that, because poor families are more visible to mandated reporters such as doctors and nurses, they are more likely to be reported to CPS.

- Worker bias—when investigating particular families, some caseworkers may not understand the cultural norms and practices of minorities; this may influence their decisions at different stages of child welfare services, including child maltreatment reporting, investigation, substantiation, and the child's removal from home and placement in foster care. A caseworker's bias may also make it more likely, for example, that he or she would remove an African-American child than a white child from a comparable home environment.

FIGURE 2.2

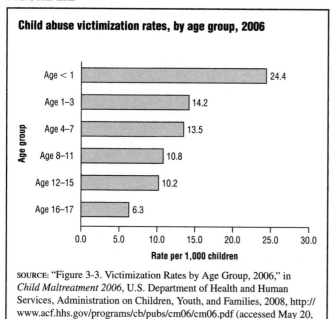

Child abuse victimization rates, by age group, 2006

SOURCE: "Figure 3-3. Victimization Rates by Age Group, 2006," in *Child Maltreatment 2006*, U.S. Department of Health and Human Services, Administration on Children, Youth, and Families, 2008, http://www.acf.hhs.gov/programs/cb/pubs/cm06/cm06.pdf (accessed May 20, 2008)

TABLE 2.8

Child abuse victims, by age group and maltreatment type, 2006

Age group	Victims	Neglect Number	%	Physical abuse Number	%	Medical neglect Number	%	Sexual abuse Number	%
Age <1	100,139	72,314	72.2	14,328	14.3	3,629	3.6	445	0.4
Age 1–3	172,940	125,997	72.9	18,731	10.8	3,948	2.3	4,558	2.6
Age 4–7	213,194	138,886	65.1	32,697	15.3	3,843	1.8	17,539	8.2
Age 8–11	170,944	103,964	60.8	29,312	17.1	3,233	1.9	18,314	10.7
Age 12–15	170,635	94,910	55.6	34,348	20.1	3,447	2.0	28,138	16.5
Age 16 and older	54,564	29,989	55.0	11,998	22.0	1,030	1.9	8,798	16.1
Unknown or missing	2,829	1,727	61.0	627	22.2	50	1.8	328	11.6
Total	**885,245**	**567,787**		**142,041**		**19,180**		**78,120**	
Percent			**64.1**		**16.0**		**2.2**		**8.8**

Age group	Psychological abuse Number	%	Other abuse Number	%	Unknown Number	%	Total maltreatments Number	%
Age <1	3,967	4.0	16,300	16.3	1,097	1.1	112,080	111.9
Age 1–3	10,262	5.9	29,016	16.8	2,114	1.2	194,626	112.5
Age 4–7	14,555	6.8	31,833	14.9	2,570	1.2	241,923	113.5
Age 8–11	13,647	8.0	25,406	14.9	1,947	1.1	195,823	114.6
Age 12–15	12,372	7.3	23,465	13.8	1,950	1.1	198,630	116.4
Age 16 and older	3,524	6.5	7,832	14.4	541	1.0	63,712	116.8
Unknown or missing	250	8.8	126	4.5	2	0.1	3,110	109.9
Total	**58,577**		**133,978**		**10,221**		**1,009,904**	
Percent		**6.6**		**15.1**		**1.2**		**114.1**

Note: Based on data from 51 states.

SOURCE: "Table 3–10. Victims by Age Group and Maltreatment Type, 2006," in *Child Maltreatment 2006*, U.S. Department of Health and Human Services, Administration on Children, Youth, and Families, 2008, http://www.acf.hhs.gov/programs/cb/pubs/cm06/cm06.pdf (accessed May 20, 2008)

FIGURE 2.3

Age differences in maltreatment, abuse, and neglect victims under the Harm Standard, 1993

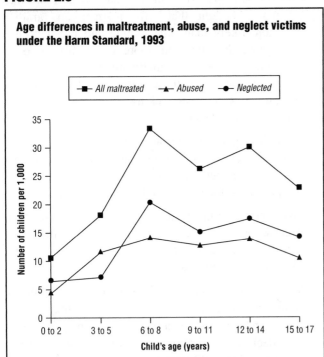

SOURCE: Andrea J. Sedlak and Diane D. Broadhurst, "Age Difference in All Maltreatment, Abuse, and Neglect under the Harm Standard," in *The Third National Incidence Study of Child Abuse and Neglect*, U.S. Department of Health and Human Services, National Center on Child Abuse and Neglect, 1996

FIGURE 2.4

Age differences in maltreatment, abuse, and neglect victims under the Endangerment Standard, 1993

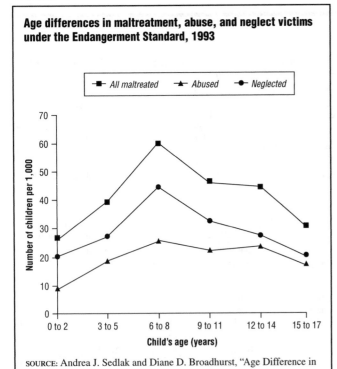

SOURCE: Andrea J. Sedlak and Diane D. Broadhurst, "Age Difference in All Maltreatment, Abuse, and Neglect under the Endangerment Standard," in *The Third National Incidence Study of Child Abuse and Neglect*, U.S. Department of Health and Human Services, National Center on Child Abuse and Neglect, 1996

FIGURE 2.5

Race and ethnicity of victims of child abuse, 2006

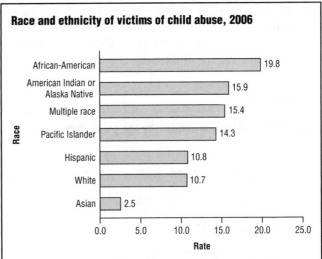

SOURCE: "Figure 3-4. Race and Ethnicity of Victims, 2006," in *Child Maltreatment 2006*, U.S. Department of Health and Human Services, Administration on Children, Youth, and Families, 2008, http://www.acf.hhs.gov/programs/cb/pubs/cm06/cm06.pdf (accessed May 20, 2008)

In *African American Children in Foster Care: Additional HHS Assistance Needed to Reduce the Proportion in Care* (July 2007, http://www.gao.gov/new.items/d07816.pdf), the U.S. Government Accountability Office (GAO) backs up Chibnall et al.'s study by finding several factors that contribute to the disproportionate number of African-American children in foster care. These factors include higher rates of poverty in the African-American community, the difficulty African-American families face in accessing support services to help prevent the removal of their children, and racial bias and misunderstandings among child welfare workers.

NIS DATA. Sedlak and Broadhurst find in *NIS-3* no significant differences in race in the incidence of maltreatment. The researchers note that this finding may be somewhat surprising, considering the overrepresentation of African-American children in the child welfare population and in those served by public agencies. They attribute this lack of race-related difference in maltreatment incidence to the broader range of children identified by *NIS-3*, compared to the smaller number investigated by public agencies and the even smaller number receiving CPS and other welfare services. *NIS-2* had also not found any disproportionate differences in race in relation to maltreatment incidence.

Children with Disabilities Are Particularly at Risk

According to the article "Assessment of Maltreatment of Children with Disabilities" (*Pediatrics*, vol. 108, no. 2, August 2001), children with disabilities are potentially at risk for maltreatment because society generally treats them as different and less valuable, thus possibly tolerating violence against them. Some parents may feel disappointment at not having a "normal" child.

Others may expect too much and feel frustrated if the child does not live up to their expectations. These children require special care and attention, and parents may not have the social support to help ease stressful situations. Caring for children with disabilities can also be expensive, creating even more stress and with it risk of maltreatment. In addition, some disabled children may not be able to distinguish between appropriate and inappropriate touching of their body, leaving them particularly vulnerable to sexual abuse.

In "Violence against Children with Disabilities: Prevention, Public Policy, and Research Implications" (Dorothy K. Marge, ed., *A Call to Action: Ending Crimes of Violence against Children and Adults with Disabilities—A Report to the Nation*, 2003), Patricia M. Sullivan calls attention to the fact that the federal government does not collect specific data on children with disabilities in its crime statistics systems or in national incidence studies mandated by law. Even though CAPTA required that national incidence studies of child maltreatment include data on children with disabilities, the latest survey, the *NIS-3*, does not satisfy this mandate. Moreover, NCANDS, which releases annual state data on maltreated children, does not gather information relating to children's disability status.

Sullivan undertook two epidemiological studies on maltreated children with disabilities. (Epidemiological studies consider individuals' sex, age, race, social class, and other demographics.) Both the incidence and prevalence of maltreatment were measured. The hospital-based study of six thousand children found a 64% prevalence rate of maltreatment among disabled children, twice the prevalence rate (32%) among nondisabled children. The school-based study included 4,954 children; 31% of disabled children had been maltreated, 3.4 times that of the nondisabled comparison group.

Family Characteristics of Victims

The only reliable information on family characteristics of victims come from NIS data, as the living arrangements data on children reported to CPS were incomplete. For example, in *Child Maltreatment 2006*, the ACYF states that in 2006 only twenty-eight states reported on living arrangements of children, and more than one-third of the reported cases had unknown or missing data and were excluded from the analysis. The following discussion comes from *NIS-3*.

FAMILY STRUCTURE. Under the Harm Standard, among children living with single parents, an estimated 27.3 per 1,000 under age eighteen suffered some type of maltreatment—almost twice the incidence rate for children living with both parents (15.5 per 1,000). (See Table 2.9.) The same rate held true for all types of abuse and neglect. Children living with single parents also had a greater risk of suffering serious injury (10.5 per 1,000) than did those living with both parents (5.8 per 1,000).

Under the Endangerment Standard an estimated 52 per 1,000 children living with single parents suffered

TABLE 2.9

Maltreatment incidence rates under the Harm Standard by family structure, 1993

[Per 1,000 children]

Harm Standard maltreatment category	Both parents	Single parent			Neither parent
		Either mother or father	Mother only	Father only	
All maltreatment:	15.5	27.3	26.1	36.6	22.9
Abuse:					
All abuse	8.4	11.4	10.5	17.7	13.7
Physical abuse	3.9	6.9	6.4	10.5	7.0
Sexual abuse	2.6	2.5	2.5	2.6	6.3
Emotional abuse	2.6	2.5	2.1	5.7	5.4
Neglect:					
All neglect	7.9	17.3	16.7	21.9	10.3
Physical neglect	3.1	5.8	5.9	4.7	4.3
Emotional neglect	2.3	4.0	3.4	8.8	3.1
Educational neglect	3.0	9.6	9.5	10.8	3.1
Severity of injury:					
Fatal	0.019	0.015	0.017	0.005	0.016
Serious	5.8	10.5	10.0	14.0	8.0
Moderate	8.1	15.4	14.7	20.5	10.1
Inferred	1.6	1.4	1.3	2.1	4.8

SOURCE: Adapted from Andrea J. Sedlak and Diane D. Broadhurst, "Incidence Rates per 1,000 Children for Maltreatment under the Harm Standard in the NIS-3 (1993) for Different Family Structures," in *The Third National Incidence Study of Child Abuse and Neglect*, U.S. Department of Health and Human Services, National Center on Child Abuse and Neglect, 1996

some type of maltreatment, compared to 26.9 per 1,000 living with both parents. (See Table 2.10.) Children in single-parent households were abused at a 45% higher rate than those in two-parent households (19.6 versus 13.5 per 1,000) and suffered more than twice as much neglect (38.9 versus 17.6 per 1,000).

FAMILY INCOME. Family income was significantly related to the incidence rates of child maltreatment. Under the Harm Standard children in families with annual incomes less than $15,000 had the highest rate of maltreatment (47 per 1,000). The figure is almost twice as high (95.9 per 1,000) using the Endangerment Standard. (See Table 2.11 and Table 2.12.) Children in families earning less than $15,000 annually also sustained more serious injuries than did children living in families earning more than that amount.

PERPETRATORS OF CHILD MALTREATMENT
CPS Data

The law considers perpetrators of child abuse to be those people who abuse or neglect children under their care. They may be parents, foster parents, other relatives, or other caretakers. People who victimize children that are not under their care are not considered to have committed child abuse, but assault, battery, rape, or other crimes.

In *Child Maltreatment 2006*, the ACYF indicates that in 2006 abuse perpetrators were more likely to be women

TABLE 2.10

Maltreatment incidence rates under the Endangerment Standard by family structure, 1993

[Per 1,000 children]

Endangerment Standard maltreatment category	Both parents	Single parent			Neither parent
		Either mother or father	Mother only	Father only	
All maltreatment	26.9	52.0	50.1	65.6	39.3
Abuse:					
All abuse	13.5	19.6	18.1	31.0	17.3
Physical abuse	6.5	10.6	9.8	16.5	9.2
Sexual abuse	3.2	4.2	4.3	3.1	6.6
Emotional abuse	6.2	8.6	7.7	14.6	7.1
Neglect:					
All neglect	17.6	38.9	37.6	47.9	24.1
Physical neglect	10.8	28.6	27.5	36.4	17.1
Emotional neglect	6.4	10.5	9.7	16.2	8.3
Educational neglect	3.0	9.6	9.5	10.8	3.1
Severity of injury:					
Fatal	0.020	0.015	0.017	0.005	0.016
Serious	5.9	10.5	10.0	14.0	8.0
Moderate	9.6	18.5	17.7	24.8	11.5
Inferred	2.1	2.5	2.0	6.0	4.7
Endangered	9.3	20.5	20.4	20.7	15.1

SOURCE: Adapted from Andrea J. Sedlak and Diane D. Broadhurst, "Incidence Rates per 1,000 Children for Maltreatment under the Endangerment Standard in the NIS-3 (1993) for Different Family Structures," in *The Third National Incidence Study of Child Abuse and Neglect*, U.S. Department of Health and Human Services, National Center on Child Abuse and Neglect, 1996

TABLE 2.11

Maltreatment incidence rates under the Harm Standard by family income, 1993

[Per 1,000 children]

Harm Standard maltreatment category	<$l5K/year	$15–29K/year	$30K+/year
All maltreatment	47.0	20.0	2.1
Abuse:			
All abuse	22.2	9.7	1.6
Physical abuse	11.0	5.0	0.7
Sexual abuse	7.0	2.8	0.4
Emotional abuse	6.5	2.5	0.5
Neglect:			
All neglect	27.2	11.3	0.6
Physical neglect	12.0	2.9	0.3
Emotional neglect	5.9	4.3	0.2
Educational neglect	11.1	4.8	0.2
Severity of injury:			
Fatal	0.060	0.002	0.001
Serious	17.9	7.8	0.8
Moderate	23.3	10.5	1.3
Inferred	5.7	1.6	0.1

SOURCE: Adapted from Andrea J. Sedlak and Diane D. Broadhurst, "Incidence Rates per 1,000 Children for Maltreatment under the Harm Standard in the NIS-3 (1993) for Different Levels of Family Income," in *The Third National Incidence Study of Child Abuse and Neglect*, U.S. Department of Health and Human Services, National Center on Child Abuse and Neglect, 1996

TABLE 2.12

Maltreatment incidence rates under the Endangerment Standard by family income, 1993

[Per 1,000 children]

Endangerment Standard maltreatment category	<$15K/year	$15–29K/year	$30K=/year
All maltreatment	95.9	33.1	3.8
Abuse:			
All abuse	37.4	17.5	2.5
Physical abuse	17.6	8.5	1.5
Sexual abuse	9.2	4.2	0.5
Emotional abuse	18.3	8.1	1.0
Neglect:			
All neglect	72.3	21.6	1.6
Physical neglect	54.3	12.5	1.1
Emotional neglect	19.0	8.2	0.7
Educational neglect	11.1	4.8	0.2
Severity of injury:			
Fatal	0.060	0.002	0.003
Serious	17.9	7.9	0.8
Moderate	29.6	12.1	1.5
Inferred	7.8	2.7	0.2
Endangered	40.5	10.3	1.3

SOURCE: Adapted from Andrea J. Sedlak and Diane D. Broadhurst, "Incidence Rates per 1,000 Children for Maltreatment under the Endangerment Standard in the NIS-3 (1993) for Different Levels of Family Income," in *The Third National Incidence Study of Child Abuse and Neglect*, U.S. Department of Health and Human Services, National Center on Child Abuse and Neglect, 1996

(57.9%) than men (42.1%). Concerning the victims, 39.9% were maltreated by their mother acting alone and 17.6% experienced maltreatment from their father acting alone. (See Figure 2.6.) Another 17.8% were maltreated by both parents. About 6.1% of the victims were maltreated by their mother and another person whose relationship with the mother was not known, and 1% were maltreated by their father and another person. One out of ten (10%) victims were maltreated by nonparental perpetrators, and another 7.6% were maltreated by unknown individuals. The ACYF indicates that 79.9% of the perpetrators were parents, whereas smaller numbers were other relatives (6.7%), unmarried partner of parents (3.8%), child day care providers (0.6%), or foster parents (0.4%). (See Figure 2.7.)

The ACYF explains that most perpetrators of child maltreatment are in their twenties and thirties. In 2006 the median age (half were older, half were younger) of female perpetrators was thirty-one years, and the median age of male perpetrators was thirty-four years. Almost half of the female perpetrators were younger than thirty (41.3% of twenty- to twenty-nine-year-olds, and 4% of those younger than twenty), whereas only about one-third of male perpetrators were (28.9% of twenty- to twenty-nine-year-olds, and 6.2% of those younger than twenty). (See Figure 2.8.)

NIS Data

In 1993 most (78%) child victims were maltreated by their birth parents. (See Table 2.13.) Parents perpetrated

FIGURE 2.6

Child abuse victims, by relationship to perpetrator, 2006

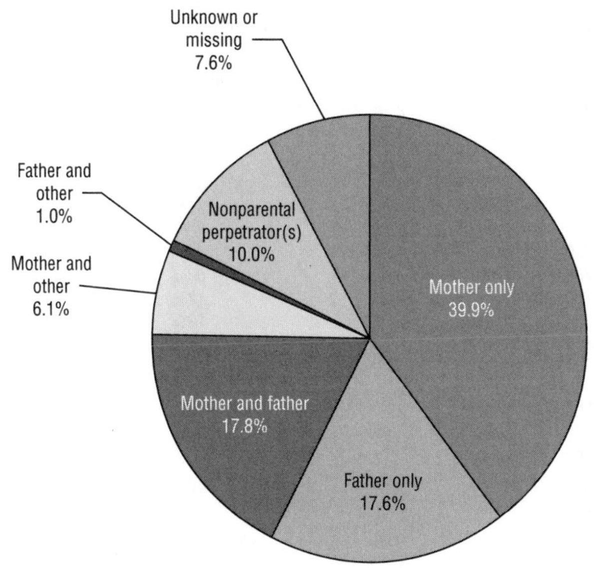

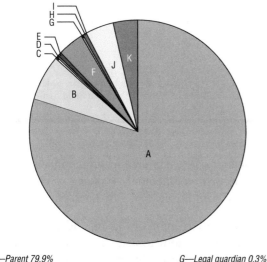

Unknown or missing 7.6%
Father and other 1.0%
Nonparental perpetrator(s) 10.0%
Mother and other 6.1%
Mother only 39.9%
Mother and father 17.8%
Father only 17.6%

SOURCE: "Figure 3-5. Victims by Perpetrator Relationship, 2006," in *Child Maltreatment 2006*, U.S. Department of Health and Human Services, Administration on Children, Youth, and Families, 2008, http://www.acf.hhs.gov/programs/cb/pubs/cm06/cm06.pdf (accessed May 20, 2008)

FIGURE 2.7

Child abuse perpetrators, by relationship to victims, 2006

I
H
G
E
D
C
K
J
F
B
A
A—Parent 79.9%
B—Other relative 6.7%
C—Foster parent 0.4%
D—Residential facility staff 0.2%
E—Child daycare provider 0.6%
F—Unmarried partner of parent 3.8%
G—Legal guardian 0.3%
H—Other professionals 0.1%
I—Friends or neighbors 0.5%
J—Other 4.1%
K—Unknown or missing 3.5%

Note: Population = 47 states.

SOURCE: "Figure 5-2. Perpetrators by Relationship to Victims, 2006," in *Child Maltreatment 2006*, U.S. Department of Health and Human Services, Administration on Children, Youth, and Families, 2008, http://www.acf.hhs.gov/programs/cb/pubs/cm06/cm06.pdf (accessed May 20, 2008)

FIGURE 2.8

Child abuse perpetrators, by age and sex, 2006

<20
20–29
30–39
40–49
>49
50%
40%
30%
20%
10%
0%
Percentage in age category
6.2
28.9
36.2
21.3
7.4
4.0
41.3
36.7
13.9
4.0
Men
Women
Sex

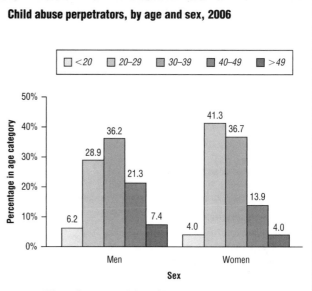

SOURCE: "Figure 5-1. Age and Sex of Perpetrators, 2006," in *Child Maltreatment 2006*, U.S. Department of Health and Human Services, Administration on Children, Youth, and Families, 2008, http://www.acf.hhs.gov/programs/cb/pubs/cm06/cm06.pdf (accessed May 20, 2008)

72% of physical abuse and 81% of emotional abuse. However, almost half (46%) of sexually abused children were violated by someone other than a parent or parent substitute. More than a quarter (29%) were sexually abused by a birth parent, and 25% were sexually abused by a parent substitute, such as a stepparent or a mother's boyfriend. Sexually abused children were the most likely to sustain fatal or serious injuries or impairments when birth parents were the perpetrators.

Overall, children were somewhat more likely to be maltreated by female perpetrators (65%) than by males (54%) in 1993. (See Table 2.14.) Among children maltreated by their natural parents, most (75%) were maltreated by their mothers, and almost half (46%) were maltreated by their fathers—with some children being maltreated by both parents. Children who were maltreated by someone other than parents and parent substitutes were more likely to have been maltreated by a male (85%) than by a female (41%). Of the other adults who maltreated children, 80% were males and 14% were females.

Neglected children differed from abused children with regard to the gender of the perpetrators in 1993. Because mothers or other females tend to be the primary caretakers, children were more likely to suffer all forms of neglect by female perpetrators (87%, versus 43% by male perpetrators). (See Table 2.14.) In contrast, children were more often abused by males (67%) than by females (40%).

REPORTING CHILD ABUSE

Mandatory Reporting

In 1974 Congress enacted the first CAPTA, which set guidelines for the reporting, investigation, and treatment

TABLE 2.13

Perpetrator's relationship to child and severity of harm, by type of maltreatment, 1993

Category	Percent children in maltreatment category	Total maltreated children	Percent of children in row with injury/impairment . . . Fatal or serious	Moderate	Inferred
Abuse:	100%	743,200	21%	63%	16%
Natural parents	62%	461,800	22%	73%	4%
Other parents and parent/substitutes	19%	144,900	12%	62%	27%
Others	18%	136,600	24%	30%	46%
Physical abuse	100%	381,700	13%	87%	a
Natural parents	72%	273,200	13%	87%	a
Other parents and parent/substitutes	21%	78,700	13%	87%	a
Others	8%	29,700	b	82%	a
Sexual abuse	100%	217,700	34%	12%	53%
Natural parents	29%	63,300	61%	10%	28%
Other parents and parent/substitutes	25%	53,800	19%	18%	63%
Others	46%	100,500	26%	11%	63%
Emotional abuse	100%	204,500	26%	68%	6%
Natural parents	81%	166,500	27%	70%	2%
Other parents and parent/substitutes	13%	27,400	b	57%	24%
Others	5%	10,600	b	b	b
Neglect:	100%	879,000	50%	44%	6%
Natural parents	91%	800,600	51%	43%	6%
Other parents and parent/substitutes	9%	78,400	35%	59%	b
Others	c	c	c	c	c
Physical neglect	100%	338,900	64%	15%	21%
Natural parents	95%	320,400	64%	16%	20%
Other parents and parent/substitutes	5%	18,400	b	b	b
Others	c	c	c	c	c
Emotional neglect	100%	212,800	97%	3%	a
Natural parents	91%	194,600	99%	b	a
Other parents and parent/substitutes	9%	b	b	b	a
Others	c	c	c	c	a
Educational neglect	100%	397,300	7%	93%	a
Natural parents	89%	354,300	8%	92%	a
Other parents and parent/substitutes	11%	43,000	b	99%	a
Others	c	c	c	c	a
All maltreatment	100%	1,553,800	36%	53%	11%
Natural parents	78%	1,208,100	41%	54%	5%
Other parents and parent/substitutes	14%	211,200	20%	61%	19%
Others	9%	134,500	24%	30%	46%

[a]This severity level not applicable for this form of maltreatment.
[b]Fewer than 20 cases with which to calculate estimate; estimate too unreliable to be given.
[c]These perpetrators were not allowed by countability requirements for cases of neglect.

SOURCE: Andrea J. Sedlak and Diane D. Broadhurst, "Distribution of Perpetrator's Relationship to Child and Severity of Harm by the Type of Maltreatment," in *The Third National Incidence Study of Child Abuse and Neglect*, U.S. Department of Health and Human Services, National Center on Child Abuse and Neglect, 1996

of child maltreatment. States had to meet these requirements to receive federal funding to assist child victims of abuse and neglect. Among its many provisions, CAPTA required the states to enact mandatory reporting laws and procedures so that CPS agencies could take action to protect children from further abuse. Each state now designates mandatory reporters, including health care workers, mental health professionals, social workers, school personnel, child care providers, and law enforcement officers. According to the Child Welfare Information Gateway, in "Mandatory Reporters of Child Abuse and Neglect" (January 2008, http://www.childwelfare.gov/systemwide/laws_policies/statutes/manda.pdf), in 2008 eighteen states and Puerto Rico mandated all people must report suspected abuse or neglect, not only designated professionals. Most states did not recognize the right for

communications between certain professionals and their clients to remain confidential—called "privileged communications"—in the case of suspected child abuse.

All states offer immunity to individuals who report incidents of child maltreatment "in good faith" or with sincerity. Besides physical injury and neglect, most states include mental injury, sexual abuse, and the sexual exploitation of minors as cases to be reported.

Who Reports Child Abuse?

In 2006 more than half of all reports of alleged child maltreatment came from professional sources—educators (16.5%); legal, law enforcement, and criminal justice personnel (15.8%); social services personnel (10%); medical personnel (8.4%); mental health personnel (4.1%);

TABLE 2.14

Perpetrator's gender, by type of maltreatment and by relationship to child, 1993

Category	Percent children in maltreatment category	Total maltreated children	Percent of children in row with perpetrator whose gender was . . .		
			Male	Female	Unknown
Abuse:	100%	743,200	67%	40%	a
Natural parents	62%	461,800	56%	55%	a
Other parents and parent/substitutes	19%	144,900	90%	15%	a
Others	18%	136,600	80%	14%	a
Physical abuse	100%	381,700	58%	50%	a
Natural parents	72%	273,200	48%	60%	a
Other parents and parent/substitutes	21%	78,700	90%	19%	a
Others	8%	29,700	57%	39%	a
Sexual abuse	100%	217,700	89%	12%	a
Natural parents	29%	63,300	87%	28%	a
Other parents and parent/substitutes	25%	53,800	97%	a	a
Others	46%	100,500	86%	8%	a
Emotional abuse	100%	204,500	63%	50%	a
Natural parents	81%	166,500	60%	55%	a
Other parents and parent/substitutes	13%	27,400	74%	a	a
Others	5%	10,600	a	a	a
All neglect:	100%	879,000	43%	87%	a
Natural parents	91%	800,600	40%	87%	a
Other parents and parent/substitutes	9%	78,400	76%	88%	a
Others	b	b	b	b	b
Physical neglect	100%	338,900	35%	93%	a
Natural parents	95%	320,400	34%	93%	a
Other parents and parent/substitutes	5%	18,400	a	90%	a
Others	b	b	b	b	b
Emotional neglect	100%	212,800	47%	77%	a
Natural parents	91%	194,600	44%	78%	a
Other parents and parent/substitutes	9%	18,200	a	a	a
Others	b	b	b	b	b
Educational neglect	100%	397,300	47%	88%	a
Natural parents	89%	354,300	43%	86%	a
Other parents and parent/substitutes	11%	43,000	82%	100%	a
Others	b	b	b	b	b
All maltreatment	100%	1,553,800	54%	65%	1%
Natural parents	78%	1,208,100	46%	75%	a
Other parents and parent/substitutes	14%	211,200	85%	41%	a
Others	9%	134,500	80%	14%	7%

[a]Fewer than 20 cases with which to calculate, estimate too unreliable to be given.
[b]These perpetrators were not allowed by countability requirements for cases of neglect.

SOURCE: Andrea J. Sedlak and Diane D. Broadhurst, "Distribution of Perpetrator's Gender by Type of Maltreatment and Perpetrator's Relationship to Child," in *The Third National Incidence Study of Child Abuse and Neglect*, U.S. Department of Health and Human Services, National Center on Child Abuse and Neglect, 1996

child day care providers (0.9%); and foster care providers (0.6%). (See Figure 2.9.) Friends and neighbors (5.3%), parents (6%), and other relatives (7.8%) encompassed nearly one-fifth of the reporters, whereas alleged victims (0.6%) and self-identified perpetrators (0.1%) rarely reported abuse. Other reports came from anonymous (8.2%) and other (8%) sources.

The percentage of neglect and abuse reports from different sources varied by the type of abuse being reported. Educational personnel were responsible for 16.5% of reports in 2006; they reported 11.5% of sexual abuse cases and 10.8% of neglect cases, and 24.2% of all physical abuse cases. (See Table 2.15.) Legal personnel, who were responsible for 15.8% of overall reporting, reported over a quarter of all sexual abuse cases (28.1%) and neglect cases (27.1%), and nearly a quarter (23.1%) of physical abuse cases. Social service personnel

were more likely to report sexual abuse than other forms of maltreatment, whereas medical personnel reported more medical neglect cases than any other source.

Failure to Report Child Maltreatment

Many states impose penalties, either a fine and/or imprisonment, for failure to report child maltreatment. A mandated reporter, such as a physician, may also be sued for negligence for failing to protect a child from harm. Even though all states have enacted legislation requiring, among other things, the mandatory reporting of child maltreatment by certain professionals, states vary in the standard for reporting. The standard to report child maltreatment varies from having "reasonable cause to suspect," to having "reason to believe," to having "observed conditions that would reasonably result," to "know or suspect."

FIGURE 2.9

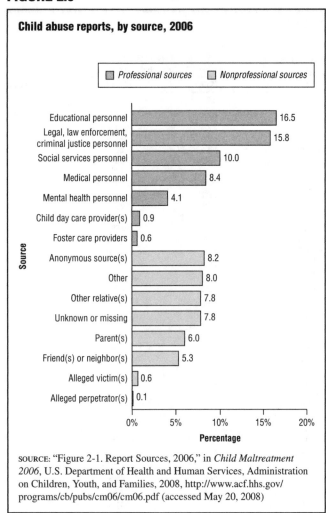

Child abuse reports, by source, 2006

Professional sources ▢ Nonprofessional sources

Source	Percentage
Educational personnel	16.5
Legal, law enforcement, criminal justice personnel	15.8
Social services personnel	10.0
Medical personnel	8.4
Mental health personnel	4.1
Child day care provider(s)	0.9
Foster care providers	0.6
Anonymous source(s)	8.2
Other	8.0
Other relative(s)	7.8
Unknown or missing	7.8
Parent(s)	6.0
Friend(s) or neighbor(s)	5.3
Alleged victim(s)	0.6
Alleged perpetrator(s)	0.1

SOURCE: "Figure 2-1. Report Sources, 2006," in *Child Maltreatment 2006*, U.S. Department of Health and Human Services, Administration on Children, Youth, and Families, 2008, http://www.acf.hhs.gov/programs/cb/pubs/cm06/cm06.pdf (accessed May 20, 2008)

The 1976 landmark California case *Landeros v. Flood et al.* (17 Cal.3d 399) illustrates a case involving a physician's failure to report child maltreatment. Eleven-month-old Gita Landeros was brought by her mother to the San Jose Hospital in California for treatment of injuries. Besides a fractured lower leg, the girl had bruises on her back and abrasions on other parts of her body. She also appeared scared when anyone approached her. At the time, Gita was also suffering from a fractured skull, but this was never diagnosed by A. J. Flood, the attending physician.

Gita returned home with her mother and subsequently suffered further serious abuse at the hands of her mother and the mother's boyfriend. Three months later Gita was brought to another hospital for medical treatment, where the doctor identified and reported the abuse to the proper authorities. After surgery for her injuries the child was placed with foster parents. The mother and boyfriend were eventually convicted of the crime of child abuse. The guardian ad litem (a court-appointed special advocate) for Gita filed a malpractice suit against Flood and the San Jose Hospital, citing painful permanent physical injury to the plaintiff as a result of the defendants' negligence.

The trial court of Santa Clara County dismissed the Landeros complaint, and the case was appealed to the California Supreme Court. The court agreed that Flood should have identified Gita's abuse and ruled that the doctor's failure to do so contributed to the child's continued suffering. Flood and the hospital were found liable. Even though this case applied specifically to a medical doctor, the principles reached by the court are applicable to other professionals. Most professionals are familiar with the court's decision in *Landeros*.

In August 2002 two-year-old Dominic James was brought to Cox South Hospital in Springfield, Missouri. Paramedics told emergency nurse Leslie Ann Brown that the boy, who was having seizure-like symptoms, had bruises on his back and to report this to the attending physician. Dominic's foster parents explained that the child got bruised by leaning back on a booster seat, so Brown did not report the bruises to the physician, nor did she include the presence of bruises on her medical reports. Dominic was hospitalized again a week later and died soon after.

In February 2003 the state of Missouri charged Brown with failure to report child abuse. In September 2003 Calvin Holden, a Green County judge, dismissed the criminal charges, stating that the Missouri statute with the "reasonable cause to suspect" standard for reporting child abuse was unconstitutionally vague in violation of the U.S. and Missouri constitutions. The state appealed the case in May 2004. In August 2004 the Missouri Supreme Court reversed Judge Holden's ruling, allowing the case to proceed to trial. However, later that year charges were dismissed against Brown after an agreement was reached requiring Cox South Hospital to revise its training for mandated reporters and implement annual refresher courses.

Why Mandated Reporters Fail to Report Suspected Maltreatment

Gail L. Zellman and C. Christine Fair explain in "Preventing and Reporting Abuse" (John E. B. Myers et al., eds., *The APSAC Handbook on Child Maltreatment*, 2002) that they conducted a national survey to determine why mandated reporters may not report suspected maltreatment. The researchers surveyed 1,196 general and family practitioners, pediatricians, child psychiatrists, clinical psychologists, social workers, public school principals, and heads of child care centers. Nearly eight out of ten (77%) survey participants had made a child maltreatment report at some time in his or her professional career. More than nine out of ten (92%) elementary school principals reported child maltreatment at some time, followed closely by child psychiatrists (90%) and pediatricians (89%). A lesser proportion of secondary school principals (84%), social workers (70%), and clinical psychologists (63%) reported child maltreatment at some time in their career.

TABLE 2.15

Types of maltreatment, by report source, 2006

Report source	Neglect		Physical abuse		Medical neglect		Sexual abuse	
	Number	%	Number	%	Number	%	Number	%
Professionals								
Educational personnel	61,099	10.8	34,240	24.2	3,217	16.9	3,991	11.5
Legal, law enforcement, criminal justice personnel	153,363	27.1	32,711	23.1	1,546	8.1	21,882	28.1
Social services personnel	71,115	12.6	14,940	10.6	2,745	14.4	11,525	14.8
Medical personnel	52,217	9.2	17,063	12.1	5,558	29.2	7,330	9.4
Mental health personnel	13,370	2.4	4,589	3.2	656	3.4	5,618	7.2
Child daycare providers	2,821	0.5	1,822	1.3	110	0.6	294	0.4
Foster care providers	1,979	0.3	622	0.4	83	0.4	804	1.0
Total professionals	355,964	62.9	105,987	74.9	13,915	73.1	56,444	72.4
Nonprofessionals								
Anonymous reporters	39,927	7.1	4,659	3.3	1,035	5.4	1,639	2.1
Other reporters	46,353	8.2	7,224	5.1	1,071	5.6	5,464	7.0
Other relatives	46,841	8.3	8,145	5.8	1,385	7.3	4,254	5.5
Parents	21,592	3.8	6,792	4.8	767	4.0	5,561	7.1
Friends or neighbors	29,081	5.1	3,593	2.5	634	3.3	1,673	2.1
Unknown reporters	23,317	4.1	3,873	2.7	141	0.7	2,064	2.6
Alleged victims	1,608	0.3	1,003	0.7	42	0.2	684	0.9
Alleged perpetrators	1,043	0.2	251	0.2	38	0.2	158	0.2
Total nonprofessionals	209,762	37.1	35,540	25.1	5,113	26.9	21,497	27.6
Total	**565,726**		**141,527**		**19,028**		**77,941**	
Total percent		100.0		100.0		100.0		100.0
Number reporting	50	50	50	50	39	39	50	50

Report source	Psychological maltreatment		Other abuse		Unknown maltreatment		Total
	Number	%	Number	%	Number	%	Number
Professionals							
Educational personnel	7,764	13.5	8,994	6.7	1,805	17.7	126,110
Legal, law enforcement, criminal justice personnel	18,720	32.6	50,645	37.8	1,981	19.4	280,848
Social services personnel	5,072	8.8	17,395	13.0	1,720	16.8	124,512
Medical personnel	2,132	3.7	8,139	6.1	1,039	10.2	93,478
Mental health personnel	3,468	6.0	2,376	1.8	22	0.2	30,099
Child daycare providers	200	0.3	424	0.3	86	0.8	5,757
Foster care providers	148	0.3	384	0.3	17	0.2	4,037
Total professionals	37,504	65.3	88,357	65.9	6,670	65.3	664,841
Nonprofessionals							
Anonymous reporters	3,866	6.7	10,411	7.8	819	8.0	62,356
Other reporters	4,718	8.2	9,433	7.0	27	0.3	74,290
Other relatives	5,017	8.7	10,532	7.9	1,155	11.3	77,329
Parents	2,609	4.5	7,599	5.7	588	5.8	45,508
Friends or neighbors	1,600	2.8	5,539	4.1	906	8.9	43,026
Unknown reporters	1,567	2.7	758	0.6			31,720
Alleged victims	440	0.8	604	0.5	56	0.5	4,437
Alleged perpetrators	92	0.2	743	0.6			2,325
Total nonprofessionals	19,909	34.7	45,619	34.1	3,551	34.7	340,991
Total	**57,413**		**133,976**		**10,221**		**1,005,832**
Total percent		100.0		100.0		100.0	
Number reporting	48	48	26	26	5	5	

SOURCE: "Table 3–7. Maltreatment Types of Victims by Report Source, 2006," in *Child Maltreatment 2006*, U.S. Department of Health and Human Services, Administration on Children, Youth, and Families, 2008, http://www.acf.hhs.gov/programs/cb/pubs/cm06/cm06.pdf (accessed May 20, 2008)

However, nearly 40% of the mandated reporters indicated that at some time in their career they had failed to report even though they had suspected child maltreatment. Almost 60% failed to report child maltreatment because they did not have enough evidence that the child had been maltreated. One-third of the mandated reporters thought the abuse was not serious enough to warrant reporting. An equal proportion of mandated reporters did not report suspected abuse because they felt they were in a better position to help the child (19.3%) or they did not want to end the treatment (19%) they were giving the child. Almost 16% failed to report because they did not think CPS would respond appropriately.

In *Confronting Chronic Neglect: The Education and Training of Health Professionals on Family Violence* (2002), Felicia Cohn, Marla E. Salmon, and John D. Stobo examine the curricula on family violence for six groups of health professionals: physicians, physician assistants, nurses, psychologists, social workers, and dentists. They find that, in fact, even though child abuse is a well-documented social and public health problem in the United States, few medical schools and residency training programs include child abuse education and other family violence education in their curricula. What training there is consists of lectures and case discussions, and the training duration varies from program to program. Suzanne P. Starling and Stephen Boos suggest in "Core Content for Residency Training in Child Abuse and Neglect" (*Child Maltreatment*, vol. 8, no. 4, 2003) offering a core curriculum in residency programs that would enable primary care physicians (including pediatricians, family doctors, and emergency-medicine doctors) to recognize, evaluate, and manage cases of child abuse and neglect. In "Pediatrician Characteristics Associated with Child Abuse Identification and Reporting: Results from a National Survey of Pediatricians" (*Child Maltreatment*, vol. 11, no. 4, 2006), Emalee G. Flaherty et al. support the idea that physicians should receive training and find in a national survey that pediatricians who received recent child abuse education were more likely to suspect and report child abuse when it existed.

In "Child Maltreatment Training in Doctoral Programs in Clinical, Counseling, and School Psychology: Where Do We Go from Here?" (*Child Maltreatment*, vol. 8, no. 3, 2003), Kelly M. Champion et al. seek to gain information on the type and amount of training psychologists received regarding child maltreatment in American Psychological Association–accredited doctoral programs. Their study examined surveys sent to training directors of doctoral programs in 1992 and 2001. Champion et al. find that doctoral programs had generally remained unchanged within these years. Few doctoral programs offered specific courses on child maltreatment in 1992 and 2001, just 13% and 11%, respectively. Even though 65% of programs in 1992 and 59% in 2001 covered child maltreatment in three or more courses, these courses were rarely required to complete a doctoral program. Twenty percent of programs in 1992 and 22% in 2001 offered training in child maltreatment in clinical settings; however, most programs reported that students completed just 1% to 10% of such training. Finally, research activities in child maltreatment decreased from 60% in 1992 to 47% in 2001.

What Happens after a Child Maltreatment Report?

CPS. On receipt of a report of suspected child maltreatment, CPS screens the case to determine its proper jurisdiction. For example, if it is determined that the alleged perpetrator of sexual abuse is the victim's parent or caretaker, CPS screens in the report and conducts further investigation. If the alleged perpetrator is a stranger or someone who is not the parent or caregiver of the victim, the case is screened out or referred elsewhere, in this case, to the police because it does not fall within CPS jurisdiction as outlined under federal law.

A state's child welfare system, under which CPS functions, consists of other components designed to ensure

FIGURE 2.10

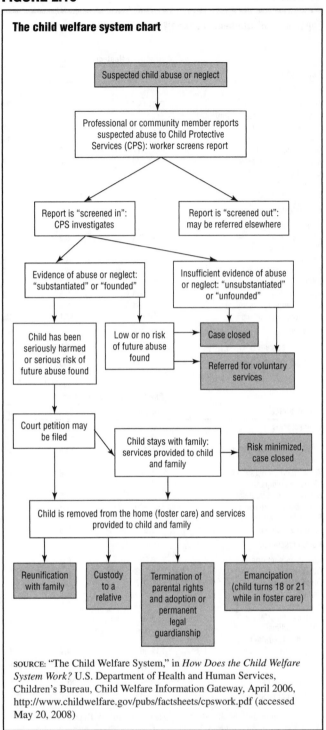

The child welfare system chart

SOURCE: "The Child Welfare System," in *How Does the Child Welfare System Work?* U.S. Department of Health and Human Services, Children's Bureau, Child Welfare Information Gateway, April 2006, http://www.childwelfare.gov/pubs/factsheets/cpswork.pdf (accessed May 20, 2008)

a child's well-being and safety. These include foster care, juvenile and family courts, and other child welfare services. CPS also oversees family reunification, granting custody to a relative, termination of parental rights, and emancipation (releasing a subject from the system because he or she is now recognized by the court as an adult). Cases of reported child abuse or neglect typically undergo a series of steps through the child welfare system. (See Figure 2.10.)

DISPOSITIONS OF INVESTIGATED REPORTS. After a CPS agency screens in a report of child maltreatment, it initiates an investigation. Some states follow one time frame for responding to all reports, whereas others follow a priority system, investigating high-priority cases within one to twenty-four hours. According to the ACYF, in *Child Maltreatment 2006*, the thirty-six states that reported response time in 2006 showed an average response time of eighty-six hours, or approximately three and a half days.

Following investigation of the report of child maltreatment, the CPS agency assigns a disposition, or finding, to the report. Before 2000 reports of alleged child maltreatment received one of three dispositions: indicated, substantiated, or unsubstantiated. In 2000 several states began implementing an alternative response program to reports of alleged child maltreatment. If the child is at a serious and immediate risk of maltreatment, CPS responds with the traditional formal investigation, which may involve removing the child from the home. If it is determined, however, that the parent will not endanger the child, CPS workers use the more informal alternative response to help the family. Instead of removing the child from the home environment, CPS steps in to assist the whole family by, for example, helping reduce stress that may lead to child abuse through provision of child care, adequate housing, and education in parenting skills. The ACYF indicates that in 2006 twelve states used the alternative response program in such cases, rather than making a formal determination of maltreatment.

Other dispositions, used by all states, include:

- A disposition of "substantiated," which means that sufficient evidence existed to support the allegation of maltreatment or risk of maltreatment

- A disposition of "indicated or reason to suspect," which means that the abuse and/or neglect could not be confirmed, but there was reason to suspect that the child was maltreated or was at risk of maltreatment

- A disposition of "unsubstantiated," which means that no maltreatment occurred or sufficient evidence did not exist to conclude that the child was maltreated or was at risk of being maltreated

Of the two million investigated reports in 2006, the ACYF states that 60.4% were unsubstantiated. More than one-fourth (25.2%) were substantiated, and 3% were indicated. (See Figure 2.11.) Another 6.3% were alternative response cases. Dispositions that were identified "closed with no finding" referred to cases in which the investigation could not be completed because the family moved out of the jurisdiction, the family could not be found, or the needed reports were not filed within the required time limit. Such dispositions accounted for 1.7% of investigated cases.

FIGURE 2.11

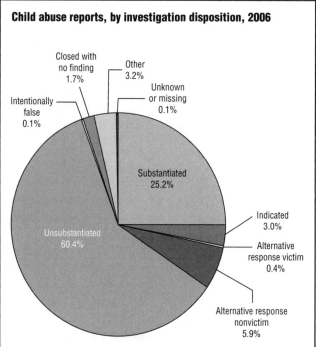

Child abuse reports, by investigation disposition, 2006

SOURCE: "Figure 2-2. Investigation Dispositions, 2006," in *Child Maltreatment 2006*, U.S. Department of Health and Human Services, Administration on Children, Youth, and Families, 2008, http://www.acf.hhs.gov/programs/cb/pubs/cm06/cm06.pdf (accessed May 20, 2008)

COURT INVOLVEMENT. The juvenile or family court hears allegations of maltreatment and decides if a child has been abused and/or neglected. The court then determines what should be done to protect the child. The child may be left in the parents' home under the supervision of the CPS agency, or the child may be placed in foster care. If the child is removed from the home and it is later determined that the child should never be returned to the parents, the court can begin proceedings to terminate parental rights so that the child can be put up for adoption. The state may also prosecute the abusive parent or caretaker when a crime has allegedly been committed.

CONTROVERSIES SURROUNDING THE CPS SYSTEM

The Debate about Family Preservation

The Adoption Assistance and Child Welfare Act of 1980 mandated: "In each case, reasonable efforts will be made (A) prior to the placement of a child in foster care, to prevent or eliminate the need for removal of the child from his home, and (B) to make it possible for the child to return to his home." However, because the law did not define the term *reasonable efforts*, states and courts interpreted the term in different ways. In many cases child welfare personnel took the "reasonable efforts" of providing family counseling, respite care, and substance abuse treatment, thus preventing the child from being removed from abusive parents.

The law was a reaction to what was seen as zealousness in the 1960s and 1970s, when children, especially African-American children, were taken from their home because their parents were poor. In the twentieth-first century, however, some feel that problems of drug or substance abuse can mean that returning the child to the home is likely a guarantee of further abuse. Others note that some situations exist where a parent's live-in partner, who has no emotional attachment to the child, may also present risks to the child.

Richard J. Gelles, a prominent family violence expert and once a vocal advocate of family preservation, had a change of heart after studying the case of fifteen-month-old David Edwards, who was suffocated by his mother after the child welfare system failed to come to his rescue. Even though David's parents had lost custody of their first child because of abuse, and despite reports of David's abuse, CPS made "reasonable efforts" to let the parents keep the child. In *The Book of David: How Preserving Families Can Cost Children's Lives* (1996), Gelles points out that CPS needed to abandon its blanket solution to child abuse in its attempt to use reasonable efforts to reunite the victims and their perpetrators. He contends that those parents who seriously abuse their children are incapable of changing their behavior.

By contrast, in "Foster Care vs. Family Preservation: The Track Record on Safety and Well-Being" (November 4, 2007, http://www.nccpr.org/newissues/1.html), the National Coalition for Child Protection Reform (NCCPR), a nonprofit organization of experts on child abuse and foster care who are committed to the reform of the child welfare system, contends that many allegedly maltreated children are unnecessarily removed from their homes—and in fact that children are in more danger when placed in foster care than when given services to help preserve the family. The NCCPR recognizes that even though there are cases in which the only way to save a child is to remove him or her from an abusive home, in many cases providing support services to the family in crisis, while letting the child remain at home, helps ensure child safety.

Joseph J. Doyle studies in "Child Protection and Child Outcomes: Measuring the Effects of Foster Care" (*American Economic Review*, forthcoming) the outcomes of foster care placement on school-age children. His results suggest that children in foster care have higher delinquency rates, teen birth rates, and lower earnings compared to other children in comparable family situations. He argues that children "on the margin of placement"—in other words, in cases of neglect or abuse where removal from the home was not a clear call—would do better if they remained at home.

Child Welfare Workforce

Child welfare caseworkers perform multiple tasks in the course of their job. Among other things, they investigate reports of child maltreatment, coordinate various services (mental health, substance abuse, etc.) to help keep families together, find foster care placements for children if needed, make regular visits to children and families, arrange placement of children in permanent homes when they cannot be safely returned to their parents or caretakers, and document all details pertaining to their cases. Caseworker supervisors monitor and support their caseworkers, sometimes taking on some of the cases when there is a staff shortage or heavy caseload.

The GAO examines in *Child Welfare: HHS Could Play a Greater Role in Helping Child Welfare Agencies Recruit and Retain Staff* (March 2003, http://www.gao.gov/new.items/d03357.pdf) the child welfare workforce and how challenges in recruiting and retaining caseworkers affect the children under their care. Among other things, the GAO focuses on exit interview documents of caseworkers who had left their jobs from seventeen states, forty counties, and nineteen private child welfare agencies. The GAO also interviewed child welfare officials and experts and conducted on-site visits to agencies in four states: California, Illinois, Kentucky, and Texas.

The GAO finds that as of 2003, CPS agencies continued to have difficulty attracting and retaining experienced caseworkers. The low pay not only made it difficult to attract qualified workers but also contributed to CPS employees leaving for better-paying jobs. Because the federal government has not set any national hiring policies, employees have college degrees that may not necessarily be related to social work. Workers whom the GAO interviewed in different states also mentioned risk to personal safety, increased paperwork, lack of supervisory support, and insufficient time to attend training as things that affected their job performance and influenced their decision to leave.

According to the GAO, in *Child Welfare: Additional Federal Action Could Help States Address Challenges in Providing Services to Children and Families* (May 2007, http://www.gao.gov/new.items/d07850t.pdf), the difficulties in recruiting and retaining caseworkers in 2007 had barely been addressed since the 2003 report. Child welfare officials in most states reported that caseloads per worker remained too high, caseworkers continued to have too many administrative responsibilities, and the effectiveness of caseworker supervision was poor.

SLIPPING THROUGH THE CRACKS. Some CPS workers at times fail to monitor the children they are supposed to protect. In Florida the Department of Children and Families could not account for the disappearance of a five-year-old foster child, Rilya Wilson, who had been missing for more than a year before the agency noticed her absence in April 2002. At around that time the agency had reportedly lost track of more than 530 children. Rilya's disappearance was only discovered after her caseworker was fired and the new caseworker could not locate the child. The former caseworker had reported that Rilya was fine, even though that caseworker had not visited the child at her foster home for months. Authorities discovered that her foster mother continued to receive welfare payments for the girl in her absence. Witnesses had also testified that the foster mother and her roommate abused the child before her disappearance. The women faced charges of aggravated child abuse, and her foster mother was convicted of fraud and sentenced to three years in jail. In March 2005 one of the caregivers was indicted on charges of murdering the girl. Rilya's foster mother eventually confessed to murdering Rilya, although her body has never been recovered.

New Jersey's child welfare system had also come to national attention because of its failure to protect adopted and foster children. In October 2003 four brothers of the Jackson family in Collingswood, New Jersey, aged nine, ten, fourteen, and nineteen, were removed from their adoptive parents' home and the couple was arrested. Investigations later revealed the brothers were systematically starved over many years. They weighed no more than forty-five pounds and stood less than four feet tall. The children reportedly subsisted on peanut butter, pancake batter, and wallboard. Authorities admitted two of the boys had fetal alcohol syndrome and two had eating disorders, which were the reasons the adoptive parents gave to neighbors for the brothers' emaciated appearance. The brothers, however, began putting on weight and height after living with other foster families.

Investigations also revealed that Division of Youth and Family Services (DYFS) workers visited the adoptive parents' home thirty-eight times in the past to check on three other foster children but never asked about the brothers. In 1995, when DYFS was notified by the oldest boy's school that he seemed malnourished, DYFS did not require a medical examination and even agreed to the adoptive mother's decision to homeschool the brothers. DYFS policies regulating foster homes required an annual medical evaluation and interview of each household member, but these never took place. In May 2004 the adoptive parents were indicted on twenty-eight counts of aggravated assault and child endangerment.

Maureen O'Hagan reports in "Judge Demands State Keep Foster-Care Promises" (Seattle Times, July 1, 2008) that in June 2008 a judge gave the Washington Department of Social and Health Services thirty days to keep the promises the state had made four years previously in the settlement of a class-action lawsuit brought on behalf of the state's foster children. The lead plaintiff in that case had been through thirty-four foster-care placements by the time she turned twelve. The June 2008 ruling required the state to immediately make progress in several areas, including reducing caseworker loads to enable workers to make monthly visits to foster children, ensure foster children are promptly screened for health problems, and facilitate regular visits between foster children and their siblings. Should the state not comply, the plaintiffs' lawyers can bring the state back to court, where the state could face fines or the agency could be placed under court governance.

These cases and others like them serve to focus public and media attention on the failures of CPS. Even though many departments are conscientiously and effectively doing their jobs, there are sometimes mistakes that result in great harm and even death to the children under their care.

Holding States Accountable

In 2006 the HHS released *Child Welfare Outcomes 2003: Annual Report—Safety, Permanency, Well-Being* (http://www.acf.hhs.gov/programs/cb/pubs/cwo03/cwo03.pdf), the sixth in a series of annual reports on states' performances in meeting the needs of at-risk children who have entered the child welfare system. The HHS finds that states were succeeding in some areas and failing in others. However, there had been significant improvement in several areas between 2000 and 2003: the percentage of children who were mistreated by a foster parent declined, the percentage of children who reentered foster care within a twelve-month period declined, the percentage of adoptions of children within twenty-four-months of entering foster care increased, and the percentage of children aged twelve and younger placed in group homes or other institutions decreased. However, the percentage of children who had entered foster care at age twelve or younger who then "aged out" of the system actually increased during this period.

According to the HHS, in *The AFGARS Report: Preliminary FY 2006 Estimates as of January 2008* (January 2008, http://www.acf.hhs.gov/programs/cb/stats_research/afcars/tar/report14.pdf), an estimated 303,000 children entered and 289,000 exited foster care in fiscal year 2006. Of those children who exited foster care, 53% were reunited with their parents or primary caretakers, 11% went to live with relatives, 17% were adopted, and 9% were emancipated (they became legal adults). (See Table 2.16.) Two percent were transferred to another CPS agency, and another 5% were put under guardianship. Two percent of foster children had run away. Another 509 children had died. As of September 30, 2006, an estimated 510,000 children remained in foster care; 129,000 of them were waiting to be adopted.

Lives Saved

Even though CPS agencies have had many problems and are often unable to perform as effectively as they should, many thousands of maltreated children have been identified, many lives have been saved, and many more

TABLE 2.16

Outcomes for children who exited foster care, fiscal year 2006

Reunification with parent(s) or primary caretaker(s)	53%	154,103
Living with other relative(s)	11%	30,751
Adoption	17%	50,379
Emancipation	9%	26,517
Guardianship	5%	15,010
Transfer to another agency	2%	6,683
Runaway	2%	5,049
Death of child	0%	509

Note: Deaths are attributable to a variety of causes including medical conditions, accidents and homicide.

SOURCE: "What Were the Outcomes for the Children Exiting Foster Care during FY 2006?" in *The AFCARS Report*, U.S. Department of Health and Human Services, Children's Bureau, January 2008, http://www.acf.hhs.gov/programs/cb/stats_research/afcars/tar/report14.pdf (accessed May 20, 2008)

have been taken out of dangerous environments. It is impossible to tally the number of child abuse cases that might have ended in death; these children have been saved by changes in the laws, by awareness and reporting, and by the efforts of the professionals who intervened on their behalf.

CHAPTER 3
CAUSES AND EFFECTS OF CHILD ABUSE

CAUSES OF CHILD ABUSE

Child abuse is primarily a problem within families. Even though abuse by nonfamily members does occur, most victims are abused by one or more of their parents. For this reason, much of the research into the causes of child abuse has focused on families and the characteristics and circumstances that can contribute to violence within them.

The 1975 National Family Violence Survey and the 1985 National Family Violence Resurvey, conducted by Murray A. Straus and Richard J. Gelles, are the most complete studies of spousal and parent-child abuse yet prepared in the United States. Unlike most studies of child abuse, the data from these surveys came from detailed interviews with the general population, not from cases that came to the attention of official agencies and professionals. Therefore, Straus and Gelles had a more intimate knowledge of the families and an awareness of incidences of child abuse that were not reported to authorities or community professionals.

Straus and Gelles believe that cultural standards permit violence in the family. They incorporated research from the two surveys and additional chapters into the book *Physical Violence in American Families: Risk Factors and Adaptations to Violence in 8,145 Families* (1990).

Understanding Factors that Contribute to Child Abuse

The factors contributing to child maltreatment are complex. In *Third National Incidence Study of Child Abuse and Neglect* (*NIS-3*; 1993), the most comprehensive federal source of information about the incidence of child maltreatment in the United States, Andrea J. Sedlak and Diane D. Broadhurst find that family structure and size, poverty, alcohol and substance abuse, domestic violence, and community violence are contributing factors to child abuse and neglect.

Even though these and other factors affect the likelihood of child maltreatment, they do not necessarily lead to abuse. It is important to understand that the causes of child abuse and the characteristics of families in which child abuse occurs are only indicators. Most parents, even in the most stressful and demanding situations, and even with a personal history that might predispose them to be more violent than parents without such a history, do not abuse their children.

Murray A. Straus and Christine Smith note in "Family Patterns and Child Abuse" (Straus and Gelles, *Physical Violence in American Families*) that a combination of several factors is more likely to result in child abuse than is a single factor alone. Also, the sum of the effects of individual factors taken together does not necessarily add up to what Straus and Smith call the "explosive combinations" of several factors interacting with one another. Nonetheless, even "explosive combinations" do not necessarily lead to child abuse.

FAMILIES AT RISK FOR CHILD MALTREATMENT

It is impossible to determine whether child maltreatment will occur, but generally a family may be at risk if the parent is young, has little education, has had several children born within a few years, and is highly dependent on social welfare. According to Judith S. Rycus and Ronald C. Hughes, in *Field Guide to Child Welfare* (1998), a family at high to moderate risk includes parents who do not understand basic child development and who may discipline inappropriately for the child's age, those who lack the necessary skills for caring for and managing a child, those who use physical punishment harshly and excessively, and those who do not appropriately supervise their children. They find that families under stresses such as divorce, death, illness, disability, unemployment, or incarceration are more likely to abuse or neglect children. Small stresses can have a cumulative effect and become explosive with a relatively minor event. For potentially abusive parents, high levels of ongoing stress, coupled with inadequate coping strategies and limited resources, produce an extremely high-risk situation for children involved.

The Centers for Disease Control and Prevention explains in the fact sheet "Understanding Child Maltreatment" (2008, http://www.cdc.gov/ncipc/pub-res/CMFactsheet.pdf) that a family may also be at risk if:

- A child in the family is age four or younger
- The family is socially isolated
- The family has a history of violence, drug or alcohol use, or chronic health problems
- The family is poor
- The surrounding community is particularly violent

Psychological Abuse

Psychological abuse can cause great harm to children but tends to be less well recognized than physical or sexual abuse or neglect. In "Family Dynamics Associated with the Use of Psychologically Violent Parental Practices" (*Journal of Family Violence*, vol. 19, no. 2, April 2004), Marie-Hélène Gagné and Camil Bouchard identify four family characteristics that are likely to result in parental psychological violence. The first involves a scapegoat child, who may be different from other family members by his or her unattractiveness, disability, having been adopted, or being the child of a former spouse. This child is typically neglected by the parents, treated harshly, and excluded from family intimacy. The second type of family has a domineering father, who intimidates the children and may even turn physically violent. The mother herself may be a victim of spousal violence. The authoritarian mother typifies the third family characteristic leading to parental psychological abuse. She controls the household, and the children are expected to do as she bids. The fourth family characteristic involves the "broken parent," who has not attained maturity and a feeling of self-worth because of a difficult past. This type of parent takes care of the children when things are going smoothly, but falls apart when difficulties arise.

Family Structure

Single-parent families appear to be at greater risk of child maltreatment. Sedlak and Broadhurst find in *NIS-3* that under the Harm Standard, children in single-parent households were at a higher risk of physical abuse and all types of neglect than were children in other family structures in 1993. (See Chapter 2 for a definition of the Harm and Endangerment Standards.) Children living with only their fathers suffered the highest incidence rates of physical abuse and emotional and educational neglect. (See

FIGURE 3.1

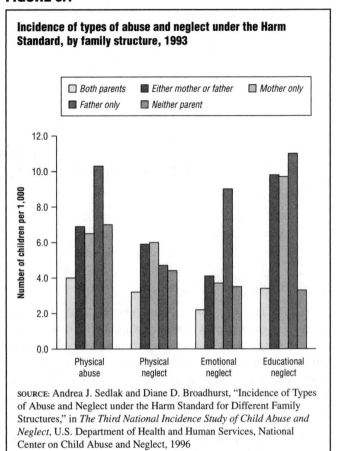

Incidence of types of abuse and neglect under the Harm Standard, by family structure, 1993

SOURCE: Andrea J. Sedlak and Diane D. Broadhurst, "Incidence of Types of Abuse and Neglect under the Harm Standard for Different Family Structures," in *The Third National Incidence Study of Child Abuse and Neglect*, U.S. Department of Health and Human Services, National Center on Child Abuse and Neglect, 1996

Figure 3.1.) Under the Endangerment Standard higher incidence rates of physical and emotional neglect occurred among children living with only their fathers than among those living in other family structures. (See Figure 3.2.)

The Problem of Substance Abuse

Child protective services (CPS) workers are faced with the growing problem of substance abuse among families involved with the child welfare system. According to the U.S. Department of Health and Human Services (HHS), in *Children Living with Substance-Abusing or Substance-Dependent Parents* (June 2, 2003, http://www.oas.samhsa.gov/2k3/children/children.pdf), approximately 70 million children under age eighteen lived with at least one parent in 2001; about 6.1 million (9%) of these children lived with one or more parents with past-year substance abuse or dependence. About one-fifth were five years old or younger (9.8% of three- to five-year-olds and 9.8% of children younger than three). (See Table 3.1.) Among these children, about 4.5 million lived with an alcoholic parent, an estimated 953,000 lived with a parent with an illicit drug problem, and approximately 657,000 lived with parents who abused both alcohol and illicit drugs. (See Figure 3.3.) The HSS notes that fathers (7.8%) were more likely than mothers (4%) to report past-year substance abuse or dependence.

FIGURE 3.2

FIGURE 3.3

Incidence of types of abuse and neglect under the Endangerment Standard, by family structure, 1993

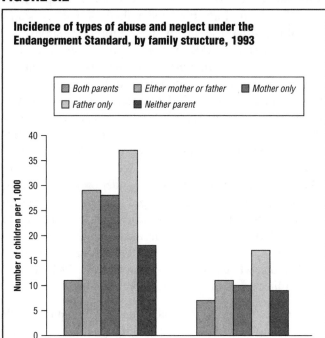

SOURCE: Andrea J. Sedlak and Diane D. Broadhurst, "Incidence of Types of Abuse and Neglect under the Endangerment Standard for Different Family Structures," in *The Third National Incidence Study of Child Abuse and Neglect*, U.S. Department of Health and Human Services, National Center on Child Abuse and Neglect, 1996

Children age 17 or younger living with one or more parents with past-year substance abuse or dependence, 2001

[In thousands]

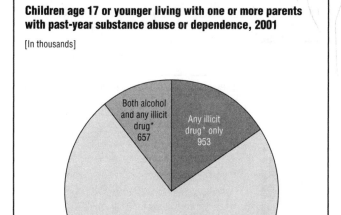

Notes: Children include biological, step, adoptive, or foster. Children aged 17 or younger who were not living with one or more parents for most of the quarter of the National Household Survey on Drug Abuse (NHSDA) interview are excluded from the present analysis. According to the 2000 Current Population Survey, this amounts to approximately 3 million or 4 percent of children aged 17 or younger. *"Any illicit drug" refers to marijuana/hashish, cocaine (including crack), inhalants, hallucinogens, heroin, or prescription-type drugs used nonmedically.

SOURCE: "Figure 1. Estimated Numbers (in Thousands) of Children Aged 17 or Younger Living with One or More Parents with Past Year Substance Abuse or Dependence: 2001," in *Children Living with Substance-Abusing or Substance-Dependent Parents*, U.S. Department of Health and Human Services, Substance Abuse and Mental Health Services Administration, Office of Applied Studies, June 2, 2003, http://www.oas.samhsa.gov/2k3/children/children.pdf (accessed May 20, 2008)

TABLE 3.1

Children age 17 or younger living with one or more parents with past-year substance abuse or dependence, by number and percentage, 2001

Ages of children (years)	Estimated numbers (in thousands)	Percentage
Younger than 3	1,078	9.8
3 to 5	1,115	9.8
6 to 11	1,816	7.5
12 to 17	2,100	9.2

Notes: Children include biological, step, adoptive, or foster. Children aged 17 or younger who were not living with one or more parents for most of the quarter of the National Household Survey on Drug Abuse (NHSDA) interview are excluded from the present analysis. According to the 2000 Current Population Survey, this amounts to approximately 3 million or 4 percent of children aged 17 or younger.

SOURCE: "Table 2. Estimated Numbers (in Thousands) and Percentages of Children Aged 17 or Younger Living with One or More Parents with Past Year Substance Abuse or Dependence: 2001," in *Children Living with Substance-Abusing or Substance-Dependent Parents*, U.S. Department of Health and Human Services, Substance Abuse and Mental Health Services Administration, Office of Applied Studies, June 2, 2003, http://www.oas.samhsa.gov/2k3/children/children.pdf (accessed May 20, 2008)

The 2004 National Survey on Drug Use and Health surveyed parents about different forms of "household turbulence" in the past year. The survey found that households in which there was past-year alcohol dependence or abuse were more likely to report turbulence. For

example, 40.4% of households containing children in which there was alcohol dependence or abuse reported that people often insulted or yelled at each other, compared to 27.3% of households with no past-year alcohol dependence or abuse. (See Figure 3.4.) Nearly a third (29.8%) of the households with alcohol problems reported that people in the household had serious arguments, compared to 18.2% of people in households with no alcohol problems. Parents in households with alcohol problems (9.9%) were also more likely than parents with no alcohol problems (3.6%) to report that one spouse hit or threatened to hit the other at least once in the past year. In other words, children living in homes where alcohol dependence or abuse was a problem were more likely to be exposed to domestic violence than children living in homes where alcohol abuse was not a problem.

Sedlak and Broadhurst note that the increase in illicit drug use since the Second National Incidence Study of Child Abuse and Neglect (1986) may have contributed to the increased child maltreatment incidence reported in *NIS-3*. Children whose parents are substance abusers

FIGURE 3.4

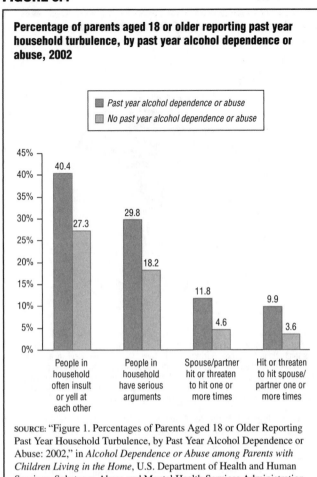

Percentage of parents aged 18 or older reporting past year household turbulence, by past year alcohol dependence or abuse, 2002

- ■ Past year alcohol dependence or abuse
- ■ No past year alcohol dependence or abuse

SOURCE: "Figure 1. Percentages of Parents Aged 18 or Older Reporting Past Year Household Turbulence, by Past Year Alcohol Dependence or Abuse: 2002," in *Alcohol Dependence or Abuse among Parents with Children Living in the Home*, U.S. Department of Health and Human Services, Substance Abuse and Mental Health Services Administration, Office of Applied Studies, February 13, 2004, http://www.oas.samhsa.gov/2k4/ACOA/ACOA.pdf (accessed May 20, 2008)

are at high risk of abuse and neglect because of the physiological, psychological, and sociological nature of addiction.

According to the Child Welfare Information Gateway, in "Substance Abuse and Child Maltreatment" (2003, http://www.childwelfare.gov/pubs/factsheets/sub abuse_childmal.cfm), about one-third to two-thirds of substantiated child maltreatment reports (those having sufficient evidence to support the allegation of maltreatment) involve substance abuse. Younger children, especially infants, are more likely to be victimized by substance-abusing parents, and the maltreatment is more likely to consist of neglect than abuse. Many children experience neglect when a parent is under the influence of alcohol or is out of the home looking for drugs. Even when the parent is at home, he or she may be psychologically unavailable to the children.

SUBSTANCE ABUSE AMONG PREGNANT WOMEN. Illicit drug use among pregnant women continues to be a national problem. Each year the National Survey on Drug Use and Health, formerly known as the National House-

hold Survey on Drug Abuse, asks female respondents aged fifteen to forty-four about their pregnancy status and illicit drug use the month before the survey. In *Results from the 2006 National Survey on Drug Use and Health: National Findings* (September 2007, http://www.oas.samhsa.gov/nsduh/2k6nsduh/2k6Results.pdf), the Substance Abuse and Mental Health Services Administration's Office of Applied Studies states that in 2005–06, 4% of pregnant women, compared to 10% of nonpregnant women, reported using illicit drugs during the past month.(See Table 3.2.) Pregnant teens were much more likely to use illicit drugs than were older pregnant women; 15.5% of pregnant women aged fifteen to seventeen reported illicit drug use the previous month, compared to just 1.8% of pregnant women aged twenty-six to forty-four. Among pregnant women, more African-Americans (6.1%) than whites (4.7%) and Hispanics (1.4%) reported using illicit drugs the previous month.

CHILDREN AT ILLICIT DRUG LABS. The rapid growth of methamphetamine use in the United States has resulted in the establishment of clandestine methamphetamine laboratories (meth labs) in many places. In years past large-scale operations, particularly in California and Mexico, produced large quantities of drugs, which were then distributed throughout various areas in the country. With more demand for methamphetamines, many small-scale businesses have started operating. Because methamphetamines can be produced almost anywhere using readily available ingredients, nearly anyone can set up a temporary laboratory, make a batch of drugs, then dismantle the apparatus. Authorities have found makeshift laboratories in places inhabited or visited by children, including houses, apartments, mobile homes, and motel rooms.

As more children are found living in or visiting home-based meth labs, CPS personnel have to deal with those children who have been exposed not only to potentially abusive people associated with the production of methamphetamines but also to dangers such as fire and explosions. Melinda Hohman, Rhonda Oliver, and Wendy Wright report in "Methamphetamine Abuse and Manufacture: The Child Welfare Response" (*Social Work*, vol. 49, no. 3, July 1, 2004) that hazardous living conditions in these labs include unsafe electrical equipment, chemical ingredients that can cause respiratory distress and possibly long-term effects such as liver and kidney disease and cancers, syringes, and the presence of firearms and pornography. Police find meth homes with defective plumbing, rodent and insect infestation, and without heating or cooling. Children living in meth labs are also likely to be victims of severe neglect and physical and sexual abuse. According to Karen Swetlow, in *Children at Clandestine Methamphetamine Labs: Helping Meth's Youngest Victims* (June 2003, http://www.ojp

TABLE 3.2

Illicit drug use in the past month among females, by age, pregnancy status, and Hispanic origin and race, 2003–04 and 2005–06

| | Total[a] | | Pregnancy status | | | |
| | | | Pregnant | | Not pregnant | |
Demographic/pregnancy characteristic	2003–2004	2005–2006	2003–2004	2005–2006	2003–2004	2005–2006
Total	10.0	9.8	4.6	4.0	10.2	10.0
Age						
15–17	16.1[b]	14.0	16.0	15.5	16.0[b]	13.9
18–25	16.0	15.7	7.8	6.5	16.4	16.3
26–44	6.7	6.7	2.1	1.8	6.9	6.9
Hispanic origin and race						
Not Hispanic or Latino	10.6	10.2	4.5	4.8	10.8	10.4
White	11.1	11.0	4.2	4.7	11.4	11.2
Black or African American	9.4	9.3	7.8	6.1	9.4	9.4
American Indian or Alaska Native	17.8[c]	10.5	*	*	18.6[b]	10.0
Native Hawaiian or other Pacific Islander	*	6.0	*	*	*	6.4
Asian	3.5	3.2	*	*	3.6	3.3
Two or more races	20.3	14.6	*	*	20.8	14.6
Hispanic or Latino	6.9	7.5	5.0c	1.4	7.0	7.9
Trimester[d]						
First	N/A	N/A	8.0	5.4	N/A	N/A
Second	N/A	N/A	3.8	3.6	N/A	N/A
Third	N/A	N/A	2.4	2.7	N/A	N/A

*Low precision; no estimate reported.
N/A: Not applicable.
Note: Illicit drugs include marijuana/hashish, cocaine (including crack), heroin, hallucinogens, inhalants, or prescription-type psychotherapeutics used non medically.
[a]Estimates in the total column are for all females aged 15 to 44, including those with unknown pregnancy status.
[b]Difference between estimate and 2005–2006 estimate is statistically significant at the 0.01 level.
[c]Difference between estimate and 2005–2006 estimate is statistically significant at the 0.05 level.
[d]Pregnant females aged 15 to 44 not reporting trimester were excluded.

SOURCE: "Table 7.52B. Illicit Drug Use in the Past Month among Females Aged 15 to 44, by Pregnancy and Demographic Characteristics: Percentages, Annual Averages Based on 2003–2004 and 2005–2006," in *Results from the 2006 National Survey on Drug Use and Health: Detailed Tables*, U.S. Department of Health and Human Services, Substance Abuse and Mental Health Services Administration, Office of Applied Studies, September 2007, http://www.oas.samhsa.gov/NSDUH/2k6nsduh/tabs/Sect7peTabs51to58.pdf (accessed May 20, 2008)

TABLE 3.3

Children involved in methamphetamine lab incidents, by selected demographics, 2000–02

| | | Number of children | | | | | |
Year	Number of meth lab-related incidents	Present	Residing in seized meth labs[a]	Affected[b]	Exposed to toxic chemicals[c]	Taken into protective custody	Injured or killed
2002	15,353	2,077	2,023	3,167	1,373	1,026	26 injured, 2 killed
2001	13,270	2,191	976	2,191	788	778	14 injured
2000	8,971	1,803	216	1,803	345	353	12 injured, 3 killed

[a]Children included in this group were not necessarily present at the time of seizure.
[b]Includes children who were residing at the labs but not necessarily present at the time of seizure and children who were visiting the site; data for 2000 and 2001 may not show all children affected.
[c]Includes children who were residing at the labs but not necessarily present at the time of seizure.

SOURCE: Karen Swetlow, "Children Involved in Methamphetamine Lab-Related Incidents in the United States," in *Children at Clandestine Methamphetamine Labs: Helping Meth's Youngest Victims*, U.S. Department of Justice, Office of Justice Programs, Office for Victims of Crime, June 2003, http://www.ojp.usdoj.gov/ovc/publications/bulletins/children/197590.pdf (accessed May 20, 2008)

.usdoj.gov/ovc/publications/bulletins/children/197590.pdf), thousands of children were living in or visiting meth labs that were seized by law enforcement nationwide between 2000 and 2002. In 2002, 1,026 children, or about half of the 2,077 children present during lab-related incidents, were taken into protective custody. (See Table 3.3.)

Poverty and Unemployment

Even though Sedlak and Broadhurst find in *NIS-3* a correlation between family income and child abuse and neglect, most experts agree that the connection between poverty and maltreatment is not easily explained. In *Depression, Substance Abuse, and Domestic Violence: Little Is Known about Co-occurrence and Combined Effects* on *Low-Income Families* (June 2004, http://www.nccp.org/publications/pdf/text_546.pdf), Sharmila Lawrence, Michelle Chau, and Mary Clare Lennon show that the problems of depression, substance abuse, and domestic violence are interrelated and that these problems are more likely to be prevalent among low-income families. They note that federally funded and community-based programs, such as Early Head Start, which are designed to help low-income parents and their infants and toddlers, recognize the connection between poverty and parental and child well-being.

Lawrence M. Berger of the University of Wisconsin, Madison, argues in "Income, Family Characteristics, and Physical Violence toward Children" (*Child Abuse and Neglect: The International Journal*, vol. 29, no. 2, February 2005) that several family factors make abuse of children more likely. He finds that in both single- and two-parent families, depression, maternal alcohol consumption, and a history of family violence put children at risk for abuse. Low income was significantly related to violence toward children, but only in single-parent families.

In "Understanding the Ecology of Child Maltreatment: A Review of the Literature and Directions for Future Research" (*Child Maltreatment*, vol. 11, no. 3, 2006), Bridget Freisthler, Darcey H. Merritt, and Elizabeth A. LaScala underscore the influence of neighborhood characteristics, such as impoverishment and housing stress, in rates of child maltreatment. The researchers also show that unemployment, child care difficulties, and alcoholism may also contribute in this atmosphere to child maltreatment.

Violent Families

Straus and Smith report that one of the most distinct findings of the National Family Violence Resurvey is that violence in one family relationship is frequently associated with violence in other family relationships. In families in which the husband struck his wife, the child abuse rate was much higher (22.3 per 100 children) than in other families (8 per 100 children). Similarly, in families in which the wife hit the husband, the child abuse rate was also considerably higher (22.9 per 100 children) than in families in which the wife did not hit the husband (9.2 per 100 children).

In *Domestic Violence, Child Abuse, and Youth Violence: Strategies for Prevention and Early Intervention* (March 14, 2005, http://www.mincava.umn.edu/link/documents/fvpf2/fvpf2.shtml), Janet Carter reviews the research and finds that domestic violence and child abuse often occur in the same families. One study finds that 50% of the men who regularly assaulted their wife also assaulted their children; another finds that 59% of mothers of abused children have also been assaulted by their partner.

TABLE 3.4

Percentage of households that experienced nonfatal intimate partner violence where children under age 12 resided, by gender of the victims, 2001–05

Households with intimate partner violence victims	Annual average	
	Number	Percent
All households with—	615,795	100%
Children	216,490	35.2
No children	303,615	49.3
Unknown	95,685	15.5
Female victim households with—	510,970	100%
Children	194,455	38.1
No children	235,940	46.2
Unknown	80,580	15.8
Male victim households with—	104,820	100%
Children	22,040	21.0
No children	67,680	64.6
Unknown	15,105	14.4

Note: The National Crime Victimization Survey (NCVS) does not ask about the extent to which young children may have witnessed the violence.

SOURCE: Shannan Catalano, "Average Annual Number and Percentage of Households Experiencing Nonfatal Intimate Partner Violence Where Children under Age 12 Resided, by Gender of Victims, 2001–2005," in *Intimate Partner Violence in the United States*, U.S. Department of Justice, Bureau of Justice Statistics, December 2007, http://www.ojp.usdoj.gov/bjs/pub/pdf/ipvus.pdf (accessed May 20, 2008)

Shannan Catalano of the Bureau of Justice Statics notes in *Intimate Partner Violence in the United States* (December 2007, http://www.ojp.usdoj.gov/bjs/intimate/ipv.htm#contents) that between 2001 and 2005, 510,970 women and 104,820 men were victims of abuse by an intimate partner. (See Table 3.4.) Children were known to reside in 38.1% of the households with female victims and 21% of the households with male victims of intimate partner violence. Experts believe these children are at high risk of being abused as well.

To determine the relationship among family stress, partner violence, caretaker distress, and child abuse, Suzanne Salzinger et al. compare in "Effects of Partner Violence and Physical Child Abuse in Child Behavior: A Study of Abused and Comparison Children" (*Journal of Family Violence*, vol. 17, no. 1, March 2002) a sample of one hundred New York City children from grades four to six who experienced physical abuse with a control group of one hundred nonabused children. They questioned each caretaker concerning stressful events that had occurred in their family during the lifetime of the subject child. These stress factors included, among other things, separation or divorce, drug abuse, alcohol abuse, deaths, serious illness in the past year, and job loss in the past year. Salzinger et al. find that in households where partner violence and child maltreatment both occurred, the children suffered physical aggression from both the perpetrator and the victim. In addition, in these households the mothers—who were typically the primary caretakers—reported that they were more likely than the fathers to physically abuse the children. Interestingly, Salzinger et al. find that family stress, not partner violence, was responsible for caretaker distress, which in turn increased the risk for child abuse.

Even if children themselves are not battered, witnessing assaults on a mother is damaging to children. In "Longitudinal Investigation of the Relationship among Maternal Victimization, Depressive Symptoms, Social Support, and Children's Behavior and Development" (*Journal of Interpersonal Violence*, vol. 20, no. 12, 2005), Catherine Koverola et al. find that maternal victimization is related to child behavior problems at age four and persists to at least age eight.

MOTHERS, FATHERS, AND SIBLINGS

A family's dynamics, stress levels, and overall situation are significant risk factors for child maltreatment, but there are other considerations as well. Many researchers have investigated how the background and temperament of the individual caregivers within a family influence the likelihood of child abuse.

Maltreatment by Mothers

Straus and Smith find that women are as likely, if not more likely, as men to abuse their children. They believe child abuse by women can be explained in terms of social factors rather than in psychological factors. Women are more likely to abuse their children because they are more likely to have much greater responsibility for raising the children, which means they are more exposed to the trials and frustrations of child rearing. Women spend more "time at risk" while tending to their children. "Time at risk" refers to the time a potential abuser spends with the victim.

To determine the connection between psychological risk factors for child maltreatment and chronic maltreatment, Louise S. Ethier, Germain Couture, and Carl Lacharité of the Université du Québec à Trois-Rivières conducted interviews and tests of a group of abusive mothers in Quebec, Canada, on three separate occasions: during the initial recruitment for an intervention program; two years later at the end of the program; and four years after the initial recruitment as a follow-up. In "Risk Factors Associated with the Chronicity of High Potential for Child Abuse and Neglect" (*Journal of Family Violence*, vol. 19, no. 1, February 2004), the researchers report that fifty-six mothers were evaluated: twenty-one mothers whose files at the social agencies had been closed for at least four months (transitory problems group), and thirty-five mothers who were still abusive (chronic group). The risk factors were categorized into two general groups: the mother's history and her characteristics as an adult. The mother's history included placement in foster care, childhood sexual abuse, running away from home in her teens, breakups with parental

relationships, parental unavailability, neglect, and physical violence. The mother's adult characteristics included family unemployment, limited social support, past intimate partner violence, low level of intellectual functioning, low level of education, and high numbers of children and partners.

Ethier, Couture, and Lacharité find that mothers who reported a history of childhood sexual abuse, placement in foster care, and running away from home during adolescence were more likely to chronically mistreat their own children. Overall, mothers exhibiting more than eight risk factors had about four times the risk for chronic child maltreatment. Those with a history of childhood sexual abuse were 3.8 times more likely to chronically mistreat their children than those without this risk factor. The risk for chronic child maltreatment was 3.6 times greater for those with a childhood history of placement in foster care and 3 times greater for those with a history of running away from home in adolescence. Ethier, Couture, and Lacharité find that the following risk factors also predisposed mothers to chronic child maltreatment: childhood neglect (0.6 times more likely than those without this risk factor), physical violence (0.7 times), and unavailability of and breakup with parental figures (0.9 and 1.5 times, respectively). Ethier, Couture, and Lacharité conclude that traumatic experiences of childhood sexual abuse (77.8% of mothers in the study), placement in foster care (80%), and running away from home during adolescence (77.3%) had the greatest adverse effects on the mother's ability to parent her children.

Carol Coohey compares in "Battered Mothers Who Physically Abuse Their Children" (*Journal of Interpersonal Violence*, vol. 19, no. 8, August 2004) four groups of mothers: those who were battered and who physically abused their children, those who were neither battered nor who physically abused their children, those who were battered but who did not physically abuse their children, and those who were not battered but who did physically abuse their children. Coohey finds that women who were assaulted by their own mother as children—not women who were battered by their partner—were the most likely to abuse their own children.

Maltreatment by Fathers

According to Katreena L. Scott and Claire V. Crooks, in "Effecting Change in Maltreating Fathers: Critical Principles for Intervention Planning" (*Clinical Psychology: Science and Practice*, vol. 11, spring 2004), even though some fathers are perpetrators of child maltreatment, little research has been done on abusive fathers. The researchers note that for intervention services to be effective, it is important to know the characteristics of abusive fathers. Abusive fathers tend to be controlling of their children. Being self-centered, they demand respect and unconditional love. They are insecure and are constantly looking for signs of defiance or disrespect. An abusive father may feel that a child has more power than he does and may misinterpret a child's action as misbehavior. He therefore inflicts physical abuse to regain control. An abusive father has a sense of entitlement, expecting his children to do as he says. Scott and Crooks point out that sexual abuse may result from the father's sense of entitlement.

An abusive father's involvement with his children is usually based on his own needs, focusing on activities that he likes instead of what the children may want to do. However, his interest in his children may come and go, depending on his emotional state. Some fathers maltreat their children because they believe in the stereotypical role of fathers as disciplinarians. Some also feel that they have to show others that they are doing a good job as a parent. Refusing to acknowledge that they may be having a tough time as a parent, they take out their frustrations on the children.

Maltreatment by Siblings

Vernon R. Wiehe explores in *What Parents Need to Know about Sibling Abuse: Breaking the Cycle of Violence* (2002) the reasons siblings hurt each other. Sibling abuse may stem from a desire to control another person or to take advantage of that person. The sibling in control typically does not know how to empathize (be aware and sensitive to the feelings of others). Wiehe notes the reason most often given for sibling abuse is that an older sibling has been put in charge of younger siblings. Some parents may expect too much from older children, relegating parental responsibilities to them. Even if an older brother or sister is capable of babysitting his or her younger siblings, he or she lacks the knowledge or skills to parent. Wiehe also points out that sibling abuse may be a learned behavior. Children who grow up in households where they see their parents abusing each other or are the recipients of such abuse may in turn use aggression toward one another. Children may also learn abusive behavior from television programs, movies, videos, and computer games.

CONSEQUENCES OF CHILDHOOD MALTREATMENT
Cycle of Violence

In "Childhood Victimization: Early Adversity, Later Psychopathology" (*National Institute of Justice Journal*, January 2000), one of the most detailed longitudinal studies (a study of the same group over a period of time) of the consequences of childhood maltreatment, Cathy Spatz Widom focuses on 908 children in a midwestern metropolitan area who were six to eleven years old when they were maltreated (between 1967 and 1971). A control group of 667 children with no history of childhood mal-

TABLE 3.5

Childhood victimization and later criminality, 1986

	Abuse/neglect group (676) %	Control group (520) %
Arrest as juvenile	31.2	19.0
Arrest as adult	48.4	36.2
Arrest as juvenile or adult for any crime	56.5	42.5
Arrest as juvenile or adult for any violent crime	21.0	15.6

Note: Numbers in parentheses are numbers of cases.

SOURCE: Cathy Spatz Widom, "Table 1. Childhood Victimization and Later Criminality," in "Childhood Victimization: Early Adversity, Later Psychopathology," *National Institute of Justice Journal*, no. 242, January 2000, http://www.ncjrs.gov/pdffiles1/jr000242b.pdf (accessed May 20, 2008)

treatment was used for comparison. Each group contained about two-thirds whites and one-third African-Americans and about an equal number of males and females. Widom examined the long-term consequences of childhood maltreatment on the subjects' intellectual, behavioral, social, and psychological development. When the two groups were interviewed for the study, they had a median age (half were older, half were younger) of about twenty-nine years.

Widom is widely known for her work on the cycle of violence theory. This theory suggests that childhood physical abuse increases the likelihood of arrest and of committing violent crime during the victim's later years. Widom finds that even though a large proportion of maltreated children did not become juvenile delinquents or criminals, those who suffered childhood abuse or neglect were more likely than those with no reported maltreatment to be arrested as juveniles (31.2% versus 19%) and as adults (48.4% versus 36.2%) when surveyed in 1986. (See Table 3.5.) The maltreated victims (21%) were also more likely than those with no reported childhood maltreatment history (15.6%) to be arrested for a violent crime during their teen years or adulthood.

Widom notes that the victims' later psychopathology (psychological disorders resulting from the childhood maltreatment) manifested itself in suicide attempts, antisocial personality, and alcohol abuse and/or dependence. When surveyed in 1989, maltreatment victims were more likely than the control individuals to report having attempted suicide (18.8% versus 7.7%) and having manifested antisocial personality disorder (18.4% versus 11.2%). Both groups, however, did not differ much in the rates of alcohol abuse and/or dependence. In "Adult Psychopathology and Intimate Partner Violence among Survivors of Childhood Maltreatment" (*Journal of Interpersonal Violence*, vol. 19, no. 10, October 2004), Ariel J. Lang et al. conducted research that also supports the association between childhood maltreatment and psychopathology in adulthood.

TABLE 3.6

Childhood victimization and later psychopathology by gender, 1989

	Abuse/neglect group %	Control group %
Females	(338)	(224)
Suicide attempt	24.3	8.6
Antisocial personality disorder	9.8	4.9
Alcohol abuse/dependence	43.8	32.8
Males	(338)	(276)
Suicide attempt	13.4	6.9
Antisocial personality disorder	27.0	16.7
Alcohol abuse/dependence	64.4	67.0

Note: Numbers in parentheses are numbers of cases.

SOURCE: Cathy Spatz Widom, "Table 3. Childhood Victimization and Later Psychopathology, by Gender," in "Childhood Victimization: Early Adversity, Later Psychopathology," *National Institute of Justice Journal*, no. 242, January 2000, http://www.ncjrs.gov/pdffiles1/jr000242b.pdf (accessed May 20, 2008)

TABLE 3.7

Involvement in criminality by history of childhood abuse and neglect and race, 1994

[In percent]

Type of arrest	Abused and neglected group (sample size=900)	Comparison group (sample size=667)
Juvenile		
Black	40.6	20.9
White	21.8	15.2
Adult		
Black	59.8	43.6
White	33.8	26.6
Violent crime		
Black	34.2	21.8
White	11.0	9.7

SOURCE: Cathy S. Widom and Michael G. Maxfield, "Exhibit 4. Involvement in Criminality by Race, in Percent," in *Research in Brief: An Update on the "Cycle of Violence,"* U.S. Department of Justice, Office of Justice Programs, National Institute of Justice, February 2001, http://www.ncjrs.gov/pdffiles1/nij/184894.pdf (accessed May 20, 2008)

Widom finds that gender plays a role in the development of psychological disorders in adolescence and adulthood. In 1989 females (24.3%) with a history of childhood maltreatment reported being more likely to attempt suicide, compared to their male counterparts (13.4%). (See Table 3.6.) However, a significantly larger percentage of male victims (27%) than female victims (9.8%) developed an antisocial personality disorder. Even though mistreated males (64.4%) and control subjects (67%) had similar proportions of alcohol abuse or dependence, females who experienced abuse or neglect were more likely than the control group to have alcohol problems (43.8% versus 32.8%).

Another phase of Widom's cycle of violence research was conducted when the maltreated and control groups had a median age of 32.5 years. Aside from collecting arrest records from federal, state, and local law enforcement, Cathy S. Widom and Michael G. Maxfield, in *An Update on the "Cycle of Violence"* (February 2001, http://www.ncjrs.gov/pdffiles1/nij/184894.pdf), also conducted interviews in 1994 with the subjects. Overall, Widom and Maxfield find that childhood abuse or neglect increased the likelihood of arrest in adolescence by 59% and in adulthood by 28%. Childhood maltreatment also increased the likelihood of committing a violent crime by 30%.

Even though earlier analysis of the maltreated group found that most of the victims did not become offenders, Widom and Maxfield's study shows that nearly half (49%) of the victims had experienced a nontraffic offense as teenagers or adults. Comparison by race shows that even though both white and African-American maltreated children had more arrests than the control group, there was no significant difference among whites in the maltreated and control groups. Among African-American

children, however, the maltreated group had higher rates of arrests. Maltreated African-Americans were nearly twice as likely as their counterparts in the control group to be arrested as juveniles (40.6% versus 20.9%). (See Table 3.7.)

Abigail A. Fagan's research in "The Relationship between Adolescent Physical Abuse and Criminal Offending: Support for an Enduring and Generalized Cycle of Violence" (*Journal of Family Violence*, vol. 20, no. 5, October 2005) supports the cycle of violence theory. She demonstrates that adolescents who are physically abused are more likely to commit violent and nonviolent crimes, use drugs, and batter their partners. Even though this relationship holds steady across racial and class backgrounds, the frequency of this behavior is moderated by family income, the area in which the adolescent lives, and family structure.

Widom and Maxfield also examined the type of childhood maltreatment that might lead to violence later in life. They find that physically abused children (21.1%) were the most likely to commit a violent crime in their teen or adult years and were closely followed by those who experienced neglect (20.2%). (See Table 3.8.) Even though their study shows that just 8.8% of children who had been sexually abused were arrested for violence, Widom and Maxfield note that the victims were mostly females, and "females less often had a record of violent offenses."

Jennie G. Noll suggests in "Does Childhood Sexual Abuse Set in Motion a Cycle of Violence against Women?: What We Know and What We Need to Learn" (*Journal of Interpersonal Violence*, vol. 20, no. 4, April 2005) that sexual abuse of females, rather than resulting

TABLE 3.8

Victims of child abuse arrested for violent crimes in later life, by type of abuse, 1994

Abuse group	Number of subjects	Percentage arrested for violent offense
Physical abuse only	76	21.1
Neglect only	609	20.2
Sexual abuse only	125	8.8
Mixed	98	14.3
Control	667	13.9

SOURCE: Cathy S. Widom and Michael G. Maxfield, "Exhibit 5. Does Only Violence Beget Violence?" in *Research in Brief: An Update on the "Cycle of Violence,"* U.S. Department of Justice, Office of Justice Programs, National Institute of Justice, February 2001, http://www.ncjrs.gov/pdffiles1/nij/184894.pdf (accessed May 20, 2008)

FIGURE 3.5

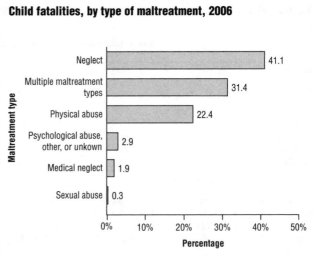

Child fatalities, by type of maltreatment, 2006

SOURCE: "Figure 4-3. Maltreatment Types of Child Fatalities, 2006," in *Child Maltreatment 2006*, U.S. Department of Health and Human Services, Administration on Children, Youth, and Families, 2008, http://www.acf.hhs.gov/programs/cb/pubs/cm06/cm06.pdf (accessed May 20, 2008)

in criminal behavior as the girl ages, sets in motion a cycle of violence against women. She argues that a girl who is sexually abused as a child is more likely than her peers to be physically or sexually assaulted in adolescence. Ultimately, these women are more likely to abuse their own children than are women who were not assaulted in childhood.

The Consequences of Neglect

When most people think of child maltreatment, they think of abuse and not neglect. Furthermore, research literature and conferences dealing with child maltreatment have generally overlooked child neglect. The congressional hearings that took place before the passage of the landmark Child Abuse Prevention and Treatment Act of 1974 focused almost entirely on examples of physical abuse. Barely three pages of the hundreds recorded pertained to child neglect.

Nonetheless, every year the federal government reports a high incidence of child neglect. According to the Administration for Children, Youth, and Families (ACYF), in *Child Maltreatment 2006* (2008, http://www.acf.hhs.gov/programs/cb/pubs/cm06/cm06.pdf), in 2006, 64.1% of all victims of child maltreatment experienced neglect, compared to 16% of all victims who were physically abused. It is important to note that these percents pertain only to children reported to CPS, and whose cases had been substantiated. Experts believe these numbers are grossly underreported. Neglect does not necessarily leave obvious physical marks like abuse does, and it often involves infants and young children who cannot speak for themselves.

Severe neglect can have devastating consequences. For example, James M. Gaudin Jr. reports in "Child Neglect: Short-Term and Long-Term Outcomes" (Howard Dubowitz, ed., *Neglected Children: Research, Practice, and Policy*, 1999) that, compared to both nonmaltreated and physically abused children, neglected children have the worst delays in language comprehension and expres-

sion. Psychologically neglected children also score lowest in intelligence quotient tests. Michael D. De Bellis of Duke University posits in "The Psychobiology of Neglect" (*Child Maltreatment*, vol. 10, no. 2, 2005) that childhood neglect might have profound affects on neuropsychological development, although the exploration of these effects is still in its infancy.

More than four out of ten (41.1%) of the children who died of child maltreatment in 2006 died of neglect alone. (See Figure 3.5.) Neglect can lead to death from causes such as malnourishment, lack of proper medical care, or abandonment. Emotional neglect, in its most serious form, can result in the "nonorganic failure to thrive syndrome," a condition in which a child fails to develop physically or even to survive. According to Gaudin, studies find that even with aggressive intervention the neglected child continues to deteriorate. The cooperation of the neglectful parents, which is crucial to the intervention, usually declines as the child's condition worsens. It is difficult to change the parental attributes that have contributed to the neglect in the first place.

Maltreated Girls Who Become Offenders

In "Childhood Victimization and the Derailment of Girls and Women to the Criminal Justice System" (Beth E. Richie, Kay Tsenin, and Cathy Spatz Widom, *Research on Women and Girls in the Justice System*, September 2000, http://www.ncjrs.gov/pdffiles1/nij/180973.pdf), Widom studied a group of girls who had experienced neglect and physical and sexual abuse before age eleven through young adulthood. Widom finds that abused and neglected girls were almost twice as likely (20%) to have been arrested as juveniles, compared to a matched control group of nonabused girls (11.4%), and almost twice as likely as the control group to be arrested as adults (28.5% versus 15.9%). Additionally, the maltreated girls were also more than twice as likely (8.2%) as the nonmaltreated girls (3.6%) to have been arrested for violent crimes. However, Widom notes that even though abused and neglected girls were at increased risk for criminal behavior, about 70% of the maltreated girls did not become criminals.

Cathy Spatz Widom, Daniel Nagin, and Peter Lambert find in "Does Childhood Victimization Alter Developmental Trajectories of Criminal Careers?" (paper presented at the annual meeting of the American Society of Criminology, Washington, DC, November 1998) that 8% of the maltreated girls developed antisocial and criminal lifestyles that carried over to adulthood. Among this group, nearly two out of five (38%) had been arrested for status offenses as juveniles, but a larger percentage had been arrested for violence (46%) and property crimes (54%). Another third (32%) had been arrested for drug crimes. None of the girls in the control group exhibited these tendencies.

Dating Violence

In "Child and Adolescent Abuse and Subsequent Victimization: A Prospective Study" (*Child Abuse and Neglect: The International Journal*, vol. 29, no. 12, December 2005), Cindy L. Rich et al. investigate the possible relationship between abuse in childhood and teen dating violence. They find that early emotional abuse by parents put adolescent women at risk. They also find that early physical abuse by a father put female adolescents at risk for sexual violence in their dating relationships. Rich et al. are careful to note that emotional abuse by both parents was actually more predictive of subsequent psychological symptoms than was physical or sexual abuse. They state, "Thus, subtler forms of abuse can be equally or more traumatic and set the stage for subsequent abuse experiences."

On the contrary, Marie-Hélène Gagné, Francine Lavoie, and Martine Hébert find in "Victimization during Childhood and Revictimization in Dating Relationships in Adolescent Girls" (*Child Abuse and Neglect: The International Journal*, vol. 29, no. 10, October 2005) that extrafamilial experiences with violence are a more important risk factor for subsequent dating violence than is abuse experienced at the hands of family members. In particular, young girls' experiences with violent or victimized peers, verbal sexual harassment by male peers, and previous dating violence all significantly contributed to the risk of subsequent dating violence.

Illicit Drug Use

Illicit drug use is associated with behaviors leading to violence, sexually transmitted diseases, other health problems, and crime. In "Childhood Abuse, Neglect, and Household Dysfunction and the Risk of Illicit Drug Use: The Adverse Childhood Experiences Study" (*Pediatrics*, vol. 111, no. 3, March 2003), Shanta R. Dube et al. study a population of 8,613 adult members of a health plan who filled out a questionnaire relating to their adverse childhood experiences (ACEs) during the first eighteen years of life. The intent of Dube et al.'s study was to determine the effects of related ACEs on various health outcomes and behaviors. ACEs included physical, emotional, or sexual abuse; physical or emotional neglect; and household dysfunction, such as a battered mother, parental separation or divorce, mental illness at home, substance abuse in the home, or an incarcerated household member.

Dube et al. find that each ACE increased two to four times the likelihood of initiation to illicit drug use by age fourteen and increased the risk of drug use into adulthood. They note that several ACEs usually occur together. Their cumulative effect on illicit drug use is strongest during early adolescence because the young teen has just been through these painful experiences and is at the same time undergoing the turmoil characteristic of that age group. However, ACEs were also found to increase the likelihood of initiation to illicit drug use among adolescents aged fifteen to eighteen and people aged nineteen and over, showing the long-term effects of these experiences. Moreover, people who had experienced more than five ACEs were seven to ten times more likely to have illicit drug use problems, specifically addiction to illicit drugs and intravenous drug use.

In "Substance Use in Maltreated Youth: Findings from the National Survey of Child and Adolescent Well-Being" (*Child Maltreatment*, vol. 12, no. 1, 2007), Ariana E. Wall and Patricia L. Kohl find that among maltreated children aged eleven to fifteen, 20% reported low levels of substance use and 9% reported moderate to high levels of use. A high level of monitoring by the current caregiver decreased the level of substance use among these youth. Wall and Kohl conclude, "Caregiver monitoring may be a key tactic in attempts to reduce the likelihood of substance use in maltreated youth."

Widom et al. find in "Long-Term Effects of Child Abuse and Neglect on Alcohol Use and Excessive Drinking in Middle Adulthood" (*Journal of Studies on Alcohol and Drugs*, vol. 68, no. 3, May 2007) that the greater likelihood that maltreated children will abuse substances continued into adulthood for women. The researchers studied individuals with documented cases of physical abuse, sexual abuse, or neglect in childhood. They note that women with histories of child abuse and neglect reported consuming larger amounts of alcohol in the past year and drank eight or more drinks in more days in the past month than did women without abuse or neglect histories.

Problems in Early Brain Development

The National Scientific Council on the Developing Child sponsors a variety of research projects that focus on the effects of stressful environments on children's developing brains. A number of research projects, such as *Excessive Stress Disrupts the Architecture of the Developing Brain* (2005, http://www.developingchild.net/pubs/wp/Stress_Disrupts_Architecture_Developing_Brain.pdf) and Dorian Friedman's *Stress and the Architecture of the Brain* (2005, http://www.developingchild.net/pubs/persp/pdf/Stress_Architecture_Brain.pdf), show that child abuse or neglect during infancy and early childhood affects early brain development.

Brain development, or learning, is the process of creating connections among neurons in the brain, called synapses. Neurons, or nerve cells, send signals to one another through synapses, which in turn form the neuronal pathways that enable the brain to respond to specific environments. An infant is born with very few synapses formed. These include synapses that are responsible for breathing, eating, and sleeping. During the early years of life the brain develops synapses at a fast rate. Scientists find that repeated experiences strengthen the neuronal pathways, making them sensitive to similar experiences that may occur later on in life. Unfortunately, if these early life experiences are of a negative nature, the development of the brain may be impaired. For example, if an infant who cries for attention constantly gets ignored, his or her brain creates the neuronal pathway that enables him or her to cope with being ignored. If the infant continually fails to get the attention he or she craves, the brain strengthens that same neuronal pathway.

Childhood abuse or neglect has long-term consequences on brain development. When children suffer abuse or neglect, their brains are preoccupied with reacting to the chronic stress. As the brain builds and strengthens neuronal pathways involved with survival, it fails to develop social and cognitive skills. Later on in life, maltreatment victims may not know how to react to kindness and nurturing because the brain has no memory of how to respond to these new experiences. They may also have learning difficulties because the brain has focused solely on the body's survival so that the thinking processes may not have been developed or may have been impaired.

Hyperarousal is another consequence of maltreatment on brain development. During the state of hyperarousal, the brain is always attuned to what it perceives as a threatening situation. The brain has "learned" that the world is a dangerous place and that it has to be constantly on the alert. The victim experiences extreme anxiety toward any perceived threat, or he or she may use aggression to control the situation. For example, children who have been physically abused may start a fight just so they can control the conflict and be able to choose their adversary. Males and older children are more likely to exhibit hyperarousal. According to Friedman, "Childhood adversity shapes a stress system that has trouble flipping the 'off' switch."

Researchers find that even though males and older children tend to suffer from hyperarousal, younger children and females are more likely to show dissociation. In the dissociative state, victims disconnect themselves from the negative experience. By "pretending" not to be there, their body and mind does not react to the abusive experience.

Childhood maltreatment can result in the disruption of the attachment process, which refers to the development of healthy emotional relationships with others. Under normal circumstances the first relationship that infants develop is with their caregivers. Such relationships form the basis for future emotional connections. In maltreated children the attachment process may not be fully developed, resulting in the inability to know oneself as well as to put oneself in another's position.

Posttraumatic Stress Disorder

Posttraumatic stress disorder (PTSD) is an anxiety disorder that sometimes develops after experiencing a terrifying event in which a person is severely physically harmed or was threatened with severe physical harm. People with PTSD may experience flashbacks (they re-experience the trauma), sleep disturbances, emotional numbness, depression, rage, memory loss, concentration problems, anxiety, and physical symptoms. The disorder can be highly distressing for sufferers.

Physical and sexual abuse in childhood can lead to the development of PTSD, which can persist into adulthood. Some psychologists, such as Judith Lewis Herman, in *Trauma and Recovery* (1997), have defined a disorder called complex PTSD, which is found among people who have been exposed to prolonged traumatic experience, as is usually the case among child abuse survivors. Sheryn T. Scott of Azusa Pacific University finds in "Multiple Traumatic Experiences and the Development of Posttraumatic Stress Disorder" (*Journal of Interpersonal Violence*, vol. 22, no. 7, 2007) that multiple lifetime traumatic events, such as physical and sexual abuse in childhood, lifetime community violence, and domestic violence increases the likelihood of developing PTSD. In other words, victimized adults who were subjected to physical or sexual abuse in childhood are more likely than other victimized adults to develop PTSD. The number of traumas, as well as their severity, is related to the severity of the symptoms developed.

DEATH

Child fatality is the most severe result of abuse and neglect. In "Risk of Death among Children Reported for Nonfatal Maltreatment" (*Child Maltreatment*, vol. 12, no. 1, 2007), Melissa Jonson-Reid, Toni Chance, and Brett Drake find that low-income children who had been reported

TABLE 3.9

Child fatalities by state, 2006

State	Child population	Child file or SDC fatalities	Agency file fatalities	Total child fatalities	Fatalities per 100,000 children
Alabama	1,114,301	24	0	24	2.15
Alaska	181,434	0	2	2	1.10
Arizona	1,628,198	16	16		0.98
Arkansas	691,186	19	19		2.75
California	9,532,614	140	140		1.47
Colorado	1,169,301	24	24		2.05
Connecticut	818,286	3	3		0.37
Delaware	203,366	0	1	1	0.49
District of Columbia	114,881	2	0	2	1.74
Florida	4,021,555	140	0	140	3.48
Georgia	2,455,020	63	63		2.57
Hawaii	298,081	4	4		1.34
Idaho	394,280	1	1		0.25
Illinois	3,215,244	58	0	58	1.80
Indiana	1,577,629	31	11	42	2.66
Iowa	710,194	6	0	6	0.84
Kansas	695,837	5	0	5	0.72
Kentucky	999,531	36	0	36	3.60
Louisiana	1,090,001	37	37		3.39
Maine	280,994	0	1	1	0.36
Maryland					
Massachusetts					
Michigan					
Minnesota	1,257,264	14	0	14	1.11
Mississippi	759,405	4	0	4	0.53
Missouri	1,416,592	43	43		3.04
Montana	217,848	1	0	1	0.46
Nebraska	445,033	3	12	15	3.37
Nevada	634,520	11	3	14	2.21
New Hampshire	297,625	1	2	3	1.01
New Jersey	2,089,338	31	1	32	1.53
New Mexico	508,930	7	7	14	2.75
New York	4,514,342	73	73		1.62
North Carolina					
North Dakota	144,934	1	1	2	1.38
Ohio	2,770,035	74	0	74	2.67
Oklahoma	894,034	26	26		2.91
Oregon	856,259	17	17		1.99
Pennsylvania	2,804,873	33	0	33	1.18
Puerto Rico	1,018,651	5	5		0.49
Rhode Island	237,451	0	0	0	0.00
South Carolina	1,039,653	10	9	19	1.83
South Dakota	194,681	1	1		0.51
Tennessee	1,442,593	22	22		1.53
Texas	6,493,965	257	257		3.96
Utah	791,198	13	0	13	1.64
Vermont	133,389	0	0	0	0.00
Virginia	1,806,847	20	20		1.11
Washington	1,526,267	21	21		1.38
West Virginia	389,071	6	9	15	3.86
Wisconsin	1,312,530	13	13		0.99
Wyoming	121,794	1	1		0.82
Total	67,311,055	1,134	242	1,376	
Weighted rate					2.04
Number reporting	48	44	31	48	48

SOURCE: Adapted from "Table 4.1. Child Fatalities, 2005–2006," in *Child Maltreatment 2006*, U.S. Department of Health and Human Services, Administration on Children, Youth, and Families, 2008, http://www.acf.hhs.gov/programs/cb/pubs/cm06/cm06.pdf (accessed May 20, 2008)

maltreated were at about twice the risk of death before age eighteen as a comparison group of other low-income children without reported maltreatment. Approximately 0.5% of the children with maltreatment reports died in childhood, compared to 0.3% of other children. Most of these deaths were preventable—if they were not the result of recurrent maltreatment, they resulted from other preventable causes, such as accidents. Among the children with maltreatment reports, the median time from the first report to the subsequent death was nine months. This study underscores the dangers that face maltreated children.

In 2006 CPS and other state agencies, including coroners' offices and fatality review boards, reported an estimated 1,376 deaths from child maltreatment. (See Table 3.9.) The

FIGURE 3.6

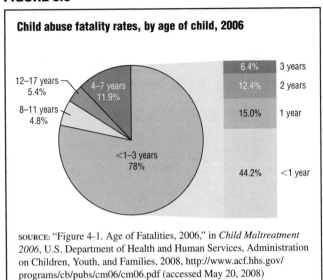

Child abuse fatality rates, by age of child, 2006

12–17 years 5.4%
8–11 years 4.8%
4–7 years 11.9%
<1–3 years 78%

6.4% 3 years
12.4% 2 years
15.0% 1 year
44.2% <1 year

SOURCE: "Figure 4-1. Age of Fatalities, 2006," in *Child Maltreatment 2006*, U.S. Department of Health and Human Services, Administration on Children, Youth, and Families, 2008, http://www.acf.hhs.gov/programs/cb/pubs/cm06/cm06.pdf (accessed May 20, 2008)

FIGURE 3.7

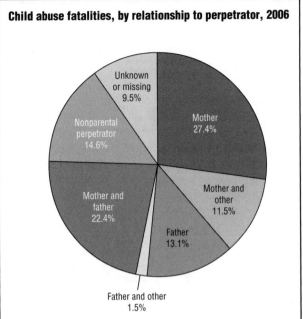

Child abuse fatalities, by relationship to perpetrator, 2006

Unknown or missing 9.5%
Nonparental perpetrator 14.6%
Mother and father 22.4%
Father and other 1.5%
Father 13.1%
Mother and other 11.5%
Mother 27.4%

SOURCE: "Figure 4-2. Perpetrator Relationships of Child Fatalities, 2006," in *Child Maltreatment 2006*, U.S. Department of Health and Human Services, Administration on Children, Youth, and Families, 2008, http://www.acf.hhs.gov/programs/cb/pubs/cm06/cm06.pdf (accessed May 20, 2008)

national fatality rate was 2.04 per 100,000 children in the general population in 2006. Texas reported the highest rate (3.96 deaths per 100,000 children), followed by West Virginia (3.86 deaths per 100,000 children). Rhode Island and Vermont were the only two states that reported no deaths resulting from child maltreatment that year.

In 2006 children three years old and younger accounted for a majority (78%) of deaths due to maltreatment. (See Figure 3.6.) Almost half (44.2%) of the deaths consisted of infants less than one year old. The ACYF reports in *Child Maltreatment 2006* that infant boys had a fatality rate of 18.5 per 100,000 and infant girls had a fatality rate of 14.7 per 100,000. Young children are more likely to be victims of child fatalities because of their small size, their dependency on their caregivers, and their inability to defend themselves.

Neglect alone was responsible for 41.1% of maltreatment deaths. (See Figure 3.5.) About a quarter (22.4%) of fatalities resulted from physical abuse. Another 31.4% of fatalities resulted from a combination of maltreatment types. The ACYF provides data on the victims' previous contact with CPS agencies. More than one out of ten (13.7%) of the victims' families had received family preservation services during the five years before the deaths occurred; 2.3% of children killed had been in foster care and were reunited with their families in the past five years.

Perpetrators of Fatalities

The ACYF states in *Child Maltreatment 2006* that 75.9% of maltreatment deaths were inflicted by one or both parents of the victims. Mothers alone accounted for

27.4% of the deaths, whereas fathers were the perpetrators in 13.1% of the deaths. (See Figure 3.7.) In about one-fifth (22.4%) of cases, both parents were responsible for causing their child's death.

Family Composition and Maltreatment Deaths

In "Household Composition and Risk of Fatal Child Maltreatment" (*Pediatrics*, vol. 109, no. 4, April 2002), Michael N. Stiffman et al. examined all information related to Missouri-resident children under five years old who died in that state within a three-year period to determine whether family composition might be a risk factor for fatal child maltreatment. The researchers used the comprehensive data of child deaths (birth through age seventeen) collected by the Missouri Child Fatality Review Panel (CFRP) system between 1992 and 1994. The CFRP data contained information on all household members and their relationship to the deceased child. For comparison, Stiffman et al. used a control group consisting of children under age five who had died of natural causes. Of the 291 injury deaths that were examined, 175 children (60%) were determined to have died of maltreatment. Fifty-five (31%) of the deaths resulted from injury caused by a parent or other caregiver. Of this group, thirty-nine of the children died from being shaken, hit, or dropped. Eleven children died from the use of physical objects, including guns. The cause of death for the remaining five children was unknown.

Stiffman et al. find that children living in households with one or more biologically unrelated adult males and boyfriends of the child's mother had the highest risk of death from maltreatment. These children were eight times more likely to die of maltreatment than children living with two biological parents with no other adults. Children residing with foster and adoptive parents, as well as with stepparents, were nearly five times as likely to suffer maltreatment deaths. Those living in households with other adult relatives present were twice as likely to die from maltreatment. However, children living with just one biological parent, with no other adult present, were not at an increased risk for fatal maltreatment.

CORPORAL PUNISHMENT: ABUSE OR NOT?

Corporal Punishment by Parents

In the United States all fifty states allow parents to use corporal punishment for purposes of disciplining their children. As long as the child does not suffer injury, the parent may use objects such as belts and the more typical spanking with the hand. When states passed child abuse laws in the 1960s, provisions allowing parents to use corporal punishment helped facilitate passage of the legislation. The Global Initiative to End All Corporal Punishment of Children reports in "States with Full Abolition" (December 2007, http://www.endcorporalpunishment.org/pages/progress/prohib_states.html) that as of 2007 corporal punishment by parents, caretakers, and teachers was completely banned in twenty-three countries around the world. Since January 2003, Canada has banned corporal punishment for children under two and over twelve years of age, as well as the use of any object, such as a paddle.

Corporal Punishment in Schools

As of 2006, among industrialized countries, only Australia (just Outback areas) and the United States allowed spanking in schools. In 2008 twenty-nine U.S. states banned corporal punishment in public schools. (See Figure 3.8.) Most of the states that allowed corporal punishment were southern states. During the 2006–07 school year, 223,190 school children were subjected to physical punishment, a decrease of 18% over the previous year (2008, http://www.stophitting.com/disatschool/statesBanning.php). Mississippi used physical punishment on the largest percentage of students (7.5%), followed by Arkansas (4.7%), and Alabama (4.5%).

Prevalence and Chronicity of Corporal Punishment

In "Parents' Discipline of Young Children: Results from the National Survey of Early Childhood Health" (*Pediatrics*, vol. 113, no. 6, June 2004), Michael Regalado et al. report on the parental use of corporal punishment for discipline in regard to the health and develop-ment of children under three years of age. Six percent of parents surveyed indicated they had spanked their children when they were four to nine months old, 29% spanked their children when they were ten to eighteen months old, and 64% spanked their children when they were nineteen to thirty-five months old. Frequent spankings were also administered by some parents (11%) of children ten to eighteen months old and nineteen to thirty-five months old (26%).

Murray A. Straus and Julie H. Stewart of the University of New Hampshire find in "Corporal Punishment by American Parents: National Data on Prevalence, Chronicity, Severity, and Duration, in Relation to Child and Family Characteristics" (*Clinical Child and Family Psychology Review*, vol. 2, no. 2, June 1999) that more than a third (35%) of parents surveyed used corporal punishment on their infants, reaching a peak of 94% of parents of children who were three to four years old. The prevalence rate of parents using corporal punishment decreased after age five, with just over 50% of parents using it on children at age twelve, 33% at age fourteen, and 13% at age seventeen. Straus and Stewart also find that corporal punishment was more prevalent among African-Americans and parents in the low socioeconomic level. It was also more commonly inflicted on boys, by mothers, and in the South.

Chronicity refers to the frequency of the infliction of corporal punishment during the year. Corporal punishment was most frequently used by parents of two-year-olds, averaging eighteen times per year. After age two, chronicity declined, averaging six times per year for teenagers.

Effects of Corporal Punishment

BEHAVIOR PROBLEMS IN ELEMENTARY SCHOOL. Studies on the spanking of children have mostly used sample populations of children aged two and older. In "Spanking in Early Childhood and Later Behavior Problems: A Prospective Study of Infants and Young Toddlers" (*Pediatrics*, vol. 113, no. 5, May 2004), Eric P. Slade and Lawrence S. Wissow of Johns Hopkins Bloomberg School of Public Health conducted the first study of its kind in the United States by following a group of children younger than two years old to test the hypothesis that "spanking frequency before age two is positively associated with the probability of having significant behavior problems four years later."

Slade and Wissow collected data on 1,966 children and their mothers who participated in the National Longitudinal Survey of Mother-Child Sample, a large-scale national study of youth aged fourteen to twenty-one years old. Some of these young people were mothers with children. Data were collected on the mother-children groups when the children were under two years of age.

FIGURE 3.8

States banning corporal punishment in schools, 2008

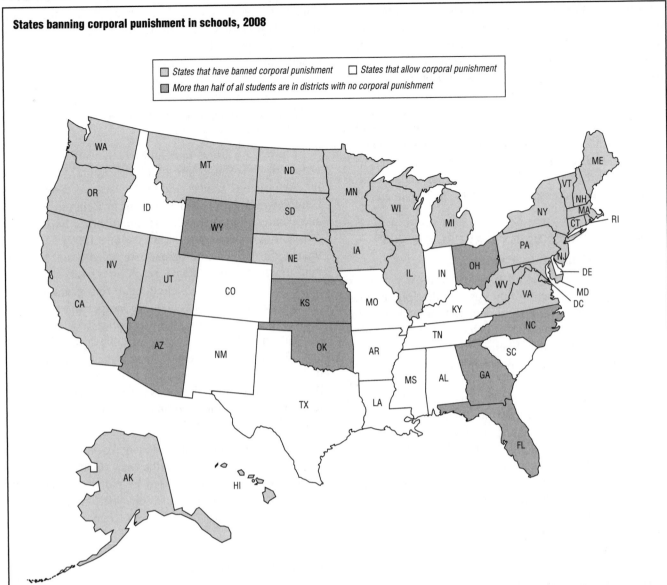

☐ States that have banned corporal punishment ☐ States that allow corporal punishment
☐ More than half of all students are in districts with no corporal punishment

SOURCE: Adapted from "States Banning Corporal Punishment," in *U.S. Corporal Punishment and Paddling Statistics by State and Race*, National Coalition to Abolish Corporal Punishment in Schools, Center for Effective Discipline, undated, http://www.stophitting.com/disatschool/statesBanning.php (accessed May 20, 2008)

Four years later, after the children had entered elementary school, Slade and Wissow interviewed the mothers to explore their hypothesis. Mothers were asked if they spanked their child the previous week and how frequently they spanked their children. They were also questioned about the child's temperament, mother-child interactions, and whether they had ever met with the child's teacher because of behavioral problems.

Slade and Wissow find that, when compared to children who were never spanked, white non-Hispanic children who were frequently spanked (five times per week) before age two were four times more likely to have behavioral problems by the time they started school. No connection was found between spanking and later behavioral problems among African-American and Hispanic

children. According to Slade and Wissow, the same results were found in studies involving children older than two years. They explain that the way white families and other ethnic groups view the spanking of children may influence the effects of spanking. For example, African-American families typically do not consider spanking as "harsh or unfair."

INCREASED RISK OF PHYSICAL ABUSE. Murray A. Straus presents in "Physical Abuse" (Murray A. Straus with Denise A. Donnelly, *Beating the Devil out of Them: Corporal Punishment in American Families and Its Effects on Children*, 2001) a model called path analysis to illustrate how physical punishment could escalate to physical abuse. Straus theorizes that parents who have been physically disciplined as adolescents are more likely to believe that it is acceptable to use violence to remedy a misbehavior. These parents tend to be depressed and to be involved in spousal violence. When a parent resorts to physical punishment and the child does not comply, the parent increases the severity of the punishment, eventually harming the child.

Corporal punishment experienced in adolescence produces the same effect on males and females. Parents who were physically punished thirty or more times as adolescents (24%) were three times as likely as those who never received physical punishment (7%) to abuse their children physically. Straus notes, however, that his model also shows that three-quarters (76%) of parents who were hit many times (thirty or more) as adolescents did not, in turn, abuse their children.

EFFECTS ON COGNITIVE DEVELOPMENT. According to Murray A. Straus and Mallie J. Paschall, in "Corporal Punishment by Mothers and Child's Cognitive Development: A Longitudinal Study" (paper presented at the Fourteenth World Congress of Sociology, Montreal, Canada, August 1998), corporal punishment is associated with a child's failure to keep up with the average rate of cognitive development. The researchers followed the cognitive development of 960 children born to mothers who participated in the National Longitudinal Study of Youth. The women were fourteen to twenty-one years old in 1979, at the start of the study. In 1986, when the women were between the ages of twenty-one and twenty-eight, those with children were interviewed regarding the way they were raising their children. The children underwent cognitive, psychosocial, and behavioral assessments. Children aged one to four were selected, among other reasons, because "the development of neural connections is greatest at the youngest ages." The children were tested again in 1990.

About seven out of ten (71%) mothers reported spanking their toddlers in the past week, with 6.2% spanking the child during the course of their interview for the study. Those who used corporal punishment reported using it an average of 3.6 times per week. This amounted to an estimated 187 spankings per year.

Straus and Paschall find that the more prevalent the corporal punishment, the greater the decrease in cognitive ability. Considering other studies, which show that talking to children, including infants, is associated with increased neural connections in the brain and cognitive functioning, Straus and Paschall hypothesize that if parents are not using corporal punishment to discipline their child, they are very likely verbally interacting with that child, thus positively affecting cognitive development.

Corporal Punishment as Effective Discipline

Some experts believe nonabusive spanking can play a role in effective parental discipline of young children. According to Robert E. Larzelere of the University of Nebraska Medical Center, in "Child Outcomes of Nonabusive and Customary Physical Punishment by Parents: An Updated Literature Review" (*Clinical Child and Family Psychology Review*, vol. 3, no. 4, December 2000), spanking can have beneficial results when it is "nonabusive (e.g., two swats to the buttocks with an open hand) and used primarily to back up milder disciplinary tactics with 2- to 6-year-olds by loving parents." Larzelere reviewed thirty-eight studies on corporal punishment to determine the effects of nonabusive and customary spanking. He describes research on customary spanking as "studies that measure physical punishment without emphasizing the severity of its use."

Generally, the thirty-eight studies were nearly equally divided in their reports of beneficial child outcomes, detrimental child outcomes, and neutral or mixed outcomes: 32%, 34%, and 34%, respectively. Larzelere examines seventeen studies he considers to be causally conclusive, that is, the research showed that nonabusive spanking was associated with the child outcomes. Nine studies in which children two to six years of age received nonabusive spankings after noncompliance with room time-out found beneficial child outcomes, such as subsequent compliance with parental orders. Of these nine studies, two studies in which parents used reasoning with the child followed by nonabusive spanking revealed a longer delay in between misbehaviors. A study involving extended disciplining by mothers showed that child compliance occurred at higher rates when the mothers used spanking as a final resort after other disciplinary measures had been tried.

Of the eight controlled longitudinal studies that examined spanking frequency, five reported negative child outcomes, such as low self-esteem. (Controlled studies refer to studies that excluded initial child misbehavior.) Larzelere notes that three of these studies showed that the detrimental effects were a result of frequent spankings.

Larzelere finds that the child's age was associated with the outcome of nonabusive spanking. Of twelve studies involving children with mean (average) ages under six, eleven reported beneficial outcomes. Among children aged seven-and-a-half to ten years, just one study reported beneficial outcomes, whereas six studies found detrimental outcomes.

Larzelere notes that confounding factors in some studies were responsible for a conclusion of detrimental child outcomes. In other words, studies that used opposing or unclear factors found negative outcomes. According to Larzelere, studies that did not show detrimental child outcomes shared three common factors: serious corporal punishment was not included in those studies, spanking was measured as a backup for other disciplinary practices and not in terms of frequency, and many children exhibited behavior problems at the start of the study.

CHAPTER 4
CHILD SEXUAL ABUSE

Many experts believe that sexual abuse is the most underreported type of child maltreatment. A victim, especially a young child, may not know what he or she is experiencing. In many cases the child was threatened to keep it secret. Adults who may be aware of the abuse sometimes get involved in a conspiracy of silence.

Child sexual abuse is the ultimate misuse of an adult's trust and power over a child. When the abuser is particularly close to the victim, the child feels betrayed and trapped in a situation in which an adult who claims to care for the child is assaulting him or her. Familial abuse, or incest, involves the use of a child for sexual satisfaction by a family member—a blood relative who is too close to marry legally. Extrafamilial abuse involves a person outside the family. Extrafamilial predators may be strangers, but they may also be people in a position of trust, such as family friends, teachers, and spiritual advisers.

WHAT IS CHILD SEXUAL ABUSE?

Federal Definition

The Child Abuse Prevention and Treatment Act (CAPTA) of 1974 specifically identified parents and caretakers as the perpetrators of sexual abuse. Sexual molestation by other individuals was considered sexual assault. The 1996 amendments to this law, however, included a more comprehensive definition, one that also included sexually abusive behavior by individuals other than parents and caregivers.

The CAPTA Amendments of 1996 defined child sexual abuse as:

- The employment, use, persuasion, inducement, enticement, or coercion of any child to engage in, or assist any other person to engage in, any sexually explicit conduct or simulation of such conduct for the purpose of producing a visual depiction of such conduct

- The rape, and in cases of caretaker or interfamilial relationships, statutory rape, molestation, prostitution, or other form of sexual exploitation of children, or incest with children

State Definitions Vary

The federal government has established a broad definition of child sexual abuse, but it leaves it up to state child abuse laws to specify detailed provisions. All states have laws prohibiting child sexual molestation and generally consider incest illegal. States also specify the age of consent, or the age at which a person can consent to sexual activity with an adult—generally between the ages of sixteen and eighteen. Sexual activity with children below the age of consent is considered statutory rape and is against the law. Table 4.1 summarizes current state laws regulating the age of consent.

HOW FREQUENT IS CHILD SEXUAL ABUSE?

Each year the National Child Abuse and Neglect Data System of the U.S. Department of Health and Human Services (HHS) collects child maltreatment data from child protective services (CPS) agencies in the fifty states and the District of Columbia, and the compiled information is released by the Administration for Children, Youth, and Families (ACYF) as *Child Maltreatment*. The federally mandated National Incidence Study of Child Abuse and Neglect (NIS) is another source that shows the extent of child sexual abuse. As of August 2008, three national incidence studies had been conducted: *NIS-1* (1980), *NIS-2* (1986), and *NIS-3* (1993). In 2003 the Keeping Children and Families Safe Act reauthorized CAPTA and authorized an additional $285 million for child abuse and neglect prevention programs. The act also directed the collection of data for *NIS-4*, which was expected to be available by the end of 2008. A third source of sexual abuse data are retrospective

TABLE 4.1

Statutory rape laws by state, 2004

State	Age of consent	Minimum age of victim	Age differential between the victim and defendant (if victim is above minimum age)	Minimum age of defendant in order to prosecute
Alabama	16	12	2	16
Alaska	16	N/A	3	N/A
Arizona	18	15	2 (defendant must be in high school and < 19)	N/A
Arkansas	16	N/A	3 (if victim is < 14)	20 (if victim is = 14)
California	18	18	N/A	N/A
Colorado	17	N/A	4 (if victim is < 15), 10 (if victim is < 17)	N/A
Connecticut	16	N/A[a]	2	N/A
Delaware	18[b]	16	N/A	N/A
District of Columbia	16	N/A	4	N/A
Florida	18	16	N/A	24 (if victim is = 16)
Georgia	16	16	N/A	N/A
Hawaii	16	14	5	N/A
Idaho	18[c]	18	N/A	N/A
Illinois	17	17	N/A	N/A
Indiana	16	14	N/A	18 (if victim is = 14)
Iowa	16	14	4	N/A
Kansas	16	16	N/A	N/A
Kentucky	16	16	N/A	N/A
Louisiana	17	13	3 (if victim is < 15), 2 (if victim is < 17)	N/A
Maine	16	14[d]	5	N/A
Maryland	16	N/A	4	N/A
Massachusetts	16	16	N/A	N/A
Michigan	16	16[e]	N/A	N/A
Minnesota	16	N/A	3 (if victim is < 13), 2 (if victim is < 16)	N/A
Mississippi	16	N/A	2 (if victim is < 14), 3 (if victim is < 16)	N/A
Missouri	17	14	N/A	21 (if victim is = 14)
Montana	16	16[f]	N/A	N/A
Nebraska	16	16[g]	N/A	19
Nevada	16	16	N/A	18
New Hampshire	16	16	N/A	N/A
New Jersey	16	13[h]	4	N/A
New Mexico	16	13	4	18 (if victim is = 13)
New York	17	17	N/A	N/A
North Carolina	16	N/A	4	12
North Dakota	18	15	N/A	18 (if victim is = 15)
Ohio	16	13	N/A	18 (if victim is = 13)
Oklahoma	16	14	N/A	18 (if victim is > 14)
Oregon	18	15	3	N/A
Pennsylvania	16	13	4	N/A
Rhode Island	16	14	N/A	18 (if victim is = 14)

studies, which are surveys of adults about their childhood experience of sexual abuse.

According to the ACYF, in *Child Maltreatment 2006* (2008, http://www.acf.hhs.gov/programs/cb/pubs/cm06/cm06.pdf), the number of sexual abuse cases reported by CPS agencies in the United States in 2006 was 78,120. (See Table 2.2 in Chapter 2.) It is important to note that these numbers represent only cases that were reported and substantiated (confirmed); unknown numbers of child sexual abuse cases are undiscovered. The secrecy surrounding child abuse makes it virtually impossible to count the cases perpetrated in the family. However, retrospective studies of adults are one attempt to get a true picture of the prevalence of child sexual abuse.

In "The Victimization of Children and Youth: A Comprehensive, National Survey" (*Child Maltreatment*, vol. 10, no. 1, February 2005), a study of a nationally representative sample of one thousand children and youth aged two to seventeen, David Finkelhor et al. find that more than half of the children had been victimized in the previous year, either by a physical assault, a property offense, a form of child maltreatment, a sexual victimization, or a form of indirect victimization, such as witnessing an act of violence. One youth out of twelve had been sexually victimized in the study year.

Determining the Extent of Child Sexual Abuse through Retrospective Studies

David Finkelhor of the University of New Hampshire is a national authority on child sexual abuse. In "Current Information on the Scope and Nature of Child Sexual Abuse" (*The Future of Children: Sexual Abuse of Children*, vol. 4, no. 2, summer–fall 1994), Finkelhor notes that surveys of adults regarding their childhood experiences (called retrospective studies) probably give the most complete estimates of the actual extent of child sexual abuse. He reviews nineteen adult retrospective surveys and finds that the proportion of adults who indicated sexual abuse during childhood ranged widely, from 2% to 62% for females and from 3% to 16% for males.

Finkelhor observes that the surveys that reported higher levels of abuse were those that asked multiple

TABLE 4.1

Statutory rape laws by state, 2004 [CONTINUED]

State	Age of consent	Minimum age of victim	Age differential between the victim and defendant (if victim is above minimum age)	Minimum age of defendant in order to prosecute
South Carolina	16	14	Illegal if victim is 14 to 16 and defendant is older than victim	N/A
South Dakota	16	10ⁱ	3	N/A
Tennessee	18	13	4	N/A
Texas	17	14	3	N/A
Utah	18	16	10	N/A
Vermont	16	16	N/A	16
Virginia	18	15	N/A	18 (if victim is = 15)
Washington	16	N/A	2 (if victim is < 12), 3 (if victim is < 14), 4 (if victim is < 16)	N/A
West Virginia	16	N/A	4 (if victim is = 11)	16, 14 (if victim is <11)
Wisconsin	18	18	N/A	N/A
Wyoming	16	N/A	4	N/A

Note: Some states have marital exemptions. This table assumes the two parties are not married to one another.

^aEngaging in *sexual intercourse* with someone who is less than 16 years of age is legal under certain circumstances. However, *sexual contact* with someone who is less than 15 years of age is illegal regardless of the age of the defendant.

^bSexual acts with individuals who are at least 16 years of age are only illegal if the defendant is 30 years of age or older.

^cIntercourse with a *female* who is less than 18 years of age is illegal regardless of the age of the defendant. However, *sexual acts not amounting to penetration* are legal under certain circumstances in cases where the victim is at least 16 years of age.

^dIt is illegal to engage in a *sexual act* with someone who is less than 14 years of age regardless of the age of the defendant. However, *sexual contact* or *sexual touching* with someone who is less than 14 years of age is legal under certain circumstances.

^eIt is illegal to engage in a *sexual penetration* with someone who is less than 16 years of age. However, *sexual contact* with someone who is at least 13 years of age is legal under certain circumstances.

^f*Sexual intercourse* with someone who is less than 16 years of age is illegal regardless of the age of the defendant. However, *sexual contact* with someone who is at least 14 years of age is legal under certain circumstances.

^gUnder the offense, "Debauching a minor," it is illegal to debauch or deprave morals by lewdly inducing someone less than 17 years of age to carnally know any other person.

^hIt is illegal to engage in a *sexual penetration* with someone who is less than 13 years of age regardless of the age of the defendant. However, *sexual contact* with someone who is less than 13 years of age is legal under certain circumstances.

ⁱEngaging in *sexual penetration* with someone who is at least 10 years of age and less than 16 years of age is legal under certain circumstances. However, *sexual contact* with someone who is less than 16 years of age is illegal regardless of the age of the defendant.

SOURCE: Asaph Glosser, Karen Gardiner, and Mike Fishman, "Table 1. State Age Requirements," in *Statutory Rape: A Guide to State Laws and Reporting Requirements*, U.S. Department of Health and Human Services, December 15, 2004, http://www.hhs.gov/opa/pubs/statutory-rape-state-laws.pdf (accessed June 2, 2008)

questions about the possibility of abuse. Multiple questions are more effective because they provide respondents various cues about the different kinds of experiences the researchers are asking about. Multiple questions also give the respondents ample time to overcome their embarrassment. Many experts accept the estimate that one out of five (20%) American women and one out of ten (10%) American men have experienced some form of childhood sexual abuse (CSA).

One of the early landmark studies of child sexual abuse was conducted in 1978 by the sociologist Diana E. H. Russell of Mills College. Russell surveyed 930 adult women in San Francisco about their early sexual experiences and reported her findings in *The Secret Trauma: Incest in the Lives of Girls and Women* (1986). Russell noted that 38% of the women had suffered incestuous and extrafamilial sexual abuse before their eighteenth birthday. About 16% had been abused by a family member.

Russell's study is still frequently cited by experts who believe that much more abuse occurs than is officially reported by government studies. They suggest the high results recorded in her study reflect the thorough-

ness of her preparation. Whereas other studies ask one question concerning CSA, she asked fourteen different questions, any one of which might have set off a memory of sexual abuse.

In *The Epidemic of Rape and Child Sexual Abuse in the United States* (2000), Diana E. H. Russell and Rebecca M. Bolen revisit the prevalence rates reported in Russell's 1978 survey. Russell and Bolen believe those rates are underestimated. The 1978 survey subjects did not include two groups regarded to be highly probable victims of child sexual abuse: females in institutions and those not living at home. Russell and Bolen also find that some women were reluctant to reveal experiences of abuse to survey interviewers, whereas others did not recall these experiences.

Are Child Sexual Abuse Cases Declining?

According to CPS agencies across the United States, reported and substantiated cases of child sexual abuse have declined since 1992. Substantiated cases of sexual abuse of children dropped from a peak of 150,000 in 1992 to less than 90,000 in 2000, a decrease of 40%. (See Figure 4.1.) The ACYF indicates that substantiated child abuse cases dropped even further to 78,120 victims in 2006.

FIGURE 4.1

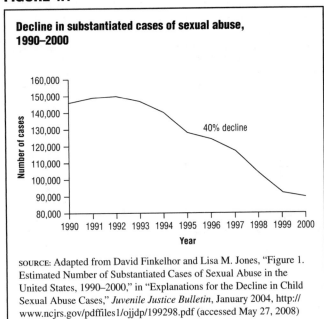

Decline in substantiated cases of sexual abuse, 1990–2000

SOURCE: Adapted from David Finkelhor and Lisa M. Jones, "Figure 1. Estimated Number of Substantiated Cases of Sexual Abuse in the United States, 1990–2000," in "Explanations for the Decline in Child Sexual Abuse Cases," *Juvenile Justice Bulletin*, January 2004, http://www.ncjrs.gov/pdffiles1/ojjdp/199298.pdf (accessed May 27, 2008)

FIGURE 4.2

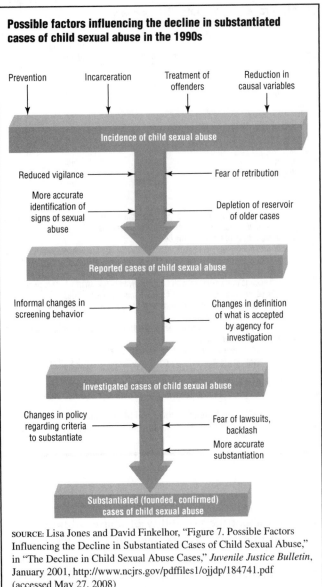

Possible factors influencing the decline in substantiated cases of child sexual abuse in the 1990s

SOURCE: Lisa Jones and David Finkelhor, "Figure 7. Possible Factors Influencing the Decline in Substantiated Cases of Child Sexual Abuse," in "The Decline in Child Sexual Abuse Cases," *Juvenile Justice Bulletin*, January 2001, http://www.ncjrs.gov/pdffiles1/ojjdp/184741.pdf (accessed May 27, 2008)

Lisa M. Jones and David Finkelhor of the University of New Hampshire examine in "The Decline in Child Sexual Abuse Cases" (*Juvenile Justice Bulletin*, January 2001) the possible factors responsible for this decline. They find that between 1990 and 1992 just three states experienced a decrease in cases of substantiated child sexual abuse, compared to fourteen states reporting increases of 20% or more. The decreasing trend started between 1992 and 1994, with twenty-two states reporting a decline of 20% or more, followed by eighteen states reporting declines between 1994 and 1996. From 1996 to 1998 thirteen states showed decreases of substantiated child sexual abuse cases.

According to Jones and Finkelhor, several factors may have influenced the decline in substantiated cases of child sexual abuse. (See Figure 4.2.) Since the 1990s the incidence of child sexual abuse may have been reduced by factors such as child victimization prevention programs, incarceration of sexual offenders, treatment programs for sex offenders, and other variables. These variables include female victimization by intimate partners and poverty. In other words, declining trends in these causal variables may play a role in the decreasing cases of child sexual abuse. Experts such as Amy M. Smith Slep and Susan G. O'Leary, in "Parent and Partner Violence in Families with Young Children: Rates, Patterns, and Connections" (*Journal of Consulting and Clinical Psychology*, vol. 73, no. 3, June 2005), and Emiko A Tajima of the University of Washington, in "Correlates of the Co-occurrence of Wife Abuse and Child Abuse among a Representative Sample" (*Journal of Family Violence*, vol. 19, no. 6, December 2004), show a 30% to 60% overlap in the victimization of children and the victimization of their mothers.

Jones and Finkelhor suggest several possible factors that could account for the drop in reports of child sexual abuse from 1991 to 1998. People might be reluctant to report their suspicions because of widely publicized cases of false accusations. The public and mandated reporters, such as health care professionals, may also have learned accurate identification of the signs of abuse. In addition, the large numbers of sexual abuse cases that had surfaced as a result of increased vigilance starting in the 1980s may have been exhausted. CPS agencies might have stopped screening certain cases, such as sexual abuse by nonfamily members, and agencies with large caseloads may have investigated only cases they deemed serious enough to warrant their time.

In "Explanations for the Decline in Child Sexual Abuse Cases" (*Juvenile Justice Bulletin*, January 2004),

FIGURE 4.3

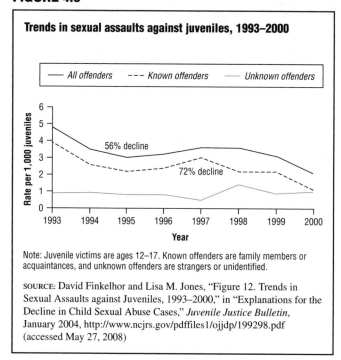

Trends in sexual assaults against juveniles, 1993–2000

Note: Juvenile victims are ages 12–17. Known offenders are family members or acquaintances, and unknown offenders are strangers or unidentified.

SOURCE: David Finkelhor and Lisa M. Jones, "Figure 12. Trends in Sexual Assaults against Juveniles, 1993–2000," in "Explanations for the Decline in Child Sexual Abuse Cases," *Juvenile Justice Bulletin*, January 2004, http://www.ncjrs.gov/pdffiles1/ojjdp/199298.pdf (accessed May 27, 2008)

FIGURE 4.4

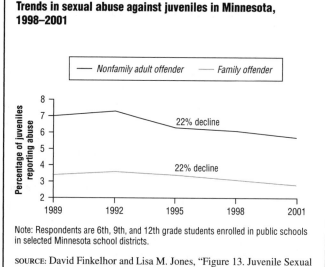

Trends in sexual abuse against juveniles in Minnesota, 1998–2001

Note: Respondents are 6th, 9th, and 12th grade students enrolled in public schools in selected Minnesota school districts.

SOURCE: David Finkelhor and Lisa M. Jones, "Figure 13. Juvenile Sexual Abuse Trends in Minnesota, 1998–2001," in "Explanations for the Decline in Child Sexual Abuse Cases," *Juvenile Justice Bulletin*, January 2004, http://www.ncjrs.gov/pdffiles1/ojjdp/199298.pdf (accessed May 27, 2008)

Finkelhor and Jones revisit the factors possibly influencing the decline. They examine, among other things, four states (Illinois, Minnesota, Oregon, and Pennsylvania) with large decreases in substantiated child sexual abuse, as well as extensive information from the 1990s. Finkelhor and Jones find little or no evidence that the decline resulted from CPS agencies not investigating certain cases or the diminishing number of older cases. They cannot determine whether or not fear of repercussions, such as lawsuits, had contributed to the decline in mandated reporting by physicians because the states had mixed results in physician reports.

Even though Finkelhor and Jones find "no solid and convincing explanation" for the decline of child sexual abuse in the 1990s, they offer two pieces of evidence that show the decline in sexual abuse cases. One piece of evidence includes the results of two self-reports of sexual assault (by nonfamily members) and sexual abuse (by family members). The second piece of evidence consists of the National Crime Victimization Survey (NCVS) and the Minnesota Student Survey. The NCVS, an annual survey of eighty thousand people over age twelve, found an overall 56% decline in self-reported sexual assault against twelve- to seventeen-year-old juveniles between 1993 and 2000, with a 72% decline by family members. (See Figure 4.3.) The Minnesota Student Survey, which was administered five times between 1989 and 2001 to over one hundred thousand students in grades six, nine, and twelve, found a slight increase in the sexual abuse trend from 1989 to 1992, then a 22% decline for sexual abuse by family and nonfamily members. (See Figure 4.4.)

WHAT MAKES A VICTIM DISCLOSE?

Rochelle F. Hanson et al. report in "Correlates of Adolescent Reports of Sexual Assault: Findings from the National Survey of Adolescents" (*Child Maltreatment*, vol. 8, no. 4, 2003) on the factors that contribute to the likelihood that an adolescent will disclose sexual abuse. The researchers also examine whether, among the different ethnic and racial groups, adolescents differ in the rates of disclosure and in the factors contributing to that disclosure.

Participants in the National Survey of Adolescents were a random sample of 4,023 U.S. adolescents aged twelve to seventeen. The sample was made up of 51.3% males and 48.7% females. A majority (70.2%) were white, non-Hispanics. The children were grouped into several age cohorts. Interviews were conducted by telephone, with the consent of the parent or guardian.

A total of 326 (8.1%) adolescents indicated that they had experienced child sexual abuse. Approximately four out of five (78.1%) of those reporting child sexual abuse were female, and one out of five (21.9%) were male. Most (58.2%) were white, 23.6% were African-American, and 9.4% were Hispanic. Other ethnic groups made up the remaining 8.8% of child sexual abuse victims.

Of the 326 victims, 30.7% had been raped, 26.8% reported fearing for their life during the assault, and 10% had suffered physical injuries. Alcohol or drugs were involved in 6.7% of the incidents. Single incidents were reported by about two-thirds (64.1%) of the victims. Three-quarters (76.4%) knew the perpetrator. Specifically, 4.3% identified their father or stepfather as the abuser, 17.5% named another relative, 52.8% reported an unrelated acquaintance, and 1.8% knew the perpetrator but did not identify the person. Nearly a quarter (23%) said the perpetrator was a stranger, and two victims did not name the perpetrator.

About two-thirds (68.1%) of the victims told interviewers they disclosed their sexual abuse to someone. Just 4.5% of those who disclosed first told a police officer or social worker. One-third (34.3%) told their mother or stepmother, and more than a third (39.3%) told a close friend. The other victims told another relative (6.1%), a teacher (1.8%), a father or stepfather (1.7%), or a doctor or other health professional (1.3%). About 3.4% indicated they disclosed the abuse to someone but did not say who it was. Another 3.9% would not say who they told of the abuse or could not remember who they first told. Overall, just 33.6% indicated they ever reported the abuse to police or other authorities.

More females (74%) than males (46.5%) disclosed to someone that they had been sexually abused. White victims (75.1%) were more likely than Hispanics (67.7%) and African-Americans (55.8%) to tell someone of their abuse. Those who feared for their life during the assault were especially likely to disclose the abuse (80.7%). Other factors that were related to high levels of disclosure were having experienced a penetration assault (72%), having suffered physical injury (70.6%), having used substances (68.2%), or having been assaulted once (67.9%). The likelihood of telling someone of the abuse was also influenced by the relationship between the victim and the perpetrator. Nearly nine out of ten (87.7%) of the victims who were sexually abused by a relative disclosed the incident, compared to those abused by a stranger (70.7%), an unrelated acquaintance (62.2%), or a father (57.1%).

Hanson et al. note that for some groups the gender of the adolescent is related to disclosure of sexual abuse, with girls more likely to do so. In this study African-American females were seven times more likely than their male counterparts to tell someone they had experienced sexual abuse, though white adolescents did not differ in disclosure of abuse based on gender. The researchers reiterate previous findings that males might fear being thought of as gay if the abuser was male. They also note that other studies show that African-American females are reluctant to disclose sexual abuse because of fear of not being believed. Even though no similar studies have been done of their male counterparts, Hanson et al. think the same reason might keep African-American male adolescents from reporting child sexual abuse.

VICTIMS
Who Is Sexually Abused?

Most studies indicate that girls are far more likely than boys to suffer sexual abuse. Under the Harm and Endangerment Standards discussed by Andrea J. Sedlak and Diane D. Broadhurst in *NIS-3*, girls were sexually abused about three times more often than boys. (See Chapter 2 for a definition of these standards.)

In "Childhood Sexual Abuse among Black Women and White Women from Two-Parent Families" (*Child Maltreatment*, vol. 11, no. 3, August 2006), a retrospective study, Maryann Amodeo et al. of Boston University examine 290 African-American and white women to determine differences in prevalence of child sexual abuse. Amodeo et al. used questionnaires and face-to-face interviews, as well as interviews with siblings, to determine whether child sexual abuse had occurred. African-American women showed a higher prevalence of child sexual abuse than did white women (34.1% and 22.8%, respectively).

Sarah E. Ullman and Henrietta Filipas of the University of Illinois find in "Ethnicity and Child Sexual Abuse Experiences of Female College Students" (*Journal of Child Sexual Abuse*, vol. 14, no. 3, 2005) racial and ethnic differences in their retrospective study using a sample of 461 female college students. Analysis of their survey reveals that African-Americans reported more sexual abuse than other groups, followed by Hispanics, whites, and Asian-Americans.

Is Sexual Abuse of Boys Underreported?

William C. Holmes and Gail B. Slap claim that sexual abuse of boys is not only common but also underreported and undertreated. In "Sexual Abuse of Boys: Definition, Prevalence, Correlates, Sequelae, and Management" (*Journal of the American Medical Association*, vol. 280, no. 21, December 2, 1998), the researchers review 149 studies of male sexual abuse. These studies, conducted between 1985 and 1997, included face-to-face interviews, telephone surveys, medical chart reviews, and computerized and paper questionnaires. The respondents included adolescents (ninth through twelfth graders, runaways, non-sex-offending delinquents, and detainees), college students, psychiatric patients, Native Americans, sex offenders (including serial rapists), substance-abusing patients, and homeless men. The researchers find that, overall, one out of five boys had been sexually abused.

Holmes and Slap note that boys younger than thirteen years of age, nonwhite, of low socioeconomic status, and not living with their fathers were at a higher risk for sexual abuse. Boys whose parents had abused alcohol, had criminal records, and were divorced, separated, or remarried were more likely to experience sexual abuse. Sexually abused boys were fifteen times more likely than boys who had never been sexually abused to live in families in which some members had also been sexually abused.

Start and Duration of Abuse

In *Sexual Assault of Young Children as Reported to Law Enforcement: Victim, Incident, and Offender Characteristics*

(July 2000, http://www.ojp.usdoj.gov/bjs/pub/pdf/saycrle .pdf), Howard N. Snyder of the National Center for Juvenile Justice finds that 20.1% of all victims of sexual assault reported to law enforcement from 1991 to 1996 were under age twelve, with 14% under six years of age. (Some researchers distinguish between child sexual abuse as perpetrated by parents or caregivers and sexual assault as committed by other individuals. In this report the term *sexual assault* included child sexual abuse.)

Patricia Tjaden and Nancy Thoennes of the Center for Policy Research in Denver, Colorado, find in *Extent, Nature, and Consequences of Rape Victimization: Findings from the National Violence against Women Survey* (January 2006, http://www.ncjrs.gov/pdffiles1/nij/210346 .pdf), a study of rape using data from the National Violence against Women Survey, that 21.6% of female rape or sexual abuse victims and 48% of male rape or sexual abuse victims were under the age of twelve when they were first raped. (See Figure 4.5.) Another 32.4% of females and 23% of males were between ages twelve and seventeen. Therefore, more than half of all female rape victims and seven out of ten male rape victims had been raped while children.

FIGURE 4.5

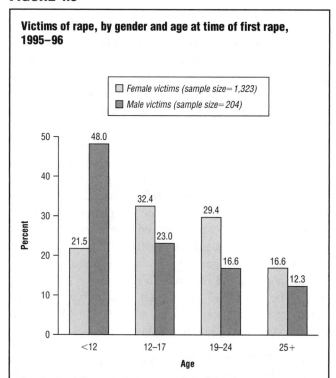

Victims of rape, by gender and age at time of first rape, 1995–96

Note: Total percentage for male victims is less than 100 due to rounding.

SOURCE: Patricia Tjaden and Nancy Thoennes, "Exhibit 10. Percentage Distribution of Female and Male Rape Victims by Age at Time of First Rape," in *Extent, Nature, and Consequences of Rape Victimization: Findings from the National Violence against Women Survey*, U.S. Department of Justice, Office of Justice Programs, National Institute of Justice, January 2006, http://www.ncjrs.gov/pdffiles1/nij/210346.pdf (accessed June 2, 2008)

In their research on male child victims, Holmes and Slap find that sexual abuse generally began before puberty. About 17% to 53% of the respondents reported repeated abuse, with some victimization continuing over periods of less than six months and some victimization enduring for eighteen to forty-eight months.

PERPETRATORS

Snyder finds that the abusers of young victims were more likely than the abusers of older victims to be family members. Sexual abusers whose victims were children five years old and younger were family members nearly half the time (48.6%), a number that decreased for those aged six to eleven (42.4%), and further decreased for victims aged twelve to seventeen (24.3%). More female victims (51.1% of those aged five years and younger and 43.8% of those aged six to eleven) were abused by family members, compared to their male counterparts (42.4% of those aged five years and younger and 37.7% of those aged six to eleven). (See Table 4.2.)

Fathers

Linda Meyer Williams and David Finkelhor indicate in *The Characteristics of Incestuous Fathers* (1992) that, generally, incestuous fathers had lonely childhoods (82%). Almost half (47%) had not lived with their own father and had changed living arrangements (43%), perhaps as a result of parental divorce or remarriage. However, their own parents' alcohol problem was no different from that of the nonabused comparison group. Incestuous fathers were far more likely to have been juvenile delinquents

TABLE 4.2

Victim-offender relationship in sexual assault, by gender of victim, 1991–96

| Victim age | Total | Offenders | | |
		Family member	Acquaintance	Stranger
Female victims	**100.0%**	**25.7%**	**59.5%**	**14.7%**
Juveniles	100.0%	33.9	58.7	7.5
0 to 5	100.0	51.1	45.9	3.0
6 to 11	100.0	43.8	51.4	4.8
12 to 17	100.0	24.3	65.7	10.0
Adults	100.0%	11.5	61.0	27.5
18 to 24	100.0	9.8	66.4	23.8
Above 24	100.0	12.9	56.9	30.2
Male victims	**100.0%**	**32.8%**	**59.8%**	**7.3%**
Juveniles	100.0%	35.8	59.2	5.0
0 to 5	100.0	42.4	54.1	3.5
6 to 11	100.0	37.7	57.7	4.6
12 to 17	100.0	23.7	68.7	7.6
Adults	100.0%	11.3	63.9	24.8
18 to 24	100.0	10.7	68.4	20.9
Above 24	100.0	11.8	60.3	27.9

SOURCE: Howard N. Snyder, "Table 7. Victim-Offender Relationship in Sexual Assault, by Victim Gender," in *Sexual Assault of Young Children As Reported to Law Enforcement: Victim, Incident, and Offender Characteristics*, U.S. Department of Justice, Bureau of Justice Statistics, July 2000, http://www.ojp .usdoj.gov/bjs/pub/pdf/saycrle.pdf (accessed June 2, 2008)

and to have been rejected by their parents. Williams and Finkelhor also find that the sex education of incestuous fathers while growing up did not come from friends or peers, but from being victims of sexual abuse. About 70% had a history of sexual abuse, with 45% having multiple abusers. Nearly three out of five were sexually abused by nonfamily adults.

Women Who Abuse

For many years, experts thought female sex abusers were uncommon. According to Craig M. Allen, in *A Comparative Analysis of Women Who Sexually Abuse Children* (1990), when women were involved in abuse, it was thought to be a situation in which a either a man had forced the woman to commit the abuse or the woman had a severe psychiatric disturbance. Some experts postulate that women are more maternal and, therefore, less likely to abuse a child. Women are also thought to have different attitudes toward sex. While men tie their feelings of self-worth to their sexual experiences, women are supposedly less concerned with sexual prowess and tend to be more empathetic toward others.

Comparing male and female offenders, Allen finds that the women reported more severe incidents of physical and emotional abuse in their past, had run away from home more often, were more sexually promiscuous than male offenders, and had more frequent incidents of being paid for sex. Because they perceived child sexual abuse as a great social deviance, female offenders were less likely to admit guilt. They were less cooperative than men during the investigations and were angrier with informants and investigators. Following disclosure, they also appeared to experience less guilt and sorrow than male offenders.

MOTHERS. The organization Making Daughters Safe Again explains in "Female-Perpetrated Sexual Abuse: Redefining the Construct of Sexual Abuse and Challenging Beliefs about Human Sexuality" (2008, http://mdsa support.homestead.com/ra.html) that sexual abuse by mothers may remain undetected because it occurs at home and is either denied or never reported. Mothers generally have more intimate contact with their children, and the lines between maternal love and care and sexual abuse are not as clear-cut as they are for fathers. Furthermore, society is reluctant to see a woman as a perpetrator of incest, portraying the woman as someone likely to turn her pain inward into depression, compared to the man who acts out his anger in sexually criminal behavior. Women's sexually abusive behavior toward their children may be disguised under the pretense of caretaking for their children.

Siblings

Sibling incest is another form of abuse that has not been well studied. However, some experts believe sibling sexual abuse is more common than father-daughter incest. Vernon R. Wiehe indicates in "Sibling Abuse" (*Understanding Family Violence: Treating and Preventing Partner, Child, Sibling, and Elder Abuse*, 1998) that the problem of sibling incest has not received much attention because of the families' reluctance to report to authorities that such abuse is happening at home, the parents' playing down the fact that "it" is indeed a problem, and the perception that it is normal for brothers and sisters to explore their sexuality.

In "Intrafamilial Sexual Abuse: Brother-Sister Incest Does Not Differ from Father-Daughter and Stepfather-Stepdaughter Incest" (*Child Abuse and Neglect: The International Journal*, vol. 26, no. 9, September 2002), Mireille Cir et al. find that there were few differences between sexual abuse perpetrated by fathers, stepfathers, or brothers in their survey of seventy-two sexually abused girls between the ages of five and sixteen. They find that penetration was much more frequent in the brother-sister incest group (70.8%) than in the stepfather-stepdaughter incest group (27.3%) or the father-daughter incest group (34.8%). They also find that nine out of ten girls abused by their brothers showed clinically significant traumatic stress. These findings indicate that sexual abuse perpetrated by a sibling should be taken seriously.

Educators

Sex between educators and students is nothing new. However, except for sensational cases, such as that of the Washington teacher Mary Kay Letourneau (1962–), who was charged with child rape of a twelve-year-old student and served a seven-and-a-half-year sentence, other cases have not received much attention. Some experts observe there seems to be a double standard in cases involving a female teacher and a male student. They point to an example in New Jersey. In 2002 the Superior Court judge Bruce A. Gaeta (1942–2008) refused to sentence Pamela Diehl-Moore (1959–) to prison for pleading guilty to sexual assault and instead ordered probation. The teacher admitted having sex for six months with a thirteen-year-old student. The judge claimed he saw no harm done to the student and that the relationship might have been a way for the boy to satisfy his sexual needs. Gaeta received public reprimand for his comments. Diehl-Moore was sentenced to three years in prison on appeal.

In 2004 Charol S. Shakeshaft of Hofstra University reported that no national study of public school educators who have abused students had ever been done. In compliance with the No Child Left Behind Act of 2001, the U.S. Department of Education commissioned Shakeshaft to conduct a national study of sexual abuse in schools. After identifying about nine hundred literature citations that discussed educator sexual misconduct and contacting over one thousand researchers, educators, and policy

TABLE 4.3

Perpetrators of sexual abuse of students in school by job title, 2000

Job title	Percent
Teacher	18
Coach	15
Substitute teachers	13
Bus driver	12
Teacher's aide	11
Other school employee	10
Security guard	10
Principal	6
Counselor	5
Total	**100**

SOURCE: Charol Shakeshaft, "Table 7. Percent of Student Targets by Job Title of Offender," in *Educator Sexual Misconduct: A Synthesis of Existing Literature*, U.S. Department of Education, Office of the Under Secretary, June 2004, http://www.ed.gov/rschstat/research/pubs/misconductreview/report.pdf (accessed June 2, 2008). Data from C. Shakeshaft, "Educator Sexual Abuse," *Hofstra Horizons*, Spring 2003, 10-13, and American Association of University Women, 2001.

makers on the issue, Shakeshaft found just fourteen U.S. and five Canadian/British empirical studies on educator sexual misconduct. (Empirical studies are based on practical observations and not theory.) With scant empirical studies on hand, she based her conclusion on two American Association of University Women *Hostile Hallways* surveys conducted in 1993 and 2001 involving 3,695 public school students in eighth and eleventh grades. Both were Shakeshaft's own work. In addition, Shakeshaft used her 2003 reanalysis of the surveys for additional data on educator sexual misconduct.

In *Educator Sexual Misconduct: A Synthesis of Existing Literature* (2004, http://www.ed.gov/rschstat/research/pubs/misconductreview/report.pdf), Shakeshaft projects the numbers in her surveys to the whole public school system. She concludes that 9.6% of public school children, accounting for 4.5 million students, have experienced sexual misconduct—ranging from being told sexual jokes, to being shown pictures of a sexual nature, to sexual intercourse—by educators. Educators included teachers and other school officials, such as principals, coaches, counselors, substitute teachers, teacher's aides, security guards, bus drivers, and other employees.

The studies Shakeshaft analyzes do not reveal the number or proportion of educators who were perpetrators of sexual misconduct. However, Shakeshaft's surveys show that perpetrators of sexual misconduct against students in schools were 18% teachers, 15% coaches, and 13% substitute teachers. (See Table 4.3.) Principals accounted for 6%, and school counselors made up 5%. Shakeshaft observes that teachers whose jobs involve dealing with individual students, such as coaches and music teachers, are more likely than other educators to sexually abuse students. With regard to the gender of the perpetrators, the different studies Shakeshaft surveys show a range of 4% to 42.8% for female educators and a range of 57.2% to 96% for male educators.

Sexual Abusers of Boys

Holmes and Slap find that more than 90% of the abusers of boys and young male adolescents in their study were male. Male abusers of older male teenagers and young male adults, however, made up 22% to 73% of perpetrators. This older age group also experienced abuse by females, ranging from 27% to 78%. Adolescent baby-sitters accounted for up to half of female sexual abusers of younger boys.

More than half of those who sexually abused male children were not family members but were known to the victims. Boys younger than six years old were more likely to be sexually abused by family and acquaintances, whereas those older than twelve were more likely to be victims of strangers. Whereas male perpetrators used physical force, with threats of physical harm increasing with victim age, female perpetrators used persuasion and promises of special favors.

Priests

Public concern about sexual abuse by priests sky-rocketed in the early twenty-first century as a result of a scandal surrounding abuse and cover-ups within the Catholic Church. Thomas F. Reilly (1942–), the attorney general of Massachusetts, explains in *The Sexual Abuse of Children in the Roman Catholic Archdiocese of Boston: A Report by the Attorney General* (July 23, 2003, news.findlaw.com/hdocs/docs/abuse/maag72303abuserpt.pdf) the culture of secrecy involving the sexual abuse of an estimated one thousand minors in the archdiocese of Boston since 1940. Reilly's eighteen-month investigation finds that "there is overwhelming evidence that for many years Cardinal [Bernard] Law and his senior managers had direct, actual knowledge that substantial numbers of children in the Archdiocese had been sexually abused by substantial numbers of its priests."

Reilly started the investigation in March 2002, soon after John Geoghan (1935–2003), a former priest in the archdiocese of Boston, was sentenced to nine to ten years in prison for sexually abusing a ten-year-old boy. Reilly's investigators found that starting in 1979 the archdiocese had received complaints of child sexual abuse against Geoghan. Church documents, which had previously been sealed, revealed that the church not only moved Geoghan from parish to parish but had also paid settlements amounting to $15 million to the victims' families. Reilly reported that the archdiocese's own files showed that 789 people had brought sexual complaints against the Boston clergy. However, Reilly believes the actual number of victims is higher. There were 237 priests and church workers who had been accused of rape and sexual assault.

EXTENT OF CHILD SEXUAL ABUSE BY PRIESTS. Responding to emerging allegations of sexual abuse by priests, in June 2002 the U.S. Conference of Catholic Bishops commissioned a study of the nature and scope of the problem of child sexual abuse in the Catholic Church. The John Jay College of Criminal Justice of the City University of New York conducted the study based on information provided by 195 dioceses, representing 98% of all diocesan priests in the United States. The researchers also collected data from 140 religious communities, accounting for about 60% of religious communities and 80% of all priests in the religious communities.

The Nature and Scope of the Problem of Sexual Abuse of Minors by Catholic Priests and Deacons in the United States (2004, http://www.usccb.org/nrb/john jaystudy/) covers the period from 1950 to 2002. Of the 109,694 priests and deacons (collectively referred to as priests) who served during this period, 4,392 (4%) allegedly abused children under age eighteen. Most (55.7%) of these priests had a single allegation of abuse. Nearly 27% had two to three allegations, 13.9% had four to nine allegations, and 3.5% had ten or more allegations.

The report shows that 10,667 individuals made allegations of child sexual abuse by priests between 1950 and 2002. About 81% of the victims were male and 19% were female. About half (50.7%) were between the ages of eleven and fourteen. More than a quarter (26.7%) were fifteen to seventeen years old, 16.5% were aged eight to ten, and 6.1% were aged seven or younger. (See Table 4.4.) The number of allegations rose steadily between 1950 and 1980 before dropping off sharply. (See Figure 4.6.)

At the time of the allegations, most of the priests were serving in the capacity of associate pastor (42.3%) or pastor (25.1%). One out of ten (10.4%) were serving as

TABLE 4.4

Victim's age at first instance of abuse by priests, 1950–2002

Age in years	Count	% of total
1	4	.0%
2	11	.1%
3	22	.2%
4	41	.5%
5	82	1.0%
6	158	1.8%
7	220	2.5%
8	369	4.1%
9	362	4.0%
10	752	8.4%
11	895	10.0%
12	1,323	14.7%
13	1,141	12.8%
14	1,188	13.2%
15	1,042	11.6%
16	769	8.6%
17	577	6.5%
Total	**8,956**	**100%**

SOURCE: "Table 4.3.2. Victim's Age at First Instance of Abuse," in *The Nature and Scope of the Problem of Sexual Abuse of Minors by Catholic Priests and Deacons in the United States*, United States Conference of Catholic Bishops, 2004, http://www.usccb.org/nrb/johnjaystudy/incident3.pdf (accessed June 2, 2008)

FIGURE 4.6

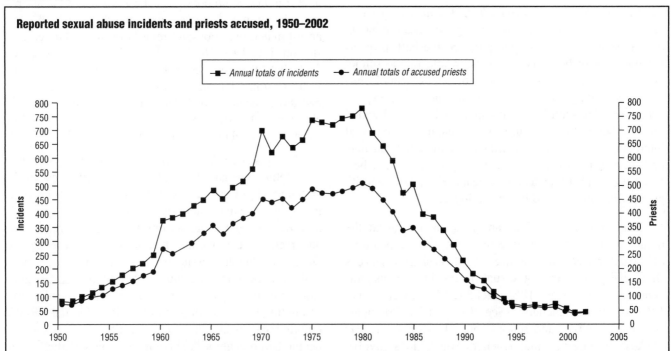

Reported sexual abuse incidents and priests accused, 1950–2002

SOURCE: "Figure 2.3.1. Annual Count of Incidents Reported and Priests Accused, by Year," in *The Nature and Scope of the Problem of Sexual Abuse of Minors by Catholic Priests and Deacons in the United States*, United States Conference of Catholic Bishops, 2004, http://www.usccb.org/nrb/johnjaystudy/prev3.pdf (accessed June 2, 2008)

TABLE 4.5

Location of abuse by priests, 1950–2002

Place	Count	Percent of cases
In school	939	10.3%
In a hotel room	675	7.4%
Retreat house	133	1.5%
Priest's home/Parish residence	3730	40.9%
Vacation house	941	10.3%
Other residences (friends, family, etc.)	49	.5%
Congregate residences	51	.6%
In victim's home	1131	12.4%
Priest's office	685	7.5%
In church	1483	16.3%
In the hospital	75	.8%
In a car	897	9.8%
Outings (camp, park, pool, etc.)	757	8.3%
Other location	571	6.3%
No record of location	2109	23.1%

Note: This is a multiple response table. The categories are not mutually exclusive since an incident of abuse may have taken place over time and in more than one place.

SOURCE: "Table 4.5.3. Location of Abuse," in *The Nature and Scope of the Problem of Sexual Abuse of Minors by Catholic Priests and Deacons in the United States*, United States Conference of Catholic Bishops, 2004, http://www.usccb.org/nrb/johnjaystudy/incident5.pdf (accessed June 2, 2008)

resident priests. Most of the abuse occurred in the priest's home or parish residence (40.9%), in church (16.3%), and in the victim's home (12.4%). (See Table 4.5.) Nearly half (49.6%) of the priests socialized with the alleged victim's family, mostly (79.6%) in the family's home.

In "Stained Glass: The Nature and Scope of Child Sexual Abuse in the Catholic Church" (*Criminal Justice and Behavior*, vol. 35, no. 5, May 2008), a follow-up study, Karen J. Terry of the John Jay College of Criminal Justice finds that many victims of abuse by priests were groomed for the abuse—7.8% of children were given gifts and 17% of children were given other enticements, such as alcohol, drugs, money, or trips. Only 7.8% of victims were threatened, usually psychologically rather than physically.

SEXUAL PREDATORS ON THE INTERNET

The Internet gives pedophiles easy access to children. According to the U.S. Department of Justice's Office for Victims of Crime, in *Internet Crimes against Children* (May 2001, http://www.ojp.usdoj.gov/ovc/publications/bulletins/internet_2_2001/welcome.html), child predators who look for victims in places where children typically congregate, such as schoolyards, playgrounds, and shopping malls, now have cyberspace to commit their criminal acts. The Internet presents an even more attractive venue because predators can commit their crime anonymously and are able to contact the same child regularly. They may groom children online for the production of child pornography. Predators have been known to prey on vulnerable children, gaining their confidence online, and

then meeting up with them for the purpose of engaging them in sex acts.

In *Computer and Internet Use in the United States: 2003* (October 2005, http://www.census.gov/prod/2005pubs/p23-208.pdf, Jennifer Cheeseman Day, Alex Janus, and Jessica Davis of the U.S. Census Bureau explain that in 2003, 80% of adolescents aged fifteen to seventeen used the Internet at some location. More than two-thirds (68.9%) of children aged ten to fourteen, 44.8% of children aged six to nine, and 23.4% of children aged three to five used the Internet. Females were slightly more likely than males to use the Internet (57% and 55.1%, respectively).

Julian Fantino notes in "Child Pornography on the Internet: New Challenges Require New Ideas" (*Police Chief*, vol. 70, no. 12, December 2003) that more and more younger children are being used in child pornography, with a large proportion being infants and preschool children. Offenders form secret clubs, sharing modes of operation and protecting one another's identity. According to Fantino, in 2003 more than one hundred thousand Web sites contained child pornography.

National Survey on the Online Victimization of Children

In *Online Victimization of Youth: Five Years Later* (2006, http://www.unh.edu/ccrc/pdf/CV138.pdf), a national survey on the risks children face on the Internet, Janis Wolak, Kimberly Mitchell, and David Finkelhor of the University of New Hampshire find that nearly one out of seven (13%) youths using the Internet in the last year had received an unwanted sexual solicitation or approach. Sexual solicitations involved requests to do sexual things the children did not want to do, and sexual approaches involved incidents in which people tried to get children to talk about sex when they did not want to or asked them intimate questions. In addition, 34% reported at least one unwanted exposure to sexual material (pictures of naked people or people having sex) while surfing the Internet the past year. Michele L. Ybarra and Kimberly J. Mitchell of the University of New Hampshire indicate in "Exposure to Internet Pornography among Children and Adolescents: A National Survey" (*CyberPsychology and Behavior*, vol. 8, no. 5, 2005) that 20% of youth between the ages of fourteen and seventeen and 8% of youth between the ages of ten and thirteen, primarily male, intentionally sought out pornographic materials on the Internet.

In a follow-up study, Kimberly J. Mitchell, Janis Wolak, and David Finkelhor of the University of New Hampshire state in "Trends in Youth Reports of Sexual Solicitations, Harassment, and Unwanted Exposure to Pornography on the Internet" (*Journal of Adolescent Health*, vol. 40, 2007) that the proportion of youth who reported online sexual solicitations declined between 2000 and

FIGURE 4.7

Online victimization of youth, 2005

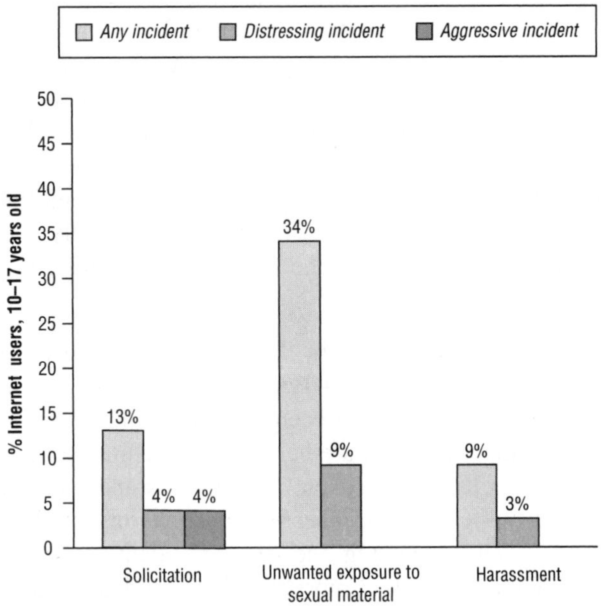

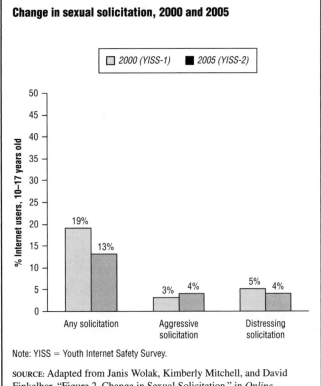

SOURCE: Janis Wolak, Kimberly Mitchell, and David Finkelhor, "Figure 1. YISS-2 Online Victimization," in *Online Victimization of Youth: Five Years Later*, National Center for Missing and Exploited Children, 2006, http://www.unh.edu/ccrc/pdf/CV138.pdf (accessed June 23, 2008)

FIGURE 4.8

Change in sexual solicitation, 2000 and 2005

Note: YISS = Youth Internet Safety Survey.

SOURCE: Adapted from Janis Wolak, Kimberly Mitchell, and David Finkelhor, "Figure 2. Change in Sexual Solicitation," in *Online Victimization of Youth: Five Years Later*, National Center for Missing and Exploited Children, 2006, http://www.unh.edu/ccrc/pdf/CV138.pdf (accessed June 23, 2008)

2005, although online harassment and unwanted exposure to pornography actually rose. The researchers find that in 2005 approximately 13% of youth were sexually solicited online, meaning that they were requested online to talk about sex—although many of these requests probably came from other youth. (See Figure 4.7.) Many of these solicitations were not intended to lure children into sexual activity. Mitchell, Wolak, and Finkelhor's best guess is that about 4% of youth were aggressively sexually solicited online, including attempts to contact the youth offline—up from 3% in 2000. (See Figure 4.8.)

However, according to Kimberly J. Mitchell, David Finkelhor, and Janis Wolak of the University of New Hampshire, in "The Internet and Family and Acquaintance Sexual Abuse" (*Child Maltreatment*, vol. 10, no. 1, 2005), nearly as many acquaintances and family members used the Internet to commit sex crimes against children as did adults who used the Internet to actually meet children. The follow-up study actually found that even though the percentage of youth who used the Internet rose between 2000 and 2006, the percentage of youth who spoke to people they knew only online dropped from 40% to 34%. (See Table 4.6.) This decline might be due to a heightened awareness of pedophiles on the Internet.

When youth were sexually solicited online, most were able to deal with the problem by blocking solicitors

or leaving sites. Most did not report feeling distressed by the experience, but about 4% of youth did report feeling upset or distressed as a result of the online solicitation. (See Figure 4.7.) In "Online 'Predators' and Their Victims: Myths, Realities, and Implications for Prevention and Treatment" (*American Psychologist*, vol. 63, 2008), Janis Wolak et al. of the University of New Hampshire indicate that when predatory offenders were charged with a crime, the pattern most often involved nonforcible sexual activity between young victims and adult men.

However, in 2006 parents, educators, and law enforcement officials sent out a warning about MySpace.com, a huge Web site designed to be an Internet chat room and hangout for teens and young adults, but which police say is attracting sexual predators. As many as fifty-eight million users post personal information on the site, including photos and Web logs (so-called blogs, containing journal-like postings from the user), sometimes with home addresses and phone numbers included. According to Jane Gordon, in "MySpace Draws a Questionable Crowd" (*New York Times*, February 26, 2006), in Connecticut police investigated several reports of sexual assaults of young girls between the ages of thirteen and fifteen that occurred after they met adult male suspects on the site. Anick Jesdanun reports in "MySpace Plans Adult Restrictions to Protect Teen Users" (*Washington Post*, June 21,

TABLE 4.6

Youth Internet use patterns, 2000 and 2005

[N = 3,001]

Description	2000 All youth (N = 1,501)	2005 All youth (N = 1,500)
Location(s) youth spent time on Internet in past year[a]		
Home	74%	91%
School	73%	90%
Friend's home[b]	68%	69%
Cellular telephone	—	17%
Other place (includes library)	37%	43%
Last time youth used Internet		
Past week	76%	86%
Past weeks	10%	6%
Past month or longer	14%	8%
Number of hours youth spent on Internet on a typical day when online		
1 hour or less	61%	45%
More than l hour to 2 hours	26%	13%
More 2 hours	13%	23%
Number of days youth went on Internet in a typical week[c]		
1 day or less	29%	8%
2 to 4 days	40%	42%
5 to 7 days	31%	49%
How youth used Internet[a]		
Went to web sites	94%	99%
Used e-mail	76%	79%
Used instant messaging	55%	68%
Went to chat rooms	56%	30%
Played games	67%	83%
Did school assignments	85%	92%
Downloaded music	—	38%
Kept online journal or blog	—	16%
Used online dating or romance sites	—	1%
Who youth talked to online[d]		
People youth knew in person offline	73%	79%
People youth knew only online	40%	34%

[a]Multiple responses possible.
[b]In Youth Internet Safety Survey-1 (YISS-1) we asked if youth used the Internet in "other households," which included friends' homes. In YISS-2 we specifically asked all youth if they used the Internet at friends' homes.
[c]Based on youth who used the Internet in the past week or past 2 weeks.
[d]Answers not mutually exclusive.
Note: Some categories do not add to 100% because of rounding and/or missing data.

SOURCE: Adapted from Janis Wolak, Kimberly Mitchell, and David Finkelhor, "Table 2. Youth Internet Use Patterns," in *Online Victimization of Youth: Five Years Later*, National Center for Missing and Exploited Children, 2006, http://www.unh.edu/ccrc/pdf/CV138.pdf (accessed June 23, 2008)

2006) that by June 2006 MySpace planned new restrictions on the interactions of adults over age eighteen and children under age sixteen on the site in response to criticisms.

In "The Relative Importance of Online Victimization in Understanding Depression, Delinquency, and Substance Use" (*Child Maltreatment*, vol. 12, no. 4, November 2007), Kimberly J. Mitchell, Michele L. Ybarra, and David Finkelhor of the University of New Hampshire find that 23% of 1,501 youth surveyed reported being the victim of either sexual solicitation or harassment online. Nearly three-quarters of these youth reported an offline victimization as well. However, youth who had been sexually solicited online were nearly twice as likely as others to report depression and substance use, indicating the serious nature of this type of victimization.

EFFECTS OF CHILD SEXUAL ABUSE

According to the American Psychological Association (APA), in "What Are the Effects of Child Sexual Abuse?" (October 31, 2006, http://www.apa.org/releases/sexabuse/effects.html), children who have been sexually abused exhibit a range of symptoms. A child may show inappropriate sexual knowledge or exhibit sexual acting out behaviors. Other immediate effects may include regressive behaviors, such as thumb sucking and/or bed wetting; sleep disturbances; eating problems; and school problems, including misconduct, problems with performing schoolwork, and failure to participate in activities.

The APA also details long-term effects of child sexual abuse. Adult victims may suffer from depression, sexual dysfunction, and anxiety. Anxiety may manifest itself in behaviors such as anxiety attacks, insomnia, and alcohol and drug abuse. Adult survivors of CSA also report revictimization as rape victims or as victims of intimate physical abuse.

High-Risk Sexual Behaviors in Adolescent Girls

In "Sexual At-Risk Behaviors of Sexually Abused Adolescent Girls" (*Journal of Child Sexual Abuse*, vol. 12, no. 2, 2003), a study of sexual at-risk behaviors of 125 female adolescents aged twelve to seventeen who had experienced sexual abuse, Caroline Cinq-Mars et al. administered a self-report questionnaire that asked about the subjects' sexual activities, not including sexual abuse experiences. Afterward, the subjects were interviewed regarding their sexual abuse experiences, including information about the perpetrator (both family and nonfamily members), frequency and duration of abuse, severity of the abuse, and whether or not they told someone of the abuse.

Among offending family members, fathers were the perpetrators in 30.4% of incidents. Stepfathers and extended family members each were responsible for 28.8% of the sexual abuse, and brothers accounted for another 9.6% of abuse. The victims experienced more than one incident of sexual abuse, with the mean (average) number of perpetrators per victim being 1.8. The mean age for the start of abuse was 9.3 years. More than one-third (36.8%) of the victims experienced sexual abuse before age eleven.

Over half (55.3%) of the participants reported being sexually active. More than half (54.5%) had their first consensual intercourse before the age of fifteen. The rate of pregnancy was 15%. Cinq-Mars et al. find three sexual abuse characteristics that were associated with the adolescents' sexual at-risk behavior. Adolescents who experienced abuse involving penetration were more than thirteen times as likely to have been pregnant and twice as likely to have more than one consensual partner in the past year. Having been abused by more than one perpetrator (in one or more incidents) was also closely associated with at-risk behaviors: pregnancy (eight times as likely), more than one consensual sexual partner (four times as likely), and irregular condom use (three times as likely). Finally, physical coercion during abuse increased the odds of pregnancy (four times as likely), more than one consensual sexual partner (five times as likely), and irregular condom use (three times as likely).

Substance Abuse

A number of studies, such as Christiane Brems et al.'s "Childhood Abuse History and Substance Use among Men and Women Receiving Detoxification Services" (*American Journal of Drug and Alcohol Abuse*, vol. 30, no. 4, November 2004), Patricia B. Moran, Sam Vuchinich, and Nancy K. Hall's "Associations between Types of Maltreatment and Substance Use during Adolescence" (*Child Abuse and Neglect: The International Journal*, vol. 28, no. 5, May 2004), and Cathy Spatz Widom et al.'s "Long-Term Effects of Child Abuse and Neglect on Alcohol Use and Excessive Drinking in Middle Adulthood" (*Journal of Studies on Alcohol and Drugs*, vol. 68, no. 3, May 2007), show that child sexual abuse increases the risk for substance abuse later in life. In "Abnormal T2 Relaxation Time in the Cerebellar Vermis of Adults Sexually Abused in Childhood: Potential Role of the Vermis in Stress-Enhanced Risk for Drug Abuse" (*Psychoneuroendocrinology*, vol. 27, no. 1–2, January 2002), Carl M. Anderson et al. of Harvard Medical School uncover how this occurs. They find that the vermis, the region flanked by the cerebellar hemispheres of the brain, may play a key role in the risk for substance abuse among adults who have experienced child abuse. The vermis develops gradually and continues to produce neurons, or nerve cells, after birth. It is known to be sensitive to stress, so that stress can influence its development.

Anderson et al. compared young adults aged eighteen to twenty-two, including eight with a history of repeated sexual abuse in childhood and sixteen others as the control group. Using functional magnetic resonance imaging technology, they measured the resting blood flow in the vermis. They find that the subjects who had been victims of sexual abuse had diminished blood flow. Anderson et al. suggest the stress experienced with repeated sexual abuse may have caused damage to the vermis, which in turn could not perform its job of controlling irritability in the limbic system. The limbic system in the center of the brain, a collection of connected clusters of nerve cells, is responsible for, among other things, regulating emotions and memory. Therefore, the damaged vermis induces a person to use drugs or alcohol to suppress the irritability.

Because the child sexual abuse subjects had no history of alcohol or substance abuse, Anderson et al. wanted to confirm their findings, which linked an impaired cerebellar vermis and the potential for substance abuse in sexual abuse survivors. After analyzing test data collected from the 537 college students recruited for the study, they find that students who reported frequent substance abuse showed higher irritability in the limbic system. They also exhibited symptoms usually associated with drug use, including depression and anger.

Robert C. Freeman, Karyn Collier, and Kathleen M. Parillo of NOVA Research Company of Bethesda, Maryland, examine in "Early Life Sexual Abuse as a Risk Factor for Crack Cocaine Use in a Sample of Community-Recruited Women at High Risk for Illicit Drug Use" (*American Journal of Drug and Alcohol Abuse*, vol. 28, no. 1, February 2002) a total of 1,478 noninjecting female sexual partners of male intravenous drug users. Nearly two-thirds (63.7%) of the women reported having used crack cocaine. The researchers find that an equal proportion of the women had suffered sexual abuse before age twelve (39.5%) and during adolescence (38.8%). Overall, nearly 22% were sexually abused during both childhood and adolescence.

While Freeman, Collier, and Parillo find a relationship between child sexual abuse and lifetime crack use, they find no direct link between sexual abuse during adolescence and lifetime crack use. However, they do find some indirect connections between the two. Female teens who were victims of sexual abuse were more likely to run away, and these runaways were more likely to use crack because of the type of people with whom they associated.

Sexual Revictimization and Self-Harming Behaviors

In "Revictimization and Self-Harm in Females Who Experienced Childhood Sexual Abuse: Results from a Prospective Study" (*Journal of Interpersonal Violence*, vol. 18, no. 12, December 2003), Jennie G. Noll et al. report on a longitudinal study (a study of the same group over a period of time) that examines the effects of child sexual abuse on female development. This was the first prospective study that followed children from the time sexual abuse was reported through adolescence and into early adulthood. Referred by CPS agencies, the participants experienced sexual abuse by a family member before the age of fourteen. The median age at the start of sexual abuse was seven to eight years, and the median duration of abuse was two years. The study consisted of eighty-four abused children and a comparison group of eighty-two nonabused children. Two yearly interviews followed the first assessment of the group. A fourth interview was conducted four to five years after the third interview.

Noll et al. note that this study was the first to provide information about the revictimization of child sexual abuse survivors not long after their abuse (seven years after the abuse when the participants were in their adolescence and early adulthood). The researchers find that participants who had been sexually abused during childhood were twice as likely as the comparison group to have experienced sexual revictimization, such as rape or sexual assault, and almost four times as likely to harm themselves through suicide attempts or self-mutilation. They also suffered 1.6 times more physical victimization, such as domestic violence. Compared to the nonabused group, the abused group reported 20% more significant lifetime traumas subsequent to being sexually abused. Significant lifetime traumas reported by the participants included separation and losses (e.g., having family or friends move away or die), emotional abuse and/or rejection by family, natural disasters, and witnessing violence.

Henrietta H. Filipas and Sarah E. Ullman of the University of Illinois, Chicago, explore in "Child Sexual Abuse, Coping Responses, Self-Blame, Posttraumatic Stress Disorder, and Adult Sexual Revictimization" (*Journal of Interpersonal Violence*, vol. 21, no. 5, 2006) what factors make child sexual abuse survivors more vulnerable to revictimization as adults. They hypothesize that self-blame, maladaptive coping responses, and posttraumatic stress disorder (PTSD) would all make survivors more likely to be revictimized. However, Filipas and Ullman find that only the extent to which adult female victims of child sexual abuse used maladaptive coping responses such as alcohol and drug use, withdrawal from people, and sexual acting out was correlated with their vulnerability to revictimization as adults.

In "Substance Use and PTSD Symptoms Impact the Likelihood of Rape and Revictimization in College Women" (*Journal of Interpersonal Violence*, May 2008), Terri L. Messman-Moore, Rose Marie Ward, and Amy L. Brown find that substance use and PTSD increase the likelihood that college women will be raped or otherwise revictimized. They argue that PTSD sufferers use drugs and alcohol or maladaptive sexual behavior to cope with PTSD symptoms and that these coping behaviors increase their risk of further victimization.

Noll et al. observe that child sexual abuse is the "strongest predictor of self-harm," even when other types of abuse are present. They surmise that the victims may have negative feelings toward their own body and want to hurt it. Noll et al. write that some researchers believe victims may want to reveal internal pains through outward manifestation of self-harm. Others wish to re-experience feelings of shame in an attempt to resolve it.

Effects of Sexual Abuse by Women

In "The Long-Term Effects of Child Sexual Abuse by Female Perpetrators: A Qualitative Study of Male and Female Victims" (*Journal of Interpersonal Violence*, vol. 19, no. 10, October 2004), Myriam S. Denov of the University of Ottawa conducted a qualitative study on the long-term effects of child sexual abuse by women. Unlike quantitative research, which involves collecting samples of quantitative data and performing some form of statistical analysis, qualitative research is based on a smaller sample of individuals and does not represent the general population. However, according to Denov, the qualitative approach "is particularly appropriate for a study of this nature as it can give depth and detail of phenomena that are difficult to convey with quantitative methods."

The study sample consisted of seven males and seven females, who ranged in age from twenty-three to fifty-nine years. The sexual abuse occurred when they were fourteen years old or younger. All participants reported at least one incident of sexual abuse by a lone female perpetrator. Five participants reported having been sexually abused by more than one lone perpetrator. Nine participants were abused by a female relative—six by their mother, two by their mother and grandmother, and one by his mother and sister. Four participants were abused by an unrelated person—three by a babysitter and one by a nun at a local church. While the study concerns abuse perpetrated by women, half (or seven) of the participants reported having also been sexually abused by a man (in a separate incident from the abuse by women)—four by their father, two by an unrelated male babysitter, and one by his older half-brother.

The sexual abuse started, on average, at age five and ended, on average, at age twelve. It lasted about six years. Five participants were abused more than once per week, three were abused once per week, and four were abused once per month. Two participants reported a single episode of abuse. All participants reported mild abuse (e.g., kissing in a sexual way and sexual invitations). In addition, ten reported moderate abuse (genital contact or fondling [without penetration] and simulated intercourse). Nine participants experienced severe abuse (such as intercourse and penetration with fingers or objects).

Denov observes that while many effects of sexual abuse by females seem similar to that by males, female sexual abuse has long-term effects that are unique. Of the fourteen study participants, just one (a male) indicated he did not feel damaged by the sexual abuse by a woman. The other thirteen said they felt damaged by the abuse. All seven participants who were also abused by males reported that the sexual abuse by women was more damaging. The effects of child sexual abuse included substance abuse (used to "silence their rage and numb the pain"), self-injury, thoughts of suicide, depression, and rage. All victims reported a great mistrust of women and a discomfort with sexual intimacy. Most of the female victims were confused about their sense of identity and self-concept. Five out of seven said that, as young girls, they did not want to grow up to be women. Four women confessed that they continued to deny their femininity, one victim admitting that she dressed in an unwomanly fashion because she would be safest to herself and to others. Twelve participants feared they might sexually abuse their own children. In fact, two men and two women reported having sexually abused children. One man and three women decided not to have children.

Effects on Boys

MALE VICTIMS' PERCEPTION OF CHILD SEXUAL ABUSE AND CLINICAL FINDINGS. In their review of nearly 150 studies of male sexual abuse, Holmes and Slap find that only 15% to 39% of victims who responded to the studies thought that they were adversely affected by the sexual abuse. The victims stressed that the adverse effects were linked to the use of force, to cases in which the perpetrator was much older than the victim, or to cases where the victim was very young. Holmes and Slap note, however, that negative clinical results (in contrast to what the studies' subjects reported) included PTSD, major depression, paranoia, aggressive behavior, poor self-image, poor school performance, substance abuse, and running away from home. They surmise that the discrepancy between the respondents' perceptions of the negative consequences of their sexual victimization and those discovered in clinical outcomes may be because of several factors: abused males may believe they have failed to protect themselves as society expects them to do, or, if they had experienced pleasure while being abused, they may be confused by their feelings about it.

Sharon M. Valente of the Research and Education Department of Veteran Affairs in Los Angeles, California, finds in "Sexual Abuse of Boys" (*Journal of Child and Adolescent Psychiatric Nursing*, vol. 18, no. 1, January–March 2005) that boys who have been sexually abused display a range of psychological consequences to the traumatic experience. She finds that common responses include anxiety, denial, dissociation, and self-mutilation. Boys who have been sexually abused are at risk for running away. According to Susan Rick of Louisiana State University Health Science Center, in "Sexually Abused Boys: A Vulnerable Population" (*Journal of Multicultural Nursing and Health*, winter 2003), sexually abused boys have "prominent symptoms such as fear, depression, guilt, self destructive behavior and hypersexuality."

A Longitudinal Study of the Effects of Child Sexual Abuse

In "The Effects of Child Sexual Abuse in Later Family Life: Mental Health, Parenting, and Adjustment of Offspring" (*Child Abuse and Neglect: The International Journal*, vol. 28, no. 5, May 2004), Ron Roberts et al. seek to determine the effects of child sexual abuse on adult mental health, parenting relationships, and the adjustment of the children of mothers who had been victims of child sexual abuse. They investigated 8,292 families, a subsample of the Avon Longitudinal Study of Parents and Children, which is a continuing study of women and their families in Avon, England. The participating women had self-reported experiences of sexual assault before adolescence. Four family groups were included:

- Single-mother families (9% of the study sample)—consist of a nonmarried woman with no partner and her children

- Biological families (79.5%)—consist of two parents and their biological children with no other children from previous relationships

- Stepmother/complex stepfamilies (4.6%)—consist of a father with at least one biological child (living in the household or visiting regularly) who is not the biological offspring of the mother

- Stepfather families (6.9%)—consist of a mother and at least one biological child (living in the household or visiting regularly) who is not the biological offspring of the father

The study reveals that more than a quarter (26%) of survivors of child sexual abuse had teen pregnancies. These women were disproportionately likely to be currently living in a nontraditional family—single-mother families (3%) and stepfather families (2.9%)—than to be living in biological families (1.3%). Roberts et al. did not have a similar finding when it came to stepmother/complex stepfamilies. In this group just 0.8% reported child sexual abuse. They surmise that a woman who has experienced child sexual abuse tends to choose a partner without children because she might feel inadequate to take care of more children.

Child sexual abuse also has consequences on the adult survivors' mental health. Mothers who reported child sexual abuse were likely to report more depression and anxiety and lower self-esteem. These mental problems in turn affect the mothers' relationship with their children and the children's adjustment. Mothers with a history of child sexual abuse reported less self-confidence and less positive relationships with their children. The children were hyperactive and had emotional, peer, and conduct problems.

THE REPRESSED MEMORY CONTROVERSY

In the early 1900s the Austrian psychoanalyst Sigmund Freud (1856–1939) first proposed the theory of repression, which hypothesizes that the mind can reject unpleasant ideas, desires, and memories by banishing them into the unconscious. Some clinicians believe memory repression explains why a victim of a traumatic experience, such as CSA, may forget the horrible incident. Some also believe forgotten traumatic experiences can be eventually recovered.

In 1988 Ellen Bass and Laura Davis published *The Courage to Heal: A Guide for Women Survivors of Child Sexual Abuse*. This book became controversial because it suggested that some women may not remember incidences of childhood abuse. Bass and Davis explain that in situations of overwhelming pain and betrayal, a child might dissociate, or separate, the memory of the experiences from conscious knowledge.

Some memory researchers do not agree, explaining that children who have suffered serious psychological trauma do not repress the memory; rather, they can never forget it. They cite the examples of survivors of concentration camps or children who have witnessed the murder of a parent who never forget. Their explanation for recovered memories is that they are inaccurate. They point to studies that have demonstrated that memory is unreliable, and that it can be manipulated to "remember" events that never happened.

In the middle of this controversy are clinicians and memory researchers who believe that the workings of the mind have yet to be fully understood. They agree that, while it is possible for a trauma victim to forget and then remember a horrible experience, it is also possible for a person to have false memories.

Dissociative Amnesia for Childhood Abuse Memories

The earliest psychiatrists recognized that memory of child sexual abuse could be "split off" from consciousness. In the late 1900s Pierre Marie Felix Janet (1859–1947) connected the new diagnosis of hysteria with traumatic experiences that were separated from consciousness. Freud also studied lost traumatic memories in relation to female patients diagnosed with hysteria. In 1896 Freud theorized in *The Aetiology of Hysteria* that sexual abuse was the cause of hysteria. Under pressure from his psychiatric colleagues, he later recanted his theory, instead arguing that women were fantasizing rather than remembering sexual abuse. However, all of these early psychiatrists recognized that memory of traumatic experience in childhood could be lost to conscious awareness.

According to James A. Chu et al. of the Harvard Medical School, in "Memories of Childhood Abuse: Dissociation, Amnesia, and Corroboration" (*American Journal of Psychiatry*, vol. 156, no. 5, May 1999), even though research shows that memories can be inaccurate and influenced by outside factors such as overt suggestions, most studies show that memory tends to be accurate when it comes to remembering the core elements of important events. Chu et al. conducted a study of ninety

female patients aged eighteen to sixty undergoing treatment in a psychiatric hospital.

A large proportion of patients reported childhood abuse: 83% experienced physical abuse, 82% were victims of sexual abuse, and 71% witnessed domestic violence. Those who had a history of any kind of abuse reported experiencing partial or complete dissociative amnesia (a type of dissociative disorder). The occurrence of physical and sexual abuse at an early age accounted for a higher level of amnesia.

Chu et al. note that contrary to the popular belief that recovered memory of childhood abuse typically occurs under psychotherapy or hypnosis, most of the patients who suffered complete amnesia for their physical and sexual abuse indicated first recalling the abuse when they were at home and alone. Most patients did not recover memory of childhood abuse as a result of suggestions during therapy. Just one or two participants (for each of the three types of abuse) reported first memory of abuse while in a therapy session. Nearly half (48% for physical abuse and 45% for sexual abuse) were not undergoing psychological counseling or treatment when they first remembered the abuse.

Critics of recovered memory note the lack of corroboration (confirmation that the abuse really occurred) in many instances of recovered memories. In this study, Chu et al. find that, among patients who tried to corroborate their abuse, more than half found physical evidence such as medical records. Nearly nine out of ten of those who suffered sexual abuse found verbal validation of such abuse.

Some studies look at participants with documented history of child sexual abuse to see whether any individuals have lost conscious awareness of the abuse for any period of time. In one such study, Robin S. Edelstein et al. find in "Individual Differences in Emotional Memory: Adult Attachment and Long-Term Memory for Child Sexual Abuse" (*Personality and Social Psychology Bulletin*, vol. 31, no. 11, 2005) that whether and how well an individual "remembered" sexual abuse was mediated by the extent to which he or she was attached to others. In fact, the more severe the abuse, the less accurately individuals who were insecurely attached to others could recall its details. Therefore, children who had received emotional support from their mother in the aftermath of child sexual abuse were better able to remember the experience in their adult life. By contrast, children who were insecurely attached to their parents because their parents were the abusers would be more likely to lose conscious awareness of the abuse.

In "'True' and 'False' Child Sexual Abuse Memories and Casey's Phenomenological View of Remembering" (*American Behavioral Scientist*, vol. 48, no. 10, 2005),

Joanne M. Hall and Lori L. Kondora review the literature on dissociative memory and find ample evidence that it is common for sexually abused children to lose conscious awareness of the abuse. The researchers point out, as have other researchers, that studies of soldiers returning from combat and World War II (1939–1945) concentration camp survivors show that people can and do fragment traumatic memory, splitting it off from daily life. They connect the debate about the authenticity of delayed sexual abuse memories with a cultural denial that sexual abuse of children occurs, because "its existence fractures cultural values about family." Hall and Kondora argue that false memories of child sexual abuse are rare, but not impossible.

Betrayal Trauma Theory

Jennifer J. Freyd proposes in *Betrayal Trauma: The Logic of Forgetting Childhood Abuse* (1996) the betrayal trauma theory to explain how children who had experienced abuse may process that betrayal of trust by mentally blocking information about it. Freyd explains that people typically respond to betrayal by distancing themselves from the betrayer. However, children who have suffered abuse at the hands of a parent or a caregiver might not be able to distance themselves from the betrayer. Children need the caregiver for their survival so they "cannot afford *not* to trust" the betrayer. Consequently, the children develop a "blindness" to the betrayal.

Jennifer J. Freyd, Anne P. Deprince, and Eileen L. Zurbriggen report in "Self-Reported Memory for Abuse Depends upon Victim-Perpetrator Relationship" (*Journal of Trauma and Dissociation*, vol. 2, no. 3, 2001) on their preliminary findings relating to the betrayal trauma theory. They find that people who had been abused by a trusted caregiver reported greater amnesia, compared to those whose abusers were not their caregivers. Greater amnesia was also more likely to be associated with the fact that the perpetrator was a caregiver than with the repeated trauma of abuse.

A Longitudinal Study of Memory and CSA

In *Resolving Childhood Trauma: A Long-Term Study of Abuse Survivors* (2000), Catherine Cameron discusses a long-term study of child sexual abuse survivors she conducted between 1986 and 1998. Cameron interviewed seventy-two women, aged twenty-five to sixty-four, during a twelve-year period. The women consisted of a group of sexual abuse survivors who sought therapy for the first time in the 1980s. On average, it had been thirty years since their first abuse occurred (thirty-six years for those who suffered amnesia). The women were in private therapy, were better educated, and were more financially well off than most survivors. Twelve imprisoned women were included in the survey. They came from a low socioeconomic background, were serving long sentences,

and had participated only in brief group therapy sessions that lasted less than a year.

Cameron sought to study amnesia as both an effect and a cause—what was it about the abuse that resulted in amnesia and how did the amnesia affect the victim later in life? Twenty-five women were amnesic and had no awareness of the abuse until recently, twenty-one were nonamnesic and unable to forget their abuse, and fourteen were partially amnesic about their abuse. The imprisoned women were not assigned a specific category because they were part of a therapy group.

About eight out of ten of the amnesic and partially amnesic women believed they did not remember the sexual abuse because the memories were too painful to live with (82%) and they felt a sense of guilt or shame (79%). More than half of each group believed the amnesia served as a defense mechanism resulting from their desire to protect the family (58%) and love for, or dependence on, the perpetrator (53%). About three-quarters (74%) thought the amnesia occurred because they felt no one would believe them or help them. More than one-third (37%) thought the amnesia had come about because they needed to believe in a "safe" world.

During the years between the abuse and the recall of the abuse, the amnesics reported experiencing the same problems as the nonamnesics, including problems with relationships, revictimization, self-abuse, and dependency on alcohol. Because the amnesics, however, had no conscious knowledge of their childhood abuse, they could not find an explanation for their problems. Cameron theorizes that the conflict between the amnesia and memories that needed release left the amnesic victims depressed and confused.

Cameron addresses the allegations that some therapists implant false memories of sexual abuse in their clients. She notes that 72% of the amnesic women in her study had begun to recall their abuse before seeking therapy. Once the survivors in her study confronted their traumatic past, they took charge of how they wanted their therapy handled. Cameron also observes that, because it is evident that recovered memories of childhood abuse are common, they should not be labeled as "false memories" nor accepted as "flawless truth," but should instead be explored by proponents of the opposing views.

Research Supporting the Repression of Memory

As of August 2008, the best study on amnesia for childhood abuse was conducted by Linda Meyer Williams. The strength of this study lies in the fact that she interviewed adults whose sexual abuse in childhood had been documented at the time that it happened. In "Recall of Childhood Trauma: A Prospective Study of Women's Memories of Child Sexual Abuse" (*Journal of Consulting and Clinical Psychology*, vol. 62, no. 6, 1994), Williams reports on detailed interviews she conducted with 129 women who, seventeen years previously, had been taken to the emergency room after being sexually abused. Williams finds that more than one out of three women did not report the sexual abuse during the interview. She concludes that most or all of these women did not remember the documented abuse. She also finds that the younger the child was at the time of the abuse, and the closer the relationship the child had with the perpetrator, the greater the likelihood that the abuse would not be remembered.

FALSE MEMORIES

In *The Myth of Repressed Memory: False Memories and Allegations of Sexual Abuse* (1994), Elizabeth Loftus and Katherine Ketcham claim that repression is not normal memory and that it is empirically unproven. The researchers do not believe that the mind can block out experiences of recurrent traumas, with the person unaware of them, and then recover them years later. Their explanation for recovered memories is that they are false memories. Loftus and Ketcham and other critics of recovered memories believe therapy to "recover" repressed memories can lead people to believe they remember things that never actually happened.

Loftus and Ketcham show that false memories can be implanted fairly easily in the laboratory. Loftus recounts assigning a term project to students in her cognitive psychology class. The project involved implanting a false memory in someone's mind. One of the students chose his fourteen-year-old brother as his test subject. The student wrote about four events his brother had suppos-

edly experienced. Three of the experiences really happened, but the fourth one was a fake event of his brother getting lost at the mall at age five. For the next five days the younger brother was asked to read about his experiences (written by his older brother) and then write down details that he could remember about them. The younger brother "remembered" his shopping mall experience quite well, describing details elaborately.

In "Make-Believe Memories" (*American Psychologist*, vol. 58, no. 11, November 2003), Loftus notes that memories can be influenced by people's imagination. She states that "imagination can not only make people believe they have done simple things that they have not done but can also lead people to believe that they have experienced more complex events." She describes a study in which participants were told to imagine performing a common task with certain objects, such as flipping a coin. The second meeting consisted of imagining doing a task without using any object. In a subsequent meeting, participants were tested on their memory of the first day's task performance. Some participants "remembered" not only tasks they had not done but also unusual ones they had not performed.

The False Memory Syndrome Foundation was founded in 1992. It is a network of people who have been accused of CSA by their adult children. They claim the accusations of abuse, and their children's recovered memories, are false. The group coined the term *false memory syndrome* (not a recognized psychological disorder) and has worked to publicize the concept of false memories of childhood abuse.

CHAPTER 5
CHILD ABUSE AND THE LAW

BEGINNINGS OF INVOLVEMENT
IN THE LAW: DISCLOSURE

What should parents do when their child says he or she has been abused? It may come as an offhand remark, as if the child is testing to see what the parents' reaction will be. Perhaps the child is engaged in sexual behavior, which is a common symptom of sexual abuse. For example, the child may go through the motions of sexual intercourse and then say that this is what a parent, stepparent, relative, or teacher at school has done. A major preschool sexual abuse case against Margaret Kelly Michaels (1961–), a teacher at the Wee Care Day Nursery in Maplewood, New Jersey, began when a boy who was having his temperature taken rectally at the pediatrician's office remarked that his teacher had been doing the same thing to him while he napped at school. The remark ultimately led to Michaels being charged with various forms of sexual abuse, and a nine-month trial ensued, at which several children testified.

Sometimes a parent realizes that something is wrong when the child's behavior changes. Some young children have an especially hard time expressing themselves verbally and may instead begin having sleep difficulties, such as nightmares and night terrors; eating problems; a fear of going to school (if that is the site of the abuse); regression; acting out, such as biting, masturbating, or sexually attacking other family members; and withdrawing. These behavior changes, however, do not necessarily mean that the child is being sexually abused. Children may also express themselves in their drawings.

The abuse may have occurred for a long time before children speak about it. Why do children keep the abuse a secret? Children who reveal their abuse through nonverbal ways may be afraid to speak out because they believe the threats of death or punishment made by their abuser. They may feel responsible for what has happened to them or fear that adults will not believe them. They may not know how to describe what has happened to them.

By contrast, children may tell about abuse when they come into contact with someone who feels safe, or who appears to already know about the abuse. Or they may tell when they are physically injured or pregnant. Sometimes children tell when they believe that if the abuse continues it will be unbearable.

If parents believe their child, particularly if the abuser is not a family member, their first reaction may be to file charges against the alleged perpetrator. Parents rarely realize how difficult and painful the process can be. Some experts claim that children psychologically need to see their abuser punished, whereas others feel children are victimized by the court process, only this time by the people who are supposed to protect them.

Is a Child's Account Reliable?

Some experts believe children do not lie about abuse. They point out that children cannot describe events unfamiliar to them. For example, the average six-year-old has no concept of how forced penetration feels or how semen tastes. Experts also note that children lie to get themselves out of trouble, not into trouble, and reporting sexual abuse is definitely trouble. Children sometimes recant or deny that any abuse has happened, after they disclosed it. Perhaps the reaction to the disclosure is unfavorable, or the pain and fear of talking about the experience are too great. The child's recanting under interrogation in a court of law may prove damaging to the case and may encourage claims that the child has made false accusations.

Kenneth V. Lanning surmises in "Criminal Investigation of Sexual Victimization of Children" (John E. B. Myers et al., eds., *The APSAC Handbook on Child Maltreatment*, 2002) that children rarely lie about sexual abuse. Some children, however, may recount what they believe in their mind to be the truth, although their account may turn out to be inaccurate. Lanning gives the following explanations for these inaccuracies:

- The child may be experiencing distorted memory because of trauma.

- The child's story might be a reflection of normal childhood fears and fantasy.

- The child may have been confused by the abuser's use of trickery or drugs.

- The child's testimony may be influenced by the suggestive questions of investigators.

- The child's account might reflect urban legends and cultural mythology.

In "Child Sexual Abuse: Can Anatomy Explain the Presentation?" (*Clinical Pediatrics*, vol. 47, no. 1, 2008), Dena Nazer and Vincent J. Palusci point out that children's accounts of sexual abuse sometimes do contain bizarre or impossible events. This does not mean that the child was not sexually abused—instead, understanding sexual abuse may be beyond a child's ability at his or her developmental stage. For example, if a child is penetrated in the course of sexual abuse, the child may perceive the painful object to be a knife. In addition, faced with sexual abuse and the high level of emotional arousal in the face of traumatic sexual abuse, children may have distorted memories of exactly what occurred.

JUVENILE COURT SYSTEM: INNOVATIONS TO HELP CHILD WITNESSES

In 2008 all fifty states had authorized juvenile family courts to intervene in child abuse cases, and all fifty states considered child abuse of any kind to be a felony and a civil crime. A felony (a serious crime) can result in a prison term; a loss in a civil suit (a noncriminal case involving private parties) can result in the payment of a fine or in losing custody of the child. Even though many states have distinct and separate juvenile courts, some states try juvenile or family cases in courts of general jurisdiction, where child protection cases are given priority over other cases on the court's docket.

Government child protective services (CPS) initiates civil court proceedings (after consultation with CPS lawyers) if it seeks to remove the child from the home, provide in-home protective services, or require the abuser to get treatment. Criminal proceedings are initiated by a government prosecutor if the abuser is to be charged with a crime, such as sexual abuse.

In civil child protection cases the accused has the right to a closed trial (a hearing with no jury and closed to the public) in which court records are kept confidential, although a few states permit jury trials. In criminal child protection cases, however, the person charged with abuse is entitled to the Sixth Amendment right to an open trial (a jury trial opened to the public), which can be waived only by the defendant.

In 1967 *In re Gault* (387 U.S. 1) substantially changed the nature of juvenile courts. Initially, children were not subject to constitutional due process rights or legal representation, and judges presiding over these courts were given unlimited power to protect children from criminal harm. The U.S. Supreme Court decided in *In re Gault* that children—whether they have committed a crime or are the victims of a crime—are entitled to due process and legal representation. However, these rights are interpreted differently among the states.

Court-Appointed Special Advocates

The federal Victims of Child Abuse Act of 1990 requires that a court-appointed special advocate (CASA) volunteer be provided to every child maltreatment victim who needs such an advocate. A CASA volunteer serves as the guardian ad litem (guardian at law) of the child during legal proceedings. The CASA volunteer's duty is to ensure that the legal system serves the best interests of the child.

According to the National CASA Association, in "History of the CASA Movement" (http://www.national casa.org/about_us/history.html), as of 2006 there were 948 CASA programs, with more than 50,000 volunteers, in all fifty states. Typically, the judge appoints a CASA volunteer, who then reviews all records pertaining to the maltreated child, including CPS reports and medical and school records. The volunteer also meets with the child, parents and family members, social workers, health care providers, school officials, and other people who may know of the child's history. The research compiled by the CASA volunteer helps the child's lawyer in presenting the case. It also helps the court in deciding what is best for the child. Each trained volunteer works with one or two children at a time, enabling the volunteer to research and monitor each case thoroughly.

Anatomically Detailed Dolls

Many legal professionals use dolls with sexual organs made to represent the human anatomy to help sexually abused children explain what has happened to them in court. Advocates of the use of dolls report that they make it easier to get a child to talk about things that can be difficult to discuss. Lori S. Holmes of CornerHouse in Minneapolis, Minnesota, notes in "Using Anatomical Dolls in Child Sexual Abuse Forensic Interviews" (*American Prosecutors Research Institute Update*, vol. 13, no. 8, 2000) that the use of anatomical dolls helps the child demonstrate internal consistency. A child who has made allegations of abuse can show the interviewer exactly what happened to him or her, thus confirming the oral disclosure. In "Anatomical Dolls: Their Use in Assessment of Children Who May Have Been Sexually Abused" (*Journal of Child Sexual Abuse*, vol. 14, no. 3, 2005), Kathleen Coulborn Faller of the University of Michigan also finds that the selective use of the dolls to help children who have trouble speaking about sexual abuse is warranted.

However, potential problems exist in using dolls. According to the affordance phenomenon, children will experiment with any opportunities provided by a new experience. Some experts believe that what might appear to be sexual behavior, such as putting a finger in a hole in the doll, may have no more significance than a child putting a finger through the hole in a doughnut. In addition, some researchers, such as Karen L. Thierry et al., in "Developmental Differences in the Function and Use of Anatomical Dolls during Interviews with Alleged Sexual Abuse Victims" (*Journal of Consulting and Clinical Psychology*, vol. 73, no. 6, December 2005), compare children's verbal details of sexual abuse with their enactments with anatomical dolls and find that children under age six using the dolls often contradict the verbal details provided without the dolls. They also find that children from three to twelve years old produce more fantastic details with the dolls than without them.

Videotaped Testimony and Closed-Circuit Television Testimony: Does It Violate the Confrontation Clause?

It is difficult for children to deal with the fear and intimidation of testifying in open court. The person who has allegedly abused and threatened them may be sitting before them, and the serious nature of the court can be intimidating to them. Videotaped testimony and closed-circuit television testimony have become common methods used to relieve the pressure on the child who must testify. According to the National Center for Prosecution of Child Abuse, in *Legislation Regarding the Use of Closed-Circuit Television Testimony in Criminal Child Abuse Proceedings* (September 12, 2002, http://www.ndaa.org/pdf/closed_cir cuit_tv_testimony.pdf), the federal government and thirty-seven states allow the use of closed-circuit television testimony instead of in-court testimony for children under age eighteen. States vary in their requirements regarding the use of closed-circuit television testimony. In some states the jury stays in the courtroom while the child, the judge, the prosecutor, the defendant, and the defense attorney are in a different room. In some states the child is alone in a room separate from the jury and other participants.

Furthermore, the National Center for Prosecution of Child Abuse notes in "Legislation Regarding the Admissibility of Videotaped Interviews/Statements in Criminal Child Abuse Proceedings" (July 2006, http://www.ndaa .org/pdf/ncpca_statute_videotaped_interviews_july_06.pdf) that the federal government and seventeen states recognize the right to use videotaped testimony taken at a preliminary hearing or deposition (testimony given under oath to be used in court at a later date) for children under age eighteen. A videotape of the pretrial interviews shows the jury how the child behaved and whether the inter-

viewer prompted the child. Often prepared soon after the abuse, videotaped interviews preserve the child's memory and emotions when they are still fresh. Because a videotaped interview presents an out-of-court statement, which the alleged abuser cannot refute face to face, it can be admitted only as a hearsay exception. (Hearsay is considered secondhand information; hearsay evidence and exceptions are further discussed later in the chapter.) Some state laws also say that, even with the videotaped testimony, the child may still be called to testify and be cross-examined.

Videotaping can cut down on the number of interviews the child must undergo, and prosecutors indicate that this method encourages guilty pleas. Videotapes can be powerful tools to deal with the problem of the child who recants his or her testimony when put on the witness stand. The case can still be prosecuted, with the jury witnessing the child's opposing statements. Experts believe that a videotape statement containing sufficient details from the child and elicited through nonleading questions makes for compelling evidence. Opponents, however, claim that this method unfairly influences the jury to think that the accused is guilty simply because the procedure is permitted, and, worse, it deprives the defendant of his or her constitutional right to confront the accuser face to face.

In June 1990 the U.S. Supreme Court upheld in *Maryland v. Craig* (497 U.S. 836) the use of closed-circuit television in a case where a six-year-old child had to testify in a case against her prekindergarten teacher, Sandra Craig, who had been charged with sexual assault and battery. Justice Sandra Day O'Connor (1930–) noted in the majority opinion that the Sixth Amendment Confrontation Clause does not guarantee an "absolute" right to a face-to-face meeting with the witness. The closed-circuit television does permit cross-examination and observation of the witness's demeanor. Justice O'Connor declared, "We are therefore confident that use of the one-way closed-circuit television procedure, where necessary to further an important state interest, does not impinge upon the truth-seeking or symbolic purposes of the Confrontation Clause."

Hearsay Evidence

With the Sixth Amendment Confrontation Clause, the hearsay rule is intended to prevent the conviction of defendants by reports of evidence offered by someone other than the witness. With a few exceptions, hearsay is inadmissible as testimony because the actual witness cannot be cross-examined and his or her demeanor cannot be assessed for credibility of testimony. Whether or not to accept the hearsay evidence from a child's reports of abuse to a parent has been frequently debated.

Some courts consider spontaneous declarations or excited utterances made by a person right after a stressful experience as reliable hearsay. Courts also allow statements individuals have made to physicians and other medical personnel for purposes of medical treatment or diagnosis. In this case it is generally assumed that people who consult with a physician are seeking treatment and, therefore, tell the physician the truth about their illness.

Hearsay evidence is especially important in cases of child sexual abuse. Cases often take years to come to trial, by which time a child may have forgotten the details of the abuse or may have made psychological progress in dealing with the trauma. The parents may be reluctant to plunge the child back into the anxious situation suffered earlier. Hearsay evidence can be crucial in determining the validity of sexual abuse charges in custody cases. In these cases juries need to know when the child first alleged abuse, to whom, under what circumstances, and whether the child ever recanted.

In *Ohio v. Roberts* (448 U.S. 56 [1980]), a case that was not about child abuse, the Supreme Court established the basis for permitting hearsay evidence: the actual witness has to be unavailable and his or her statement has to be reliable enough to permit another person to repeat it to the jury. Many judges have chosen to interpret unavailability on physical standards rather than on the emotional unavailability that children who are afraid to testify may exhibit. Furthermore, legal experts insist that the reliability of a statement does not refer to whether the statement appears to be truthful, but only that it has sufficient reliability for the jury to decide whether it is true.

After *Ohio v. Roberts*, many courts decided that spontaneous statements of child abuse victims, especially victims of sexual assault, fulfilled the hearsay requirements. In *White v. Illinois* (502 U.S. 346 [1992]), the Supreme Court found that a four-year-old girl's statements to her babysitter, her mother, a police officer, an emergency room nurse, and a doctor fulfilled the hearsay requirements because they were all either spontaneous declarations or made for medical treatment. In *Bugh v. Mitchell* (329 F.3d 496 [2003]), the Sixth Circuit U.S. Court of Appeals ruled that a child's statements to her mother, a counselor, a county social services supervisor, and a doctor about sexual abuse by her father were admissible as hearsay evidence because a three-year-old would have limited ability to lie about the circumstances of an attack. However, in *Carpenter v. State* (786 N.E.2d 696 [2003]) the Indiana Supreme Court decided that out-of-court statements made by a three-year-old who had been sexually assaulted by her father to her mother and grandfather were inadmissible because the state could not establish the precise time of alleged molestation or whether the child's statements occurred immediately after the alleged molestation.

CRAWFORD V. WASHINGTON OVERRULES OHIO V. ROBERTS. In *Crawford v. Washington* (541 U.S. 36 [2004]), the U.S. Supreme Court overturned its ruling in *Ohio v.*

Roberts, which held that the Sixth Amendment right of confrontation does not prohibit hearsay evidence if a judge deems that evidence reliable and trustworthy. In 1999 Michael Crawford stabbed a man who allegedly attempted to rape his wife. During the trial the state introduced an out-of-court, tape-recorded statement to police by his wife, who was present during the assault. The state wanted to show that Crawford did not stab the man in self-defense as he had told police. His wife did not testify during the trial because of Washington's spousal privilege, which prohibits one spouse from testifying against the other without the other's consent. The trial court found the wife's statement to be reliable and trustworthy and accepted it as evidence. Crawford was convicted of assault with a deadly weapon.

On Crawford's appeal, the Washington Court of Appeals reversed the trial court ruling. The Washington Supreme Court subsequently reinstated the conviction. The U.S. Supreme Court agreed to hear the case to determine whether the state's use of the wife's statement violated the Confrontation Clause. In reversing the judgment of the Washington Supreme Court, the Supreme Court held that when a hearsay statement is "testimonial," the Confrontation Clause bars the state from using that statement against a criminal defendant unless the person who made the statement is available to testify at trial, or the defendant had a previous opportunity to cross-examine that person.

Even though the Court stated, "We leave for another day any effort to spell out a comprehensive definition of 'testimonial,'" it gave as an example of a testimonial statement that which is made during police interrogations (e.g., the pretrial statement of Crawford's wife). The Court added that its *Crawford* ruling holds regardless of whether or not the statement is a hearsay exception or is judged reliable, thus overruling *Ohio v. Roberts*. The case was sent back to the Washington Supreme Court for further proceedings. *Crawford* was not a child abuse case, but it has major implications in child abuse cases.

CRAWFORD V. WASHINGTON IS INTERPRETED BY A CALIFORNIA COURT. In a California case the defendant Seum Sisavath was convicted of, among other things, several child sexual abuse charges involving two sisters, aged four and eight. The younger child was not at trial because she was found incompetent to testify. Based on the hearsay testimonies of an officer who responded to the mother's call to police and of an investigator from the district attorney's office who attended a videotaped interview of the younger child, the court admitted the statements. Sisavath was found guilty of most of the sexual charges and sentenced to thirty-two years to life. The defendant petitioned the California Court of Appeals.

While the appeal was pending, the U.S. Supreme Court decided *Crawford v. Washington*. Consequently, the appeals court ruled in *People v. Sisavath* (No. 671573-4) that the testimonial hearsay statements against the defendant were inadmissible under *Crawford* because they violated the Confrontation Clause of the Sixth Amendment. Because the U.S. Supreme Court did not define *testimonial*, the appeals court observed, "It is more likely that the Supreme Court meant simply that if the statement was given under circumstances in which its use in a prosecution is reasonably foreseeable by an objective observer, then the statement is testimonial.... We have no occasion here to hold, and do not hold, that statements made in every MDIC [Multidisciplinary Interview Center] interview are testimonial under *Crawford*. We hold only that Victim 2's [younger victim's] statements in the MDIC interview in this case were testimonial. [The MDIC is a facility specially designed and staffed for interviewing children suspected of being victims of abuse.]"

EFFECT ON CHILD ABUSE CASES. Because child abuse cases typically rely on evidence such as videotaped testimony and statements to physicians, parents, counselors, and other adults in the aftermath of an assault, the effects of *Crawford* may be substantial. In fact, Michael H. Graham of the University of Miami argues in "Special Report: *Crawford v. Washington*" (*Criminal Law Bulletin*, vol. 41, no. 6, November–December 2006) that *Crawford* will have its biggest effect on child physical and sexual abuse cases.

Even though children cannot be expected to understand that their statements to physicians and counselors will be used at trial, Myrna Raeder of Southwestern University explains in "Remember the Ladies and the Children Too: *Crawford*'s Impact on Domestic Violence and Child Abuse Cases" (*Brooklyn Law Review*, vol. 71, fall 2005) that courts, in the aftermath of *Crawford*, have interpreted statements as testimonial using an "objective standard." In other words, if an adult could reasonably be expected to understand that statements made would be used at trial, the statements have been ruled as inadmissible unless the child is present. Raeder argues that statements made to physicians, counselors, and even parents are all being interpreted by courts as testimonial, and therefore not acceptable as evidence under *Crawford*. Videotaped interviews by forensic teams have also generally been found to be testimonial, and therefore may fall into disuse as a result of *Crawford*. Raeder concludes that "post-Crawford, if a child does not testify, the chances of winning at trial plummet."

In fact, many child sexual abuse convictions were overturned after the *Crawford* decision. According to Erin Thompson, in "Child Sex Abuse Victims: How Will Their Stories Be Heard after *Crawford v. Washington*?" (*Campbell Law Review*, vol. 27, spring 2005), convictions in *People v. Espinoza* (No. B200912 [Cal. App. 2008]), *People v. Vigil* (104 P.3d 258, 263–65 [Colo. App. 2004]), *In the Interest of R.A.S.* (No. 03CA1209 [Colo. App. 2004]), and *Snowden v. State* (156 Md. App. 139; 846 A.2d 36 [2004]) were all overturned because the perpetrators had been convicted based on videotaped testimony, with no opportunity for cross-examination of the child witnesses. The reversal of these convictions reflects the difficulty faced by prosecutors in child abuse cases in the aftermath of *Crawford*.

DIFFICULTIES IN PROSECUTING CHILD ABUSERS

For the prosecutor's office, child abuse can present many problems. The foremost is that the victim is a child. This becomes an even greater problem when the victim is young (from birth to age six), because the question of competency arises. More and more studies have examined children's reliability in recalling and retelling past events. Researchers find that different settings and interview techniques may result in children remembering different details at different times.

The prosecutor may also worry about the possible harm the child may suffer in having to relive the abuse and in being interrogated by adversarial defense attorneys. For instance, if the child is an adolescent making accusations of sexual abuse, the defendant's attorney may accuse the teenage victim of seducing the defendant or having willingly taken part in the acts.

Other factors that prosecutors must consider include the slowness of the court process and the possibility that the case may be delayed, not just once, but several times. This is hard enough for adults to tolerate, but it is particularly difficult for children. The delay prolongs the child's pain. Children may become more reluctant to testify or may no longer be able to retell their stories accurately. There is a far greater difference between a thirty-one-year-old testifying about something that happened when he or she was twenty-six and an eleven-year-old retelling an event that happened at six years of age. Prosecutors are also obliged to keep the child's best interests in mind and to try and preserve the family.

In "Child Maltreatment and the Justice System: Predictors of Court Involvement" (*Research on Social Work Practice*, vol. 15, no. 5, 2005), Andrea J. Sedlak et al. find that several factors made it more likely that child maltreatment cases reported to child protective services, the sheriff's office, the prosecutor's office, or dependency court were prosecuted. The researchers note that cases involving a male perpetrator and a female victim or victims were the most likely to be prosecuted, with sexual abuse being the type of maltreatment with the highest likelihood of prosecution. Abuse cases with multiple victims, especially when a parent abused his or her own child as well as another child, were the most likely to be prosecuted. Cases with a disabled victim were less likely than other cases to be prosecuted.

Prosecuting Child Sexual Abuse

According to Nazer and Palusci, prosecuting a child sexual abuse case is particularly challenging. A child who has been physically abused will often display unmistakable signs of the abuse, such as broken bones. Sexual abuse does not necessarily leave such visible marks. So the abuse is less likely to have been noticed by others and is more difficult to verify once an accusation has been made.

Many other difficulties exist. For example, physical abusers will sometimes admit to having "disciplined" their children by striking them or have actually been seen committing abusive acts in public. Sexual abusers almost never admit to their actions when confronted, and their abuse always takes place in secret. Another major difficulty is that young children who have little or no knowledge of sex may have trouble understanding, let alone explaining in a court room, what was done to them.

In "How Long to Prosecute Child Sexual Abuse for a Community Using a Children's Advocacy Center and Two Comparison Communities?" (*Child Maltreatment*, vol. 13, no. 1, 2008), Wendy A. Walsh et al. examined the effect of the particular difficulties encountered in child sexual abuse cases on the length of time it took to resolve them. The researchers find that less than half (44%) of child sexual abuse cases in the legal system were resolved within one year, and nearly a third (30%) remained unresolved at the two-year mark. Only one out of five were resolved within six months, the American Bar Association standard for felony cases. Walsh et al. speculate that child sexual abuse cases may take longer because of the presence of many factors that make prosecution difficult, including a lack of familial commitment to prosecution, the potentially severe criminal and social sanctions for defendants, and the tendency for evidence to be sparse. The researchers also note that the long process can be extremely stressful for children and possibly stand in the way of their process of recovery.

According to Wendy A. Walsh et al., in "Prosecuting Child Sexual Abuse: The Importance of Evidence Type" (*Crime and Delinquency*, 2008), the cases the most likely to have charges filed had at least some of these types of evidence: a child disclosure, a corroborating witness, an offender confession, or an additional report against the alleged perpetrator. Cases lacking physical evidence were twice as likely to be filed if there was a corroborating witness. Regardless of whether a child disclosed the abuse or not, a case was much more likely to be filed if there were at least two types of evidence present. This study underlines the difficulties in prosecuting child sexual abuse cases.

Are Children Competent Witnesses?

Traditionally, judges protected juries from incompetent witnesses, which in the early years of the United States were considered to include women, slaves, and children. Children in particular were believed to live in a fantasy world, and their inability to understand terms such as *oath*, *testify*, and *solemnly swear* denied them the right to appear in court. In 1895 the U.S. Supreme Court established in *Wheeler v. United States* (159 U.S. 523) the rights of child witnesses. The Court explained:

> There is no precise age which determines the question of competency. This depends on the capacity and intelligence of the child, his appreciation of the difference between truth and falsehood, as well as of his duty to tell the former. The decision of this question rests primarily with the trial judge, who sees the proposed witness, notices his manner, his apparent possession or lack of intelligence, and may resort to any examination which will tend to disclose his capacity and intelligence, as well as his understanding of the obligations of an oath. . . . To exclude [a child] from the witness stand . . . would sometimes result in staying the hand of justice.

As a result of this ruling, the courts formalized the *Wheeler* decision, requiring judges to interview all children to determine their competency. It was not until 1974 that the revised Federal Rules of Evidence abolished the competency rule so that children may testify at trial in federal courts regardless of competence.

In state courts judges sometimes still apply the competency rule regardless of state laws that may have banned it. In the 1987 Margaret Kelly Michaels case, the judge chatted with each child witness before he or she testified, holding a red crayon and asking questions such as, "If I said this was a green crayon, would I be telling the truth?"

CHILDREN CAN BE UNRELIABLE WITNESSES IF SUBJECTED TO SUGGESTED EVENTS. In "Children's Eyewitness Reports after Exposure to Misinformation from Parents" (*Journal of Experimental Psychology: Applied*, vol. 7, no. 1, March 2001), Debra Ann Poole and D. Stephen Lindsay examine children's eyewitness reports after the children were given misinformation by their parents and show that children may not be able to distinguish fact from fiction when subjected to suggested events before formal interviews.

A total of 114 children aged three to eight participated, on a one-to-one basis, in four science activities with a man called "Mr. Science." Three interviews were conducted afterward. The first interview occurred right after the science activities in which an interviewer asked each child nonsuggestive questions about the activities. About three and a half months later the children's parents read them a story, in three instances, about their science experience. The story included two science activities they had experienced and two others that they had not experienced. The story also included an event in which the child experienced unpleasant touching by Mr. Science. In reality this event did not happen. The children were then interviewed. The final step in the interview consisted of a source-monitoring procedure, in which the children were reminded of their actual experiences, as well as the story, to help them distinguish fact from fiction. A final interview was conducted after another month. This time the children were not given any misinformation.

The interview conducted soon after the science activities showed that the children recalled their experiences, with the amount of events reported increasing with the age of the child. When prompted for more information, the amount of new information reported also increased with age. The reports resulting from the promptings remained accurate.

In the interview that occurred soon after the children were read the storybook with misleading suggestions, 35% (forty children) reported fifty-eight suggested events in free recall (without prompting from the interviewer), including seventeen events relating to the unpleasant touching by Mr. Science. In the last interview a month later, with no additional misinformation given the children, 21% (twenty-four children) reported twenty-seven suggested events, including nine suggested events that involved unpleasant touching. Even when the children were prompted to provide more information about their experiences, they continued to report false events. Poole and Lindsay conclude that, because children's credibility as eyewitnesses depends on their ability to distinguish their memories from other sources, interviewers will have to develop better procedures to help them do so.

STATUTE OF LIMITATIONS AND RECOVERED MEMORY
Suing Alleged Abusers

According to Anita Lipton, in "Recovered Memories in the Courts" (Sheila Taub, ed., *Recovered Memories of Child Sexual Abuse: Psychological, Social, and Legal Perspectives on a Contemporary Mental Health Controversy*, 1999), between 1983 and 1998 many individuals who had recovered memories of childhood sexual abuse sued their alleged abusers. During those years a total of 589 lawsuits based on repressed memory were filed, of which 506 were civil and 83 were criminal. Following a sharp rise in 1992, the year the False Memory Syndrome Foundation was created, the number of lawsuits dropped rapidly after 1994.

EXCEPTION TO STATUTE OF LIMITATIONS IN CASES OF REPRESSED MEMORY. A statute of limitations is a law that sets the time within which criminal charges or civil claims can be filed and after which one loses the right to sue or make a claim. Most states provide for extensions of the statute of limitations, either through state law or judicial tolling doctrines. A tolling doctrine is a rule that suspends the date from which a statutory period starts to run. An example is the minority tolling doctrine, which provides that a statutory period does not begin to run until the child becomes an adult. For instance, in 2003, in response to revelations of clergy abuse, Illinois extended the statute of limitations in cases of childhood sexual abuse, allowing prosecutors twenty years from the time the victim turns eighteen to bring criminal charges. Victims wishing to bring a civil suit have up to ten years from the time they discover abuse and its connection to their injuries. In June 2008 the New York State Assembly passed legislation that would extend the statute of limitations in child abuse cases from age twenty-three until age twenty-eight. The speaker of the house called on the senate to also pass the measure.

One of the legal issues contested in cases of childhood sexual abuse of repressed memory is how long the statute of limitations should run. In 1991 Paula Hearndon sued her stepfather, Kenneth Graham, for sexually abusing her from 1968 to 1975 (when she was between the ages of eight and fifteen). According to Hearndon, the traumatic amnesia she experienced because of the abuse lasted until 1988. Because of Florida's four-year statute of limitations, the lawsuit did not proceed.

However, in *Hearndon v. Graham* (767 So. 2d 1179, 1184 [2000]) the Florida Supreme Court ruled 5–2 that memory loss resulting from the trauma of childhood sexual abuse should be considered an exception to the statute of limitations. The court, while observing that disagreements about recovered memory exist, stated, "It is widely recognized that the shock and confusion resultant from childhood molestation, often coupled with authoritative adult demands and threats for secrecy, may lead a child to deny or suppress such abuse from his or her consciousness."

U.S. SUPREME COURT RULES ON CALIFORNIA'S RETROACTIVE CHANGE IN STATUTE OF LIMITATIONS. In 2003 the U.S. Supreme Court heard arguments in a case that involved California's statute of limitations. In 1998 Marion Stogner was charged with the alleged sexual molestation of his two daughters between 1955 and 1973. Even though the statute of limitations had expired, prosecutors brought criminal charges under a 1994 state law that had removed the statute of limitations for the time the crime was committed. In the trial court Stogner claimed that the Ex Post Facto Clause of the U.S. Constitution forbids revival of prosecution that was previously time-barred. The trial court agreed, but the California Court of Appeals, in *People v. Stogner v. California* (No. A084772 [1999]), reversed the ruling, saying that the 1994 law was not unconstitutional as an Ex Post Facto law. (Article 1 of the U.S. Constitution forbids the passing of an Ex Post Facto law—that is, a law that applies retroactively.)

On the defendant's second appeal, the California Court of Appeals, in *Stogner v. Superior Court* (114 Cal. Rptr. 2d 37, 41 [2001]), held that the 1994 law allows the prosecution of Stogner's alleged crimes committed between 1955 and 1973. In June 2003 the U.S.

Supreme Court ruled on *Stogner v. California* (539 U.S. 607). By a 5–4 vote the Court reversed the appeals court decision, concluding that "a law enacted after expiration of a previously applicable limitations period violates the *Ex Post Facto* Clause when it is applied to revive a previously time-barred prosecution."

LEGAL PROTECTIONS FOR CHILDREN
Child Pornography

Even though the First Amendment protects pornography, it does not protect child pornography. Since 1982 child pornography has been banned by the U.S. Supreme Court ruling *New York v. Ferber* (458 U.S. 747), which held that pornography depicting children engaged in sexually explicit acts can be banned, whether or not it is obscene, because of the state's interest in protecting children from sexual exploitation. In other words, such images are not protected by the First Amendment.

The Child Pornography Prevention Act of 1996 (CPPA) attempted to legally define child pornography. The CPPA, in part, banned any visual depiction that "is, or appears to be, of a minor engaging in sexually explicit conduct." The "appears to be" portion of the law was intended to combat virtual child pornography, which includes computer-generated images and images using youthful-looking adults. The CPPA also prohibited the advertisement or promotion of any sexually explicit image that "conveys the impression" that children are performing sexual acts.

In 2002 the U.S. Supreme Court ruled that the CPPA was unconstitutional, because it prohibits free speech that is not child pornography based on *Ferber*. In *Ashcroft v. Free Speech Coalition et al.* (535 U.S. 234), the Court ruled 6–3 that banning virtual child pornography is unconstitutional because, unlike *Ferber*, actual children are not used in its production. Moreover, the Court claimed that the government cannot prohibit material fit for adults just because children might get hold of it. The Court also struck down the government's argument that child pornography whets the appetites of pedophiles and encourages them to commit unlawful acts. As to that part of the law that bans material that "conveys the impression" it contains children performing sexual acts, the justices noted that anyone found in possession of such "mislabeled" material could be prosecuted.

In 2003 Congress passed the Child Obscenity and Pornography Prevention Act, which was designed to meet the constitutional challenges raised by CPPA. This act banned computer-generated sex images of children.

Ending the "Incest Exception"

According to the organization PROTECT, in "Betrayal of Trust: Child Sexual Abuse Loopholes in American Law" (July 2006, http://www.protect.org/miscStories/item002.shtml), as of 2006 thirty-four states had a "incest exception" in their criminal codes and sentencing guidelines. Put simply, these loopholes allow a person who commits incest (sexual abuse of a biological family member, sometimes one's own child) to receive a lighter sentence, if any at all, compared to a person who sexually abuses an unrelated child. In some states a family member who commits incest with a child is charged with a misdemeanor. In other states the molester can get off with probation and therapy. Often, the offender is not required to stay away from the child he or she abused. Andrew Vachss first brought up the incest exception issue in "Our Endangered Species: A Hard Look At How We Treat Children" (*Parade*, March 29, 1998). Vachss is an advisory board member of the National Association to Protect Children, which is an organization working to change incest laws in different states.

In 1999 a bill was introduced in Congress that would have banned states from treating rape committed by a biological relative as a lesser crime than the rape of a stranger. That legislation was not enacted, and, as of 2008, no such federal law had been passed. In the meantime, the National Association to Protect Children decided to fight the incest exception one state at a time. In 2002 the association was instrumental in changing North Carolina's archaic incest law of 1879. Before the new legislation, a father who raped his child was found guilty of a minor felony, which was punishable by probation, and an uncle who raped his niece was required to perform forty-five days of community service for the misdemeanor offense of incest. In April and May 2003 Arkansas and Illinois, respectively, reformed their incest laws to impose stricter penalties for offenders. Under Arkansas's old incest laws an adult who raped a child in his or her own family was considered guilty of incest and was either fined or put under probation. In Illinois the laws had been deliberately revised in 1981 with a view to keeping families together, imposing a punishment of probation or two years of counseling rather than jail time for incestuous offenders. In January 2006 California repealed its incest exception law, enacted in 1981, which had allowed judges to grant probation only to men and women convicted of abusing family members.

Protecting Fetuses and Infants

In November 1997 the South Carolina Supreme Court held in *Whitner v. South Carolina* (328 S.C. 1, 492 S.E.2d 777) that pregnant women who use drugs can be criminally prosecuted for child maltreatment. The court found that a viable fetus (potentially capable of surviving outside the womb) is a person covered by the state's child abuse and neglect laws. Cornelia Whitner's newborn tested positive for cocaine. She was prosecuted, plead guilty to child neglect, and was sentenced to eight years in prison in 1992. The ruling was appealed to the

South Carolina Supreme Court by Whitner. The South Carolina Supreme Court upheld the conviction, the first time the highest court of any state upheld the criminal conviction of a woman charged with such an offense.

In March 1998 Malissa Ann Crawley, who was charged with the same criminal offense, began serving a five-year prison sentence in South Carolina. In June 1998 the U.S. Supreme Court refused to hear appeals by Whitner and Crawley.

Whitner's lawyer had argued that if a woman could be prosecuted for child abuse for having used drugs while pregnant, what was to keep the law from prosecuting her for smoking or drinking alcohol or even for failing to obtain prenatal care? Other critics of the law argued that women who are substance abusers, fearing prosecution, might not seek prenatal care and counseling for their drug problems, which would further endanger the child.

In another South Carolina case Regina McKnight, a crack cocaine addict, was arrested in 1999 after giving birth to a stillborn. In 2001 she was convicted of homicide by child abuse and was sentenced to twelve years in prison. The jury found her guilty of killing a viable fetus, which is considered a child under South Carolina law. In January 2003 the South Carolina Supreme Court ruled in *State v. Regina D. McKnight* (No. 25585) against McKnight. The court pointed out that the state legislature amended the homicide by child abuse statute in 2000, about three years after the court held in *Whitner v. South Carolina* that the term *child* includes a viable fetus. The court added, "The fact that the legislature was well aware of this Court's opinion in *Whitner*, yet failed to omit 'viable fetus' from the statute's applicability, is persuasive evidence that the legislature did not intend to exempt fetuses from the statute's operation." In October 2003 the U.S. Supreme Court refused to hear McKnight's case.

The Child Abuse Prevention and Treatment Act requires that all states have ways to address the needs of drug-addicted infants or infants suffering from symptoms resulting from prenatal drug exposure. Tiffany Scott indicates in "Repercussions of the 'Crack Baby' Epidemic: Why a Message of Care Rather Than Punishment Is Needed for Pregnant Drug-Users" (*National Black Law Journal*, vol. 19, no. 2, 2006–07) that as of 2006 twenty states had a child welfare law on the books that regulated maternal drug use. The District of Columbia and twenty-three states had laws requiring the mandatory reporting of drug-exposed infants. After receiving a report of a drug-exposed infant, CPS typically visits the mother, sometimes removing the infant from her custody on a temporary or permanent basis. South Dakota mandates the reporting of substance-ingesting pregnant women for child abuse to law enforcement instead of to social services. Failure to report such cases of child abuse is a crime punishable by up to six months in prison.

In "Punishment of Pregnant Women" (2007, http://advocatesforpregnantwomen.org/issues/punishment_of_pregnant_women/), the National Advocates for Pregnant Women reports that since the Supreme Court's refusal to consider McKnight's case, South Carolina has led the way in the prosecution of pregnant women for behaviors that harmed their unborn children. In 2006 alone, Jennifer Lee Arrowood was arrested for "homicide by child abuse" after giving birth to a stillborn son was attributed to her drug use; Carolyn Michelle Wright was charged with "unlawful neglect" after testing positive for cocaine when she was in the hospital giving birth; Betty L. Staley was charged with "unlawful neglect" after her newborn tested positive for cocaine; and Hannah Lauren Jolly was charged with "unlawful neglect" after her newborn tested positive for marijuana and cocaine.

In 2004 President George W. Bush (1946–) signed the Unborn Victims of Violence Act into law, making it a crime to harm a fetus in the commission of federal crimes. In 2005 six states passed laws making it a crime to kill a viable fetus. In "New Wave of 'Fetal Protectionism' Decried" (*Lexington Herald-Leader* [Kentucky], July 10, 2006), Rick Montgomery states that in 2006 Arkansas lawmakers were debating making smoking a crime for pregnant women.

Critics of fetal-rights legislation argue that these laws disregard the rights of women. According to Scott, some critics argue that maternal drug laws disproportionately target African-American women. They believe such legislation may lead to greater restrictions on the activities and decisions of pregnant women—for example, could it become a crime to fail to take prenatal vitamins, to play sports, or to make informed medical decisions contrary to a doctor's advice? Quoted by Montgomery, Lynn M. Paltrow, the executive director of the National Advocates for Pregnant Women, said, "What we're seeing is a political trend in which the fetuses are coming first, and the rights of women ... are coming last."

In 2007 the New Mexico Supreme Court agreed to hear the case of *New Mexico v. Martinez*. The state was appealing a lower court's ruling that Martinez could not be prosecuted for drug use during pregnancy. Physicians, scientists, child welfare organizations, the American Civil Liberties Union (ACLU), and other medical and scientific organizations filed briefs with the court opposing making drug addiction during pregnancy a crime. In May 2007 the court decided it should not have taken the appeal from the state to begin with, leaving the lower appellate court's finding that the state's child abuse laws do not apply to pregnant women. The ACLU notes in "New Mexico v. Martinez" (March 9, 2007, http://www.aclu.org/womensrights/crimjustice/29772res20070309.html) that New Mexico and the appellate courts of twenty other states had found that child abuse laws do not allow states to prosecute pregnant women for behavior the state believes might harm their fetuses.

DRUG TESTING OF PREGNANT WOMEN. In 1989 a public hospital in Charleston, South Carolina, offered to work with city officials and police to test pregnant women suspected of drug use. The women were not told they were being screened for drugs or that they would be turned over to police if they tested positive. Many of the women were prosecuted and subsequently imprisoned for child abuse.

In 1993 ten women who had been subjected to the "search and arrest" policy of the hospital and police filed a lawsuit, charging that "warrantless and nonconsensual drug tests conducted for criminal investigatory purposes were unconstitutional searches" prohibited by the Fourth Amendment. In 1997, in *Ferguson v. City of Charleston*, the U.S. District Court upheld the policy. In 1999 on appeal, the U.S. Court of Appeals for the Fourth Circuit affirmed the judgment of the district court, saying that the searches constitute a "special needs" exception to the Fourth Amendment, which justifies searches done for non–law enforcement ends, in this case, the medical interests of the mothers and infants, even though law enforcement means were used.

The U.S. Supreme Court reviewed the ruling by the Fourth Circuit Court to determine whether the policy involved searches justified by "special needs." In *Ferguson v. City of Charleston* (532 US 67 [2001]), the Court ruled 6–3 that the policy was unconstitutional, noting, "While the ultimate goal of the program may well have been to get the women in question into substance abuse treatment and off drugs, the immediate objective of the searches was to generate evidence for law enforcement purposes in order to reach that goal. Given that purpose and given the extensive involvement of law enforcement officials at every stage of the policy, this case simply does not fit within the closely guarded category of 'special needs.'"

The Court remanded (sent back) the case to the Fourth Circuit Court to determine whether or not the women gave informed consent to the hospital to test them for drugs. In October 2002 the appellate court noted that eight of the women did not provide informed consent to the drug testing; therefore, the search and arrest policy violated their Fourth Amendment rights. The city of Charleston appealed to the U.S. Supreme Court, but the Court declined to rehear the case.

Child Abuse Laws Relating to Domestic Violence

Some state and local laws impose penalties for domestic violence when children are present. For example, Steve Christian explains in "Children's Exposure to Domestic Violence: Is It Child Abuse?" (*NCSL State Legislative Report*, vol. 27, no. 1, January 2002) that Utah and Georgia enacted statutes creating a new crime of child maltreatment when domestic violence is witnessed by a child.

TABLE 5.1

Action taken by prosecutors in cases of children and domestic violence, by scenario

Scenario	Would report at least sometimes	Would prosecute at least sometimes
Mom abuses children	94% (n=90)	100% (n=82)
Mom fails to protect from abuse	63% (n=87)	77.5% (n=80)
Mom fails to protect from exposure	40% (n=86)	25% (n=73)

Note: n=sample size.

SOURCE: Debra Whitcomb, "Table 1. Prosecutors' Responses to Scenarios Involving Children and Abuse," in "Prosecutors, Kids, and Domestic Violence Cases," *National Institute of Justice Journal*, no. 248, March 2002, http://www.ncjrs.gov/pdffiles1/jr000248.pdf (accessed June 26, 2008)

Alaska amended its definition of child maltreatment in 1998 to include exposure to domestic violence.

In "Prosecutors, Kids, and Domestic Violence Cases" (*National Institute of Justice Journal*, no. 248, March 2002), Debra Whitcomb reports on a study she conducted involving a survey of prosecutors to determine their responses to cases where children witness domestic violence. The survey asked 128 prosecutors across the country how they would respond to three domestic violence cases in which children were present. A majority (94%) of prosecutors stated they would report a battered mother to CPS if she were found abusing the child. (See Table 5.1.) All indicated they would prosecute the abusing mother. Prosecutors would more likely report a battered mother if she failed to protect her child from abuse (63%) than if she failed to protect the child from witnessing the domestic violence (40%). More than three times as many prosecutors would charge the mother with a crime for the child's abuse (77.5%) than for exposure to family violence (25%).

Battered women with children are often further traumatized by CPS's removal of their children. Diana J. English, Jeffrey L. Edleson, and Mary E. Herrick find in "Domestic Violence in One State's Child Protective Caseload: A Study of Differential Case Dispositions and Outcomes" (*Children and Youth Services Review*, vol. 27, no. 11, November 2005) that when cases were referred to CPS, those with indications of domestic violence were significantly more likely to have their children placed in foster care.

In December 2001 Jack B. Weinstein (1921–), a federal judge, ruled that New York City's Administration for Children's Services (ACS) violated the constitutional rights of mothers and their children by removing the children simply because the mothers were victims of domestic violence. In this first case of its kind, fifteen battered women had filed the class action suit *Nicholson v. Scoppetta* (205 FRD 92, 95, 100 [ED NY 2001]). In January 2002 Weinstein issued in *In re Nicholson* (181 F. Supp. 2d 182, 188) an injunction ordering the ACS to stop separating a child from his or her battered mother unless the child "is in imminent danger." The injunction asserted that the government "may not penalize a mother, not otherwise unfit, who is battered by her partner, by separating her from her children; nor may children be separated from the mother, in effect visiting upon them the sins of their mother's batterer."

CHAPTER 6

THE PREVALENCE OF DOMESTIC VIOLENCE

WHO IS ABUSED?

Shannan Catalano of the Bureau of Justice Statics (BJS) reports in *Intimate Partner Violence in the United States* (December 2007, http://www.ojp.usdoj.gov/bjs/intimate/ipv.htm#contents) that the National Crime Victimization Survey found that in 2005, 3.6 of every 1,000 women were victims of nonfatal intimate partner violence. (See Figure 6.1.) Most of these women were victims of simple assault (assault without a weapon). The rate of violent intimate partner victimization had steadily decreased since 1993, when the rate was 9.8 per 1,000 women.

Who were these women? Sarah Romans et al. of the University of Toronto find in "Who Is Most At Risk for Intimate Partner Violence?: A Canadian Population-Based Study" (*Journal of Interpersonal Violence*, vol. 22, no. 12, 2007) that there was little difference between men and women in the frequency with which they reported an incident of physical or sexual abuse in an intimate relationship during the previous five years. However, women were much more likely than men to have experienced repeated violence or severe forms of violence, such as being choked or beaten, during that time frame. The researchers also note that risk factors for intimate partner violence included a younger age, being divorced, separated, or single, having children living in the household, and having poor physical health. A lower income or minority status put women, but not men, at a higher risk for intimate partner violence. Still, Romans et al. explain that classification is not exclusive. Just about anyone, rich or poor, male or female, may be a victim of domestic violence.

WHO ARE THE ABUSERS?

Like victims of domestic abuse, batterers come from all socioeconomic groups and all ethnic backgrounds. They may be male or female, young or old, but by definition they share one common characteristic: they all have a personal relationship with their victim.

During 2005 men who had been abused were slightly more likely to have been victimized by a stranger (54.1%) than a nonstranger (42.8%), whereas women were more likely to be victimized by someone they knew (64.4%) as opposed to a stranger (34.1%). (See Table 6.1.) Two-thirds (67%) of rape and sexual assault victims knew their assailant. Catalano reports that rates of violent victimization by an intimate partner toward women increase as household incomes go down.

Single people were victimized by violent crime much more often than married or widowed people in 2005. Never-married people who were victimized experienced violent crime at a rate of 37.4 per 1,000 people, and divorced or separated people experienced violent crime at a rate of 31.7 per 1,000 people. (See Table 6.2.) These rates were more than three times higher than the rates of violent crime experienced by married and widowed people. Married people experienced violent crime at a rate of 10.3 per 1,000 people, whereas widowed people (who tend to be older, on average) experienced violent crime at a rate of 6.1 per 1,000 people.

Women as Abusers

Amy Holtzworth-Munroe points out in "Female Perpetration of Physical Aggression against an Intimate Partner: A Controversial New Topic of Study" (*Violence and Victims*, vol. 20, no. 2, April 2005) that until the early twenty-first century, "it was politically incorrect to even consider studying female aggression when conducting research on marital violence." However, as surveys reveal, a substantial minority of perpetrators of intimate partner violence are women. Intimate partner violence has traditionally been understood as a method to gain power and control in a relationship. Research indicates, however, that this model may be useful mainly for understanding male batterers. By contrast, Poco Kernsmith of Wayne State University notes in "Exerting Power or Striking Back: A Gendered Comparison of Motivations for Domestic Violence Perpetration" (*Violence and Victims*, vol. 20, no. 2,

FIGURE 6.1

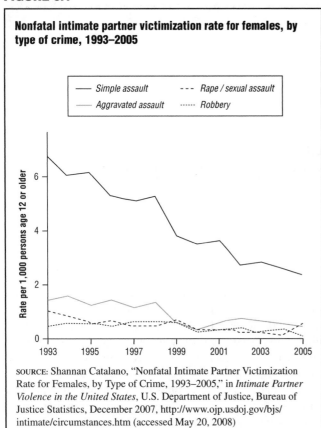

Nonfatal intimate partner victimization rate for females, by type of crime, 1993–2005

— Simple assault - - - Rape / sexual assault
— Aggravated assault ······ Robbery

Rate per 1,000 persons age 12 or older

1993 1995 1997 1999 2001 2003 2005

SOURCE: Shannan Catalano, "Nonfatal Intimate Partner Victimization Rate for Females, by Type of Crime, 1993–2005," in *Intimate Partner Violence in the United States*, U.S. Department of Justice, Bureau of Justice Statistics, December 2007, http://www.ojp.usdoj.gov/bjs/intimate/circumstances.htm (accessed May 20, 2008)

April 2005) that female batterers "appear more motivated by the desire to maintain personal liberties in a relationship where they have been victimized."

Motivation for battering is important to consider; so, too, is the impact and pattern of abuse. L. Kevin Hamberger of the Medical College of Wisconsin addresses these issues in "Men's and Women's Use of Intimate Partner Violence in Clinical Samples: Toward a Gender-Sensitive Analysis" (*Violence and Victims*, vol. 20, no. 2, April 2005). Even though some surveys find that women initiate domestic violence nearly as often as men, Hamberger argues that in evaluating these results, research must also assess the impact and context of intimate partner violence. In his review, he used a model that included gender differences in key elements of partner violence, including the initiation of the pattern of violence in the relationship, how often each partner initiates violence, the physical and mental health effects of domestic violence, behavioral and emotional responses to being victimized by violence, and the motivations of the batterer. He concludes that, even in relationships in which women also use violence against their partners, "women are disproportionately victimized by partner violence compared to men."

ESTIMATES OF DOMESTIC VIOLENCE

Because domestic violence is often unreported, it is impossible to be certain exactly how many domestic assaults

occur each year. Variations in definitions of violence and abuse, the types of questions posed by researchers, and the context in which they are asked compound the difficulty. For example, when victims are questioned in the presence of their abuser, or even other family members, they are often more reluctant to report instances of violence. Studies on the subject are sometimes contradictory, but most show that domestic violence remains a growing concern. Many researchers fear that available data represent only a fraction of a problem of massive proportions.

To understand why there are so many varying estimates of domestic violence, it is necessary to consider the surveys, studies, and reports themselves. Richard J. Gelles of the University of Pennsylvania notes in "Estimating the Incidence and Prevalence of Violence against Women" (*Violence against Women*, vol. 6, no. 7, July 2000) that the source and purpose of the research, the definition of abuse used, the population surveyed, and the survey setting, as well as the political agendas of the surveyors and researchers, may elicit different data and varying interpretations of these data.

The 1975 National Family Violence Survey and the 1985 National Family Violence Resurvey are among the most analyzed and cited data in the literature about intimate partner violence. The strength of these surveys lies in their ability to measure violent behavior that respondents might not classify as criminal. Using data from both surveys, Murray A. Straus and Richard J. Gelles estimate in "Societal Change and Change in Family Violence from 1975 to 1985 as Revealed by Two National Surveys" (*Journal of Marriage and the Family*, vol. 48, August 1986) that about 1.6 million women were severely beaten by their partners in 1985, down from 2.1 million in 1975.

The National Crime Victimization Surveys (NCVS; published by the BJS) and the Uniform Crime Reports (UCR; published by the Federal Bureau of Investigation [FBI]) are valuable sources of information on crime, including violent crime by intimate partners such as rape and sexual assault. Both studies measure the amount and prevalence of crime in the United States. The NCVS is a national survey that asks Americans about crimes they have personally suffered, including those that were not reported to the police. By its nature it cannot include coverage of murder. The UCR is a compilation of crime statistics reported by law enforcement agencies across the United States. Crimes that were not reported to the police are not included. Because they are based on different sources of data, the surveys give different results, and neither can be assumed to measure the true amount of intimate partner violence because some people will not report that it is occurring. However, one advantage of these surveys is that they enable researchers to observe trends in interpersonal violence over time. For example, NCVS data show that the rate of nonfatal intimate vio-

TABLE 6.1

Victim population by personal characteristics, type of crime, and victim/offender relationship, 2005

Characteristic	Total victimizations	Percent of all victimizations					
		Nonstrangers					
		Total	Intimate	Other relative	Friend or acquaintance	Stranger	Don't know relationship
Both genders							
Crimes of violence	100.0%	51.8%	9.0%	5.8%	36.9%	45.8%	2.4%
Rape/sexual assault[a]	100.0	67.0	26.1	6.2*	34.7	31.4	1.6*
Robbery	100.0	30.4	4.8*	1.9*	23.7	66.5	3.1*
Assault	100.0	54.2	8.9	6.4	38.9	43.5	2.4
Aggravated	100.0	49.7	5.3	6.9	37.6	47.3	3.0*
Simple	100.0	55.6	10.0	6.2	39.3	42.2	2.2
Male							
Crimes of violence	100.0	42.8	2.6	4.6	35.6	54.1	3.1
Rape/sexual assault	100.0*	0.0*	0.0*	0.0*	0.0*	100.0*	0.0*
Robbery	100.0	23.2	3.2*	2.1*	17.9	73.6	3.2*
Assault	100.0	46.5	2.5	5.0	39.0	50.3	3.1
Aggravated	100.0	42.4	1.1*	5.5	35.7	53.6	4.0*
Simple	100.0	48.0	3.0	4.9	40.1	49.2	2.8
Female							
Crimes of violence	100.0	64.4	18.1	7.6	38.7	34.1	1.5*
Rape/sexual assault[a]	100.0	72.8	28.3	6.7*	37.7	25.5	1.7*
Robbery	100.0	49.5	9.0*	1.5*	39.0	47.6	3.0*
Assault	100.0	65.1	18.0	8.3	38.8	33.6	1.3*
Aggravated	100.0	62.2	12.4	9.1*	40.7	36.5	1.3*
Simple	100.0	65.8	19.5	8.0	38.3	32.9	1.3*
All Races							
Crimes of violence	100.0	51.8	9.0	5.8	36.9	45.8	2.4
Rape/sexual assault[a]	100.0	67.0	26.1	6.2*	34.7	31.4	1.6*
Robbery	100.0	30.4	4.8*	1.9*	23.7	66.5	3.1*
Assault	100.0	54.2	8.9	6.4	38.9	43.5	2.4
Aggravated	100.0	49.7	5.3	6.9	37.6	47.3	3.0*
Simple	100.0	55.6	10.0	6.2	39.3	42.2	2.2
White only							
Crimes of violence	100.0	50.4	8.4	5.8	36.2	47.2	2.3
Rape/sexual assault[a]	100.0	55.9	15.4*	3.7*	36.8	41.6	2.4*
Robbery	100.0	30.7	6.1*	2.7*	21.9	65.7	3.6*
Assault	100.0	52.8	8.5	6.2	38.1	45.1	2.2
Aggravated	100.0	45.5	4.9	6.8	33.8	51.8	2.8*
Simple	100.0	54.8	9.5	6.1	39.3	43.2	2.0
Black only							
Crimes of violence	100.0	58.8	10.0	6.4	42.3	38.5	2.7*
Rape/sexual assault[a]	100.0	89.3	46.7*	13.9*	28.7*	10.7*	0.0*
Robbery	100.0	26.9	2.0*	0.0*	25.0*	70.4	2.6*
Assault	100.0	63.3	8.7	7.2	47.4	33.7	3.0*
Aggravated	100.0	63.0	3.0*	5.8*	54.2	33.7	3.4*
Simple	100.0	63.5	12.1	8.1*	43.3	33.7	2.8*
Other race only[b]							
Crimes of violence	100.0	42.5	4.7*	2.9*	34.9	55.3	2.2*
Rape/sexual assault[a]	100.0*	100.0*	57.7*	0.0*	42.3*	0.0*	0.0*
Robbery	100.0	32.3*	0.0*	0.0*	32.3*	67.7*	0.0*
Assault	100.0	42.6	3.5*	3.8*	35.2	54.4	3.0*
Aggravated	100.0*	27.4*	0.0*	15.7*	11.8*	72.6*	0.0*
Simple	100.0	47.5	4.7*	0.0*	42.8	48.6	4.0*
Two or more races[c]							
Crimes of violence	100.0	59.7	21.6	7.4*	30.7	36.8	3.5*
Rape/sexual assault[a]	100.0	62.9*	33.7*	0.0*	35.5*	30.8*	0.0*
Robbery	100.0	100.0*	0.0*	0.0*	100.0*	0.0*	0.0*
Assault	100.0	58.3	21.5	7.9*	28.9	37.9	3.7*
Aggravated	100.0	74.4*	31.1*	7.0*	36.2*	17.1*	8.6*
Simple	100.0	54.0	18.9*	8.1*	26.9	43.6	2.4*

lence against females declined drastically between 1993 and 2005. (See Figure 6.1.)

As a joint effort of the National Institute of Justice and the Centers for Disease Control and Prevention, the National Violence against Women Survey (NVAWS) collected data about intimate and nonintimate partner violence during the 1990s. The NVAWS and NCVS are considered the most reliable sources of data about intimate partner violence, even though their differing approaches make data comparisons difficult. For example, the NCVS is a survey about crime, and because some

TABLE 6.1

Victim population by personal characteristics, type of crime, and victim/offender relationship, 2005 [CONTINUED]

		Percent of all victimizations					
		Nonstrangers					
Characteristic	**Total victimizations**	**Total**	**Intimate**	**Other relative**	**Friend or acquaintance**	**Stranger**	**Don't know relationship**
Ethnicity							
Crimes of violence	100.0	51.8	9.0	5.8	36.9	45.8	2.4
Rape/sexual assault[a]	100.0	67.0	26.1	6.2*	34.7	31.4	1.6*
Robbery	100.0	30.4	4.8*	1.9*	23.7	66.5	3.1*
Assault	100.0	54.2	8.9	6.4	38.9	43.5	2.4
Aggravated	100.0	49.7	5.3	6.9	37.6	47.3	3.0*
Simple	100.0	55.6	10.0	6.2	39.3	42.2	2.2
Hispanic							
Crimes of violence	100.0	41.9	10.6	6.7	24.7	53.5	4.5*
Rape/sexual assault[a]	100.0*	38.6*	25.4*	0.0*	13.2*	61.4*	0.0*
Robbery	100.0	18.4*	3.0*	3.0*	12.4*	75.9	5.7*
Assault	100.0	46.9	11.3	7.8	27.8	48.6	4.5*
Aggravated	100.0	47.9	8.5*	12.6*	26.7	48.8	3.3*
Simple	100.0	46.4	12.4	5.8*	28.2	48.5	5.1*
Non-Hispanic							
Crimes of violence	100.0	53.5	8.7	5.6	39.2	44.4	2.1
Rape/sexual assault[a]	100.0	73.6	26.2	7.6*	39.7	24.5	2.0*
Robbery	100.0	33.5	5.3*	1.7*	26.5	64.0	2.5*
Assault	100.0	55.4	8.5	6.1	40.8	42.6	2.0
Aggravated	100.0	49.9	4.6	5.3	40.0	47.1	2.9*
Simple	100.0	57.0	9.6	6.3	41.1	41.2	1.7

Note: Detail may not add to total shown because of rounding.
*Estimate is based on about 10 or fewer sample cases.
[a]Includes verbal threats of rape and threats of sexual assault.
[b]Includes American Indian, Eskimo, Asian Pacific Islander If only one of these races is given.
[c]Includes all persons of any race, indicating two or more races.

SOURCE: "Table 43a. Personal Crimes of Violence, 2005: Percent Distribution of Victimizations, by Characteristics of Victims, Type of Crime, and Victim/Offender Relationship," in *Criminal Victimization in the United States, 2005 Statistical Tables*, U.S. Department of Justice, Office of Justice Programs, Bureau of Justice Statistics, December 2006, http://www.ojp.usdoj.gov/bjs/pub/pdf/cvus05.pdf (accessed June 26, 2008)

victims do not consider instances of intimate partner violence as a crime, they are less likely to disclose them in the NCVS.

The NCVS defines an intimate partner as a spouse, former spouse, or a current or former boyfriend or girlfriend, either of the same sex or the opposite sex. (See Table 6.3.) In *Criminal Victimization in the United States, 2005 Statistical Tables* (December 2006, http://www.ojp .usdoj.gov/bjs/pub/pdf/cvus05.pdf), the BJS states that in 2005, 9% of all violent crimes, including rape, sexual assault, aggravated assault (assault with a weapon), and simple assault victimizations (assault without a weapon and resulting in minor injuries), were committed against intimate partners. (See Table 6.1.) However, women were disproportionately likely to be victimized by their intimate partners. Nearly one out of five (18.1%) violent crimes against women were committed by intimate partners, whereas only 2.6% of violent crimes against men were committed by intimates.

Far more women than men are murdered by their intimate partners, as well. The FBI reports in *Crime in the United States, 2006* (September 2007, http://www.fbi .gov/ucr/cius2006/index.html) that in 2006, 11.9% of murders were committed by family members. In that year, 567

wives were killed by their husband and 123 husbands were killed by their wife. (See Table 6.4.) In addition, 450 girlfriends were killed by their boyfriend and 150 boyfriends were killed by their girlfriend.

National Violence against Women Survey

The NVAWS collected information from interviews with eight thousand men and eight thousand women to assess their experiences as victims of various types of violence, including domestic violence. The NVAWS asked survey respondents about physical assaults and rape, but excluded other sexual assaults, murders, and robberies.

In *Extent, Nature, and Consequences of Intimate Partner Violence: Findings from the National Violence against Women Survey* (July 2000, http://www.ncjrs.gov/ pdffiles1/nij/181867.pdf), Patricia Tjaden and Nancy Thoennes of the Center for Policy Research in Denver, Colorado, find that intimate violence is pervasive in American society, with women suffering about three times as much of this violence as men. They estimate that in 1998, 22.3 million (22.1%) of women had been physically assaulted by a loved one during the course of their lifetime, whereas 6.9 million (7.4%) men had been physically assaulted by intimates over their lifetime. Women were also more likely to become victims of rape,

TABLE 6.2

Victims age 12 and over, by type of crime and marital status of victims, 2005

Type of crime	Rate per 1,000 persons age 12 and over			
	Never married	Married	Widowed	Divorced or separated
All personal crimes	**39.0**	**10.8**	**6.9**	**32.8**
Crimes of violence	37.4	10.3	6.1	31.7
Completed violence	12.8	2.5	2.9	10.9
Attempted/threatened violence	24.6	7.8	3.2	20.8
Rape/sexual assault	1.4	0.2*	0.8*	1.5
Rape/attempted rape	0.9	0.2*	0.2*	1.3*
Rape	0.5	0.1*	0.2*	0.8*
Attempted rapeª	0.4*	0.1*	0.0*	0.5*
Sexual assaultᵇ	0.6	0.0*	0.5*	0.2*
Robbery	4.8	1.0	1.4*	3.8
Completed/property taken	3.2	0.6	1.4*	2.4
With injury	1.1	0.2*	1.1*	0.7*
Without injury	2.1	0.5	0.2*	1.7
Attempted to take property	1.6	0.4	0.0*	1.4*
With injury	0.4*	0.1*	0.0*	0.7*
Without injury	1.2	0.2*	0.0*	0.7*
Assault	31.2	9.0	4.0	26.4
Aggravated	7.7	2.4	0.5*	5.2
With injury	2.7	0.6	0.2*	1.6
Threatened with weapon	5.0	1.8	0.3*	3.6
Simple	23.5	6.6	3.6	21.2
With minor injury	6.1	1.1	0.7*	6.0
Without injury	17.4	5.5	2.9	15.2
Purse snatching/pocket picking	1.5	0.5	0.8*	1.1*
Population age 12 and over	**79,664,210**	**122,198,090**	**14,312,360**	**26,079,910**

Note: Detail may not add to total shown because of rounding. Excludes data on persons whose marital status was not ascertained.
*Estimate is based on about 10 or fewer sample cases.
ªIncludes verbal threats of rape.
ᵇIncludes threats.

SOURCE: "Table 11. Personal Crimes, 2005: Victimization Rates for Persons Age 12 and over, by Type of Crime and Marital Status of Victims," in *Criminal Victimization in the United States, 2005 Statistical Tables*, U.S. Department of Justice, Office of Justice Programs, Bureau of Justice Statistics, December 2006, http://www.ojp.usdoj.gov/bjs/pub/pdf/cvus05.pdf (accessed June 26, 2008)

TABLE 6.3

Definition of an intimate partner by source of report

Intimate partner relationships involve current spouses, former spouses, current boy/girlfriends, or former boy/girlfriends. Individuals involved in an intimate partner relationship may be of the same gender. The FBI does not report former boy/girlfriends in categories separate from current boy/girlfriends. Rather, they are included in the boy/girlfriend category during the data collection process.

	National Crime Victimization Survey categories	Supplementary Homicide Reports categories
Intimate	Spouse	Husband/wife
	Ex-spouse	Common-law husband or wife
	Boyfriend/girlfriend	Ex-husband/ex-wife
	Ex-girlfriend/ex-boyfriend	Boyfriend/girlfriend
		Homosexual relationship
Friend/ acquaintance	Friend/ex-friend	Acquaintance
	Roommate/boarder	Friend
	Schoolmate	Neighbor
	Neighbor	Employee
	Someone at work/customer	Employer
	Other non-relative	Other known
Other family	Parent or stepparent	Mother/father
	Own child or stepchild	Son/daughter
	Brother/sister	Brother/sister
	Other relative	In-law
		Stepfather/stepmother
		Stepson/stepdaughter
		Other family
Stranger	Stranger	Stranger
	Known by sight only	

SOURCE: Adapted from Callie Marie Rennison and Sarah Welchans, "Definitions of Intimate Partner," in *Intimate Partner Violence*, U.S. Department of Justice, Office of Justice Programs, Bureau of Justice Statistics, May 2000, http://www.ojp.usdoj.gov/bjs/pub/pdf/ipv.pdf (accessed June 26, 2008)

---

stalking, and physical assault by intimates than their male counterparts at some time during their lifetime. Furthermore, women physically assaulted by their partners averaged 6.9 assaults by the same person, as opposed to men, who averaged 4.4 assaults.

During the twelve months that preceded the interview, women also reported higher rates of rape, stalking, and physical assault than did men. Tjaden and Thoennes estimate based on NVAWS data that about 1.5 million (1.5%) of the surveyed women and 834,732 (0.9%) of the men reported they had been raped and/or physically assaulted by a partner in the twelve months preceding the survey. In other words, approximately 4.8 million women and 2.9 million men are assaulted by a partner every year.

The rates of violence between intimate partners varied by race. Whereas 15% of Asian and Pacific Islanders

reported violence, 37.5% of Native Americans and Alaskan Natives, 29.1% of African-Americans, and 24.8% of whites reported having been victimized by an intimate partner in their lifetime.

Tjaden and Thoennes conclude that most partner abuse and violence is not reported to the police. Women reported 17.2% of rapes, 26.7% of physical assaults, and 51.9% of stalking incidents to police, whereas men reported 13.5% of physical assaults and 36.2% of stalking incidents. Many victims said they felt the police would not or could not do anything on their behalf. These expressions of helplessness and hopelessness—feeling that others in a position to assist would be unwilling or unable to do so—is a common characteristic shared by many victims of intimate partner violence.

STATISTICS FOR VIOLENCE IN SAME-SEX COUPLES ARE PROBLEMATIC. Tjaden and Thoennes also find that same-sex couples who lived together reported experiencing far more intimate violence in their lifetime than heterosexual cohabitants. Among women, 39.2% of the same-sex cohabitants and 21.7% of the opposite-sex cohabitants reported being raped, physically assaulted, or stalked by a partner during their lifetime. Among men, the comparative figures were 23.1% and 7.4%, respectively.

TABLE 6.4

Murder circumstances by relationship, 2006

Circumstances	Total murder victims	Husband	Wife	Mother	Father	Son	Daughter	Brother	Sister	Other family	Acquaintance	Friend	Boyfriend	Girlfriend	Neighbor	Employee	Employer	Stranger	Unknown
Total	**14,990**	**123**	**567**	**115**	**114**	**283**	**179**	**80**	**22**	**298**	**3,465**	**339**	**150**	**450**	**127**	**13**	**10**	**1,905**	**6,750**
Felony type total:	**2,436**	**2**	**25**	**8**	**9**	**11**	**3**	**2**	**1**	**27**	**646**	**37**	**2**	**15**	**14**	**3**	**0**	**583**	**1,048**
Rape	32	0	1	0	0	0	0	0	0	0	16	0	0	1	1	1	0	6	6
Robbery	1,041	0	0	1	4	0	0	0	1	8	212	12	0	1	5	0	0	392	405
Burglary	79	0	3	0	0	0	0	0	0	4	21	0	0	3	3	0	0	17	28
Larceny-theft	14	1	0	0	0	0	0	0	0	0	5	0	0	1	0	0	0	2	5
Motor vehicle theft	15	0	0	0	2	0	0	0	0	1	4	0	0	0	1	0	0	4	3
Arson	27	0	2	1	0	1	2	2	0	1	1	1	0	1	1	0	0	0	14
Prostitution and commercialized vice	8	0	0	0	0	0	0	0	0	0	1	0	0	0	0	0	0	5	2
Other sex offenses	18	0	0	0	0	0	0	0	0	2	10	0	0	0	0	0	0	3	3
Narcotic drug laws	796	0	0	0	0	2	0	0	0	7	302	18	1	0	0	0	0	77	389
Gambling	4	0	0	0	0	0	0	0	0	0	0	0	0	0	0	0	0	2	2
Other—not specified	402	1	19	6	3	8	1	0	0	4	74	6	1	8	3	2	0	75	191
Suspected felony type	**58**	**1**	**0**	**1**	**0**	**0**	**3**	**0**	**0**	**0**	**10**	**0**	**0**	**2**	**0**	**0**	**0**	**4**	**37**
Other than felony type total:	**7,273**	**105**	**473**	**81**	**80**	**236**	**147**	**65**	**16**	**211**	**2,233**	**235**	**123**	**366**	**98**	**6**	**9**	**946**	**1,843**
Romantic triangle	103	4	5	0	0	2	1	0	0	0	63	2	1	10	0	0	0	9	6
Child killed by babysitter	27	0	0	0	0	1	0	0	0	0	24	0	0	0	0	0	0	0	2
Brawl due to influence of alcohol	107	2	2	0	2	2	1	4	0	4	32	13	2	5	2	0	0	23	13
Brawl due to influence of narcotics	51	1	0	1	0	1	1	1	0	3	25	4	2	2	2	0	0	4	4
Argument over money or property	198	1	6	2	1	2	2	3	0	8	97	15	0	0	4	0	3	23	31
Other arguments	3,607	78	297	46	60	37	13	46	10	128	1,217	151	93	275	58	4	4	449	641
Gangland killings	118	0	0	0	0	0	0	0	0	0	32	2	0	0	0	0	0	17	67
Juvenile gang killings	865	0	0	0	1	0	0	0	0	1	200	2	0	0	0	0	0	179	482
Institutional killings	22	0	0	0	0	0	0	0	0	0	13	0	0	0	0	0	0	8	8
Sniper attack	2	0	0	0	0	0	0	0	0	0	0	0	0	0	0	0	0	1	1
Other—not specified	2,173	19	163	32	16	191	129	11	6	67	530	46	25	74	32	2	2	240	588
Unknown	**5,223**	**15**	**69**	**25**	**25**	**36**	**26**	**13**	**5**	**60**	**576**	**67**	**25**	**67**	**15**	**4**	**1**	**372**	**3,822**

Note: The relationship categories of husband and wife include both common-law and ex-spouses. The categories of mother, father, sister, brother, son, and daughter include stepparents, stepchildren, and stepsiblings. The category of acquaintance includes homosexual relationships and the composite category of other known to victim.

SOURCE: "Expanded Homicide Data Table 9. Murder Circumstances by Relationship, 2006," in *Crime in the United States, 2006*, U.S. Department of Justice, Federal Bureau of Investigation, September 2007, http://www.fbi.gov/ucr/cius2006/offenses/expanded_information/data/shrtable_09.html (accessed June 26, 2008)

Even though survey findings indicated that members of same-sex couples have experienced more intimate partner violence than have members of heterosexual couples, the reported violence does not necessarily occur within the same-sex relationship. When comparing intimate partner victimization rates among same-sex and opposite-sex cohabitants by the gender of the perpetrator, Tjaden and Thoennes find that 30.4% of the same-sex women cohabitants reported being victimized by a male partner sometime in their lifetime, whereas 11.4% reported being victimized by a female partner. The researchers conclude that same-sex cohabiting women were three times more likely to report being victimized by a male partner than by a female partner. In comparison, women who lived with men were nearly twice as likely to report being victimized by a male than same-sex cohabiting women were to report being victimized by a female partner.

According to Tjaden and Thoennes, male same-sex partners reported more partner violence than men who lived with women. About 23% of men who lived with men said they had been raped, sexually assaulted, or stalked by a male cohabitant, as opposed to just 7.4% of men who reported comparable experiences with female cohabitants. This finding confirms the widely held observation that violence and abuse in intimate partner relationships is primarily inflicted by men, whether the victimized partner is male or female.

In comparison with the research on intimate partner violence between men and women, the literature about same-sex violence is sparse, in part because many respondents may consider disclosing same-sex relationships risky and revealing partner violence within them even more sensitive. Furthermore, not all people who engage in same-sex relationships identify themselves as homosexual, leading to more questions about the quality of data gathered. The research that examines same-sex partner violence reveals that it is quite similar to heterosexual partner violence—abuse arises in the attempts of one partner to exert control over the other, and it escalates throughout the course of the relationship.

National Crime Victimization Surveys

The NCVS are ongoing federal surveys that interview eighty thousand people from a representative sample of households biannually to estimate the amount of crime committed against people over age twelve in the United States. Even though the surveys cover all types of crime, they were extensively redesigned in 1992 to produce more accurate reports of rape, sexual assault, and other violent crimes committed by intimates or family members. Both *Intimate Partner Violence in the United States* by Catalano and *Criminal Victimization, 2006* (December 2007, http://www.ojp.usdoj.gov/bjs/pub/pdf/cv06.pdf) by Michael

TABLE 6.5

Victim and offender relationship in violent crimes, 2006

	Violent crime	
Relationship with victim	Number	Percent
Male victims		
Total	3,187,880	100%
Nonstranger	1,577,580	50%
Intimate	144,350	5
Other relative	154,530	5
Friend/acquaintance	1,278,700	40
Stranger	1,495,580	47%
Relationship unknown	114,720	4%
Female victims		
Total	2,906,850	100%
Nonstranger	2,038,910	70%
Intimate	595,740	21
Other relative	276,150	10
Friend/acquaintance	1,167,020	40
Stranger	833,840	29%
Relationship unknown	34,100	1%*

Note: Percentages may not total to 100% because of rounding.
*Based on 10 or fewer sample cases.

SOURCE: Michael Rand and Shannan Catalano, "Table 6. Victim and Offender Relationship, 2006," in *Criminal Victimization, 2006*, U.S. Department of Justice, Bureau of Justice Statistics, December 2007, http://www.ojp.usdoj.gov/bjs/pub/pdf/cv06.pdf (accessed June 26, 2008)

Rand and Shannan Catalano of the BJS are based on NCVS survey results.

Rand and Catalano find that the rate of violent crime was 23.3 per 1,000 people aged twelve and older in 2006. Even though the number of violent crimes remained fairly steady between 2005 and 2006, the numbers are still staggering: 3.7 million violent crimes were committed in 2006 (rape/sexual assault, robbery, aggravated assault, and simple assault). Nearly three-quarters of a million violent crimes—595,740 women and 144,350 men—were committed against intimate partners. (See Table 6.5.)

According to Catalano, between 2001 and 2005, 22% of violent crimes against females and 4% of violent crimes against males were perpetrated by intimate partners. Of those women attacked by an intimate partner, 7.2% were raped; 1.9% were sexually assaulted; 62.7% were hit, slapped, or knocked down; and 54.9% were grabbed, held, or tripped. (See Table 6.6.) Male victims were more likely than female victims to be attacked with a weapon: 8% were attacked by a knife and 4.5% were hit by a thrown object. Over half of both female and male victims were threatened with harm (59.3% and 55.3%, respectively). (See Table 6.7.) Females reported their partners threatened to kill them more often than males did (26.9% and 15.1%, respectively). Catalano notes that female victims of intimate partner violence were more likely than male victims to be injured (51.3% and 41.5%, respectively).

According to the BJS, in *Criminal Victimization in the United States, 2005 Statistical Tables*, 47.4% of all

TABLE 6.6

Type of attack used in intimate partner violence, by gender, 2001–05

Type of attack	Percent of victims of nonfatal intimate partner violence who were attacked	
	Female	Male
Raped	7.2%	0.8%*
Sexual assault	1.9	0.9
Attacked with firearm	0.5*	—
Attacked with knife	2.5	8*
Hit by thrown object	2.1	4.5*
Attacked with other weapon	0.8*	1.8*
Hit, slapped, knocked down	62.7	62.2
Grabbed, held, tripped	54.9	26

*Based on 10 or fewer sample cases.
—Information is not provided because the small number of cases is insufficient for reliable estimates.
Note: Detail may not add to total because victims may have reported more than one type of attack.

SOURCE: Shannan Catalano, "Type of Attack," in *Intimate Partner Violence in the United States*, U.S. Department of Justice, Bureau of Justice Statistics, December 2007, http://www.ojp.usdoj.gov/bjs/intimate/injury.htm (accessed May 20, 2008)

TABLE 6.7

Type of threat used in intimate partner violence, by gender, 2001–05

Type of threat	Percent of victims of nonfatal intimate partner violence, 2001-2005	
	Female	Male
Threatened to kill	26.9%	15.1%*
Threatened to rape	0.5*	—
Threatened with harm	59.3	55.3
Threatened with a weapon	17.6	22.9
Threw object at victim	7.5	7.4*
Followed/surrounded victim	5.9	1.8*
Tried to hit, slap, or knock down victim	14.1	12.6*

*Based on 10 or fewer sample cases.
Note: Detail may not add to total because victims may have reported more than one type of threat.
—Information is not provided because the small number of cases is insufficient for reliable estimates.

SOURCE: Shannan Catalano, "Type of Threat," in *Intimate Partner Violence in the United States*, U.S. Department of Justice, Bureau of Justice Statistics, December 2007, http://www.ojp.usdoj.gov/bjs/intimate/injury.htm (accessed May 20, 2008)

violent victimizations were reported to the police in 2005, including 62.4% of aggravated assaults, 42.3% of simple assaults, and 38.3% of rape and sexual assaults. (See Table 6.8.) Female victims were more likely to report violent offenses than male victims. Hispanic women were the most likely to report violent crimes (60.3%), followed by African-American women (58.3%) and white women (53.9%). (See Table 6.9.) Hispanic men (43.5%) were more likely than either white men (42.8%) or African-American men (41.5%) to report violent crime. However, as mentioned earlier, women are known to seriously underreport sexual assaults and rapes.

National Family Violence Survey

The National Family Violence Survey, which is considered by many to be the source of the most important research on family violence, was originally conducted in 1975 for the Family Research Laboratory at the University of New Hampshire, Durham. In the 1985 study Murray A. Straus and Richard J. Gelles found that the rate of assaults by husbands on wives had dropped slightly during the decade, from 121 instances per 100,000 couples in 1975 to 113 instances per 100,000 couples in 1985. Furthermore, the rate of severe violence, such as hitting, kicking, or using a weapon had declined by 21%, from thirty-eight to thirty per one hundred thousand couples.

The study's most controversial finding indicated that women were initiating domestic violence at a rate equal to men. The 1985 study reported that in half of the cases, the abuse was mutual. After reassessing their data in 1990 and again in 1993, Straus and Gelles concluded that even though there were similar levels of abuse between men and women, men were six times more likely to inflict serious injury.

In "Change in Spouse Assault Rates from 1975 to 1992: A Comparison of Three National Surveys in the United States" (paper presented at the Thirteenth World Congress of Sociology, Bielefeld, Germany, July 1994), Murray A. Straus and Glenda Kaufman Kantor compare the rates of abuse from the 1975 National Family Violence Survey and the 1985 National Family Violence Resurvey and a 1992 survey conducted by Kantor. When the researchers reclassified "minor assault" to include pushing, grabbing, shoving, and slapping, and "severe assault" to include behavior likely to cause serious injury, such as kicking, punching, beating, and threatening with a weapon, they found some startling results.

The rates of reclassified minor assaults, which were considered less likely to cause injuries requiring medical treatment, decreased for husbands between the 1975 and 1985 surveys, yet remained constant for wives. The researchers find the same trend held true for severe assaults by husbands versus those by wives. Even though the rate of severe assaults by men against their wives declined 50% in the seventeen years from 1975 to 1992, severe assaults by women remained fairly steady. Straus and Kantor conclude that the reason for the decline in severe assaults by husbands was that over time men became increasingly aware that battering was a crime and grew reluctant to admit the abuse. At the same time, women had been encouraged not to tolerate abuse and to report it, accounting for an increase in the reporting of even minor instances of abuse.

When abuse was measured based on separate reports by men and women, Straus and Kantor find that minor assaults by husbands decreased from 1975 to 1985. Based

TABLE 6.8

Victimizations by type of crime and victims' decision to report or not report the incident to police, 2005

Sector and type of crime	Number of victimizations	Percent of victimizations reported to the police			
		Total	Yes[a]	No	Not known and not available
All crimes	**23,440,720%**	**100.0%**	**41.3%**	**57.4%**	**1.3%**
Personal crimes	**5,400,790**	**100.0%**	**46.9%**	**51.3%**	**1.8%**
Crimes of violence	5,173,720	100.0	47.4	50.7	1.8
Completed violence	1,658,660	100.0	61.5	37.4	1.1*
Attempted/threatened violence	3,515,060	100.0	40.8	57.0	2.1
Rape/sexual assault	191,670	100.0	38.3	61.7	0.0*
Rape/attempted rape	130,140	100.0	42.1	57.9	0.0*
Rape	69,370	100.0	45.2*	54.8	0.0*
Attempted rape[b]	60,770	100.0	38.7*	61.3	0.0*
Sexual assault[c]	61,530	100.0	30.2*	69.8	0.0*
Robbery	624,850	100.0	52.4	46.9	0.7*
Completed/property taken	415,320	100.0	60.5	38.5	1.0*
With injury	142,830	100.0	73.8	26.2	0.0*
Without injury	272,490	100.0	53.6	44.9	1.5*
Attempted to take property	209,530	100.0	36.4	63.6	0.0*
With injury	64,450	100.0	39.6*	60.4	0.0*
Without injury	145,090	100.0	35.0	65.0	0.0*
Assault	4,357,190	100.0	47.1	50.8	2.1
Aggravated	1,052,260	100.0	62.4	36.6	1.0*
With injury	330,730	100.0	76.2	23.8	0.0*
Threatened with weapon	721,530	100.0	56.0	42.5	1.5*
Simple	3,304,930	100.0	42.3	55.3	2.4
With minor injury	795,240	100.0	59.0	39.2	1.8*
Without injury	2,509,690	100.0	37.0	60.4	2.6
Purse snatching/pocket picking	227,070	100.0	35.2	63.6	1.2*
Completed purse snatching	43,550	100.0	51.2*	48.8*	0.0*
Attempted purse snatching	3,260*	100.0*	0.0*	100.0*	0.0*
Pocket picking	180,260	100.0	32.0	66.5	1.5*
Property crimes	**18,039,930**	**100.0%**	**39.6%**	**59.3%**	**1.1%**
Household burglary	3,456,220	100.0	56.3	42.6	1.1
Completed	2,900,460	100.0	57.1	41.9	0.9*
Forcible entry	1,068,430	100.0	74.7	24.7	0.5*
Unlawful entry without force	1,832,030	100.0	46.9	52.0	1.2*
Attempted forcible entry	555,760	100.0	51.7	46.2	2.1*
Motor vehicle theft	978,120	100.0	83.2	15.9	0.8*
Completed	774,650	100.0	92.4	7.1	0.4*
Attempted	203,470	100.0	48.2	49.4	2.3*
Theft	13,605,590	100.0	32.3	66.6	1.1
Completed	13,116,270	100.0	32.0	66.9	1.1
Less than $50	4,079,120	100.0	18.6	80.5	0.9*
$50–$249	4,656,120	100.0	27.6	71.5	0.9
$250 or more	3,231,440	100.0	52.7	46.2	1.1*
Amount not available	1,149,590	100.0	39.0	58.3	2.7*
Attempted	489,320	100.0	38.6	59.5	1.8*

Note: Detail may not add to total shown because of rounding.

*Estimate is based on about 10 or fewer sample cases.

[a]Figures in this column represent the rates at which victimizations were reported to the police, or "police reporting rates."

[b]Includes verbal threats of rape.

[c]Includes threats.

SOURCE: "Table 91. Personal and Property Crimes, 2005: Percent Distribution of Victimizations, by Type of Crime and Whether or Not Reported to the Police," in *Criminal Victimization in the United States, 2005 Statistical Tables*, U.S. Department of Justice, Office of Justice Programs, Bureau of Justice Statistics, December 2006, http://www.ojp.usdoj.gov/bjs/pub/pdf/cvus05.pdf (accessed June 26, 2008)

on the husbands' reports, these rates continued to decline from 1985 to 1992, but wives reported an increase over the same period. Men also reported a decrease in the rate of severe abuse between 1975 and 1985, whereas women reported no change. In contrast, between 1985 and 1992 men reported a slight increase in the rate of severe abuse, whereas women reported a sharp drop of 43%. These findings appear to contradict Straus and Kantor's hypothesis that the rate change was a result of men's reluctance to report abuse and women's greater freedom to report it.

According to women, minor abuse perpetrated by wives against their husbands declined from 1975 to 1985 but increased substantially from 1985 to 1992. Men, however, said the rate of minor abuse by their wives increased over both periods. Women also reported that the rate of severe assaults against their husbands remained steady during the first decade but increased between 1985 and 1992. Husbands reported a steady decrease in severe assaults by their wives during both periods.

TABLE 6.9

Violent victimizations reported to the police, by type of crime, and gender and race or ethnicity of victims, 2005

Characteristic	Percent of all victimizations reported to the police	
	Crimes of violence[a]	Property crimes
Total	**47.4 %**	**39.6 %**
Male		
White only	42.8	39.6
Black only	41.5	44.0
Other race only[b]	49.0	37.2
Two or more races[c]	25.9*	42.1
Female		
White only	53.9	38.8
Black only	58.3	44.7
Other race only[b]	58.1	30.2
Two or more races[c]	49.3	31.6
Male		
Hispanic	43.5	37.8
Non-Hispanic	42.3	40.3
Female		
Hispanic	60.3	36.8
Non-Hispanic	53.5	39.6

*Estimate is based on about 10 or fewer sample cases.
Excludes data on persons whose ethnicity was not ascertained.
[a]Includes data on rape and sexual assault, not shown separately
[b]Includes American Indian, Eskimo, Asian Pacific Islander if only one of these races is given
[c]includes all persons of any race, indicating two or more races

SOURCE: "Table 91b. Violent Crimes, 2005: Percent of Victimizations Reported to the Police, by Type of Crime and Gender and Race or Ethnicity of Victims," in *Criminal Victimization in the United States, 2005 Statistical Tables*, U.S. Department of Justice, Office of Justice Programs, Bureau of Justice Statistics, December 2006, http://www.ojp.usdoj.gov/bjs/pub/pdf/cvus05.pdf (accessed June 26, 2008)

TABLE 6.10

Intimate homicide victims, by gender, 1976–2005

	Male	Female
1976	1,304	1,587
1977	1,248	1,421
1978	1,159	1,473
1979	1,229	1,498
1980	1,169	1,543
1981	1,232	1,558
1982	1,093	1,477
1983	1,067	1,456
1984	947	1,432
1985	927	1,542
1986	946	1,581
1987	891	1,482
1988	816	1,568
1989	862	1,410
1990	820	1,485
1991	734	1,492
1992	662	1,436
1993	638	1,563
1994	654	1,401
1995	521	1,311
1996	476	1,299
1997	413	1,202
1998	460	1,302
1999	381	1,195
2000	382	1,232
2001	344	1,187
2002	339	1,182
2003	330	1,156
2004	344	1,155
2005	329	1,181

SOURCE: James Alan Fox and Marianne W. Zawitz, "Intimate Homicide Victims by Gender," in *Homicide Trends in the United States*, U.S. Department of Justice, Bureau of Justice Statistics, July 2007, http://www.ojp.usdoj.gov/bjs/homicide/tables/intimatestab.htm (accessed June 26, 2008)

DRAWING CONCLUSIONS FROM THE DATA. Straus and Kantor observe that the large decrease in severe assaults by husbands was supported by FBI statistics showing an 18% drop in the number of women killed by their husbands during that period. The researchers speculate that strides made over several years, such as justice system interventions to punish abusive husbands, along with the greater availability of shelters and restraining orders, played a role in the decline of severe abuse. The lack of change in minor assaults by husbands may reflect the emphasis that has been placed on severe assaults, which could allow men to mistakenly assume that an occasional slap or shove does not constitute abusive behavior.

To explain the increase in minor assaults by women, Straus and Kantor suggest that there had been no effort to condemn assaults by wives, and with increasing gender equality, women might feel entitled to hit as often as their male partners. The decrease in severe abuse by wives as reported by their husbands, which is inconsistent with the wives' responses, might reflect men's reluctance to admit they have been victims of abuse.

ABUSED TO DEATH

In 2005, 1,181 women and 329 men were killed by an intimate partner. (See Table 6.10.) Even though these statistics sound alarming, they reflect a positive trend in domestic homicides. Since 1976, when the FBI began keeping statistics on intimate murders, the number of men and women killed by an intimate partner has dropped significantly. The number of men killed by an intimate declined from 1,304 in 1976 to 329 in 2005, a decrease of 75%, and the number of women killed was stable until 1993, when it began to decline. (See Figure 6.2.)

According to James Alan Fox and Marianne W. Zawitz, in *Homicide Trends in the United States* (July 2007, http://www.ojp.usdoj.gov/bjs/homicide/homtrnd.htm#contents), the number of white females killed by an intimate increased during most of the 1980s but then declined after 1987. In 1997 it reached its lowest point in two decades. This decline, however, did not hold true across all relationship categories. The intimate homicide rate for white girlfriends in 2006 was higher than it was in 1976, and even though the homicide rate for white wives and former wives had declined somewhat, it had not declined as much as that for white husbands and former husbands. (See Figure 6.3.) The intimate homicide rates among African-Americans

FIGURE 6.2

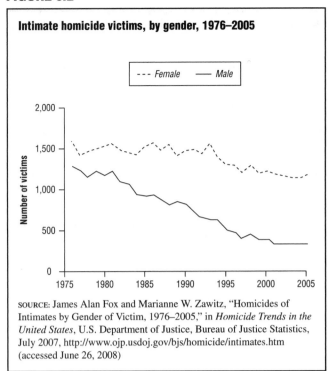

Intimate homicide victims, by gender, 1976–2005

SOURCE: James Alan Fox and Marianne W. Zawitz, "Homicides of Intimates by Gender of Victim, 1976–2005," in *Homicide Trends in the United States*, U.S. Department of Justice, Bureau of Justice Statistics, July 2007, http://www.ojp.usdoj.gov/bjs/homicide/intimates.htm (accessed June 26, 2008)

FIGURE 6.3

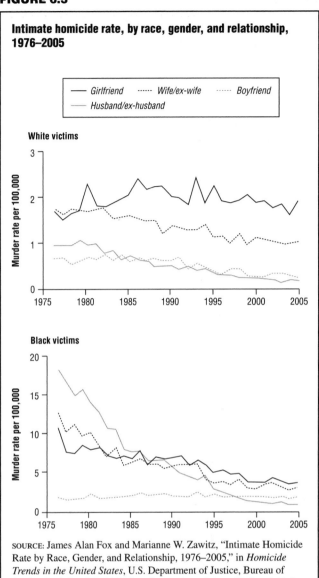

Intimate homicide rate, by race, gender, and relationship, 1976–2005

SOURCE: James Alan Fox and Marianne W. Zawitz, "Intimate Homicide Rate by Race, Gender, and Relationship, 1976–2005," in *Homicide Trends in the United States*, U.S. Department of Justice, Bureau of Justice Statistics, July 2007, http://www.ojp.usdoj.gov/bjs/homicide/intimates.htm (accessed June 26, 2008)

dropped more dramatically for all relationship categories, with the steepest decline experienced by husbands and the most modest decrease experienced by girlfriends.

Of all intimate homicides committed during this period, guns were used in a majority of the murders, although other weapons such as knives were also used. (See Figure 6.4 and Table 6.11.) In the period between 1990 and 2005 more than two-thirds of all victims of murder at the hands of their spouse or former spouse were killed by guns. However, almost half (47%) of the boyfriends murdered by their partner and one out of five (20%) of the girlfriends murdered by their partner were killed with knives.

In "How Can Practitioners Help an Abused Woman Lower Her Risk of Death?" (*National Institute of Justice Journal*, no. 250, November 2003), Carolyn Rebecca Block of the Illinois Criminal Justice Information Authority investigates what factors present in abusive relationships might indicate a threat of the violence escalating to homicide. She finds that certain types of past violence directed against female intimates indicate an increased risk of homicide, especially choking. She also finds that recently abused women are more likely to be killed—half of women who were killed in 1995 and 1996 by their partners had experienced violence in the previous thirty days before the survey. Increasingly frequent violent incidents posed a higher risk of homicide.

Jacquelyn C. Campbell et al. evaluate in "Assessing Risk Factors for Intimate Partner Homicide" (*National Institute of Justice Journal*, no. 250, November 2003) the risk factors among abused women for being killed by their intimate partners. The researchers find that abused women whose abusers owned guns and who had threatened to kill them were at a high risk of being killed by their intimate partners. (See Figure 6.5.) Other high-risk factors for homicide include extreme jealousy, attempts to choke, and marital rape. Campbell et al. hope that the "danger assessment" tool they use may assist women and advocates for battered women to better assess the level of risk in abusive relationships.

FIGURE 6.4

Intimate homicide victims, by gender and type of weapon, 1976–2005

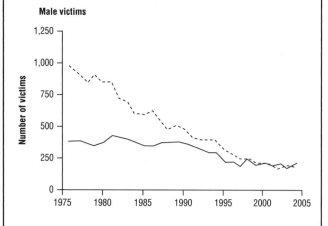

Male victims

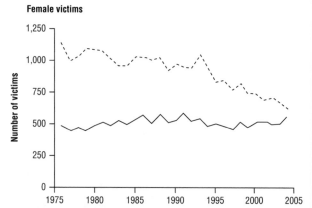

Female victims

SOURCE: James Alan Fox and Marianne W. Zawitz, "Intimate Homicide Victims by Type of Weapon, 1976–2005," in *Homicide Trends in the United States*, U.S. Department of Justice, Bureau of Justice Statistics, July 2007, http://www.ojp.usdoj.gov/bjs/homicide/intimates.htm (accessed June 26, 2008)

TABLE 6.11

Intimate homicides, by relationship and weapon type, 1990–2005

Relationship of victim to offender	Total	Gun	Knife	Blunt object	Force	Other weapon
Husband	100%	69%	26%	2%	1%	3%
Ex-husband	100	86	10	1	0	3
Wife	100	68	14	5	10	4
Ex-wife	100	77	12	3	5	3
Boyfriend	100	45	47	3	3	3
Girlfriend	100	56	20	5	14	5

SOURCE: James Alan Fox and Marianne W. Zawitz, "Homicides by Relationship and Weapon Type, 1990–2005," in *Homicide Trends in the United States*, U.S. Department of Justice, Bureau of Justice Statistics, July 2007, http://www.ojp.usdoj.gov/bjs/homicide/intimates.htm (accessed June 26, 2008)

FIGURE 6.5

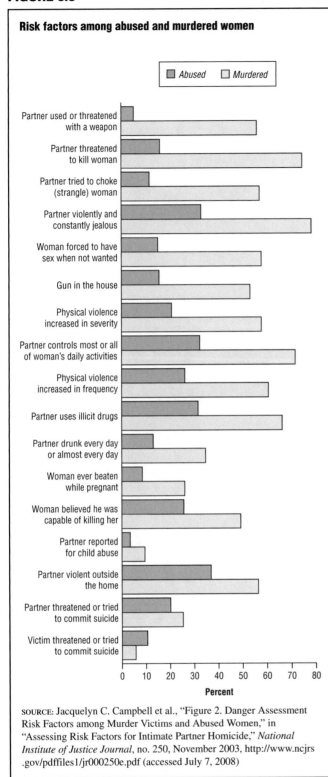

Risk factors among abused and murdered women

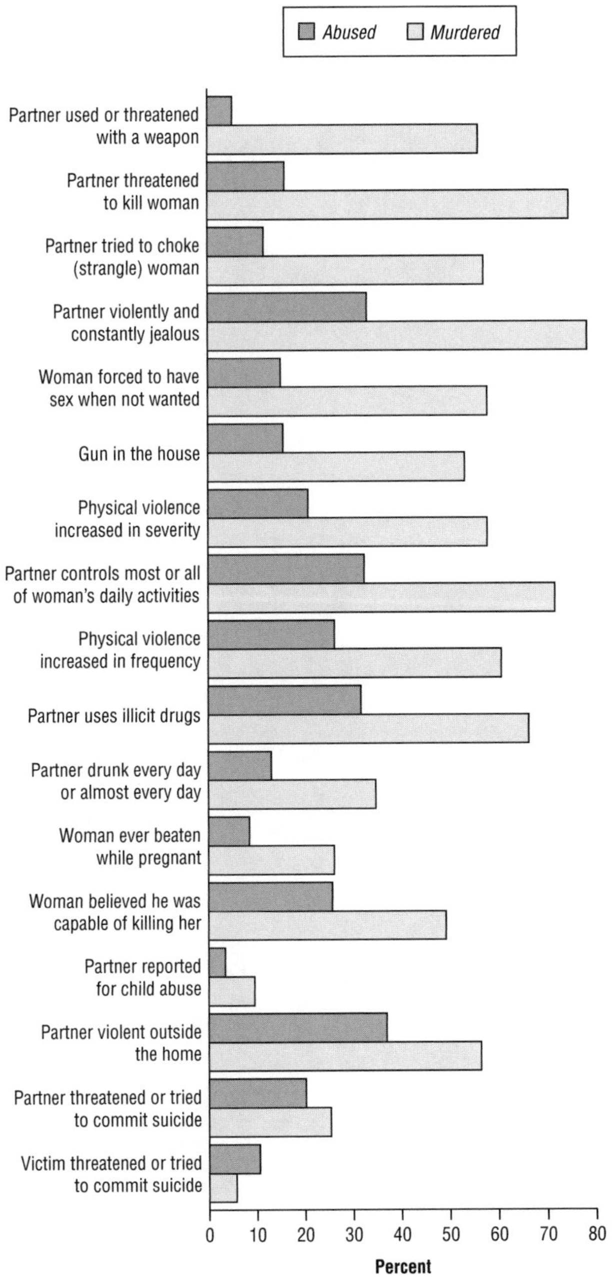
Abused
Murdered
Partner used or threatened with a weapon
Partner threatened to kill woman
Partner tried to choke (strangle) woman
Partner violently and constantly jealous
Woman forced to have sex when not wanted
Gun in the house
Physical violence increased in severity
Partner controls most or all of woman's daily activities
Physical violence increased in frequency
Partner uses illicit drugs
Partner drunk every day or almost every day
Woman ever beaten while pregnant
Woman believed he was capable of killing her
Partner reported for child abuse
Partner violent outside the home
Partner threatened or tried to commit suicide
Victim threatened or tried to commit suicide
0
10
20
30
40
50
60
70
80
Percent

SOURCE: Jacquelyn C. Campbell et al., "Figure 2. Danger Assessment Risk Factors among Murder Victims and Abused Women," in "Assessing Risk Factors for Intimate Partner Homicide," *National Institute of Justice Journal*, no. 250, November 2003, http://www.ncjrs.gov/pdffiles1/jr000250e.pdf (accessed July 7, 2008)

CHAPTER 7

CAUSES, EFFECTS, AND PREVENTION
OF DOMESTIC VIOLENCE

SOCIOLOGICAL THEORIES ON THE CAUSES OF DOMESTIC VIOLENCE

Researchers have studied domestic violence for about thirty years. Even though scholars from different intellectual traditions have varying theories on the causes of domestic violence, sociological explanations have gained wide acceptance.

Murray A. Straus explains in "A General Systems Theory Approach to a Theory of Violence between Family Members" (*Social Science Information*, vol. 12, no. 3, June 1973) that the general systems theory views violence as a system rather than as a result of individual mental disturbance. It describes a system of violence that operates at the individual, family, and societal levels. It views domestic violence as having many causes, including stereotyped family violence imagery learned in childhood and the fact that these stereotyped images are continually reaffirmed through social and cultural interactions. In fact, violent acts might generate positive feedback—in other words, they might achieve the desired results—leading to a perpetuation of violence.

According to the resource theory of domestic violence, the more resources (social, personal, and economic) a person can command, the more power he or she can potentially call on. The individual who is rich in terms of these resources has less need to use force in an open manner. In contrast, a person with little education, low job prestige and income, or poor interpersonal skills may use violence to compensate for a real or perceived lack of resources and to maintain dominance. For example, the 1985 National Family Violence Survey, which surveyed 6,002 households, showed that serious physical acts of wife abuse are more likely to occur in poorer homes. In the survey, families living at or below the poverty level had a rate of marital violence 500% greater than more affluent families. In "Neighborhood Environment, Racial Position, and Domestic Violence Risk:

Contextual Analysis" (*Public Health Reports*, vol. 118, no. 1, January–February 2003), Deborah N. Pearlman et al. of Brown University find a complex but strong relationship between poverty and domestic violence and speculate that one explanation for the increased risk of domestic violence in poorer neighborhoods might be differences in law enforcement availability and practices—that is, economically deprived communities might have less police notification, attention, and documentation.

The subculture of violence theory posits that some groups within society hold values that permit, and even encourage, the use of violence. Offered as an explanation of why some segments of society and some cultures are more violent than others, this theory is perhaps the most widely accepted theory of violence. In fact, some researchers believe attitudes about violence are shaped early in life, long before the first punch is thrown in a relationship. In "The Attitudes towards Violence Scale: A Measure for Adolescents" (*Journal of Interpersonal Violence*, vol. 14, no. 11, November 1999), Jeanne B. Funk et al. asked junior high and high school students attending an inner-city public school in a midwestern city about their attitudes toward violence. The researchers find that males endorsed more pro-violence attitudes independent of age, grade level, and ethnicity than did those students who identified themselves as victims of violence. African-American teenagers endorsed reactive violence (violence used in response to actual or perceived threats) at higher levels than other groups. Hispanics endorsed culture of violence measures, reflecting a pervasive identification with violence as a valued activity, at slightly higher levels than the teenagers as a group. Culture of violence measures included the belief that the world is a dangerous place where the best way to ensure survival is to be vigilant and prepared to take the offensive. Whites scored lower on measures of reactive violence as well as on total pro-violence attitudes. Funk et al. conclude that a combination of biological, environmental, and social influences are responsible for these findings.

FEMINIST THEORIES

Feminist theories of violence against women emphasize that patriarchal structures of gender-based inequalities of power in society are at the root of the problem. That is, the violence, rather than being an individual psychological problem, is instead an expression of male domination of females. Violence against women, in the feminist view, includes a variety of control tactics meant to control women.

Learned Gender Roles

Pointing to history, some feminist researchers see wife abuse as a natural consequence of women's second-class status in society. Among the first to express this viewpoint were R. Emerson Dobash and Russell Dobash in *Violence against Wives: A Case against the Patriarchy* (1979). The researchers argue that men who assaulted their wives were actually living up to roles and qualities expected and cherished in Western society (aggressiveness, male dominance, and female subordination) and that they used physical force as a means to enforce these roles. Many sociologists and anthropologists believe men are socialized to exert power and control over women. Some men may use both physical and emotional abuse to attain the position of dominance in the spousal relationship. Kristin L. Anderson and Debra Umberson state in "Gendering Violence: Masculinity and Power in Men's Accounts of Domestic Violence" (*Gender and Society*, vol. 15, no. 3, June 2001), a study of thirty-three male batterers, that "violence is ... an effective means by which batterers reconstruct men as masculine and women as feminine."

Donna Chung of the University of South Australia concludes in "Violence, Control, Romance, and Gender Equality: Young Women and Heterosexual Relationships" (*Women's Studies International Forum*, vol. 28, no. 6, 2005) that patriarchal belief systems combine with heterosexual norms and sometimes result in violence. She examines dating violence with a view to discerning the "structural factors" that influence the violent actions of young people within relationships. She argues that the "micropractices" of heterosexual relationships embody power relations between the genders. This inequality in power relationships at times results in intimate partner violence.

In "Girlfriend Abuse as a Form of Masculinity Construction among Violent, Marginal Male Youth" (*Men and Masculinities*, vol. 6, no. 1, July 2003), a study of thirty male adolescents, primarily gang members, Mark Totten of the Youth Services Bureau of Ottawa, Canada, finds another link between patriarchy and violence. He concludes that underprivileged males in society use violence toward women in response to their lack of access to the traditional benefits of patriarchy. Totten posits that the ideals of patriarchy—and the inability of these disenfranchised boys to wield any patriarchal power outside of their gangs or family groups—leads them to be violent toward their girlfriends as one way to define their masculinity. He states that "violence was one of the few resources over which they had control." However, he also suggests that "men with more resources can commit different, less visible forms of abuse."

STRUCTURE OF INTERPERSONAL RELATIONSHIPS THEORY

As seen in the previous discussion, many theories about the cause of domestic violence overlap somewhat. According to Joseph H. Michalski of the University of Western Ontario, in "Making Sociological Sense out of Trends in Intimate Partner Violence" (*Violence against Women*, vol. 10, no. 6, June 2004), many of the insights of other theories need to be integrated into a more comprehensive theory of the impact of the structure of relationships on domestic violence. He suggests that key risk factors of domestic violence include:

- Social isolation of the couple
- Separate peer support networks
- Inequality between partners
- Lack of relational distance, or a high degree of intimacy within a couple
- The centralization of authority—in other words, patriarchal dominance within a family
- Exposure to violence and violent networks

In "Explaining Intimate Partner Violence: The Sociological Limitations of Victimization Studies" (*Sociological Forum*, vol. 20, no. 4, December 2005), Michalski argues that distinctions need to be drawn between different types of violence in relationships. He indicates that there is a predatory type of violence, including what he calls "intimate terrorism," which may in fact be a type of male violence meant to control women. He also identifies "situational couple violence," which is violence that is in response to a particular conflict within a couple that has a fairly egalitarian relationship. The causes for each of these types of violence, he states, are very different.

DOES SUBSTANCE ABUSE CAUSE DOMESTIC VIOLENCE?

The role of alcohol and drug abuse in family violence is documented in many studies, and it is a factor in physical violence and stalking, according to researchers such as Pam Wilson et al., in "Severity of Violence against Women by Intimate Partners and Associated Use of Alcohol and/or Illicit Drugs by the Perpetrator" (*Journal of Interpersonal Violence*, vol. 15, no. 9, 2000). Even though researchers generally do not consider alcohol and drug use to be the cause of violence, they find that it can contribute to, accelerate, or increase aggression. A variety

TABLE 7.1

Violent victimizations, by offenders who appeared to be under the influence of drugs and/or alcohol and by type of crime, 2005

Perceived drug or alcohol use by offender	Percent of victimizations					
				Assault		
	Crimes of violence	Rape/sexual assault[a]	Robbery	Total	Aggravated	Simple
Total victimizations	100.0%	100.0%	100.0%	100.0%	100.0%	100.0%
Total (perceived to be under the influence of drugs or alcohol)	27.5	35.5	22.5	27.8	30.7	26.9
Under the influence of alcohol	14.1	10.5*	5.1*	15.6	14.9	15.8
Under the influence of drugs	7.0	16.7*	10.6	6.0	6.4	5.9
Under the influence of both drugs and alcohol	4.6	5.1*	5.4*	4.4	6.5	3.8
Under the influence of one, not sure which	1.6	3.2*	0.9*	1.6	2.7*	1.3
Not available whether drugs or alcohol	0.2*	0.0*	0.4*	0.2*	0.3*	0.1*
Not on alcohol or drugs	23.4	23.8	13.1	24.8	23.1	25.4
Don't know or not ascertained	49.2	40.6	64.4	47.4	46.2	47.7

Note: Detail may not add to total shown because of rounding.
*Estimate is based on about 10 or fewer sample cases.
[a]Includes verbal threats of rape and threats of sexual assault.

SOURCE: "Table 32. Personal Crimes of Violence, 2005: Percent Distribution of Victimizations by Perceived Drug or Alcohol Use by Offender," in *Criminal Victimization in the United States, 2005 Statistical Tables*, U.S. Department of Justice, Office of Justice Programs, Bureau of Justice Statistics, December 2006, http://www.ojp.usdoj.gov/bjs/pub/pdf/cvus05.pdf (accessed June 26, 2008)

of data sources establish a correlation (a complementary or parallel relationship) between substance abuse and violence, but a correlation does not establish a causation. In theory, and possibly even in practice, substance abuse may promote or provoke domestic violence, but both may also be influenced by other factors, such as environmental, biological, and situational stressors. Based on available research, it remains unclear whether substance abuse is a key factor in most domestic violence incidents.

In 2005, 14.1% of victims of violent assaults believed the offender had been using alcohol, 7% believed the offender had been using drugs, and 4.6% believed the offender had been under the influence of both. (See Table 7.1.) Another 1.6% thought the offender was under the influence of either drugs or alcohol. Only 23.4% of victims believed the offender had not used any drugs or alcohol, whereas another 49.2% reported they did not know.

According to Shannan Catalano of the Bureau of Justice Statistics, in *Intimate Partner Violence in the United States* (December 2007, http://www.ojp.usdoj .gov/bjs/intimate/ipv.htm#contents), 42.1% of victims of intimate partner violence stated the perpetrator had used alcohol or drugs. (See Figure 7.1.) Because these victims knew the perpetrator intimately, the proportion of victims who answered they did not know if the perpetrator was under the influence was smaller, at 22.9%. A third (35%) said the perpetrator had not used alcohol or drugs. Even though anecdotal evidence suggests that alcohol and drugs appear to be linked to violence and abuse, in controlled studies the connection is not as clear. In *Alcohol and Intimate Partner Violence* (March 2005, http://pubs .niaaa.nih.gov/publications/Social/Module8IntimatePartner Violence/Module8.html), the National Institute on Alcohol

FIGURE 7.1

Average annual percent of nonfatal intimate partner victimizations, by offender alcohol and drug use and victim gender, 2001–05

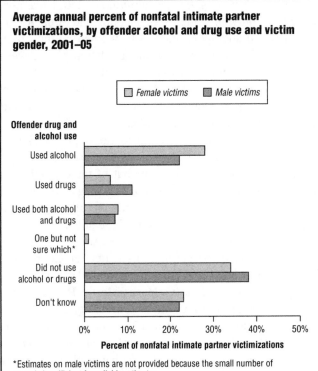

*Estimates on male victims are not provided because the small number of cases is insufficient for reliable estimates.

SOURCE: Shannan Catalano, "Average Annual Percent of Nonfatal Intimate Partner Victimizations, by Offender Alcohol and Drug Use and Victim Gender, 2001–2005," in *Intimate Partner Violence in the United States*, U.S. Department of Justice, Bureau of Justice Statistics, December 2007, http://www.ojp.usdoj.gov/bjs/intimate/circumstances .htm (accessed May 20, 2008)

Abuse and Alcoholism states that "alcohol is not a clearly identified direct cause of [intimate partner violence], though it clearly is a correlate and may be a contributing factor."

Richard J. Gelles and Mary M. Cavanaugh suggest in "Association Is Not Causation: Alcohol and Other Drugs Do Not Cause Violence" (Donileen R. Loseke, Richard J. Gelles, and Mary M. Cavanaugh, eds., *Current Controversies on Family Violence*, 2005) that substance abuse is not a cause of family violence—rather, it is often used as an excuse for family violence. Gelles and Cavanaugh argue that even though substantial evidence has linked alcohol and drug use to violence, there is little scientific evidence that alcohol or other drugs, such as cocaine, have pharmacological properties that produce violent and abusive behavior. The researchers maintain that alcoholism may be associated with intimate violence, but it is not a primary cause of the violence. They cite experiments using college students as subjects that have found that when the students thought they were consuming alcohol, they acted more aggressively than if they were told they had been given nonalcoholic drinks. According to Gelles and Cavanaugh, it is the expectation of the effects of alcohol that influences behavior, not the actual liquor consumed.

In "Risky Mix: Drinking, Drug Use, and Homicide" (*National Institute of Justice Journal*, no. 250, November 2003), a study of patterns of alcohol and drug use in murders and attempted murders of women by their partners, Phyllis Sharps et al. show a relationship between substance use and violence. They find that in the year before the violent incident, female victims used alcohol and drugs less frequently and consumed smaller amounts than did their male partners. Sharps et al. also note that during the homicide or attempted homicide, 31.3% of perpetrators consumed alcohol, 12.6% used drugs, and 26.2% used both. Less than one out of three (29.9%) of perpetrators used neither alcohol nor drugs. In contrast, perpetrators who abused their partners without attempting to kill them consumed alcohol 21% of the time, drugs 6.7% of the time, and both 5.8% of the time. Nearly two-thirds (65.8%) of perpetrators used neither alcohol nor drugs. Sharps et al. conclude that increased substance use results in more serious violence. Martie P. Thompson and J. B. Kingree of Clemson University agree. They find in "The Roles of Victim and Perpetrator Alcohol Use in Intimate Partner Violence Outcomes" (*Journal of Interpersonal Violence*, vol. 21, no. 2, 2006) that alcohol use among male batterers led to a significant increase in the likelihood that their partners would suffer injury in a violent incident.

Does Treatment Help?

According to Gregory L. Stuart et al., in "Reductions in Marital Violence Following Treatment for Alcohol Dependence" (*Journal of Interpersonal Violence*, vol. 18, no. 10, October 2003), after intensive inpatient treatment of male batterers for alcoholism, both alcohol consumption and levels of violence within families decreased. Not only did the frequency of husband-to-wife physical and psychological abuse decrease but also the frequency of wife-to-husband marital violence decreased significantly.

Gregory L. Stuart of Brown Medical School reviews in "Improving Violence Intervention Outcomes by Integrating Alcohol Treatment" (*Journal of Interpersonal Violence*, vol. 20, no. 4, April 2005) empirical and theoretical evidence to conclude that not only do most men in batterer intervention programs have problems with abusing alcohol but also that these men are at high risk for continuing to batter their intimate partners. He argues that combining alcohol treatment with batterer intervention programs would significantly improve recidivism rates.

DOES PREGNANCY EXACERBATE DOMESTIC VIOLENCE?

Research about intimate partner violence reveals that violence does not stop when women become pregnant. The Division of Reproductive Health at the Centers for Disease Control and Prevention (CDC) gathers data about the health of expectant mothers using its Pregnancy Risk Assessment Monitoring System (PRAMS). An analysis of PRAMS data (February 2006, http://www.cdc.gov/ReproductiveHealth/Products&Pubs/PDFs/Physical%20Violence.pdf) reveals that between 4% and 8% of women report being abused by their husband or partner in the year before they gave birth. Jana L. Jasinski of the University of Central Florida states in "Pregnancy and Domestic Violence: A Review of the Literature" (*Trauma, Violence, and Abuse*, vol. 5, no. 1, January 2004) that this estimate is too low because PRAMS asks limited questions about domestic violence and asks about abuse rather than about particular behaviors. Still, she argues, pregnancy does not appear to increase the risk of domestic violence, although more research into this question is needed.

Studies such as Julie Gazmararian et al.'s "Prevalence of Violence against Pregnant Women" (*International Journal of Gynecology and Obstetrics*, vol. 275, no. 24, June 1996) and Gazmararian et al.'s "Violence and Reproductive Health: Current Knowledge and Future Research Directions" (*Maternal and Child Health Journal*, vol. 4, no. 2, June 2000) estimate that higher rates of abuse of pregnant women—as many as 324,000 women per year and rates as high as 20% of pregnant women—have been reported. According to Gazmararian et al., in "Prevalence of Violence against Pregnant Women," higher abuse rates were reported later in pregnancy, with 7.4% to 20% of that violence occurring in the third trimester. The lowest rates were reported in a study of women with a higher socioeconomic status who were treated in a private clinic. The assailants were mainly intimate or former intimate partners, parents, or other family members. Two studies that also examined violence in the period after birth found that violence was more prevalent after birth than during pregnancy.

Jasinski suggests that violence directed toward pregnant women is usually part of an ongoing pattern of domestic violence. However, some factors do seem to increase the risk of violence for pregnant women. In "Prevalence of Violence against Pregnant Women," Gazmararian et al. find that women with unwanted pregnancies had 4.1 times the risk of experiencing physical violence by a husband or boyfriend during the months before delivery than did women with desired pregnancies. Loraine Bacchus, Gill Mezey, and Susan Bewley find in "A Qualitative Exploration of the Nature of Domestic Violence in Pregnancy" (*Violence against Women*, vol. 12, no. 6, June 2006) that abuse of pregnant women centered around financial worries, the woman's inability to be as physically and emotionally available during pregnancy, the lack of support of a male partner, and doubts about paternity. In "Police-Reported Intimate Partner Violence during Pregnancy: Who Is At Risk?" (*Violence and Victims*, vol. 20, no. 5, 2005), Sherry Lipsky et al. of the University of Washington, Seattle, find that certain factors put pregnant women at risk for police-reported intimate partner violence, including unmarried status, public health program use, smoking or alcohol use while pregnant, and having previously been pregnant or given birth.

According to Phyllis W. Sharps, Kathryn Laughon and Sandra K. Giangrande, in "Intimate Partner Violence and the Childbearing Year: Maternal and Infant Health Consequences" (*Trauma, Violence, and Abuse*, vol. 8, no. 2, 2007), intimate partner violence during pregnancy is associated with poorer maternal and infant health. Abuse during pregnancy is associated with an increased risk of preterm delivery, low birth-weight infants, and infant death. Abused pregnant women were more likely to experience vaginal bleeding, severe nausea and/or vomiting, dehydration, and kidney infections and/or uterine tract infections.

In "Pregnancy-Associated Violent Deaths: The Role of Intimate Partner Violence" (*Trauma, Violence, and Abuse*, vol. 8, no. 2, 2007), Sandra L. Martin et al. of the University of North Carolina, Chapel Hill, find that intimate partners are responsible for many, if not most, murders of pregnant women. Research in many U.S. cities indicates that about one out of twenty women killed by intimate partners is pregnant. Unsurprisingly, pregnant women who had previously experienced intimate partner violence were at a much higher risk for fatal violence.

EXPERIENCING VIOLENCE AS A CHILD

Research demonstrates a relationship between having been a victim of violence and becoming violent in future relationships. In fact, Shelby A. Kaura and Craig M. Allen of Iowa State University note in "Power and Dating Violence Perpetration by Men and Women" (*Journal of Interpersonal Violence*, vol. 19, no. 5, May 2004), a study of 352 male and 296 female undergraduate college students, that witnessing parental violence was the strongest predictor of perpetrating dating violence. Another study of college students found exceedingly high rates of abuse during college, especially of students who had been victimized in childhood or adolescence. During the first year of college, 23% of women who had not been victimized in the past were victimized physically, sexually, or both. However, 32% of students who had been victimized in childhood were abused in their first year of college, 42% of students who had been victimized in adolescence were abused, and 66% of students who were abused during both childhood and adolescence were abused during their first year of college (See Table 7.2.)

TABLE 7.2

College victimization, by prior victimization status

Victimization status	Type of abuse	Year 1 (%)	Year 2 (%)	Year 3 (%)	Year 4 (%)
None before college	Only physical	7	11	7	5
	Only sexual	13	4	8	5
	Physical and sexual	3	4	5	5
	Total	**23**	**19**	**20**	**16**
Childhood victimization but no adolescent victimization	Only physical	10	10	12	6
	Only sexual	17	4	13	11
	Physical and sexual	5	7	5	8
	Total	**32**	**21**	**30**	**25**
Adolescent victimization but no childhood victimization	Only physical	16	16	15	13
	Only sexual	22	13	12	14
	Physical and sexual	4	7	7	4
	Total	**42**	**36**	**34**	**31**
Childhood and adolescent victimization	Only physical	17	16	20	18
	Only sexual	27	17	16	12
	Physical and sexual	22	20	16	12
	Total	**66**	**53**	**52**	**42**

SOURCE: "Exhibit 1. College Student Study—College Victimization, by Prior Victimization Status," in *Research in Brief: Violence against Women: Identifying Risk Factors*, Office of Justice Programs, National Institute of Justice, November 2004, http://www.ncjrs.gov/pdffiles1/nij/197019.pdf (accessed June 28, 2008)

TABLE 7.3

Adult victimization, by whether sexually abused in childhood or adolescence

Prior victimization status	Sexually abused as adults (%)	Experienced some domestic violence (%)	Experienced severe domestic violence (%)
Not sexually abused in childhood or adolescence (=46)	28	60	42
Sexually abused in childhood but not in adolescence (=82)	38	62	42
Sexually abused in adolescence but not in childhoodi (=14)	50	79	64
Sexually abused in childhood and adolescence (=82)	75	97	84

SOURCE: "Exhibit 3. Child Sexual Abuse Study—Adult Victimization, by Prior Victimization Status," in *Research in Brief: Violence against Women: Identifying Risk Factors*, Office of Justice Programs, National Institute of Justice, November 2004, http://www.ncjrs.gov/pdffiles1/nij/197019.pdf (accessed June 28, 2008)

Another study looked at whether adults who experienced sexual abuse or domestic violence had been abused in childhood or adolescence. Over a quarter (28%) of adults who had not been abused before reaching adulthood were sexually abused as adults, whereas 75% of those who had been abused in childhood and adolescence were sexually abused as adults. (See Table 7.3.) Six out of ten women who had not been abused in childhood or adolescence experienced some domestic violence in adulthood, but nearly all (97%) of women who had been sexually abused in childhood and adolescence experienced some domestic violence in adulthood.

Dating Violence in Adolescence

Dating violence encompasses physical, sexual, or psychological violence in a dating relationship. Experiencing dating violence puts victims at a greater risk for engaging in risky sexual behavior, anorexia or bulimia, substance abuse, and suicide. It can also be an indicator that an adolescent is at risk for victimization in intimate relationships in adulthood.

According to Erika L. Lichte and Laura A. McCloskey of Harvard University, in "The Effects of Childhood Exposure to Marital Violence on Adolescent Gender-Role Beliefs and Dating Violence" (*Psychology of Women Quarterly*, vol. 28, no. 4, 2004), adolescents who were exposed to domestic violence during their childhood were in fact more likely to justify being violent in dating relationships. However, Lichte and McCloskey find that even more important in predicting dating violence was an adolescent's belief in traditional models of male-female relationships and the belief that violence was sometimes justified.

Mireille Cyr, Pierre McDuff, and John Wright of the Université de Montréal examined dating violence among a group of adolescent girls who had been sexually abused

as children and reported their findings in "Prevalence and Predictors of Dating Violence among Adolescent Female Victims of Child Sexual Abuse" (*Journal of Interpersonal Violence*, vol. 21, no. 8, 2006). Dating violence was more prevalent among these young women than other studies had found in a general population of female adolescents. Nearly half of the sexual abused teens reported that they had experienced physical violence in a dating relationship in the previous year. Certain characteristics of the abuse the girls had suffered made it even more likely for them to be the victims of physical violence, namely if the sexual abuse included penetration or physical violence. Cyr, McDuff, and Wright argue that difficulties that sexually abused youth have with intimate relationships, including a fear of intimacy and ambivalent attachment, might explain the higher levels of dating violence among this group.

The CDC's Youth Risk Behavior Surveillance system surveys students in grades nine to twelve on their experience of dating violence. Almost one out of ten (9.9%) students said they had been hit, slapped, or physically hurt on purpose by their boyfriend or girlfriend during the past year. (See Table 7.4.) Males were more likely to say they had experienced dating violence than were females, across all race and ethnic groups and age groups. A slightly smaller proportion of students said they had been forced to have sexual intercourse, but it was still an alarming 7.8%. Females were much more likely to say they had been forced to have sexual intercourse than were males across all race and ethnic groups and age groups.

AGE AND DOMESTIC VIOLENCE
Intimate Partner Violence Declines with Increasing Age

Studies show that intimate partner violence declines with advancing age. Analyzing National Crime Victimization Survey data, Catalano finds that in 2004 women aged twenty to twenty-four had 11.5 intimate partner victimizations per 1,000 women, compared to just 1.3 per 1,000 among women aged fifty and older. In "Nonlethal Intimate Partner Violence against Women: A Comparison of Three Age Cohorts" (*Violence against Women*, vol. 9, no. 12, 2003), Callie Rennison and Michael R. Rand also find lower rates of intimate partner violence in women over age fifty-four. They believe lower rates might be because of several factors, such as homicides of younger women, earlier divorces from abusive partners, or the turning of older perpetrators to other forms of victimization, such as psychological abuse or economic domination.

Effects of Abuse among Older Adults

In "The Nature and Impact of Domestic Violence across Age Cohorts" (*Affilia*, vol. 20, no. 3, 2005), Dina J. Wilke and Linda Vinton of Florida State University indicate that there were no differences among abused

TABLE 7.4

Percentage of high school students who experienced dating violence and who were ever physically forced to have sexual intercourse, by sex, race/ethnicity, and grade, 2007

	Dating violence[a]			Forced to have sexual intercourse[b]		
	Female	Male	Total	Female	Male	Total
Category	%	%	%	%	%	%
Race/ethnicity						
White[c]	7.4	9.3	8.4	11.0	3.2	7.0
Black[c]	13.2	15.2	14.2	13.3	7.8	10.5
Hispanic	10.1	12.0	11.1	11.4	6.2	8.8
Grade						
9	6.3	10.5	8.5	9.2	4.1	6.6
10	8.8	9.1	8.9	13.1	3.4	8.2
11	10.2	10.8	10.6	12.0	5.0	8.5
12	10.1	14.1	12.1	10.9	5.7	8.3
Total	**8.8**	**11.0**	**9.9**	**11.3**	**4.5**	**7.8**

[a]Hit, slapped, or physically hurt on purpose by their boyfriend or girlfriend during the 12 months before the survey.
[b]When they did not want to.
[c]Non-Hispanic.

SOURCE: "Table 11. Percentage of High School Students Who Experienced Dating Violence and Who Were Ever Physically Forced to Have Sexual Intercourse, by Sex, Race/Ethnicity, and Grade—United States, Youth Risk Behavior Survey, 2007," in "Youth Risk Behavior Surveillance—United States, 2007," *Morbidity and Mortality Weekly Report*, vol. 57, no. SS-4, June 6, 2008, http://www.cdc.gov/HealthyYouth/yrbs/pdf/yrbss07_mmwr.pdf (accessed June 28, 2008)

women of different ages in the severity of the abuse, the kind of injuries received, substance abuse at the time of the incidents, the likelihood that women would report the violence, or the rates of childhood abuse or depression. However, older women, on average, had endured abuse for a longer time. They were also more likely to be currently in violent relationships and to have health and mental health problems than were younger women.

WHY DO ABUSED WOMEN STAY?

One of the most frequently asked questions about abused women is: Why do they stay? Some authors and advocates argue that the relevant questions for battered women themselves are different. They believe this question implies there is something wrong with the woman for staying, rather than placing the blame where it belongs: on the batterer. Ola W. Barnett of Pepperdine University argues in "Why Battered Women Do Not Leave, Part 1" (*Trauma, Violence, and Abuse*, vol. 1, no. 4, 2000) that better questions might be: "Why does he beat her?" or "Why does society let him get away with it?" or "What can be done to stop him?"

However, not all women stay in abusive relationships. Many leave abusive relationships and situations without turning to the police or support organizations. Even though their number is unknown, most women who leave without asking for help usually have strong personal support systems of friends and family or employment and earnings that enable them to live economically independent of their abusive partner. Yet, there can be little question that a large percentage of women remain with their abuser. There are as many reasons women

stay as there are consequences and outcomes of abusive relationships.

Women's Reasons to Stay

Women stay in abusive relationships for a variety of reasons. A major reason women stay is their economic dependency on their batterer. Many women feel they are better off with a violent husband than facing the challenge of raising children on their own. Some harbor deep feelings for their abusive partner and believe that over time they can change their partner's behavior. Others mistakenly interpret their abuser's efforts to control their life as expressions of love. Some frequently reported practical considerations include:

- Most women have at least one dependent child who must be cared for.

- Many are unemployed.

- Their parents are either distant, unable, or unwilling to help.

- The women may fear losing mutual friends and the support of family, especially in-laws.

- Many have no property that is solely their own.

- Some lack access to cash, credit, or any financial resources.

- If the woman leaves, then she risks being charged with desertion and losing her children and joint assets.

- She may face a decline in living standards for herself and her children, and the children, especially older ones, may resent this reduced living standard.

- The woman and/or children may be in poor health.

- The abuser may have threatened or harmed her pets, as noted by Catherine A. Faver and Elizabeth B. Strand in "To Leave or to Stay? Battered Women's Concern for Vulnerable Pets" (*Journal of Interpersonal Violence*, vol. 18, no. 12, December 2003).

In "'We Don't Have Time for Social Change': Cultural Compromise and the Battered Woman Syndrome" (*Gender and Society*, vol. 17, no. 5, October 2003), Bess Rothenberg of Clemson University argues that women are victimized and coerced into staying in violent relationships by a combination of different forces. According to Rothenberg, women are victimized first and foremost by violent abusers; second, by a society that sanctions the right of men to hit women and socializes women into staying in abusive relationships; third, by representatives of institutions who are in a position to help but who instead ignore the plight of battered women (e.g., doctors, police, the criminal justice system, clergy, and therapists); and fourth, by the everyday realities of being a woman in a patriarchal system that expects women to raise children and denies them access to education, job skills, and good employment.

Similarly, April L. Few and Karen H. Rosen examine in "Victims of Chronic Dating Violence: How Women's Vulnerabilities Link to Their Decisions to Stay" (*Family Relations*, vol. 54, no. 2, April 2005) why women stay in abusive dating relationships and describe a combination of "relational" and "situational" vulnerabilities that work together to influence a woman's decision to stay. They define relational vulnerabilities as one's beliefs about what behaviors and interactions are normal in an intimate relationship. Situational vulnerabilities refer to the degree to which a woman was experiencing stress at the beginning of the abusive relationship (either as a consequence of life changes or as a consequence of feeling like one is getting too old for marriage or parenthood). Few and Rosen find that an accumulation of vulnerabilities, combined with lacking protective factors such as high self-esteem, a social support system, and healthy coping skills, made it more likely a woman would stay in a chronically abusive dating relationship.

The Role of Self-Blame

Ola W. Barnett, Tomas E. Martinez, and Mae Keyson explain in "The Relationship between Violence, Social Support, and Self-Blame in Battered Women" (*Journal of Interpersonal Violence*, vol. 11, no. 2, June 1996) that battered women often hold distorted beliefs and perceptions that tend to keep them in abusive relationships. Some women blame themselves for the violence; they believe that they cause the abuse and that they should be able to prevent it by changing their behavior. Others see the abuse as normal and rationalize the violence as "not that bad."

Escalating levels of violence in a relationship often lead to greater use of violence by the woman as a means of self-defense or retaliation. This can result in still more self-blame, because the woman feels she is at fault for the violence. It may also deter her from seeking help and prompt her to believe no help is available. External sources of support may be less inclined to help a woman who presents the problem as her fault; as a result, the self-blaming woman may receive less assistance from health and social service agencies and organizations. Breaking this vicious cycle requires counselors or advisers who can help the woman shift the blame to her abusive mate. In fact, some researchers, such as Kate Cavanagh of the University of Glasgow in "Understanding Women's Responses to Domestic Violence" (*Qualitative Social Work*, vol. 2, no. 3, 2003), suggest that even though women may blame themselves when the abuse begins, as the frequency and severity of violence increases, they do eventually begin to assign the blame to the perpetrator.

The Role of Fear

Many women fear that attempting to end an abusive relationship will lead to even worse violence. Research shows this fear of reprisal is well founded. As Lenore E. Walker explains in *Terrifying Love: Why Battered Women Kill and How Society Responds* (1989), batterers often panic when they think women are going to end the relationship. In the personal stories women told Walker, they repeatedly related that after calling the police or asking for a divorce, their partners' violence escalated.

Walker observes that in an abusive relationship it is often the man who is desperately dependent on the relationship. Battered women are likely to feel that the batterer's sanity and emotional stability are their responsibility—that they are their partner's only link to the normal world. Walker alleges that almost 10% of abandoned batterers committed suicide when their partners left them.

It appears, however, that more batterers become homicidal than suicidal. Angela Browne, in "When Battered Women Kill," and Kirk Williams, in "Resource Availability for Women at Risk and Partner Homicide" (both published in *Law and Society Review*, vol. 23, 1989), find that more than 50% of all female homicide victims were murdered by a former abusive male partner. Barnett emphasizes that evidence consistently demonstrates that after women leave abusive partners they often continue to be assaulted, stalked, and threatened and that leaving provokes some batterers to kill their partners. In "How Can Practitioners Help an Abused Woman Lower Her Risk of Death?" (*National Institute of Justice Journal*, no. 250, November 2003), Carolyn Rebecca Block of the Illinois Criminal Justice Information Authority concurs that an attempt to leave can escalate domestic violence. She finds that 45% of homicides of a woman by a man were in response to the woman trying to leave her abusive partner.

The Battered Woman Syndrome

In *The Battered Woman* (1979), Lenore E. Walker claims that abused women suffer from a constellation of symptoms—the so-called battered woman syndrome—that keeps them from leaving abusive partners. She argues that a psychological condition known as learned helplessness plays a significant role in keeping women in abusive relationships. Even though Walker recognizes, as do other multiple-victimization theorists, that women are victims of a patriarchal society and institutions that fail to advocate for abused women, she emphasizes the psychological problems women develop in response to abuse.

The concept of learned helplessness was articulated by Martin E. P. Seligman. In *Helplessness: On Depression, Development, and Death* (1992), Seligman describes how he conducted an experiment in which he taught dogs to fear the sound of a bell. He did so by restraining a dog, ringing the bell, and then subjecting the dog to a painful (but not dangerous) shock. This process was repeated many times.

Next, to test the effectiveness of the training, Seligman placed the dog in a cage with a floor that could be electrified. One wall of the cage was low enough that the dog could jump over it if it wished. Seligman then rang the bell and administered shocks through the floor. He expected that the dog would jump out of the cage. However, most of the dogs did not. Seligman theorized this was because their earlier experience, where they had been shocked with no possibility of escape, had taught them that they were helpless.

Seligman called this learned helplessness. He and other psychologists theorize that it also occurs in humans, with similar effects. In *Battered Woman*, Walker contends that battered women have learned through their life experiences that they are helpless to escape or avoid violence. These battered women are conditioned to believe that they cannot predict their safety and that nothing can be done to fundamentally change their situation. They become passive, submissive, depressed, overwhelmingly fearful, and psychologically paralyzed. Walker emphasizes that even though they do not respond with total helplessness, they narrow their choices, choosing the ones that seem to have the greatest likelihood of success.

In "The Battered Woman Syndrome Is a Psychological Consequence of Abuse" (Richard J. Gelles and Donileen R. Loseke, eds., *Current Controversies on Family Violence*, 1993), Walker claims that battered woman syndrome is common among severely abused women and that it is part of the recognized pattern of psychological symptoms called posttraumatic stress dis-

order (PTSD). Normally, fear and the responses to fear abate once the feared object or circumstance is removed. People who have suffered a traumatic event, however, often continue to respond to the fear with flashbacks and violent thoughts long after the event has passed. Symptoms of PTSD may include difficulty in thinking clearly and a pessimistic outlook, memory distortions, intrusive memories, sleep and eating disorders, and medical problems associated with persistent high levels of stress. Over time, the more aggressive symptoms diminish and are replaced by more passive, constrictive symptoms, making the affected women appear helpless. The abused woman's outlook often improves, however, when she regains some degree of power and control in her life.

Women Are Not Helpless

Beginning in the 1980s a number of critics emerged who argued that the emphasis on psychological problems of abuse victims was an inadequate explanation of domestic violence. Lee H. Bowker surmises in "A Battered Woman's Problems Are Social, Not Psychological" (Gelles and Loseke, eds., *Current Controversies on Family Violence*, 1993) that women remain trapped in violent marriages because of conditions in the social system rather than because they suffer from psychological problems. According to Bowker, battered women are not as passive as they are portrayed in abuse literature and routinely take steps to make their life safer or to escape abuse. Bowker views husbands' unwillingness to stop being dominant and a lack of support from traditional social institutions as the factors that delay battered women in escaping from abuse.

External Barriers to Leaving

Barnett suggests that battered women face many obstacles to leaving abusive relationships. She states that many of these barriers are external—in other words, not because of an individual or psychological problem with the abused woman. Barnett outlines many external obstacles to an abused woman's quest to leave her partner, including:

- The patriarchal structure of society—when men control all of a family's resources, women may be economically powerless.

- Problems with the criminal justice system—the U.S. criminal justice system is underfunded and tends not to enforce legislation prohibiting the abuse of women. The lack of adequate funding keeps battered women from getting legal assistance. Police decisions to arrest or not arrest batterers tend to be inconsistent; when police do not arrest, it impedes women's attempts to leave and leaves them vulnerable to further abuse. Barnett notes that only a quarter of batterers are arrested, about one-third of those arrested are prosecuted, and only 1% of those prosecuted serve jail time beyond the time served at arrest. Orders of protection are ineffective because most judges will not enforce them.

- Child custody and visitation—women fear losing their children if they report intimate partner violence. A report of domestic violence can trigger an investigation by child protective services. When women do retain custody of their children, judges usually do not take intimate partner violence into account when writing visitation orders. Court-ordered visitation is often used by abusers as an opportunity for further battering.

Internal and Psychological Barriers to Leaving

In "Why Battered Women Do Not Leave, Part 2" (*Trauma, Violence, and Abuse*, vol. 2, no. 1, 2001), Barnett outlines several internalized socialization beliefs (normal, learned beliefs about how society and relationships work) as well as psychological factors induced by trauma that serve as obstacles to battered women leaving their abuser. Barnett emphasizes that many of these beliefs are detrimental to all women—but battered women are particularly vulnerable. Among them are:

- Gender-role socialization—society values male traits more than female traits and often devalues female gender roles. As girls age into adolescence, they begin to lose self-confidence as they turn to romantic relationships for a sense of self-worth. When an adult woman values her ability to form a relationship with a male partner over other characteristics, losing the relationship may seem worse than staying and enduring the abuse.

- Distorted beliefs and perceptions—as previously mentioned, battered women tend to hold some distorted beliefs that keep them in abusive relationships. Common distorted thought patterns among battered women include a belief that violence is commonplace and not abusive, a belief that they caused the abuse, a lack of recognition that children are harmed more by witnessing intimate partner violence than by living with a single parent, and a belief that they can and should help the abuser to change.

- PTSD—this is a prolonged psychological reaction to a traumatic event. The level of psychological distress abused women experience can keep them from being able to escape the violence.

- Impaired problem-solving abilities—many factors can impede the problem-solving abilities of battered women, including postconcussion syndrome resulting from head injuries and the cognitive distortions of PTSD.

- Prior victimization effects—women who have been abused during their childhood have an increased risk of becoming involved with an abusive intimate partner in adulthood. This may be because these women

have difficulty judging how trustworthy people are, or they hold a distorted belief that they cannot escape violence.

WHAT CAN A WOMAN DO?

Cavanagh gathered qualitative data from interviews with the female partners of violent men to illustrate that battered women try to end the violence in their relationships in many ways, even if they stay—complicating the notion of the battered woman as passive and helpless. She finds that women worked to stop the violence by talking with their partner about the violence, developing strategies for avoiding the violence (e.g., being affectionate or feigning agreement with the abuser), challenging the violence (e.g., fighting back, verbally or physically), telling other people about the violence, and leaving (usually temporarily) the relationship. Cavanagh argues that abused women almost always actively fight the abuse: "At some points in time the struggle to change took second place to the struggle to survive but not even women subjected to the extremes of abuse totally 'gave up.'"

Avoidance

For their landmark book *Intimate Violence* (1988), Richard J. Gelles and Murray A. Straus interviewed 192 women who suffered minor violence and 140 who suffered severe violence and asked which long-range strategies they used to avoid violence. Fifty-three percent of the minor-violence victims and 69% of the severe-violence victims learned to avoid issues they thought would anger their partner. Others learned to read a change in their partner's facial expressions or body language as one of the first signs of impending abuse. Avoidance worked for about 68% of those women who suffered minor abuse, but this tactic was successful for less than one-third of the more severely abused victims.

Leaving

Some battered women do leave their husband. Gelles and Straus find that 70% had left their spouse in the year preceding the interview. Only about half of those who left, however, reported that this was a "very effective" method of ending the abuse. In fact, for one out of eight women it only made things worse. Batterers put incredible pressure on their partner to return. Often, when the women returned they were abused more severely than before—as revenge or because the men learned that, once again, they could get away with this behavior. Women who returned also risked losing the aid of personal and public support systems, because these people perceived that their help or advice was useless or ignored.

Just Say "No"

Many researchers believe there is real truth to the statement that men abuse because they can. A wife who will not permit herself to be beaten from the first act of minor abuse, such as a slap or push, is the most successful in stopping it. Gelles and Straus note that simply eliciting a promise to stop was by far the most effective strategy women could undertake—especially in cases of minor violence. Threatening to divorce or leave the home worked in about 40% of the minor-abuse cases, but this strategy worked in less than 5% of the severe-abuse situations. Physically fighting back was the most unsuccessful method. It worked in fewer than 2% of the minor-abuse cases and in less than 1% of the severe-abuse cases.

HEALTH EFFECTS OF DOMESTIC VIOLENCE

There are often urgent and long-term physical and health consequences of domestic violence. Short-term physical consequences include mild to moderate injuries, such as broken bones, bruises, and cuts. More serious medical problems include sexually transmitted diseases, miscarriages, premature labor, and injury to unborn children, as well as damage to the central nervous system sustained as a result of blows to the head, including traumatic brain injuries, chronic headaches, and loss of vision and hearing. The medical consequences of abuse are often unreported or underreported because women are reluctant to disclose abuse as the cause of their injuries, and health professionals are uncomfortable inquiring about it.

In "Does Physical Intimate Partner Violence Affect Sexual Health" (*Trauma, Violence, and Abuse*, vol. 8, no. 2, April 2007), Ann L. Coker of the University of Texas Health Science Center undertook a systematic review of studies that looked at whether domestic violence affected women's sexual health. She found that a causal connection could be made between intimate partner violence and unplanned pregnancies and abortions, sexually transmitted infections, sexual dysfunction, such as lack of sexual pleasure, and sexual risk taking, including failure to use condoms or partner nonmonogamy.

Abused women are also at risk for health problems not directly caused by the abuse. Jacquelyn Campbell et al. compare in "Intimate Partner Violence and Physical Health Consequences" (*Archives of Internal Medicine*, vol. 162, no. 10, 2002) the physical health problems of abused women to a control group of women who had never suffered abuse. The researchers find that abused women suffered from 50% to 70% more gynecological, central nervous system, and stress-related problems. Examples of stress-related problems included chronic fear, headaches, back pain, gastrointestinal disorders, appetite loss, and increased incidence of viral infections such as colds. Even though women who most recently suffered physical abuse reported the most health problems, Campbell et al. find evidence that abused women remain less healthy over time.

Posttraumatic Stress Disorder

Women who have been abused are at risk for developing PTSD. According to the National Institute of Health, in "Post-Traumatic Stress Disorder" (June 26, 2008, http://www.nimh.nih.gov/health/publications/anxiety-disorders/post-traumatic-stress-disorder.shtml), PTSD symptoms include startling easily, emotional numbness (especially in relationships), irritability or aggressiveness, avoidance of situations that are similar to the traumatic event, and reliving the trauma in flashbacks and nightmares.

The development of PTSD may lead to some of the adverse health outcomes associated with intimate partner violence. Studies such as Mary Ann Dutton et al.'s "Intimate Partner Violence, PTSD, and Adverse Health Outcomes" (*Journal of Interpersonal Violence*, vol. 21, no. 7, 2006) and Stephanie J. Woods's "Intimate Partner Violence and Post-Traumatic Stress Disorder Symptoms in Women: What We Know and Need to Know" (*Journal of Interpersonal Violence*, vol. 20, no. 4, 2005) show that victims of intimate partner violence have up to five times a greater likelihood of having or developing PTSD, as well as a host of other mental health problems such as depression and substance abuse. Some researchers estimate that between 31% and 84% of all battered women develop PTSD. The more severe the violence, the higher the likelihood that a woman will develop the disorder.

According to Dutton et al., "PTSD ... appears to be a linchpin in the relationship between exposure to violence and negative health outcomes." The researchers postulate that PTSD, which has been shown to lead to negative health behaviors, has consequences on battered women's health. These consequences may result from not adhering to a doctor's instructions or from specific coping strategies to deal with PTSD. In addition, biological responses to PTSD may contribute to an increase in blood pressure or a suppression of the immune system.

WHEN WOMEN KILL THEIR PARTNERS

James Alan Fox and Marianne W. Zawitz indicate in *Homicide Trends in the United States* (July 2007, http://www.ojp.usdoj.gov/bjs/homicide/homtrnd.htm#contents) that in 2005, 1,181 women and 329 men were killed by an intimate partner. The researchers note that the number of males killed by intimate partners dropped 74.8% between 1976 and 2005. Researchers and advocates for battered women attribute this dramatic decline to the widespread availability of support services for women, including shelters, crisis counseling, hotlines, and legal measures such as protection and restraining orders. These services offer abused women options for escaping violence and abuse other than taking their partner's life. Other factors that may have contributed to the decline are the increased ease of obtaining divorce and the generally improved economic conditions for women.

Factors That Influence Wives to Murder Their Husbands

In *When Battered Women Kill* (1987), one of the first studies of wives who murdered their abusive partners, Angela Browne compares forty-two women charged with murdering or seriously injuring their spouse with 205 abused women who had not killed their husband. Browne's findings suggest a link between homicide potential and three things: marital rape, murder and suicide threats, and drug use. In her study, more than 75% of women who had committed homicide claimed they were forced to have sexual intercourse with their husband, compared to 59% in the group of women who had not killed their husband. Some 39% of the former group had been raped more than twenty times, compared to 13% of the latter group. One woman Browne interviewed said, "It was as though he wanted to annihilate me ... as though he wanted to tear me apart from the inside out and simply leave nothing there."

In addition, men murdered by their spouse had often threatened to kill their partner. In Browne's study 83% of the men killed by their spouse had threatened to kill their spouse, compared to 59% of the men whose spouse did not kill them. Men killed by their spouse had used guns to frighten their spouse and were sometimes killed with their own weapon. Nearly two-thirds (61%) of this group also threatened to kill themselves. Many of the threats were made when women tried to leave the relationship or when the men were depressed. Browne questioned whether the suicide threats were genuine expressions of wishes to die or whether they were used to manipulate the women in efforts to make them feel guilty and prevent them from leaving.

Legal Defense

In legal cases involving battered women who kill their abuser, the defendants often admit to the murder and reveal a history of physical abuse. The charge is usually first- or second-degree murder, which is murder with malicious intent either with or without premeditation. The outcome of these trials depends on three main issues: self-defense, equal force, and immediate versus imminent danger. Expert witnesses are crucial in an abused woman's trial to explain how these issues are different for cases involving battered women than for other homicide cases.

SELF-DEFENSE. Women often plead that they killed in self-defense, a plea that requires proof that the woman used such force as was necessary to avoid imminent bodily harm. Self-defense was originally intended to cover unexpected attacks by strangers and did not take into account a past history of abuse or a woman's fear of renewed violence. Traditionally applied, a self-defense plea does not exonerate a woman who kills during a lull

in the violence, for example, when the drunken abuser passes out.

According to Diane R. Follingstad et al. of the University of South Carolina, in "The Impact of Elements of Self-Defense and Objective versus Subjective Instructions on Jurors' Verdicts for Battered Women Defendants" (*Journal of Interpersonal Violence*, vol. 12, no. 5, October 1997), many observers feel that self-defense law is problematic, inadequate, and/or not appropriate for use in self-defense cases of battered women. Traditionally, self-defense permits an individual to use physical force when he or she reasonably believes it is necessary to counteract imminent or immediate danger of serious bodily harm. Furthermore, a person must use only a reasonable amount of force to stop the attack and cannot be the one who provoked the encounter or initiated the violence. To justify the use of reciprocal deadly force, most jurisdictions require that the defendant reasonably believes the attacker is using or is about to use deadly force.

Advocates for battered women have succeeded in convincing many courts to accept a subjective standard of determining whether a battered woman who killed her husband was protecting her own life. This concession allows the court to judge the circumstances of the crime in relation to the special needs of battered women and not according to the strict definition of self-defense. This looser definition is especially important for women who killed during a lull in the violence, because a strict interpretation of imminent danger does not provide legal justification for their actions.

Gena Rachel Hatcher explains in "The Gendered Nature of Battered Woman Syndrome: Why Gender Neutrality Does Not Mean Equality" (*New York University Annual Survey of American Law*, vol. 10, no. 27, March 2003) that for this modified definition of self-defense to work, the court must first be subjective in understanding the woman's circumstances. Next, it must be objective in deciding that, given the situation, she truly did act in a reasonable manner. Courts have already accepted the notion that self-defense does not require perfect judgment in a violent situation, only reasonableness. In *Brown v. United States* (256 U.S. 335 [1921]), Justice Oliver Wendell Holmes (1841–1935) said: "Detached reflection cannot be demanded in the presence of an uplifted knife." Battered women and their advocates have asked the courts to revise their definitions of imminent danger and appropriate force in cases involving domestic violence.

EQUAL FORCE. Self-defense permits the use of equal force, which is defined as the least amount of force necessary to prevent imminent bodily harm or death. Women, however, who are generally physically weaker than men and who know the kind of physical damage their batterer can inflict, may justifiably feel that they are protecting their life when shooting an unarmed man. In

State v. Wanrow (88 Wash.2d 221, 559 P.2d 548 [1977]), the Washington Supreme Court ruled that it was permissible to instruct the jury that the objective standard of self-defense does not always apply.

Yvonne Wanrow was sitting up at night fearful that a male neighbor, who she thought had molested the child in her care, was going to make good on his threats to break into the house where she was staying. When the large, intoxicated man did enter, Wanrow, who was incapacitated with a broken leg, shot him. The court ruled:

> The respondent was entitled to have the jury consider her actions in the light of her own perceptions of the situation, including those perceptions which were the product of our nation's "long and unfortunate history of sex discrimination." Until such time as the effects of that history are eradicated, care must be taken to assure that our self-defense instructions afford women the right to have their conduct judged in light of the individual physical handicaps which are the product of sex discrimination. To fail to do so is to deny the right of the individual woman involved to trial by the same rules which are applicable to male defendants.

IMMEDIATE VERSUS IMMINENT DANGER. Traditionally, self-defense required that the danger be immediate, meaning that the danger was present at the moment the decision to respond was made, to justify the use of force, as noted by Kimberly Kessler Ferzan of Rutgers University in "Defending Imminence: From Battered Women to Iraq" (*Arizona Law Review*, vol. 46, 2004). Accepting imminent danger, or danger that is about to occur, as justification for action permits the jury to understand the motivations and dynamics of a battered woman's behavior. A history of abuse may explain why a defendant might react to the threat of violence more quickly than a stranger would in the same circumstances. In *Wanrow*, the Washington Supreme Court found that "it is clear that the jury is entitled to consider all of the circumstances surrounding the incident in determining whether the defendant had reasonable grounds to believe grievous bodily harm was about to be inflicted."

LEGAL OUTCOMES. Whether a woman will be convicted depends largely on the jury's attitude, or the judge's disposition when it is not a jury trial, and the amount of background and personal history of abuse that the judge or jury is permitted to hear. Juries that have not heard expert witnesses present the battered woman defense are often unsympathetic to women who kill their abusive partner.

In "Jurors' Decisions in Trials of Battered Women Who Kill: The Role of Prior Beliefs and Expert Testimony" (*Journal of Applied Psychology*, vol. 24, 1994), Regina Schuller, Vicki L. Smith, and James M. Olson find that jurors who learned about battered woman syndrome from expert testimony were more likely to believe the defendant feared for her life, that she was in danger,

and that she was trapped in the abusive relationship. Equipped with knowledge and understanding of battering and its effects, jurors handed down fewer murder convictions than were issued by a control group of jurors who were not given this specialized information.

PREVENTION OF DOMESTIC VIOLENCE
Empowerment of Battered Women

Researchers and advocates find that one of the most effective ways to deal with partner violence is by giving the victim the power, encouragement, and support to stop it. In "Estrangement, Interventions, and Male Violence toward Female Partners" (*Violence and Victims*, vol. 12, no. 1, spring 1997), Desmond Ellis and Lori Wight of York University assert that abused women want the violence to stop and most, if not all, attempt to do something to stop it. They find evidence showing that empowerment of abused women is related to a decrease in the likelihood of further violence. The interventions Ellis and Wight recommend to promote gender equality include:

- Social service agencies such as counselors or shelters to provide information and support

- Mediation to facilitate a woman's control over the process

- Prosecution with an option to drop the charges, which also facilitates control by female victims

- Separation, which indicates the woman's strength in decision making

Ellis and Wight find that separation or divorce is one of the most effective strategies for ending abuse. Levels of violence after separation vary with the type of legal separation or divorce proceedings. Women who participate in mediation before separation are less likely to be harmed, either physically or emotionally, than women whose separation is negotiated by lawyers. Ellis and Wight find that other legal proceedings, such as restraining orders and protection orders, were relatively ineffective in protecting female abuse victims.

In "Survivor Preferences for Response to IPV Disclosure" (*Clinical Nursing Research*, vol. 14, no. 3, 2005), Jacqueline Dienemann, Nancy Glass, and Rebecca Hyman examine how intimate partner violence survivors want to be treated when disclosing the violence to health care professionals. The researchers find that surveyed survivors want to be treated with respect and concern when disclosing intimate partner violence. They also want health care professionals to document the abuse and provide protection. The women say they want to retain control over their options. They believe health care professionals should listen, present choices, and ultimately leave the decision about what to do up to the victim herself.

CHAPTER 8
RAPE AND STALKING

Historically, because women have been viewed as the possessions of their fathers and husbands, sexual abuse of a woman has been considered a violation of a man's property rights rather than a violation of a woman's human rights. However, primarily through the efforts of women's advocacy groups worldwide, in most countries rape is no longer viewed as a violation of family honor but as an abuse and violation of women. In most countries rape is now considered a crime. The United Nations' (UN) Declaration on the Elimination of Violence against Women (December 20, 1993, http://www.unhchr.ch/huridocda/huridoca.nsf/(Symbol)/A.RES.48.104.En?Opendocument) specifically names marital rape, sexual abuse of female children, selling women into slavery or prostitution, and other acts of sexual violence against women in its condemnation of "any act of gender-based violence that results in, or is likely to result in, physical, sexual or psychological harm or suffering to women, including threats of such acts, coercion or arbitrary deprivation of liberty, whether occurring in public or in private life." In December 2007 the UN adopted a resolution to intensify efforts to eliminate rape and sexual violence.

RAPE IN THE UNITED STATES

In *Extent, Nature, and Consequences of Rape Victimization: Findings from the National Violence against Women Survey* (January 2006, http://www.ncjrs.gov/pdffiles1/nij/210346.pdf), an analysis of data from the National Violence against Women Survey (NVAWS), Patricia Tjaden and Nancy Thoennes of the Center for Policy Research in Denver, Colorado, estimate that 302,091 women are raped each year and that 17.7 million women have been raped in their lifetime, compared to 92,748 men who are raped each year and 2.8 million men who have been raped in their lifetime. (See Table 8.1.) Native American and Alaskan Native women have the highest rate of having been raped in their lifetime (34.1%), followed by African-American women (18.8%),

non-Hispanic white women (17.9%), and Hispanic women (11.9%). (See Table 8.2.)

Tjaden and Thoennes find that most female victims of rape had been raped by a current or former intimate partner. One out of five (20.2%) had been raped by a spouse or former spouse, 4.3% by a cohabiting partner or former partner, and 21.5% by a date or former date. (See Figure 8.1.) Male victims tended to be raped by acquaintances. Only 4.1% of males had been raped by a spouse or former spouse, 3.7% by a current or former cohabitating partner, and 2.7% by a date or former date. In fact, Tjaden and Thoennes note that 7.7% of all women, but only 0.4% of all men, had ever been raped by a current or former intimate partner.

Justice System Outcomes

Tjaden and Thoennes find that the overwhelming majority of rapes are unreported to police, and women raped by intimate partners are even less likely to report rapes to the police than are women raped by nonintimate partners. Only 18% of women raped by intimates reported the rape, compared to 20.9% of women raped by nonintimates. (See Table 8.3.) Of the women who did not report to the police, 22.1% said they were too afraid of the rapist, 18.1% said they were too ashamed, 17.7% said it was a minor incident, 12.6% said the police could not do anything, and 11.9% said the police would not believe them. (See Table 8.4.) Almost one out of ten (8.6%) said it was because the perpetrator was a husband, family member, or friend.

When women did call the police, police took a report only 79.8% of the time, and in 8.3% of the cases, the police did nothing. (See Table 8.3.) In 46.4% of the cases the perpetrator was arrested or detained. The perpetrator was prosecuted in only 32.1% of reported cases; only 36.4% of those prosecutions resulted in a conviction. Of those convicted rapists, 33.3% did not go to jail.

TABLE 8.1

Women and men raped during their lifetime and/or in a selected 12-month period in 1995–96

| | Percentage | | Number[a] | |
| | | | Women
(100,697,000) | Men
(92,748,000) |
Rape timeframe	Women[b]	Men[b]		
Raped in lifetime[c]	17.6	3.0	17,722,672	2,782,440
Raped in previous 12 months	0.3	0.1	302,091	92,748

[a]Estimates are based on women and men age 18 and older.
[b]Sample size=8,000.
[c]Difference between women and men is statistically significant.
Notes: Lifetime prevalence rates for women in this exhibit are based on survey records of 6,999 women who were administered a version of the survey questionnaire that contains separate questions about attempted rape and completed rape. The remaining 1,001 women were administered versions of the questionnaire that combine questions about attempted rape and completed rape. Because it is impossible to distinguish attempted rape and completed rape from the combined questions, the corresponding 1,001 survey records were excluded when attempted rape and completed rape rates for women were calculated. The 1,001 survey records also were excluded when the total lifetime rape rate for women presented here was calculated.

SOURCE: Patricia Tjaden and Nancy Thoennes, "Exhibit 1. Percentage and Number of Women and Men Who Were Raped in Lifetime and Previous 12 Months," in *Extent, Nature, and Consequences of Rape Victimization: Findings from the National Violence against Women Survey*, U.S. Department of Justice, Office of Justice Programs, National Institute of Justice, January 2006, http://www.ncjrs.gov/pdffiles1/nij/210346.pdf (accessed June 2, 2008)

TABLE 8.2

Women and men who were raped in their lifetime, by race/ethnicity, 1995–96

Victims' gender	Non-Hispanic white (%)	Hispanic white (%)	African-American (%)	American Indian/Alaska Native (%)	Mixed race (%)	Asian/Pacific Islander (%)
Women[a]	17.9 (n=6,217)	11.9 (n=235)	18.8 (n=780)	34.1 (n=88)	24.4 (n=397)	6.8 (n=133)
Men	2.8 (n=6,250)	—[b] (n=174)	3.3 (n=659)	—[b] (n=105)	4.4 (n=406)	—[b] (n=165)

[a]Difference between Hispanic white and mixed-race women and between American Indian/Alaska Native and all other non-Asian/Pacific Islander women is statistically significant.
[b]Estimates were not calculated on five or fewer victims.
Notes: Rates for women in this exhibit are based on 8,000 records of survey data. n=sample size.

SOURCE: Patricia Tjaden and Nancy Thoennes, "Exhibit 8. Percentage of Women and Men Who Were Raped in Lifetime by Race/Ethnicity," in *Extent, Nature, and Consequences of Rape Victimization: Findings from the National Violence against Women Survey*, U.S. Department of Justice, Office of Justice Programs, National Institute of Justice, January 2006, http://www.ncjrs.gov/pdffiles1/nij/210346.pdf (accessed June 2, 2008)

RAPE BY AN INTIMATE PARTNER

Rape has little to do with the sexual relations associated with love and marriage. Rape is an act of violence by one person against another. It is an act of power that aims to hurt at the most intimate level. Rape is a violation, whether it occurs at the hands of a stranger or within the home at the hands of an abusive husband or partner.

Judith McFarlane and Ann Malecha of Texas Woman's University report in *Sexual Assault among Intimates: Frequency, Consequences and Treatments* (October 2005, http://www.ncjrs.gov/pdffiles1/nij/grants/211678.pdf) that intimate partner sexual assault is common and that as many as a quarter of women surveyed report being sexually assaulted by an intimate partner at some time. Sexual assault is especially common among physically abused women; 68% of the abused women in the research study also reported sexual assault. Four out of five (79%) of these women reported multiple assaults. The consequences for these women were severe. After a sexual assault by an intimate partner, 27% of the women increased their use of alcohol, drugs, or cigarettes, 15% contracted a sexually transmitted disease, and 22% reported threatening or attempting suicide within ninety days of the initial assault. The children of these mothers also suffer from depression and exhibit more behavioral problems than other children.

Because rape frequently occurs in relationships plagued by other types of abusive behavior, some researchers view it as just another expression of intimate partner violence. Amy D. Marshall and Amy Holtzworth-Munroe of Indiana University investigated the relationship between two forms of sexual aggression—coerced sex (persuading or pressuring the victim into having sex) and threatened/forced sex—and husbands' physical and psychological aggressiveness. They report their findings in "Varying Forms of Husband Sexual Aggression: Predictors and Subgroup Differences" (*Journal of Family Psychology*, vol. 16, no. 3, 2002). The researchers interviewed 164 couples and evaluated husbands using their own self-reports and their wife's reports on three measures: the revised Conflict Tactics Scale, a questionnaire called the Sexual Experiences Survey, and the Psychological Maltreatment of Women Inventory, a fifty-eight-item measure of psychological abuse.

Marshall and Holtzworth-Munroe find that "husbands' physical and psychological aggression predicted husbands' sexual coercion, but only physical aggression predicted threatened/forced sex." Husbands who were rated as generally violent and antisocial engaged in the most threatened and forced sex. Interestingly, even the subtype of physically nonviolent men was found to have engaged in some sexual coercion in the year preceding the study. The researchers conclude that their findings underscore the need to consider sexual aggression as a form of intimate partner abuse. They also call for research to determine the extent to which sexual coercion precedes and predicts threatened and forced sex and whether this association holds true for all relationships or only for those relationships in which there are other forms of violence.

MARITAL RAPE

Attitudes about Marital Rape

Historically, wives were considered the property of the husband, and therefore rape of a wife was viewed as

FIGURE 8.1

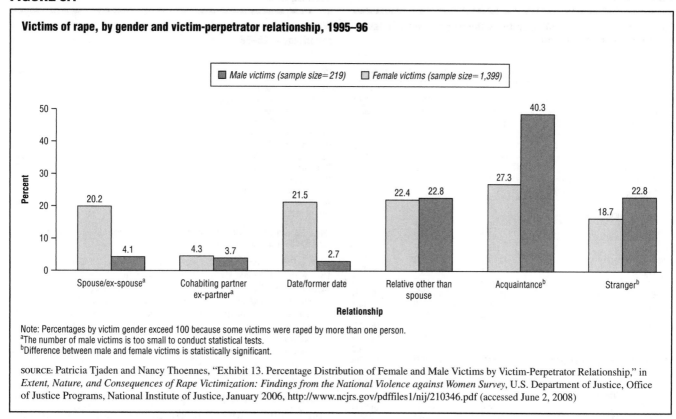

Victims of rape, by gender and victim-perpetrator relationship, 1995–96

Note: Percentages by victim gender exceed 100 because some victims were raped by more than one person.
[a]The number of male victims is too small to conduct statistical tests.
[b]Difference between male and female victims is statistically significant.

SOURCE: Patricia Tjaden and Nancy Thoennes, "Exhibit 13. Percentage Distribution of Female and Male Victims by Victim-Perpetrator Relationship," in *Extent, Nature, and Consequences of Rape Victimization: Findings from the National Violence against Women Survey*, U.S. Department of Justice, Office of Justice Programs, National Institute of Justice, January 2006, http://www.ncjrs.gov/pdffiles1/nij/210346.pdf (accessed June 2, 2008)

impossible. No husband still living with his wife was prosecuted for marital rape in the United States until 1978—and at that time, marital rape was a crime in only five states, as reported by Jennifer A. Bennice and Patricia A. Resick of the University of Missouri, St. Louis, in "Marital Rape: History, Research, and Practice" (*Trauma, Violence, and Abuse*, vol. 4, no. 3, July 2003). By 1993 marital rape under some conditions was recognized in all fifty states. In thirty-three states, however, there are exemptions from prosecution if, for example, the husband does not use force or if the woman is legally unable to consent because of a severe disability. There is still a tendency in the legal system to consider marital rape far less serious than either stranger or acquaintance rape.

Public attitudes toward rape in marriage have been slow to change, with many people believing that marital rape is not "real rape." Kathleen C. Basile of Georgia State University examines in "Attitudes toward Wife Rape: Effects of Social Background and Victim Status" (*Violence and Victims*, vol. 17, no. 3, 2002) variables that might predict specific attitudes about wife rape: beliefs about the occurrence and frequency of forced sex by a husband on his wife and whether respondents would classify various scenarios as constituting rape. Basile chose to analyze data from a nationally representative telephone survey of 1,108 adults to produce more widely applicable findings.

Survey respondents were asked whether they "think husbands ever use force, like hitting, holding down, or using a weapon, to make their wives have sex when the wife doesn't want to" to find out if they thought wife rape occurs. Respondents who answered "yes" to this question were asked how often they thought this occurs to gauge their perceptions of the frequency of wife rape. They also listened to descriptions of three scenarios of forced sex: two scenarios involved forced sex between husband and wife and the other was a woman forced to have sex with someone with whom she was previously intimate. The respondents were asked whether they considered each scenario to be an instance of rape.

Basile finds that 73% of respondents believed that wife rape occurs, 18% thought it does not occur, and 5% were unsure. Among those who thought wife rape occurs, 38% said it happens often, and an additional 40% felt it happens somewhat often. Fifteen percent felt wife rape is infrequent and 4% said it is a rare occurrence. The older the respondents, the less likely they were to believe that wife rape occurs, and white respondents were 2.5 times more likely to believe that wife rape occurs than African-Americans and other minorities. Women thought wife rape occurs more frequently than did men and, predictably, victims were more than twice as likely as nonvictims to feel that wife rape occurs.

Even though Basile finds that, overall, Americans were more likely than not to recognize forced sex on a

TABLE 8.3

Female rape cases, by justice system outcomes and victims' level of intimacy with rapist, 1995–96

Outcome	Intimate (%)	Nonintimate (%)	Total
Rape was reported to police	(n=461)	(n=273)	(n=734)
Yes	18.0	20.9	19.1
No	82.0	79.1	80.9
Identity of reporter[a, b]	(n=84)	(n=57)	(n=141)
Victim	78.3	59.6	70.2
Other	21.7	40.4	29.8
Police response	(n=84)	(n=57)	(n=141)
Took report	79.8	73.7	75.9
Arrested/detained perpetrator	46.4	40.4	43.3
Referred case to prosecutor/court[b]	40.5	24.6	33.3
Referred victim to victim services[b]	39.3	29.8	34.8
Gave victim advice[b]	42.9	19.2	32.6
Did nothing	8.3	12.2	9.9
Perpetrator was prosecuted[a]	(n=81)	(n=54)	(n=135)
Yes	32.1	44.4	37.0
No	67.9	55.6	63.0
Perpetrator was convicted[b,c]	(n=33)	(n=21)	(n=54)
Yes	36.4	61.9	46.2
No	63.6	38.1	53.8
Perpetrator was sentenced to jail[d]	(n=12)	(n=13)	(n=25)
Yes	66.7	84.6	76.0
No	33.3	15.4	24.0
Victim obtained restraining order[b]	(n=452)	(n=257)	(n=709)
Yes	17.7	4.7	13.0
No	82.3	95.3	87.0
Perpetrator violated restraining order[e]	(n=80)	(n=11)	(n=91)
Yes	68.8	45.5	65.9
No	31.3	54.5	34.1

Note: Estimates are based on the most recent rape since age 18.
n=sample size.
[a]Estimates are based on responses from victims whose rape was reported to the police.
[b]Difference between intimates and nonintimates is statistically significant.
[c]Estimates are based on responses from victims whose rapist was prosecuted.
[d]Estimates are based on responses from victims whose rapist was convicted.
[e]Estimates are based on responses from victims who obtained a restraining order.

SOURCE: Patricia Tjaden and Nancy Thoennes, "Exhibit 21. Percentage Distribution of Female Rape Victims by Justice System Outcomes and Whether Rapist Was Intimate or Nonintimate," in *Extent, Nature, and Consequences of Rape Victimization: Findings from the National Violence against Women Survey*, U.S. Department of Justice, Office of Justice Programs, National Institute of Justice, January 2006, http://www.ncjrs.gov/pdffiles1/nij/210346.pdf (accessed June 2, 2008)

TABLE 8.4

Women's failure to report rape to the police by reason for not reporting, 1995–96

Reason	Percent
Reported to someone else	1.5
One-time incident, last incident	2.9
Did not want perpetrator arrested	2.9
Did not want police or court involved	3.5
Too young to understand	4.4
Handled it myself	7.7
Perpetrator was husband, family member, friend	8.6
Police would not believe me or would blame me	11.9
Police could not do anything	12.6
Minor incident; not a crime or police matter	17.7
Too ashamed or embarrassed	18.1
Fear of rapist	22.1

Notes: Estimates are based on the most recent rape since age 18. Total percentages exceed 100 because some victims had multiple responses.

SOURCE: Patricia Tjaden and Nancy Thoennes, "Exhibit 22. Percentage Distribution of Female Victims Who Did Not Report Rape to the Police by Reason for Not Reporting," in *Extent, Nature, and Consequences of Rape Victimization: Findings from the National Violence against Women Survey*, U.S. Department of Justice, Office of Justice Programs, National Institute of Justice, January 2006, http://www.ncjrs.gov/pdffiles1/nij/210346.pdf (accessed June 2, 2008)

wife by her husband as rape, the variations she discovered in attitudes toward the two marital rape scenarios prompted her to observe that many Americans still feel victims play some part in their own victimization.

In "The Effect of Participant Sex, Victim Dress, and Traditional Attitudes on Causal Judgments for Marital Rape Victims" (*Journal of Family Violence*, vol. 20, no. 3, June 2005), Mark A. Whatley of Valdosta State University also investigates attitudes toward whether marital rape victims "deserved" to be raped. Participants in the study read a fiction account of a marital rape in which the victim was dressed either somberly or seductively. Male participants in the study rated the victim more "deserving" of the attack than did female participants. The seductively dressed victim was rated more responsible for the attack by all participants. Participants who held more traditional attitudes toward marriage were more likely to hold the victim responsible than were participants with more egalitarian attitudes toward marriage.

HOW OFTEN DOES MARITAL RAPE OCCUR? Available data about marital rape and intimate partner violence in general are limited. Callie Marie Rennison of the Bureau of Justice Statistics (BJS) cautions in *Intimate Partner Violence and Age of Victim, 1993–99* (October 2001, http://www.ojp.usdoj.gov/bjs/pub/pdf/ipva99.pdf) that marital status may relate directly to a survey respondent's willingness to reveal violence at the hands of an intimate partner or spouse. For example, a married woman may be afraid to report her husband as the offender or she may be in a state of denial—unable to admit to herself or to others that her husband has victimized her.

In the landmark study *Rape in Marriage* (1990), Diana E. H. Russell reports on interviews with a random sample of 930 women in the San Francisco area. Of all the women who had been married, 14% had been raped by their spouse at least once. Of this number, one-third reported being raped once, one-third reported between two and twenty incidents, and one-third said they had been raped by their spouse more than twenty times.

According to Russell, the first incident of rape usually occurred in the first year of marriage. Data from the NVAWS confirm that most rapes perpetrated against women by intimate partners occur in ongoing, not terminated, relationships. Only 6.3% of rapes by intimate partners occur exclusively after the end of the relationship,

FIGURE 8.2

Women who were raped by a former intimate partner by point in relationship when rape(s) occurred, 1995–96

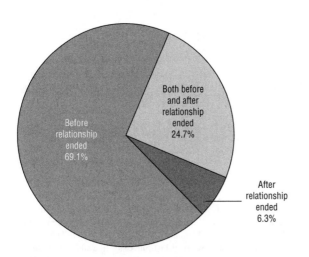

Note: Estimates are based on responses from women who were raped by a former spouse/cohabiting partner since age 18. If a woman was raped by more than one former spouse/cohabiting partner since age 18, information about the former spouse/cohabiting partner who raped her most recently was used.

SOURCE: Patricia Tjaden and Nancy Thoennes, "Exhibit 16. Percentage Distribution of Female Former Intimate Partner Rape Victims by Point in Relationship When Rape(s) Occurred," in *Extent, Nature, and Consequences of Rape Victimization: Findings from the National Violence against Women Survey*, U.S. Department of Justice, Office of Justice Programs, National Institute of Justice, January 2006, http://www.ncjrs.gov/pdffiles1/nij/210346.pdf (accessed June 2, 2008)

69.1% occur before the relationship has ended, and 24.7% occur both before and after a relationship has ended. (See Figure 8.2.) Even though marital rape occurred more frequently in spousal relationships where emotional and physical abuse were present, it could also happen in marriages where there was little other violence.

According to the BJS, in *Criminal Victimization in the United States, 2005 Statistical Tables* (December 2006, http://www.ojp.usdoj.gov/bjs/pub/pdf/cvus05.pdf), the perpetrator of rapes and sexual assaults is often an intimate partner. In 2005, 26.1% of rapes and sexual assaults counted in the survey were perpetrated by an intimate partner. Over one-third (34.7%) were perpetrated by a friend or acquaintance and 31.4% were perpetrated by a stranger. Shannan Catalano of the BJS states in *Intimate Partner Violence in the United States* (December 2007, http://www.ojp.usdoj.gov/bjs/intimate/ipv.htm#contents) that between 2001 and 2005, 7.2% of women were raped and 1.9% were sexually assaulted by their intimate partner.

EFFECTS OF MARITAL RAPE. Contrary to the traditional belief that victims of marital rape suffer few or no consequences, research reveals that women may suffer serious long-term medical and psychological consequences from this form of abuse. In *Marital Rape* (March 1999), a review of the relevant research, Raquel Kennedy Bergen reports rape-related genital injuries, such as lacerations (tears), soreness, bruising, torn muscles, fatigue, vomiting, unintended pregnancy, and infection with sexually transmitted diseases. Victims who had been battered before, during, or after the rape suffered broken bones, black eyes, bloody noses, and knife wounds, as well as injuries sustained when they were kicked, punched, or burned.

The short-term psychological effects are similar to those experienced by other victims of sexual assault and include anxiety, shock, intense fear, suicidal thinking, depression, and posttraumatic stress disorder (PTSD). However, marital rape victims reportedly suffer higher rates of anger and depression than women raped by strangers, perhaps because the violence was perpetrated by a person they had loved and trusted to not harm them. Long-term consequences include serious depression, sexual problems, and emotional pain that lasts years after the abuse. Jennifer A. Bennice et al. note in "The Relative Effects of Intimate Partner Physical and Sexual Violence on PTSD Symptomatology" (*Violence and Victims*, vol. 18, no. 1, February 2003) that marital rape survivors are more likely than other battered women to suffer the debilitating effects of PTSD, even when controlling for the severity of the beatings.

As is true with other violent acts, marital rape prompts some women to leave their husband. Bergen reports that women from selected ethnic groups, such as Hispanics, appeared less likely to characterize forced sex as rape and consequently were less likely to accuse or flee their spouse. The fact that married women do leave their abuser, however, was confirmed by an analysis of National Crime Victimization Surveys data that compared marital status of survey respondents from one survey with the next. Rennison finds that over a six-month period, more than one-third (38%) of women who had been violently victimized by a spouse had separated or divorced from their husband six months later.

ACQUAINTANCE RAPE

According to a number of widely publicized studies, young women are at high risk of sexual assault by acquaintances or boyfriends. Studies find rates ranging from a low of 15% for rape to a high of 78% for unwanted sexual aggression. For example, in "Rates and Risk Factors for Sexual Violence among an Ethnically Diverse Sample of Adolescents" (*Archives of Pediatrics and Adolescent Medicine*, vol. 158, no. 12, December 2004), Vaughn I. Rickert et al. find that of their sample of 689 adolescents and young adults, 30% reported having had an unwanted sexual experience in the past year, including verbal sexual coercion, rape, or attempted rape by a date or acquaintance. Other studies, such as Victoria L. Banyard et al.'s "Revisiting Unwanted Sexual Experiences on Campus: A 12-Year

Follow-Up" (*Violence against Women*, vol. 11, no. 4, April 2005), indicate that the number of rapes on college campuses has remained fairly steady since the late 1980s. Researchers surmise that acquaintance rape is especially underreported because the victims believe that nothing can or will be done, feel unsure about how to define the occurrence, or are uncertain about whether the action qualified as abuse.

Date rape is considered a form of acquaintance rape (as opposed to intimate partner rape), especially if the perpetrator and victim have not known one another for long and the abuse begins early in the relationship. In "Adolescent Dating Violence and Date Rape" (*Current Opinion in Obstetrics and Gynecology*, vol. 14, no. 5, October 2002), a review of research and literature about date rape, Vaughn I. Rickert, Roger D. Vaughan, and Constance M. Wiemann observe that female teens aged sixteen to nineteen years old and women aged twenty to twenty-four are not only four times as likely to be raped as women of other ages but also that teens who have experienced rape or attempted rape during adolescence are twice as likely to experience an additional assault when they are college age.

Rickert, Vaughan, and Wiemann also focus on high-risk subgroups of adolescents that, although less often studied, appear to experience high rates of date rape and other dating violence. They cite academically under-performing teens as at high risk, with 67% of female students and 33% of male students in a high school dropout prevention program admitting to having experienced or perpetrated dating violence, including sexual abuse and rape.

College Rape

In *Sexual Victimization of College Women* (December 2000, http://www.ncjrs.gov/pdffiles1/nij/182369.pdf), Bonnie S. Fisher, Francis T. Cullen, and Michael G. Turner find a disturbingly high rate of rapes among college women. Their study was based on a national telephone survey of 4,446 randomly selected women attending colleges and universities in the fall of 1996. Respondents were asked between late February and early May 1997 if they had experienced sexual victimization "since school began in fall 1996." The researchers find that in that period of almost seven months, 2.8% of the women had experienced either an attempted or completed rape. They suggest that the data show that nearly 5% of women college students are victimized in a given calendar year and that the percentage of attempted or completed rape victimizations of college women during their college careers approaches one in four. Fisher, Cullen, and Turner conclude that even though the 2.8% figure might "seem" low, "from a policy perspective, college administrators might be disturbed to learn that for every 1,000 women

FIGURE 8.3

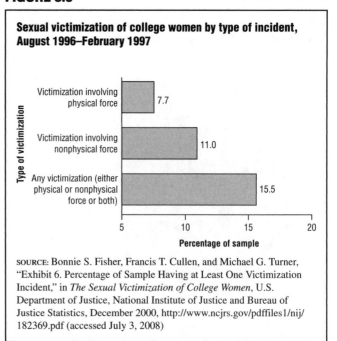

Sexual victimization of college women by type of incident, August 1996–February 1997

SOURCE: Bonnie S. Fisher, Francis T. Cullen, and Michael G. Turner, "Exhibit 6. Percentage of Sample Having at Least One Victimization Incident," in *The Sexual Victimization of College Women*, U.S. Department of Justice, National Institute of Justice and Bureau of Justice Statistics, December 2000, http://www.ncjrs.gov/pdffiles1/nij/182369.pdf (accessed July 3, 2008).

attending their institutions, there may well be 35 incidents of rape in a given academic year.... For a campus with 10,000 women, this would mean the number of rapes could exceed 350."

Fisher, Cullen, and Turner also asked respondents about other types of sexual victimization. They find that 1.7% of their sample had been victims of completed sexual coercion (unwanted sexual penetration with the threat of punishment or promise of reward), 1.3% had been victims of attempted sexual coercion, 1.9% had been victims of unwanted completed sexual contact with force or the threat of force, and 1.8% had been victims of completed sexual contact without physical force. Smaller percentages of women had been sexually threatened. Figure 8.3 displays the data slightly differently, showing that 7.7% of college women surveyed had experienced sexual victimization involving physical force, 11% had experienced sexual victimization involving nonphysical force, and 15.5% had experienced any victimization since the start of the academic year.

Fisher, Cullen, and Turner also find that fewer than 5% of the rapes and attempted rapes had been reported to police, and even lower percentages of other types of sexual victimization were reported. (See Table 8.5.) These numbers confirm other researchers' findings, including those of Bonnie S. Fisher et al. in "Reporting Sexual Victimization to the Police and Others: Results from a National-Level Study of College Women" (*Criminal Justice and Behavior*, vol. 30, no. 1, February 2003), that students overwhelmingly do not report acquaintance rapes or attempted rapes. According to the Centers for Disease Control and Prevention, the term *hidden rape* has

TABLE 8.5

College women's reasons for not reporting sexual victimization to police, by type of incident, 1996

Type of incident	Incident was not reported %	Reason for not reporting incident*											
		Did not want family to know %	Did not want other people to know %	Lack of proof that incident happened %	Fear of being treated hostilely by police %	Fear of being treated hostilely by other parts of justice system %	Not clear it was a crime or that harm was intended %	Did not know how to report %	Police wouldn't think it was serious enough %	Police wouldn't want to be bothered %	Afraid of reprisal by assailant or other %	Did not think it was serious enough to report %	Other %
Completed or attempted													
Completed rape	95.2	44.4	46.9	42.0	24.7	6.2	44.4	13.6	27.2	25.9	39.5	65.4	7.4
Attempted rape	95.8	32.4	32.4	30.9	8.8	1.5	39.7	7.4	33.8	13.2 (9)	25.0 (17)	76.5 (52)	1.5 (1)
Completed sexual coercion	100.0	41.9	43.8	33.3	8.6	1.9	58.1	14.3	24.8	21.9	31.4	71.4	1.9
Attempted sexual coercion	100.0	21.2	19.5	15.9	2.7	2.7	46.9	6.2	28.3	18.6	11.5	86.7	0
Completed sexual contact with force or threat of force	99.2	19.5	16.4	21.9	9.4	0	37.5	7.0	37.5	30.5	22.7	81.3	3.1
Completed sexual contact without force	98.5	4.7	11.7	18.0	4.7	1.6	43.0	5.5	29.7	18.8	12.5	91.4	0.8
Attempted sexual contact with force or threat of force	97.0	13.8	21.9	23.1	8.8	6.3	37.5	10.0	31.3	22.5	23.8	80.0	2.5
Attempted sexual contact without force	99.3	7.2	10.2	18.1	4.4	1.4	39.6	6.1	22.9	18.4	10.9	88.4	2.7
Threats													
Threat of rape	90.5	26.3	34.2	31.6	13.2	7.9	39.5	13.2	34.2	31.6	26.3	65.8	2.6
Threat of contact with force or threat of force	90.0	22.2	20.0	20.0	8.9	4.4	51.1	13.3	37.8	26.7	17.8	68.9	4.4
Threat of penetration without force	100.0	20.0	22.0	24.0	4.0	4.0	46.0	6.0	30.0	30.0	12.0	88.0	2.0
Threat of contact without force	98.7	6.8	8.1	21.6	8.1	6.8	31.1	2.7	21.6	9.5	13.5	83.8	0

*Percentages may be greater than 100 because a respondent could give more than one response.

SOURCE: Bonnie S. Fisher, Francis T. Cullen, and Michael G. Turner, "Exhibit 12. Reasons for Not Reporting Incident to the Police, by Type of Victimization," in *The Sexual Victimization of College Women*, U.S. Department of Justice, National Institute of Justice and Bureau of Justice Statistics, December 2000, http://www.ncjrs.gov/pdffiles1/nij/182369.pdf (accessed July 3, 2008)

been used to describe this finding of widespread unreported and underreported sexual assault. Anecdotal reports from college and university administrators suggest that many female students who have been raped not only fail to report the offense but also drop out of school.

Influence of Alcohol on Sexual Assault

Alcohol reduces inhibitions and, in some cases, enhances aggression, so it is not surprising that researchers examine the link between alcohol and sexual assault. In "Alcohol and Sexual Assault in a National Sample of College Women" (*Journal of Interpersonal Violence*, vol. 14, no. 6, June 1999), Sarah E. Ullman, George Karabatsos, and Mary P. Koss examine how drinking before an assault influenced the severity of the attack.

The researchers administered a questionnaire to 3,187 college-age women, more than half of whom had been victims of rape, attempted rape, unwanted sexual contact, or sexual coercion. They measured the participants' alcohol use, the severity of the sexual attack, the social context in which the assault occurred, and the victims' familiarity with the offender. As expected, victims who reported getting drunk more often also reported more severe assaults ("more severe" meaning, for example, the completion of the rape but not necessarily a more aggressive, forceful, or violent attack) than those who were drunk less often. Neither the victim's family income nor how well the victim knew the offender was related to the severity of the attack, although older women experienced more severe victimization.

Ullman, Karabatsos, and Koss also find that alcohol's role in predicting the severity of an attack did not vary according to how well the victim knew her attacker or whether a social situation, such as a party, was the setting for the assault—with one exception. Unplanned social situations were associated with more severe assaults when offenders were not drinking before the assault than when they were drinking. The victim's use of alcohol was related to the severity of the attack in cases where the rapist was not drinking. According to Ullman, Karabatsos, and Koss, this finding suggests that intoxicated victims may be targeted by offenders, who perceive an opportunity to engage in sex without having to use coercive behaviors.

As anticipated, Ullman, Karabatsos, and Koss find that victims who abused alcohol or offenders and victims who used alcohol before the attack suffered higher rates of severe assaults (completion of the rape). They also find that offender drinking was related to more aggressive offender behavior and more severe victimization, suggesting that more violent assaults occurred when assailants had been drinking. Conversely, victim drinking was related to less offender aggression and violence, possibly because force was not needed to complete the rape of intoxicated victims.

Not all researchers find that the use of alcohol by offenders increases the severity of sexual assaults. Leanne R. Brecklin and Sarah E. Ullman of the University of Illinois, Chicago, find in "The Role of Offender Alcohol Use in Rape Attacks: An Analysis of National Crime Victimization Survey Data" (*Journal of Interpersonal Violence*, vol. 16, no. 1, January 2001) that alcohol use of offenders did not affect victim physical injury or need for medical attention. They also find that alcohol use was related to less completed rape. They suggest, however, that alcohol use might be indirectly associated with injury outcomes, because offenders using alcohol were more likely to assault in more dangerous situations (assaulting at night and outdoors, and attacking strangers).

According to Ullman, Karabatsos, and Koss, of the 54.2% of women who had experienced some sexual victimization, 53.4% reported that their assailants were using alcohol at the time of the incident, and 42% reported that they themselves were using alcohol. Nearly four out of ten (39.7%) of the assaults occurred during dates with men that the women knew well or moderately well. Most assaults were committed without weapons, although 40% of the men used physical force. More than 90% of the victims said they attempted to resist the assault.

Overall, Ullman, Karabatsos, and Koss's findings indicate that alcohol use by victims and offenders before an assault plays direct and indirect roles in the severity of assaults, but generally the woman's drinking behavior contributes less strongly to the outcome of the attack.

Sexual Coercion

Sexual coercion is generally considered any situation in which one person uses verbal or physical methods to obtain sex or sexual activity without consent of the other. In "College Women's Experiences of Sexual Coercion: A Review of Cultural, Perpetrator, Victim, and Situational Variables" (*Trauma, Violence, and Abuse*, vol. 5, no. 2, April 2004), Leah E. Adams-Curtis and Gordon B. Forbes of Millikin University argue that coercive sexual behavior must be understood within prevalent sexual values on college campuses, including attitudes toward women, beliefs about sexual behavior, rape-supporting beliefs, coercion-supporting peer groups such as fraternities and athletic teams, gender concepts of both victims and perpetrators, and sexual promiscuity and its link with alcohol.

Adams-Curtis and Forbes posit that sexual coercion has its roots in traditional sex roles and expectations. Perpetrators of sexual coercion are not psychopaths, but men not particularly different from other men. Instead, the researchers state, "We view sexual coercion as a complex, multiply determined, social behavior that has its origins in normal heterosexual interactions. . . . The factors influencing the progression from normal sexual negotiations to coercive sexuality are often commonplace elements of college life." They recommend that work be done to change traditional concepts of masculinity and femininity that result in the large percentages of college women being coerced into unwanted sexual activity.

Debra L. Oswald and Brenda L. Russell agree. They surmise in "Perceptions of Sexual Coercion in Heterosexual Dating Relationships: The Role of Aggressor Gender and Tactics" (*Journal of Sex Research*, vol. 42, no. 1, February 2006) that college students do not perceive coercive behaviors (verbal pressure, purposeful intoxication, or physical force) as "highly problematic." Instead, men who coerce women are viewed as sexually aggressive; women who coerce men are viewed as promiscuous.

Fraternities and Athletics

In 2006 a stripper hired for a team party accused three Duke University lacrosse players of raping her in a bathroom on March 13 of that year. The university's president canceled the rest of the lacrosse team's season. The case set off racial tensions in Durham, North Carolina, as the woman accuser was a student of North Carolina Central University, a historically black college. Even though the charges against all three students were dropped in April 2007, a national discussion about athletes on campus and rape had been set in motion.

The relationship between athletics, fraternities, and rape is not a new dynamic. Several studies find that peer support of violence and social ties with abusive peers are predictors of abuse against women. In addition, training for violent occupations such as athletics and the military can "spill over" into personal life. Athletic training is sex-segregated, promotes hostile attitudes toward rivals, and rewards athletes for physically dominating others. Todd W. Crosset et al. report in "Male Student-Athletes and Violence against Women: A Survey of Campus Judicial Affairs Offices" (*Violence against Women*, vol. 2, no. 2, June 1996) on data that they gathered from the judicial affairs offices of the ten Division I schools with the largest athletic programs. Even though male student athletes made up just 3% of the student population, they accounted for 35% of the reported perpetrators.

In "Dating Aggression, Sexual Coercion, and Aggression-Supporting Attitudes among College Men as a Function of Participation in Aggressive High School Sports" (*Violence against Women*, vol. 12, no. 5, May 2006), Gordon B. Forbes et al. indicate that participation in aggressive male sports in high school was a risk factor in perpetrating dating violence in college. In a study of 147 men, the researchers find that men who had been involved in aggressive sports in high school engaged in more psychological and physical aggression and sexual coercion in their dating relationships. They were also more accepting of violence, caused their partners more physical injury, and were more hostile toward women. According to Forbes et al., the results

indicate "that participation in aggressive high school sports is one of the multiple developmental pathways leading to relationship violence."

Mary Koss and Hobart H. Cleveland of the University of Arizona, Tucson, in "Athletic Participation, Fraternity Membership, and Date Rape: The Question Remains—Self-Selection or Different Causal Processes?" (*Violence against Women*, vol. 2, no. 2, June 1996), try to determine whether date rape is more likely to be perpetrated by athletes and fraternity members. They speculate that a fraternity-sponsored party draws acquaintances of the same social network together, whereas the fraternity controls the limited physical space with little supervision. Together, these circumstances create an environment that legitimizes the actions of the members, thereby minimizing the chance of reporting as well as the credibility of women who do report sexual misconduct. Koss and Cleveland conclude that there is low reporting of fraternity rape.

The members of fraternities and athletic teams are frequently blamed as perpetrators of college rapes. Stephen E. Humphrey and Arnold S. Kahn of James Madison University examine in "Fraternities, Athletic Teams, and Rape: Importance of Identification with a Risky Group" (*Journal of Interpersonal Violence*, vol. 15, no. 12, December 2000) the question of whether fraternity members and male athletes are more likely to perpetrate sexual assaults than other college males. They argue that one reason that previous studies have yielded conflicting results is that they treat all sports teams and fraternities as the same, but that "there is evidence that fraternities vary widely in their attitudes toward women and their behavior toward them." They conclude that some "high-risk groups" had higher levels of sexual aggression and hostility toward women, as well as more support for sexual violence than did other "low-risk groups." In other words, the members of some fraternities and athletic teams are more likely to perpetrate sexual assault, whereas others are not.

Date Rape Drugs

Even though alcohol abuse remains a significant problem on college campuses, other drugs, such as flunitrazepam, have made resistance to attacks practically impossible. A hypnotic sedative ten times more powerful than diazepam, flunitrazepam has been used to obtain nonconsensual sex from many women. Mixed in a drink, it causes memory impairment, confusion, and drowsiness. A woman may be completely unaware of a sexual assault until she wakes up the next morning. The only way to determine if a victim has been given flunitrazepam is to test for the drug within two or three days of the rape, and few hospital emergency departments routinely screen for this drug. Health educators, high school guidance counselors, resident advisers at colleges, and scores of newspaper and magazine articles advise women not to accept drinks at parties or to leave drinks sitting unattended.

TABLE 8.6

Trends in annual use of "date rape drugs" by grade, 1991–2007

	1991	1992	1993	1994	1995	1996	1997	1998	1999	2000	2001	2002	2003	2004	2005	2006	2007	2006–2007 change
Any illicit drug[a]																		
8th grade	11.3	12.9	15.1	18.5	21.4	23.6	22.1	21.0	20.5	19.5	19.5	17.7	16.1	15.2	15.5	14.8	13.2	−1.6
10th grade	21.4	20.4	24.7	30.0	33.3	37.5	38.5	35.0	35.9	36.4	37.2	34.8	32.0	31.1	29.8	28.7	28.1	−0.7
12th grade	29.4	27.1	31.0	35.8	39.0	40.2	42.4	41.4	42.1	40.9	41.4	41.0	39.3	38.8	38.4	36.5	35.9	−0.5
Ecstasy (MDMA)[b]																		
8th grade	—	—	—	—	—	2.3	2.3	1.8	1.7	3.1	3.5	2.9	2.1	1.7	1.7	1.4	1.5	+0.1
10th grade	—	—	—	—	—	4.6	3.9	3.3	4.4	5.4	6.2	4.9	3.0	2.4	2.6	2.8	3.5	+0.7
12th grade	—	—	—	—	—	4.6	4.0	3.6	5.6	8.2	9.2	7.4	4.5	4.0	3.0	4.1	4.5	+0.4
Rohypnol[c]																		
8th grade	—	—	—	—	—	1.0	0.8	0.8	0.5	0.5	0.7	0.3	0.5	0.6	0.7	0.5	0.7	+0.1
10th grade	—	—	—	—	—	1.1	1.3	1.2	1.0	0.8	1.0	0.7	0.6	0.7	0.5	0.5	0.7	+0.1
12th grade	—	—	—	—	—	1.1	1.2	1.4	1.0	0.8	0.90	1.6	1.3	1.6	1.2	1.1	1.0	−0.1
GHB[d, e]																		
8th grade	—	—	—	—	—	—	—	—	—	1.2	1.1	0.8	0.9	0.7	0.5	0.8	0.7	−0.1
10th grade	—	—	—	—	—	—	—	—	—	1.1	1.0	1.4	1.4	0.8	0.8	0.7	0.6	−0.1
12th grade	—	—	—	—	—	—	—	—	—	1.9	1.6	1.5	1.4	2.0	1.1	1.1	0.9	−0.2
Ketamine[d, f]																		
8th grade	—	—	—	—	—	—	—	—	—	1.6	1.3	1.3	1.1	0.9	0.6	0.9	1.0	+0.1
10th grade	—	—	—	—	—	—	—	—	—	2.1	2.1	2.2	1.9	1.3	1.0	1.0	0.8	−0.2
12th grade	—	—	—	—	—	—	—	—	—	2.5	2.5	2.6	2.1	1.9	1.6	1.4	1.3	0.0

—Indicates data not available.

[a]For 12th graders only: Use of "any illicit drug" includes any use of marijuana, LSD, other hallucinogens, crack, other cocaine, or heroin; or any use of other narcotics, amphetamines, sedatives (barbiturates), or tranquilizers not under a doctor's orders. For 8th and 10th graders only: The use of other narcotics and sedatives (barbiturates) has been excluded because these younger respondents appear to overreport use (perhaps because they include the use of nonprescription drugs in their answers).

[b]For 8th and 10th graders only: Data based on one of two forms in 1996; *N* is one half of *N* indicated. Data based on one third of *N* indicated in 1997–2001 due to changes in the questionnaire forms. Data based on two of four forms beginning in 2002; *N* is one half of *N* indicated. For 12th graders only: Data based on one of six forms in 1996–2001; *N* is one sixth of *N* indicated. Data based on two of six forms beginning in 2002; *N* is two sixths of *N* indicated.

[c]For 8th and 10th graders only: Data based on one of two forms in 1996; *N* is one half of *N* indicated. Data based on three of four forms in 1997–1998; *N* is two thirds of *N* indicated. Data based on two of four forms in 1999–2001; *N* is one third of *N* indicated. Data based on one of four forms beginning in 2002; *N* is one sixth of *N* indicated. For 12th graders only: Data based on one of six forms in 1996–2001; *N* is one sixth of *N* indicated. Data based on two of six forms beginning in 2002; *N* is two sixths of *N* indicated. Data for 2001 and 2002 are not comparable due to changes in the questionnaire forms.

[d]For 8th and 10th graders only: Data based on one of four forms; *N* is one third of *N* indicated.

[e]For 12th graders only: Data based on two of six forms in 2000; *N* is two sixths of *N* indicated. Data based on three of six forms in 2001; *N* is three sixths of *N* indicated. Data based on one of six forms beginning in 2002; *N* is one sixth of *N* indicated.

[f]Data based on two of six forms in 2000; *N* is two sixths of *N* indicated. Data based on three of six forms beginning in 2001; *N* is three sixths of *N* indicated.

SOURCE: Adapted from Lloyd D. Johnston et al., "Table 2. Trends in Annual Prevalence of Use of Various Drugs in Grades 8, 10, and 12," in *Monitoring the Future: National Results on Adolescent Drug Use, Overview of Key Findings, 2007*, National Institutes of Health, National Institute on Drug Abuse, April 2008, http://monitoringthefuture.org/pubs/monographs/overview2007.pdf (accessed July 3, 2008).

Flunitrazepam is legally prescribed outside of the United States for short-term treatment of severe sleep disorders, but it is neither manufactured nor approved for sale in the United States. The importation of the drug was banned in March 1996, and the U.S. Customs and Border Protection began seizing quantities of flunitrazepam at U.S. borders. In response to reported abuse, the manufacturers reformulated the drug as green tablets that can be detected in clear liquids and are visible in the bottom of a cup. Anyone convicted of slipping a controlled substance, including flunitrazepam, to an individual with intent to commit a violent act, such as rape, faces a prison term of up to twenty years and a fine as high as $2 million.

According to Lloyd D. Johnston et al. of the University of Michigan, in *Monitoring the Future: National Results on Adolescent Drug Use, Overview of Key Findings, 2007* (April 2008, http://monitoringthefuture.org/pubs/monographs/overview2007.pdf), flunitrazepam has a low prevalence rate that remained steady between 2006 and 2007. Less than 1% of eighth and tenth graders had used the drug within the past year; 1% of twelfth graders had used it. (See Table 8.6.) Still, given the drug's association with committing crime, even the use of the drug by one in one hundred high schoolers is cause for concern.

Two other drugs are also used as date rape pills. Gamma hydroxybutyric acid (also known as "liquid ecstasy") enhances the effects of alcohol, which reduces the drinker's inhibitions. It also causes a form of amnesia. Ketamine hydrochloride (also known as "Special K") is an animal tranquilizer used to impair a person's natural resistance impulses. Table 8.6 shows that the annual prevalence of use of both of these drugs ranged from 0.6% to 1.3% for eighth, tenth, and twelfth graders in 2007, generally slightly down from the previous year. During 2002 anecdotal reports about another dangerous drug surfaced—a combination of ecstasy and sildenafil (a prescription drug used to treat erectile dysfunction); this combination was dubbed "sextasy." According to media reports, the drugs are taken together by male teens because sildenafil offsets impotence, a potential side effect of ecstasy use. Public health officials are alarmed by this off-label use of sildenafil and fear that it may contribute to increased rates of sexually transmitted diseases and sexual assault. In 2007, 1.5% of eighth graders, 3.5% of tenth graders, and 4.5% of twelfth graders had used ecstasy in the past twelve months, up from the previous year. (See Table 8.6.)

RAPE AMONG LESBIANS AND GAY MEN

Lesbians and gay men have been victims of rape and sexual abuse at rates comparable to or higher than rates in the heterosexual community. In "Comparing Violence over the Lifespan in Samples of Same-Sex and Opposite Sex Cohabitants" (*Violence and Victims*, vol. 14, no. 4, winter 1999), Patricia Tjaden, Nancy Thoennes, and Christine J. Allison find that cohabiting lesbians were nearly twice as likely as women living with male partners to have been forcibly raped as a minor (16.5% versus 8.7%) and nearly three times as likely to report being raped as an adult (25.3% versus 10.3%). They also find that 15.4% of cohabiting gay men were raped as minors, whereas 10.8% were raped as adults. The rate of rape for heterosexual men living with female partners was insignificant.

Tjaden, Thoennes, and Allison find that cohabiting gay men usually had been raped by strangers and acquaintances, whereas cohabiting females usually had been raped by intimate partners. A vast majority of the rape victims, regardless of gender or sexual preference, were raped by men.

Gay and lesbian cohabitants were also significantly more likely to report being physically assaulted as a child by an adult caretaker. Among gay men, 70.8% reported such violence, compared to 50.3% of heterosexual cohabitants. Among women, the figures were 59.5% and 37.5%, respectively. Gay and lesbian cohabitants also experienced higher levels of physical assault in adulthood.

Tjaden, Thoennes, and Allison indicate that same-sex cohabiting partners reported significantly more intimate partner violence than did cohabiting heterosexuals. About 32% of gay respondents said they had been raped or physically assaulted by a spouse or cohabiting partner at some point in their life, compared to just 7.7% of heterosexual men. Among lesbian cohabitants, 39.2% reported having been physically assaulted by a spouse or cohabiting partner, compared to 20.3% of women living with a male partner. The researchers note that lesbian cohabitants were also more than twice as likely to report having been victimized by male intimate partners than by female intimate partners, with 30.4% of the lesbian cohabitants

raped or physically assaulted by male intimates. Only 11.4% of that group said they were raped or physically assaulted by female intimate partners. The same group reported less violence by their female partners than did heterosexual women living with males, which leads Tjaden, Thoennes, and Allison to conclude that women are far more likely to be assaulted by male intimate partners than by female intimate partners.

STALKING

Many abused women who leave their partner feel threatened and remain in physical danger of further attacks. One form of threatening behavior—stalking—is generally defined as harassment that involves repeated visual or physical proximity; nonconsensual communication; verbal, written, or implied threats; or a combination of these acts that would cause a reasonable person fear. Stalking is a series of actions, usually escalating from legal but annoying acts, such as following or repeatedly phoning the victim, to violent or even fatal actions. In "Policy and Legislation on Stalking" (October 25, 2007, http://www.ojp.gov/nij/topics/crime/stalking/policy-legislation.htm), the U.S. Department of Justice estimates that there are more than two million felony stalking cases and four million misdemeanor stalking cases each year.

Not all stalking incidents involve abusive couples or intimate relationships. A stalker may fixate on an acquaintance or a stranger as the object of obsession. Celebrity stalking cases have been highly publicized, but they account for a small percentage of stalking incidents. Stalking most often involves intimates or former intimates and starts or continues after a victim leaves the relationship. It is a widespread problem. Kathleen C. Basile et al. estimate in "Stalking in the United States: Recent National Prevalence Estimates" (*American Journal of Preventive Medicine*, vol. 31, no. 2, August 2006) that nearly one out of twenty-two adults, or almost ten million, have been stalked in their lifetime. Four out of five stalking victims are women.

Women are much more likely to be stalked than are men. According to Tjaden and Thoennes, in *Stalking in America: Findings from the National Violence against Women Survey* (April 1998, http://www.ncjrs.gov/pdffiles/169592.pdf), one out of twelve American women and one out of forty-five American men had been stalked at some point in their life. An estimated 1% of all women respondents and 0.4% of all male respondents were stalked in the twelve months before the NVAWS. These percentages represent over 1 million women and 370,000 men who are stalked annually in the United States.

Stalkers: Who Are They?

No data have been collected since the 1996 NVAWS on the details of stalking incidents. However, Basile et al.'s study demonstrates that prevalence rates remain virtually unchanged. As such, the NVAWS's detailed findings are valid and worth studying in the absence of more recent detailed data.

Even though stalking is considered a "gender-neutral" crime, most victims are women and the main perpetrators are men. Young adults are the primary targets—in 1996, 52% of victims were between the ages of eighteen and twenty-nine. (See Figure 8.4.) Another 22% were between ages thirty and thirty-nine when the stalking began, and 15% were forty years old or older. Recent data back up the assertion that stalking victims are primarily younger adults. Basile et al. report that 6.5% of adults aged eighteen to twenty-four reported ever having been stalked, compared to 5.7% of those aged twenty-five to thirty four, 5.5% of those aged thirty-five to forty-four, 5.2% of those aged forty-five to fifty-four, and 1.7% of those aged fifty-five and older.

As suspected, the NVAWS found that most victims knew their stalker. Only 23% of female victims and 36% of male victims were stalked by a stranger between 1995 and 1996. (See Figure 8.5.) Most women were stalked by an intimate partner. Overall, 62% of female and 32% of male victims were stalked by a current or former intimate. Figure 8.5 shows the relationship between stalkers and victims: female victims were stalked by a spouse and former spouse nearly three times as often as male victims.

Most stalkers follow or spy on their victim, place unwanted phone calls, and send unwanted letters or other items. Tjaden and Thoennes note in *Stalking in America* that the pattern of harassment is similar whether the victim is male or female. Eighty-two percent of all female stalking victims and 72% of all male stalking victims reported being followed or spied on or found the stalker standing outside their home or workplace. Sixty-one percent of the females and 42% of the males

FIGURE 8.4

Victim's age when first stalked, 1996

Note: Based on responses from 797 male and female victims. Percentages do not total 100 due to rounding.

SOURCE: "Victim's Age When First Stalked," in *Stalking and Domestic Violence: The Third Annual Report to Congress under the Violence against Women Act*, U.S. Department of Justice, Violence Against Women Grants Office, July 1998

FIGURE 8.5

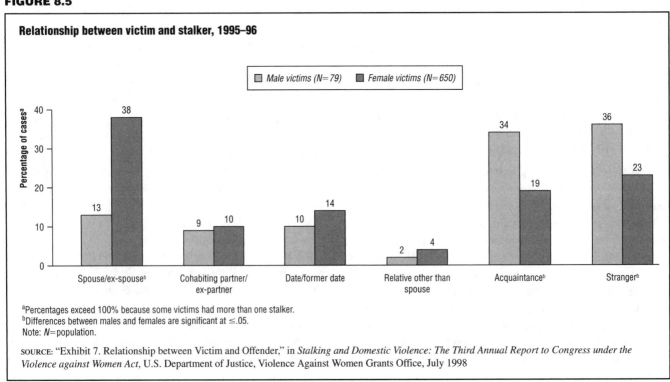

Relationship between victim and stalker, 1995–96

[a]Percentages exceed 100% because some victims had more than one stalker.
[b]Differences between males and females are significant at ≤.05.
Note: *N*=population.

SOURCE: "Exhibit 7. Relationship between Victim and Offender," in *Stalking and Domestic Violence: The Third Annual Report to Congress under the Violence against Women Act*, U.S. Department of Justice, Violence Against Women Grants Office, July 1998

FIGURE 8.6

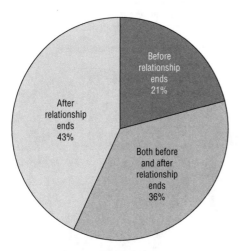

Point in intimate relationship when stalking of women occurred, 1996

Before relationship ends
21%

After relationship ends
43%

Both before and after relationship ends
36%

Note: Based on responses from 263 female victims.

SOURCE: "Point in Intimate Relationship When Stalking of Women Occurs," in *Stalking and Domestic Violence: The Third Annual Report to Congress under the Violence against Women Act*, U.S. Department of Justice, Violence Against Women Grants Office, July 1998

reported receiving phone calls from the stalker. Twenty-nine percent of the women and 30% of the men reported property damage by the stalker, and 9% of the women and 6% of the male victims said the stalker either killed or threatened to kill their family pet.

When the Violence Occurs

Victims' advocates and counselors have long held that women are at the greatest risk of violence when they end a relationship with a batterer. This assumption is based on findings that divorced or separated women report more intimate partner violence than married women. In addition, interviews conducted with men who killed their partner reveal that the violence escalated or was precipitated by separation or threats of separation from their partner.

Many female stalking victims (43%) reported that the stalking began after ending their relationship with an intimate partner, although another 36% said they were stalked both before and after the breakup. (See Figure 8.6.) Twenty-one percent of the victims said the stalking occurred before they terminated their relationship.

According to Tjaden and Thoennes, in *Extent, Nature, and Consequences of Intimate Partner Violence: Findings from the National Violence against Women Survey* (July 2000, http://www.ncjrs.gov/pdffiles1/nij/181867.pdf), separated women are nearly four times more likely to report rape, physical assault, or being stalked by their spouse than women who live with their husband. In comparison, men

who live apart from their spouse are nearly three times as likely to report being victimized by their wife than men who live with their spouse. These findings support the widely held belief that there is an increased risk of partner violence for both men and women once an abusive relationship ends.

Whereas 42.8% of all stalking victims said the stalking began after they ended their relationship, only 6.3% of rape victims and 4.2% of physical assault victims reported that victimization began after they terminated their relationship. (See Figure 8.7.) These findings suggest that most rapes and violent assaults against women by their partner begin during a relationship. In contrast, stalking is more likely to begin after the relationship is terminated.

Legal Response to Stalking

Tjaden and Thoennes note in *Stalking in America* that about half (53.1%) of the stalking victims in the NVAWS reported stalking to the police. In most cases the victim made the report. Police were significantly more likely to arrest or detain a suspect stalking a female victim (25.1%) than one stalking a male victim (16.7%). Other police responses included referrals to the prosecutor or court (23.3%), referral to victim services (13.8%), and advice on self-protective measures (33.2%). In 18.9% of the cases police did nothing.

Of those victims who reported their stalking to the police, Tjaden and Thoennes report that about half were satisfied with the actions subsequently taken by the police, and about the same proportion indicated they felt police interventions had improved their situation or that the police had done all they could. Victims who thought police actions were inadequate had hoped that their assailant would be jailed (42%) or that their complaint would be treated more seriously (20%). Another 16% had wanted police to do more to protect them from their assailant.

According to Tjaden and Thoennes, victims who chose not to report their stalking to the police said they felt their stalking was not a police matter (20%), they believed police would be unable to help them (17%), or they feared reprisal from their stalker (16%).

Not unexpectedly, because women were more likely to be stalked by an intimate partner with a history of violence, female victims were significantly more likely than male victims to obtain protective or restraining orders. According to the Violence against Women Grants Office, in *Stalking and Domestic Violence: The Third Annual Report to Congress under the Violence against Women Act* (1998), of those who obtained protective orders, 68.7% of the women and 81.3% of the men said their stalker violated the order.

Carol E. Jordan et al. studied the disposition of stalking cases and published their results in "Stalking: An

FIGURE 8.7

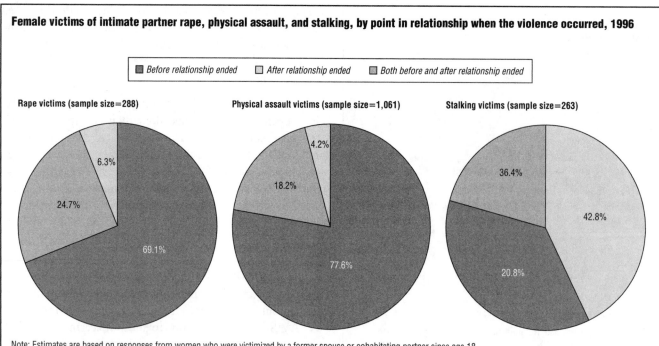

Female victims of intimate partner rape, physical assault, and stalking, by point in relationship when the violence occurred, 1996

■ *Before relationship ended* □ *After relationship ended* ▨ *Both before and after relationship ended*

Rape victims (sample size=288)

6.3%
24.7%
69.1%

Physical assault victims (sample size=1,061)

4.2%
18.2%
77.6%

Stalking victims (sample size=263)

36.4%
42.8%
20.8%

Note: Estimates are based on responses from women who were victimized by a former spouse or cohabiting partner since age 18.

SOURCE: "Exhibit 10. Distribution of Female Victims of Intimate Partner Rape, Physical Assault, and Stalking, by Point in Relationship When the Violence Occurred," in *Stalking and Domestic Violence: The Third Annual Report to Congress under the Violence against Women Act*, U.S. Department of Justice, Violence Against Women Grants Office, July 1998

Examination of the Criminal Justice Response" (*Journal of Interpersonal Violence*, vol. 18, no. 2, February 2003). They examine the cases of 346 males charged with stalking from fiscal year 1999 and find that most misdemeanor and felony charges of stalking were dismissed. Only 28.5% of the charged stalkers were convicted. Jordan et al. conclude that even though most stalking cases are dismissed, those cases that are not dismissed have a fair chance of resulting in conviction.

Antistalking Legislation

All states and the District of Columbia have laws making stalking a crime, but whether it is a felony or a misdemeanor varies by state. In 1996 the Interstate Stalking Punishment and Prevention Act, which is part of the National Defense Authorization Act of 1997, made interstate stalking a felony. This federal statute addresses cases that cross state lines. In the past interstate offenses were difficult for state law enforcement agencies to take action against. In 2005 the Violence against Women Act was renewed, criminalizing stalking by surveillance and expanding the definition of "accountable harm" to include substantial emotional harm to the victim.

Several state legislatures have amended their antistalking laws after constitutional challenges or judicial interpretations of the law made it difficult to prosecute

alleged stalkers. For example, in 1996 the Texas Court of Criminal Appeals ruled in *Long v. Texas* (931 SW2d 285) that the 1993 Texas antistalking law was unconstitutional because it addressed conduct protected by the First Amendment. Legislators amended the statute in January 1997 to stipulate that to violate the statute, an alleged offender must knowingly engage in conduct that he or she "reasonably believes the other person will regard as threatening."

According to the Department of Justice's Office for Victims of Crime, the variation in state stalking laws has to do with the type of repeated behavior that is prohibited, and whether by definition stalking must include a threat. Laws are also based on the victim's reaction to the stalking and the stalker's intent. In *Strengthening Antistalking Statutes* (January 2002, http://www.ojp.usdoj .gov/ovc/publications/bulletins/legalseries/bulletin1/ncj18 9192.pdf), the Department of Justice details state legislative changes to better define prohibited conduct so that supreme courts would not find the statutes "unconstitutionally vague." For example, the Oregon legislature removed the term *legitimate purpose* from its statute when its supreme court determined it did not adequately describe the prohibited behavior. Similarly, the Kansas Supreme Court sought increased precision when it requested that the state's stalking statute provide measures of behaviors such as "alarm, annoy, and harassment," arguing that actions that alarm or annoy one person may not alarm or annoy another.

Cyberstalking

Cyberstalking (online harassment and threats that can escalate to frightening and even life-threatening offline violence) is a relatively recent phenomenon. Brian H. Spitzberg and Greg Hoobler note in "Cyberstalking and the Technologies of Interpersonal Terrorism" (*New Media and Society*, vol. 4, no. 1, 2002), a study of college students, that almost one-third responded that they had experienced some degree of computer-based harassment and pursuit. The researchers state that "it stands to reason that if there are classes of people who elect, or are driven obsessively, to pursue intimacy with others that these pursuers will seek whatever means are available that might increase their access to the objects of their pursuit, and that people's increasing exposure on and through the computer will make them more accessible as victims."

In January 2006 a federal anticyberstalking law was signed into law by President George W. Bush (1946–) as part of the reauthorized Violence against Women Act. It prohibited anyone from using a telephone or telecommunications device (including a computer) "without disclosing his identity and with intent to annoy, abuse, threaten, or harass any person."

Even though the extent of the problem is difficult to measure, by 1999 cyberstalking had generated enough concern to warrant the report *Cyberstalking: A New Challenge for Law Enforcement and Industry* (August 1999, http://www.usdoj.gov/criminal/cybercrime/cyberstalking .htm) by the U.S. attorney general to Vice President Al Gore (1948–). The attorney general's report cautions that even though cyberstalking does not involve physical contact, it should not be considered less dangerous than physical stalking. In *Stalking and Domestic Violence: Report to Congress* (May 2001, http://www.ncjrs.gov/pdffiles1/ojp/186157 .pdf), the Department of Justice compares the similarities and differences between offline and online stalking. Most stalking cases, offline and online, involve stalking by former intimate partners, although there are cases of stranger stalking in each. Stalking victims, offline and online, are most often women, whereas stalkers are most often men. Most stalkers are motivated by a desire to control the victim.

The Department of Justice also notes major differences. Cyberstalking is actually easier for the stalker than offline stalking; the online environment lowers barriers to harassment and threats. Offline stalking, for example, requires the perpetrator to be in the same area as the victim, whereas cyberstalkers can be anywhere. In addition, the online environment makes it easy for a cyberstalker to "encourage third parties to harass or threaten a victim." For example, a stalker can impersonate a victim online and post inflammatory messages, causing others to send threatening messages back to the victim.

In "A Study on Cyberstalking" (*FBI Law Enforcement Bulletin*, vol. 72, no. 3, March 2003), Robert D'Ovidio and James Doyle analyze basic demographic information about cyberstalkers. Four out of five (80%) cyberstalkers were males, 74% of them were white, 13% Asian-American, 8% Hispanic, and 5% African-American. Cyberstalkers were typically young; the average age was twenty-four, and about a quarter of offenders were juveniles.

CASES MAKE HEADLINE NEWS. The attorney general's report recounts three of many serious instances of cyberstalking that attracted attention in the media and among policy makers. The first successful prosecution under California's cyberstalking law was in Los Angeles, where a fifty-year-old man stalked a twenty-eight-year-old woman who had refused his advances. He posted her name and telephone number online along with messages saying she wanted to be raped. The Internet posts prompted men to knock on the woman's door, often during the night, in the hopes of fulfilling the fantasy her stalker had posted. In April 1999 the accused pleaded guilty to stalking and solicitation of sexual assault and was sentenced to a six-year prison term.

Another California case involved an honors graduate student at the University of San Diego who entered a guilty plea after sending, over the course of a year, hundreds of violent and menacing e-mail messages to five female university students he had never met. The third case cited in the report was prosecuted in Massachusetts, where a man repeatedly harassed a coworker via e-mail and attempted to extort sexual favors from the victim.

In July 2002 the CBS News program *48 Hours* investigated a lethal case of cyberstalking that shocked the nation. In 1999 a twenty-year-old New Hampshire resident named Amy Boyer was killed by a cyberstalker she had met, but never befriended or dated, years earlier in the eighth grade. Unknown to Boyer, her stalker had apparently obsessed over her for years and had constructed a Web site that described his stalking of Boyer and his plans to kill her. He used an investigation service to discover where she worked and ambushed her as she left, shooting her and then killing himself. Boyer's death inspired her parents to speak out and champion anticyberstalking laws.

LAW ENFORCEMENT AND CYBERSTALKING.

Cyberspace has become a fertile field for illegal activity. By the use of new technology and equipment which cannot be policed by traditional methods, cyberstalking has replaced traditional methods of stalking and harassment. In addition, cyberstalking has led to offline incidents of violent crime. Police and prosecutors need to be aware of the escalating numbers of these events and devise strategies to resolve these problems through the criminal justice system.

—Linda Fairstein, chief of the Sex Crimes Prosecution Unit, Manhattan District Attorney's Office

According to D'Ovidio and Doyle, cyberstalking presents some unique law enforcement challenges. Offenders are often able to use the anonymity of online communication to avoid detection and accountability for their actions. Appropriate interventions and recourse are unclear because often the stalker and his victim have never been in physical proximity to one another. Complicating the situation, the identity of the stalker may be difficult to determine. Furthermore, many law enforcement agencies are unprepared to investigate cyberstalking cases because they lack the expertise and training. The attorney general's study finds that some victims had been advised by law enforcement agents to simply "turn off their computers" or to "come back should the offender confront or threaten them offline."

Finally, some state and local law enforcement agencies are frustrated in their efforts to track down cyberstalkers by the limits of their statutory authority. For example, the Cable Communications Policy Act of 1984 bars the release of cable subscriber information to law enforcement agencies without advance notice to the subscriber and a court order. Because a growing number of Internet users receive services via cable, the act inadvertently grants those wishing to remain anonymous for purposes of cyberstalking some legal protection from investigation. The attorney general's report calls for modifications to the act to include provisions to help law enforcement agents gain access to the identifying information they need while maintaining privacy safeguards for cable customers. "It may be ironic," write Spitzberg and Hoobler, "that to combat the risks of cyberstalking, law enforcement may need the very tools of electronic surveillance and intrusion that are currently the source of many citizens' fundamental fears of privacy invasion."

CHAPTER 9
DOMESTIC VIOLENCE, LAW ENFORCEMENT, AND COURT RESPONSES TO DOMESTIC VIOLENCE

POLICE RESPONSE TO DOMESTIC VIOLENCE

Family disturbance calls constitute most of the calls received by police departments throughout the country. Historically, such calls were not been taken seriously, which reflects society's attitude about domestic violence at the time. For instance, in the mid-1960s Detroit police dispatchers were instructed to screen out family disturbance calls unless they suspected "excessive" violence. A 1975 police guide, *The Function of the Police in Crisis Intervention and Conflict Management*, taught officers to avoid arrest at all costs and to discourage the victim from pressing charges by emphasizing the consequences of testifying in court, the potential lost income, and other detrimental aspects of prosecution.

Changes in society's tolerance for domestic violence mean that these approaches to domestic violence no longer enjoy official support (although they may still influence the actions of individual officers). By 2008 every state had moved to authorize probable cause arrests (arrest before the completion of the investigation of the alleged violation or crime) without a warrant in domestic violence cases. (A warrant is a written legal document authorizing a police officer to make a search, seizure, or arrest.) Many police departments have adopted pro-arrest or mandatory arrest policies. Pro-arrest strategies include a range of sanctions from issuing a warning, to mandated treatment, to prison time.

The police are often an abuse victim's initial contact with the judicial system, making the police response particularly important. The manner in which the police handle a domestic violence complaint will likely color the way the victim views the entire judicial system. Not surprisingly, when police project the blame for intimate partner violence on victims, the victims may be reluctant to report further abuse.

In *Criminal Victimization in the United States, 2005 Statistical Tables* (December 2006, http://www.ojp.usdoj .gov/bjs/pub/pdf/cvus05.pdf), which analyzes data from the National Crime Victimization Survey (NCVS), the Bureau of Justice Statistics (BJS) reports that in 2005, 47.4% of all violent crimes were reported to the police. Out of violent crimes reported to the police, the police came to the aid of victims in 78.2% of cases, the victim went to the police 3.2% of the time, and the police did not come 11% of the time. (See Table 9.1.) Police came to the aid of more victims of robbery (84.8%) and aggravated assault (79%), while coming less often to the aid of victims of purse snatching or pocket picking (64.2%).

The BJS notes that in 2005, 54.6% of female victims of violence had reported the crime to the police. (See Table 9.2.) However, only 38.5% of female victims of rape or sexual assault reported the crime.

REPORTING DOMESTIC VIOLENCE TO THE POLICE

It is well established that a significant amount of intimate partner violence is unreported or underreported. In the past most women did not report incidents of abuse to the police. In the 1985 National Family Violence Resurvey, Murray A. Straus and Richard J. Gelles find that only 6.7% of all husband-to-wife assaults were reported to police. When the assaults are categorized by severity as measured on a Conflict Tactics Scale, only 3.2% of minor violence cases and 14.4% of severe violence cases were reported.

The women who chose not to report their abuse cited a variety of reasons, including fear of retaliation, loss of income, or loss of their children to child protection authorities. When abuse is reported to law enforcement agencies, it is often by health care professionals from whom the woman has sought treatment for her injuries. In many states health professionals are mandated by law to report all instances of domestic violence to law enforcement authorities.

TABLE 9.1

Police response to a reported incident, by type of crime, 2005

Type of crime	Number of incidents		Percent of incidents					
		Total	Police came to victim	Victim went to police	Contact with police-don't know how	Police did not come	Not known if police came	Police were at the scene
Crimes of violence	**2,100,200**	**100.0%**	**78.2%**	**3.2%**	**0.0%***	**11.0%**	**2.9%**	**4.7%**
Rape/sexual assault[a]	70,700	100.0%	74.7	13.3*	0.0*	8.0*	0.0*	3.9*
Robbery	287,260	100.0%	84.8	1.1*	0.0*	8.0*	5.1*	1.1*
Aggravated assault	522,910	100.0%	79.0	3.5*	0.0*	12.0	3.8*	1.7*
Simple assault	1,219,320	100.0%	76.5	2.9*	0.0*	11.4	2.2*	6.9
Purse snatching/pocket picking	79,970	100.0%	64.2	9.2*	0.0*	26.6*	0.0*	0.0*
Property crimes	**6,998,740**	**100.0%**	**66.5%**	**4.6%**	**0.1%***	**24.7%**	**2.6%**	**1.5%**
Household burglary	1,906,390	100.0%	81.4	2.3	0.3*	13.4	1.6*	1.0*
Motor vehicle theft	786,800	100.0%	70.2	2.6*	0.0*	21.1	4.0*	2.0*
Theft	4,305,550	100.0%	59.2	5.9	0.0*	30.3	2.8	1.7

Note: Detail may not add to total shown because of rounding.
*Estimate is based on about 10 or fewer sample cases.
[a]Includes verbal threats of rape and threats of sexual assault.

SOURCE: "Table 106. Personal and Property Crimes, 2005: Percent Distribution of Police Response to a Reported Incident,by Type of Crime," in *Criminal Victimization in the United States, 2005 Statistical Tables*, U.S. Department of Justice, Office of Justice Programs, Bureau of Justice Statistics, December 2006, http://www.ojp.usdoj.gov/bjs/pub/pdf/cvus05.pdf (accessed June 26, 2008)

TABLE 9.2

Violent victimizations reported to police by type of crime, victim-offender relationship, and gender of victims, 2005

Type of crime	Percent of all victimizations reported to the police								
	All victimizations			Involving strangers			Involving nonstrangers		
	Both genders	Male	Female	Both genders	Male	Female	Both genders	Male	Female
Crimes of violence	**47.4%**	**42.4%**	**54.6%**	**45.9%**	**39.7%**	**59.3%**	**49.2%**	**46.8%**	**51.4%**
Completed violence	61.5	59.0	64.9	61.7	56.3	74.8	61.2	63.8	59.1
Attempted/threatened violence	40.8	34.5	49.7	38.6	31.7	52.9	43.4	39.2	47.4
Rape/sexual assault[a]	38.3	35.8*	38.5	56.1	35.8*	61.9*	28.3*	0.0*	28.3*
Robbery	52.4	45.9	69.6	47.7	42.9	66.1	70.7	65.8	74.8
Completed/property taken	60.5	55.5	70.6	57.5	53.8	68.2	70.3	65.0*	74.1
With injury	73.8	67.7	84.9	70.4	64.2	82.4*	100.0*	100.0*	100.0*
Without injury	53.6	49.3	62.4	49.0	48.2	52.3*	64.3	54.9*	70.2*
Attempted to take property	36.4	30.9	65.2*	30.4	26.6	58.0*	71.8*	67.6*	78.3*
With injury	39.6*	36.9*	100.0*	35.2*	35.2*	0.0*	65.9*	51.7*	100.0*
Without injury	35.0	27.7*	62.2*	28.2*	21.9*	58.0*	74.3*	76.0*	72.0*
Assault	47.1	41.8	54.7	45.1	38.9	58.2	49.1	45.8	52.5
Aggravated	62.4	59.4	67.5	58.3	55.4	65.1	67.6	66.1	69.5
With injury	76.2	75.0	78.4	80.2	77.0	90.6*	72.1	71.7	72.4
Threatened with weapon	56.0	52.2	62.5	49.7	45.6	58.0	65.2	63.3	67.6
Simple	42.3	35.6	51.2	40.2	32.5	55.8	44.2	39.6	48.5
With minor injury	59.0	54.4	66.0	54.8	48.4	69.3	62.4	60.8	64.2
Attempted threat without weapon	37.0	29.2	47.0	35.9	27.6	52.2	38.0	31.5	43.8

Note: Detail may not add to total shown because of rounding.
*Estimate is based on about 10 or fewer sample cases.
[a]Includes verbal threats of rape and threats of sexual assault

SOURCE: "Table 93. Violent Crimes, 2005: Percent of Victimizations Reported to the Police, by Type of Crime, Victim-Offender Relationship and Gender of Victims," in *Criminal Victimization in the United States, 2005 Statistical Tables*, U.S. Department of Justice, Office of Justice Programs, Bureau of Justice Statistics, December 2006, http://www.ojp.usdoj.gov/bjs/pub/pdf/cvus05.pdf (accessed June 26, 2008)

Table 9.2 shows that in 2005 women who were victims of violent crime at the hands of strangers were more likely to report the crime than were women who were victimized by nonstrangers (59.3% and 51.4%, respectively). People who reported crimes of violence to the police reported various reasons for doing so, including to prevent further crimes by offender against the victim (19.6%) or anyone else (10.4%), to stop or prevent that incident (20.1%), to punish the offender (8.1%), to catch or find the offender (7.4%), or simply because it was a crime (15.1%). (See Table 9.3.)

People who did not report violent crime to the police often said it was a personal matter (20.3%), the police

TABLE 9.3

Reasons for reporting victimizations to the police, by type of crime, 2005

Type of crime	Number of reasons for reporting	Total	Percent of reasons for reporting				
			Stop or prevent this incident	Needed help due to injury	To recover property	To collect insurance	To prevent further crimes by offender against victim
All personal crimes	**2,399,330**	**100.0%**	**19.7%**	**2.3%**	**3.5%**	**0.0%***	**19.4%**
Crimes of violence	2,292,200	100.0%	20.1	2.4	2.6	0.0*	19.6
Completed violence	797,780	100.0%	15.4	4.9	6.0	0.0*	20.1
Attempted/threatened violence	1,494,410	100.0%	22.7	1.0*	0.7*	0.0*	19.4
Rape/sexual assault[a]	88,740	100.0%	16.6*	3.4*	3.4*	0.0*	17.2*
Robbery	381,620	100.0%	7.9*	0.8*	12.6	0.0*	11.8
Completed/property taken	260,590	100.0%	7.8*	1.1*	17.3	0.0*	11.0*
With injury	67,940	100.0%	12.5*	0.0*	4.1*	0.0*	4.8*
Without injury	192,650	100.0%	6.1*	1.5*	21.9	0.0*	13.2*
Attempted to take property	121,040	100.0%	8.3*	0.0*	2.6*	0.0*	13.5*
With injury	44,810	100.0%	8.7*	0.0*	0.0*	0.0*	8.7*
Without injury	76,220	100.0%	8.0*	0.0*	4.1*	0.0*	16.2*
Assault	1,821,840	100.0%	22.9	2.7	0.4*	0.0*	21.4
Aggravated	596,840	100.0%	17.4	2.6*	0.8*	0.0*	19.5
Simple	1,225,000	100.0%	25.6	2.7*	0.2*	0.0*	22.3
Purse snatching/pocket picking	107,130	100.0%	9.7*	0.0*	23.5*	0.0*	13.8*
All property crimes	**9,314,820**	**100.0%**	**9.0%**	**0.3%***	**21.8%**	**4.4%**	**10.6%**
Household burglary	2,897,810	100.0%	12.4	0.2*	17.9	3.5	14.3
Completed	2,621,910	100.0%	11.6	0.2*	19.8	3.7	14.4
Forcible entry	1,309,190	100.0%	11.8	0.2*	18.5	4.1	15.3
Unlawful entry without force	1,312,720	100.0%	11.3	0.2*	21.1	3.4	13.5
Attempted forcible entry	275,900	100.0%	20.1	0.0*	0.0*	0.8*	13.7
Motor vehicle theft	1,080,350	100.0%	5.7	0.5*	34.1	8.4	7.1
Completed	945,560	100.0%	4.3	0.6*	38.4	8.9	5.9
Attempted	134,790	100.0%	15.8*	0.0*	4.0*	4.8*	15.7*
Theft	5,336,660	100.0%	7.8	0.3*	21.4	4.2	9.4
Completed	5,090,700	100.0%	7.5	0.4*	22.4	4.2	8.9
Attempted	245,970	100.0%	14.4*	0.0*	2.1*	2.5*	18.9

Type of crime	Percent of reasons for reporting							
	To prevent crime by offender against anyone	To punish offender	To catch or find offender	To improve police surveillance	Duty to notify police	Because it was a crime	Some other reason	Not available
All personal crimes	**10.5%**	**7.7%**	**7.1%**	**3.0%**	**6.2%**	**15.3%**	**3.7%**	**1.7%**
Crimes of violence	10.4	8.1	7.4	3.1	6.2	15.1	3.3	1.6*
Completed violence	8.1	10.9	9.4	1.9*	3.6*	16.1	2.1*	1.6*
Attempted/threatened violence	11.6	6.6	6.4	3.8	7.5	14.6	4.0	1.6*
Rape/sexual assault[a]	17.6*	9.0*	5.6*	0.0*	5.8*	18.1*	3.3*	0.0*
Robbery	10.3	6.0*	14.1	2.7*	6.0*	23.4	2.4*	2.1*
Completed/property taken	5.2*	6.4*	12.0*	2.8*	4.3*	27.8	1.2*	3.0*
With injury	0.0*	0.0*	22.2*	5.0*	0.0*	39.8*	0.0*	11.6*
Without injury	7.0*	8.7*	8.4*	2.1*	5.8*	23.6	1.7*	0.0*
Attempted to take property	21.2*	5.0*	18.6*	2.6*	9.5*	13.8*	5.0*	0.0*
With injury	16.9*	0.0*	16.9*	0.0*	18.7*	16.6*	13.4*	0.0*
Without injury	23.7*	8.0*	19.6*	4.1*	4.1*	12.2*	0.0*	0.0*
Assault	10.1	8.5	6.1	3.4	6.2	13.3	3.5	1.6*
Aggravated	11.4	9.8	10.2	5.6*	6.8	13.8	1.3*	0.7*
Simple	9.4	7.8	4.1	2.3*	5.9	13.0	4.6	2.0*
Purse snatching/pocket picking	13.1*	0.0*	0.0*	0.0*	6.7*	19.0*	10.5*	3.7*

would not want to be bothered (5.5%) or would be ineffective or biased (4%), and fear of reprisal (3.8%). (See Table 9.4.) Reasons varied according to whether the crime was perpetrated by a stranger or a nonstranger. For example, 31.1% of rape and sexual assault victims who were violated by a nonstranger and who did not report the crime to police said they did not report the victimization because it was a private or personal matter; no one raped by a stranger gave this reason. (See Table 9.5.) Similarly, 27% of people assaulted by a nonstranger and who did

not report the crime said it was because it was a private or personal matter, whereas only 15.3% of nonreporters who were assaulted by a stranger gave this reason.

Shannan Catalano of the BJS reports in *Intimate Partner Violence in the United States* (December 2007, http://www.ojp.usdoj.gov/bjs/intimate/report.htm) that in 2004–05, 62.1% of female victims of intimate partner violence and 64.3% of male victims reported the violence to police. The percentage of both men and women who reported the violence to the police had risen since 1994–95.

TABLE 9.3

Reasons for reporting victimizations to the police, by type of crime, 2005 [CONTINUED]

Type of crime	Percent of reasons for reporting							
	To prevent crime by offender against anyone	To punish offender	To catch or find offender	To improve police surveillance	Duty to notify police	Because it was a crime	Some other reason	Not available
All personal crimes	10.5%	7.7%	7.1%	3.0%	6.2%	15.3%	3.7%	1.7%
Household burglary	7.2	5.0	9.1	7.9	6.2	12.7	2.3	1.2*
Completed	7.3	5.6	9.2	7.6	6.3	11.4	1.9	1.1*
Forcible entry	7.0	6.2	8.5	8.9	5.7	10.8	1.3*	1.7*
Unlawful entry without force	7.6	5.0	9.8	6.3	6.9	12.0	2.5*	0.4*
Attempted forcible entry	6.6*	0.0*	8.0*	10.8*	5.5*	25.4	6.2*	2.8*
Motor vehicle theft	5.0	4.6	8.5	7.1	6.3	10.6	0.6*	1.4*
Completed	4.1	4.3	9.0	5.6	6.4	10.4	0.7*	1.6*
Attempted	11.1*	7.4*	5.4*	18.1*	5.6*	12.1*	0.0*	0.0*
Theft	6.7	4.2	6.7	6.8	6.8	20.6	3.2	2.0
Completed	6.5	4.1	6.7	6.8	6.8	20.3	3.4	2.0
Attempted	9.4*	5.3*	6.4*	6.1*	6.9*	26.9	0.0*	1.0*

Note: Detail may not add to total shown because of rounding.
Some respondents may have cited more than one reason for reporting victimizations to the police.
*Estimate is based on about 10 or fewer sample cases.
ªIncludes verbal threats of rape and threats of sexual assault

SOURCE: "Table 101. Personal and Property Crimes, 2005: Percent of Reasons for Reporting Victimizations to the Police, by Type of Crime," in *Criminal Victimization in the United States, 2005 Statistical Tables*, U.S. Department of Justice, Office of Justice Programs, Bureau of Justice Statistics, December 2006, http://www.ojp.usdoj.gov/bjs/pub/pdf/cvus05.pdf (accessed June 26, 2008)

Between 2001 and 2005 African-American females were the most likely to report intimate partner violence to police (70.2%), whereas African-American males were the least likely (46.5%). (See Figure 9.1.). Hispanic males were much more likely than non-Hispanic males to report intimate partner violence (86.2% and 53.2%, respectively), whereas Hispanic females were slightly more likely than non-Hispanic females to report (66.3% and 58.6%, respectively). (See Figure 9.2.)

Male and female victims of intimate partner violence who did not report the violence to police differed in the reasons they did not report. Nearly four out of ten (39.2%) male victims said they did not report because it was a private matter, compared to 21.8% of female victims. (See Table 9.6.) By contrast, female victims were much more likely to state they feared reprisal (12.4% and 5.3%, respectively). Other reasons reported included to protect the offender, because victims viewed it as a minor crime, or because victims believed the police were ineffective or would not do anything.

In *The Reporting of Domestic Violence and Sexual Assault by Nonstrangers to the Police* (March 2005, http://www.ncjrs.gov/pdffiles1/nij/grants/209039.pdf), Richard Felson and Paul-Philippe Paré use data from the NCVS to examine the effects of the gender of the victim and the relationship between victim and offender on the victim's decision to report or not report a physical or sexual assault to the police. They find that victims are just as likely to report assaults by intimate partners as they are to report assaults by other people they know. Sexual assaults are less likely to be reported than are physical assaults.

Marsha E. Wolf et al., in "Barriers to Seeking Police Help for Intimate Partner Violence" (*Journal of Family Violence*, vol. 18, no. 2, April 2003), interviewed forty-one battered women to find out what kept them from calling police. The factors cited included the idea that they must have physical proof that battering had occurred, the desire to avoid a humiliating physical examination in the case of rape or sexual abuse, cultural attitudes about domestic violence, poor self-esteem, being physically prevented from calling the police by the batterer, poor police response when battering was previously reported, and fears of possible retaliation by the batterer or removal of children from the home by child protective services. These women also came up with a "wish list" for how they wanted police to treat them when they called about domestic violence. This list, in the words of Wolf et al., "reflects the women's desires to have responsive police who treat victims with dignity, listen to them, and send appropriate messages to victims and batterers."

OUTCOME OF POLICE INTERVENTION

In the early 1970s it was legal for the police to make probable cause arrests without a warrant for felonies, but only fourteen states permitted it for misdemeanors. Because the crime of simple assault and battery is a misdemeanor in most states, family violence victims were forced to initiate their own criminal charges against a batterer. By 2008, however, all states authorized warrantless probable cause misdemeanor arrests in domestic violence cases. However, more than half of the states have added qualifiers, such as visible signs of injury or

TABLE 9.4

Reasons for not reporting victimizations to the police, by type of crime, 2005

Type of crime	Number of reasons for not reporting	Total	Percent of reasons for not reporting								Percent of reasons for not reporting				
			Reported to another official	Private or personal matter	Object recovered; offender unsuccessful	Not important enough	Insurance would not cover	Not aware crime occurred until later	Unable to recover property; no ID no.	Lack of proof	Police would not want to be bothered	Police inefficient, ineffective, or biased	Fear of reprisal	Too inconvenient or time consuming	Other reasons
All personal crimes	**3,447,480**	**100.0%**	**13.0%**	**19.8%**	**20.1%**	**6.4%**	**0.1%***	**0.8%***	**0.8%***	**5.2%**	**5.8%**	**3.9%**	**3.7%**	**4.0%**	**16.3%**
Crimes of violence	3,271,670	100.0	13.2	20.3	20.1	6.4	0.1	0.5*	0.6*	4.7	5.5	4.0	3.8	4.2	16.7
Completed violence	828,580	100.0	11.4	15.7	11.9	3.8*	0.0*	0.8*	1.7*	6.9	8.2	6.9	5.0	3.3*	24.2
Attempted/threatened violence	2,443,100	100.0	13.8	21.9	22.8	7.3	0.1	0.3*	0.2*	3.9	4.6	3.0	3.4	4.6	14.1
Rape/sexual assault[a]	142,410	100.0	18.2*	22.0*	3.7*	0.0*	0.0*	0.0*	0.0*	0.0*	13.5*	4.0*	3.2*	1.7*	33.7
Robbery	392,510	100.0	2.3*	13.3	21.1	0.0*	0.0*	1.7*	4.6*	17.5	9.9	7.7*	1.2*	6.4*	14.2
Completed/property taken	229,230	100.0	1.4*	9.8*	18.5	0.0*	0.0*	3.0*	6.3*	15.3*	14.1*	9.6*	2.0*	6.9*	13.1*
With injury	60,390	100.0	0.0*	0.0*	11.3*	0.0*	0.0*	11.3*	6.3*	26.9*	8.1*	6.8*	0.0*	8.1*	21.2*
Without injury	168,840	100.0	1.9*	13.4*	21.1*	0.0*	0.0*	0.0*	6.2*	11.2*	16.2*	10.6*	2.7*	6.4*	10.2*
Attempted to take property	163,280	100.0	3.6*	18.2*	24.8	0.0*	0.0*	0.0*	2.3*	20.6*	4.1*	5.0*	0.0*	5.7*	15.6*
With injury	38,960	100.0	7.7*	27.5*	9.7*	0.0*	0.0*	0.0*	9.7*	29.0*	0.0*	0.0*	0.0*	8.5*	8.0*
Without injury	124,320	100.0	2.3*	15.3*	29.5	0.0*	0.0*	0.0*	0.0*	18.0*	5.3*	6.6*	0.0*	4.9*	18.0*
Assault	2,736,760	100.0	14.5	21.3	20.8	7.6	0.1	0.3*	0.0*	3.1	4.4	3.5	4.2	4.1	16.2
Aggravated	497,490	100.0	7.5	23.9	24.9	7.3*	0.0*	0.0*	0.0*	7.0*	1.9*	4.4*	4.2*	6.5*	12.5
Simple	2,239,270	100.0	16.1	20.7	19.9	7.7	0.1*	0.4*	0.0*	2.2	5.0	3.3	4.2	3.5	17.0
Purse snatching/pocket picking	175,810	100.0	9.6*	10.6*	21.5	6.1*	0.0*	7.8*	5.1*	16.2*	11.1*	1.8*	1.7*	0.0*	8.4*
All property crimes	**14,073,950**	**100.0%**	**8.6%**	**5.1%**	**26.7%**	**3.9%**	**3.0%**	**5.6%**	**7.4%**	**13.0%**	**8.7%**	**2.9%**	**0.6%**	**3.9%**	**10.4%**
Household burglary	2,023,280	100.0	4.2	4.2	20.2	5.5	4.6	7.6	7.9	16.4	7.8	4.5	0.9*	3.9	12.2
Completed	1,710,040	100.0	3.9	5.0	18.2	3.9	4.9	7.8	9.4	16.7	7.9	4.2	1.0*	4.4	12.7
Forcible entry	381,430	100.0	2.7*	4.1*	9.5*	2.3*	6.6*	5.3*	9.5*	15.9	9.5*	6.6*	2.2*	7.0*	18.8
Unlawful entry without force	1,328,610	100.0	4.3	5.3	20.7	4.3	4.4	8.5	9.4	17.0	7.5	3.5	0.7*	3.7	10.9
Attempted forcible entry	313,240	100.0	5.8*	0.0*	31.5	14.5	2.9*	6.4*	0.0*	14.8	7.4	6.7*	0.0*	0.9*	9.2*
Motor vehicle theft	211,600	100.0	1.3*	9.5*	31.2	0.0*	5.5*	4.8*	2.3*	9.0*	7.9*	6.2*	4.4*	4.1*	13.8*
Completed	81,870	100.0	0.0*	20.0*	6.3*	0.0*	6.8*	0.0*	6.0*	7.1*	3.7*	9.5*	11.3*	8.0*	21.4*
Attempted	129,730	100.0	2.2*	2.9*	46.9	0.0*	4.6*	7.8*	0.0*	10.2*	10.5*	4.2*	0.0*	1.7*	9.0*
Theft	11,839,070	100.0	9.5	5.2	27.8	3.7	2.7	5.3	7.5	12.5	8.9	2.6	0.5	3.9	10.0
Completed	11,455,860	100.0	9.7	5.2	27.3	3.7	2.7	5.3	7.7	12.7	8.9	2.5	0.5	3.9	9.9
Attempted	383,210	100.0	4.9*	3.4*	42.6	5.7*	2.8*	5.3*	0.0*	7.4*	9.3*	3.2*	0.7*	2.8*	12.0

Note: Detail may not add to total shown because of rounding.
Some respondents may have cited more than one reason for not reporting victimizations to the police.
*Estimate is based on about 10 or fewer sample cases.
[a]Includes verbal threats of rape and threats of sexual assault.

SOURCE: "Table 102. Personal and Property Crimes, 2005: Percent of Reasons for Not Reporting Victimizations to the Police, by Type of Crime," in *Criminal Victimization in the United States, 2005 Statistical Tables*, U.S. Department of Justice, Office of Justice Programs, Bureau of Justice Statistics, December 2006.

TABLE 9.5

Reasons for not reporting violent victimizations to the police, by victim-offender relationship and type of crime, 2005

Relationship and type of crime	Number of reasons for not reporting	Total	Percent of reasons for not reporting													
			Reported to another official	Private or personal matter	Object recovered; offender unsuccessful	Not important enough	Insurance would not cover	Not aware crime occurred until later	Unable to recover property; no ID no.	Lack of proof	Police would not want to be bothered	Police inefficient, ineffective, or biased	Fear of reprisal	Too inconvenient or time consuming	Other reasons
Involving strangers															
Crimes of violence	1,689,490	100.0%	10.4%	13.7%	24.6%	6.5%	0.2%*	0.5%*	1.1%*	7.6%	6.5%	5.4%	4.6%	5.6%	13.3%
Rape/sexual assault[a]	41,910	100.0%	49.6*	0.0*	12.7*	0.0*	0.0*	0.0*	0.0*	0.0*	19.9*	6.9*	11.0*	0.0*	0.0*
Robbery	302,810	100.0%	3.0*	8.5*	18.1	0.0*	0.0*	0.0*	6.0*	19.0	11.7*	10.0*	1.5*	8.3*	13.9
Assault	1,344,770	100.0%	10.8	15.3	26.4	8.2	0.2*	0.6*	0.0*	5.3	5.0	4.3	5.0	5.2	13.6
Involving nonstrangers															
Crimes of violence	1,582,190	100.0%	16.2	27.4	15.3	6.3	0.0*	0.4*	0.0*	1.5*	4.4	2.6	3	2.8	20.3
Rape/sexual assault[a]	100,500	100.0%	5.1*	31.1*	0.0*	0.0*	0.0*	0.0*	0.0*	0.0*	10.8*	2.8*	0.0*	2.4*	47.7
Robbery	89,700	100.0%	0.0*	29.7*	31.4*	0.0*	0.0*	7.6*	0.0*	12.5*	3.9*	0.0*	0.0*	0.0*	14.9*
Assault	1,391,980	100.0%	18.1	27.0	15.3	7.1	0.0*	0.0*	0.0*	0.9*	3.9	2.7	3.4	3.0	18.7

Note: Detail may not add to total shown because of rounding.
Some respondents may have cited more than one reason for not reporting victimizations to the police.
*Estimate is based on about 10 or fewer sample cases.
[a]Includes verbal threats of rape and threats of sexual assault.

SOURCE: "Table 104. Personal Crimes of Violence, 2005: Percent of Reasons for Not Reporting Victimizations to the Police, by Victim–Offender Relationship and Type of Crime," in *Criminal Victimization in the United States, 2005 Statistical Tables*, U.S. Department of Justice, Office of Justice Programs, Bureau of Justice Statistics, December 2006, http://www.ojp.usdoj.gov/bjs/pub/pdf/cvus05.pdf (accessed June 26, 2008)

FIGURE 9.1

Percent of nonfatal intimate partner victimizations reported to police, by victim race and gender, 2001–05

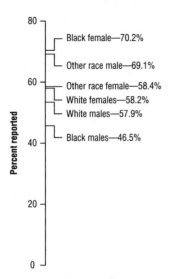

Black female—70.2%
Other race male—69.1%
Other race female—58.4%
White females—58.2%
White males—57.9%
Black males—46.5%

SOURCE: Shannan Catalano, "Percent of Nonfatal Intimate Partner Victimizations Reported to Police, by Victim Race and Gender, 2001–2005," in *Intimate Partner Violence in the United States*, U.S. Department of Justice, Bureau of Justice Statistics, December 2007, http://www.ojp.usdoj.gov/bjs/intimate/report.htm (accessed May 20, 2008)

FIGURE 9.2

Percent of nonfatal intimate partner victimizations reported to police, by victim ethnicity and gender, 2001–05

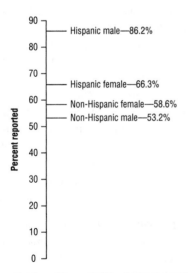

Hispanic male—86.2%
Hispanic female—66.3%
Non-Hispanic female—58.6%
Non-Hispanic male—53.2%

SOURCE: Shannan Catalano, "Percent of Nonfatal Intimate Partner Victimizations Reported to Police, by Victim Ethnicity and Gender, 2001–2005," in *Intimate Partner Violence in the United States*, U.S. Department of Justice, Bureau of Justice Statistics, December 2007, http://www.ojp.usdoj.gov/bjs/intimate/report.htm (accessed May 20, 2008)

TABLE 9.6

Intimate partner violence victims who failed to report their victimization to the police, by reasons for not reporting and by gender, 2001–05

Reason victimizations not reported	Percent of victims who did not report the victimization	
	Female victims	Male victims
Private or personal matter	22.8%	39.2%
Afraid of reprisal	12.4	5.3*
Protect offender	14.4	15.6
Minor crime	8.4	8.5*
Police will not do anything	7.9	—
Police ineffectiveness	2.7	2*
Inconvenient	3.4	1.4*
Reported to another official	3.1	—*
Police biased	1.3*	1.2*
Not clear a crime occurred	1.9*	8.6*
Don't know why I did not report it	0.6*	1.2*
Other reason given	22	17.1

—Information is not provided because the small number of cases is insufficient for reliable estimates.
*Based on 10 or fewer sample cases.
Note: Detail may not add to 100% because victims may report more than one reason and because of values not shown in instances when the small number of cases in category is insufficient for reliable estimates.

SOURCE: Shannan Catalano, "Reasons for Not Reporting," in *Intimate Partner Violence in the United States*, U.S. Department of Justice, Bureau of Justice Statistics, December 2007, http://www.ojp.usdoj.gov/bjs/intimate/report.htm (accessed May 20, 2008)

police to inform victims of their rights, which include the acquisition of protection orders and referral to emergency and shelter facilities and transportation.

In "Determining Police Response to Domestic Violence Victims" (*American Behavioral Scientist*, vol. 36, no. 5, May–June 1993), a landmark study of four precincts of the Detroit Police Department and their responses to domestic violence in 1993, Eve S. Buzawa and Thomas Austin document several factors that affected police decisions to arrest offenders:

- The presence of bystanders or children during the abuse

- The presence of guns and sharp objects as weapons

- An injury resulting from the assault

- The offender and victim sharing the same residence whether they were married or not

- The victim's desire to have the offender arrested (of the victims who expressed such a desire, arrests were made in 44% of the cases; when the victim did not want the offender arrested, arrests were made in only 21% of the cases)

Mandatory Arrests

Arrest gained popularity as a tactic after the publication of the first in a series of six studies funded by the National Institute of Justice known as the Spouse Assault Replication Program. All the studies were designed to explain how arrest in domestic violence cases could serve

a report of the violence within eight hours of the incident. Most state codes authorizing warrantless arrests require

Domestic Violence, Law Enforcement, and Court Responses to Domestic Violence

as a deterrent to future violence. Lawrence W. Sherman and Richard A. Berk, the authors of the influential first study in the series, "The Specific Deterrent Effects of Arrest for Domestic Assault" (*American Sociological Review*, vol. 49, 1984), find that "the arrest intervention certainly did not make things worse and may well have made things better."

Even though Sherman and Berk caution about generalizing the results of a small study dealing with a single police department in which few police officers properly followed the test procedure, they conclude that in instances of domestic violence, an arrest is advisable except in cases where it would be clearly counterproductive. At the same time, Sherman and Berk recommend allowing police a certain amount of flexibility when making decisions about individual situations, on the premise that police officers must be permitted to rely on professional judgment based on experience.

Sherman and Berk's study had a tremendous impact on police practices, although J. David Hirschel, Ira W. Hutchison III, and Charles W. Dean explain in "The Failure of Arrest to Deter Spouse Abuse" (*Journal of Research in Crime and Delinquency*, vol. 29, no. 1, 1992) that the five other Spouse Assault Replication Program studies found arrest had little or no effect on domestic violence recurrence. Some police departments have adopted a presumptive arrest policy. This policy means that an arrest should be made unless clear and compelling reasons exist not to arrest. Presumptive arrest provisions forbid officers from basing the decision to arrest on the victim's preference or on a perception of the victim's willingness to testify or participate in the proceedings. Proponents point out that arresting an offender gives the victim a respite from fear and an opportunity to look for help. Furthermore, they claim it prevents bias in arrests.

By the 1990s as many as one out of three police precincts had adopted a mandatory arrest policy in domestic abuse cases. In "The Influence of Mandatory Arrest Policies, Police Organizational Characteristics, and Situational Variables on the Probability of Arrest in Domestic Violence Cases" (*Crime and Delinquency*, vol. 51, no. 4, 2005), David Eitle of the Florida International University finds that mandatory police arrest policies do result in more arrests when called to the scene of a domestic assault. In addition, he notes that these policies reduce somewhat the overrepresentation of African-Americans among those arrested. However, do these arrests reduce violence against women?

Some studies suggest that mandatory arrest policies have positive effects. For example, Jacquelyn C. Campbell et al. explain in "Risk Factors for Femicide in Abusive Relationships: Results from a Multisite Case Control Study" (*American Journal of Public Health*, vol. 93, no. 7, July 2003) that previous arrest for battering actually decreased women's risk of being subsequently killed by the batterer. According to Christopher D. Maxwell, Joel H. Garner, and Jeffrey A. Fagan, in "The Effects of Arrest on Intimate Partner Violence: New Evidence from the Spouse Assault Replication Program" (July 2001, http://www.ncjrs.gov/pdffiles1/nij/188199.pdf), arrest of batterers is consistently related to subsequent reduced aggression against their intimate partner.

However, Debra Houry, Sudha Reddy, and Constance Parramore of Emory University suggest in "Characteristics of Victims Coarrested for Intimate Partner Violence" (*Journal of Interpersonal Violence*, vol. 21, no. 11, 2006) that some battered women's advocates do not support mandatory arrest. They fear that poor and minority families are treated more harshly than middle-class families and that if the police arrive and both spouses are bloodied by the fight, both will be arrested, forcing the children into foster care. In fact, Mary A. Finn and Pamela Bettis of Georgia State University state in "Punitive Action or Gentle Persuasion" (*Violence against Women*, vol. 12, no. 3, 2006) that "mandatory and preferred arrest policies may be resulting in a backlash for victims who are arrested along with their batterers. Officers justified arrest of both parties, citing that such was required by law and the desire to force both parties to obtain counseling for their relationship."

In "The Voices of Domestic Violence Victims: Predictors of Victim Preference for Arrest and the Relationship between Preference for Arrest and Revictimization" (*Crime and Delinquency*, vol. 49, no. 2, April 2003), David Hirschel and Ira W. Hutchinson find support for a police policy of taking victim preferences into account in the decision to arrest. Victims based their preferences for arrest on the seriousness of the violence and the perpetrator's previous abusive behavior; in fact, victims proved to be good judges of the seriousness of the violence and the likelihood of it recurring. The researchers indicate that victims who wanted their abuser arrested were more likely to suffer subsequent abuse than were victims who did not want their batterer arrested. Hirschel and Hutchinson state that "based on these data, victim desire for arrest of the offender would appear to be a factor that police should take into account in determining subsequent action."

DO MANDATORY ARREST POLICIES DISEMPOWER THE VICTIM? Paula C. Barata and Frank Schneider examine in "Battered Women Add Their Voices to the Debate about the Merits of Mandatory Arrest" (*Women's Studies Quarterly*, vol. 32, no. 3–4, 2004) the debate about mandatory arrest policies from a different angle: from the victim's viewpoint. They find that a large proportion of battered women actually support a mandatory arrest policy, although they "were more likely to see the benefits of mandatory arrest for other victims/survivors than for themselves." Barata and Schneider hypothesize that battered women's support for mandatory arrest policies in their own situations was influenced by factors such as love for their battering partner, their fear of retaliatory abuse, or their worries about money.

Battered women whose partner had been arrested generally described a pattern of initial decreased violence when the batterer was removed from the home, but an increase in violence when the abuser, who was potentially angry about being arrested, returned home. Nearly four out of ten (38.5%) of the women interviewed believed the threat of another arrest would decrease the violence in the long run.

However, despite their disbelief in deterrence, a majority of women still thought that domestic violence was a crime, not a family problem, and several participants liked mandatory arrest policies because they proved to the abuser that assault is wrong and will be punished by the legal system. In fact, most of the battered women interviewed by Barata and Schneider did not view mandatory arrest policies as disempowering. The researchers argue that this is for two reasons: first, victims do not want the responsibility for deciding if their battering partner will be arrested and were relieved when the decision was taken out of their hands, and second, victims of battering do not believe they have much influence over the decision to arrest, even without a mandatory arrest policy in place. Also, the vast majority of women believed mandatory arrest policies made police take their abuse more seriously.

JoAnn Miller of Purdue University also studied victims' perceptions of empowerment or disempowerment as a result of arrest. In "An Arresting Experiment: Domestic Violence Victim Experiences and Perceptions" (*Journal of Interpersonal Violence*, vol. 18, no. 7, July 2003), she examined two concepts of power: personal power (control of economic and social resources) and legal power (perceived empowerment in response to police intervention). Miller finds that women did not use their sense of personal power (derived from an independent income) to end domestic violence. However, she notes that victims' perception of legal power (derived from their satisfaction with the police action taken) could be used to feel safer and to control interactions with a violent partner in the future. In Miller's view, mandatory arrest policies tend to undermine victims' personal power because they do not take into account victims' needs.

Victims' Attitudes toward Police Response

In "Perceptions of the Police by Female Victims of Domestic Partner Violence" (*Violence against Women*, vol. 9, no. 11, November 2003), Robert Apsler, Michele R. Cummins, and Steven Carl investigate "what female victims of domestic violence wanted from the police, the extent to which they perceived they obtained what they wanted, and how helpful they found the actions of the police." They find that women in the study were satisfied with the police response to their call. The women believed the police had been helpful, and more than 80% of them said they would definitely call the police for help in the future. Apsler, Cummins, and Carl emphasize that the particular police department involved in the study had recently instituted policies specifically designed to help battered women.

NOT ALL VICTIMS WHO SEEK POLICE ATTENTION ARE THE SAME

Another study by Apsler, Cummins, and Carl points out the need for a police response tailored to individual victims' needs. In "Fear and Expectations: Differences among Female Victims of Domestic Violence Who Come to the Attention of Police" (*Violence and Victims*, vol. 17, no. 4, August 2002), Apsler, Cummins, and Carl report that one-quarter of women who had come to a police department requesting intervention in a violent intimate partner dispute said they were afraid of their abuser. Another 6% were fairly afraid, 12% said they were slightly afraid, and 36% claimed they were not at all afraid of their abuser. Taken together, these latter two groups accounted for nearly half of participants reporting little or no fear of their abuser.

The results were similar in terms of participants' expectations of future abuse. Apsler, Cummins, and Carl find that just 21% of victims thought future abuse was likely, and well over half of women surveyed said future abuse was not at all likely or only slightly likely. These findings challenge long-standing beliefs that the victims who tend to come to the attention of the police are those who most fear future abuse.

Interestingly, there were no statistically significant relationships found between victims' expectations of future violence and whether they lived with their abuser, had children under eighteen years old, or were able to support themselves financially. A less surprising result was that victims' expectations of future abuse strongly influenced their desired future relationship with their offender. A strong majority (90%) of the participants who thought future abuse was fairly likely or likely wanted to permanently separate from the offenders. In contrast, only about half of the women who thought further abuse was not at all likely wanted permanent separation.

Apsler, Cummins, and Carl conclude that the differences between victims of domestic violence and their varied expectations when seeking police attention point to a need for law enforcement agencies to offer a variety of police responses tailored to victims' needs. For example, they suggest that mandatory arrest of victims' aggressors might not help as a universally applicable strategy for all victims, especially women who do not fear further abuse. By contrast, fearful victims might be reassured and experience greater security if police maintained regular, ongoing contact with them following the incident. Apsler, Cummins, and Carl add that police follow-up might also send a powerful message to perpetrators—that they are under surveillance and that future violations will not be tolerated.

PROTECTION ORDERS
What Are They?

An abuse victim in any state may go to court to obtain a protection order. Also referred to as "restraining orders" or "injunctions," civil orders of protection are legally binding court orders that prohibit an individual who has committed an act of domestic violence from further abusing the victim. Even though the terms are often used interchangeably, restraining orders usually refer to short-term or temporary sanctions, whereas protection orders have longer duration and may be permanent. These orders generally prohibit harassment, contact, communication, and physical proximity to the victim. Protection orders are common and readily obtained, but they are not always effective.

All states and the District of Columbia have laws that allow an abused adult to petition the court for an order of protection. States also have laws to permit people variously related to the abuser to file for protection orders. Relatives of the victim, children of either partner, couples in dating relationships, same-sex couples, and former spouses are among those who can file for a protection order in a majority of the states, the District of Columbia, and Puerto Rico. In Hawaii and Illinois, those who shelter an abused person can also obtain a protective order against the abuser.

Petitioners may file for protection orders in circumstances other than violent physical abuse, including sexual assault, marital rape, harassment, emotional abuse, and stalking. Protection orders are valid for varying lengths of time depending on the state. In thirty states the orders are in force for six months to a year. In Illinois and Wisconsin the orders last two years, and in California and Hawaii they are in effect for three years. Furthermore, some states have extended the time during which a general or incident-specific protective order is effective. For example, a no-contact order issued against a stalker convicted in California remains in effect for ten years. In Iowa five-year protection orders are issued and additional five-year extensions may be obtained. New Jersey offers permanent protective orders, and a conviction for stalking serves as an application for a permanent restraining order. Judges in Connecticut may issue standing criminal restraining orders that remain in effect until they are altered or revoked by the court.

Protection orders give victims an option other than filing a criminal complaint. Issued quickly, usually within twenty-four hours, they provide safety for the victim by barring or evicting the abuser from the household. Statutes in most states make violating a protection order a matter of criminal contempt, a misdemeanor, or even a felony. However, this judicial protection has little meaning if the police do not maintain records and follow through with arrest should the abuser violate the order.

The "full faith and credit" provision of the Violence against Women Act was passed to establish nationwide enforcement of protection orders in courts throughout the country. States, territories, and tribal lands were ordered to honor protection orders issued in other jurisdictions—although the act did not mandate how these orders were to be enforced. According to Christina DeJong and Amanda Burgess-Proctor of Michigan State University, in "A Summary of Personal Protection Order Statutes in the United States" (*Violence against Women*, vol. 12, no. 1, January 2006), most states have amended their state domestic violence codes or statutes to reflect the new requirement, although the states vary widely on how easy it is for battered women to get their protection orders enforced. Courts and law enforcement agencies in most states have access to electronic registries of protection orders, both to verify the existence of an order and to assess whether violations have occurred.

Effects of Protection Orders

In "Protection Orders and Intimate Partner Violence: An 18-Month Study of 150 Black, Hispanic, and White Women" (*American Journal of Public Health*, vol. 94, no. 4, April 2004), Judith McFarlane et al. report on their study of the effects on intimate partner violence of the application for and receipt of a two-year protection order against abusers. The researchers interviewed 150 women over an eighteen-month period to determine whether protection orders diminished violence. Even though almost half (44%) of the women reported at least one violation of the order, McFarlane et al. find significant reductions in physical assaults, stalking, and threats of assault over time among all women who applied for a protection order, even if they had not been granted the order. McFarlane et al. hypothesize that it was not the protection order itself that led to the diminished violence but the contact with the criminal justice system that exposed the battering to public view.

Victoria L. Holt et al. come to a similar conclusion in "Do Protection Orders Affect the Likelihood of Future Partner Violence and Injury?" (*American Journal of Preventive Medicine*, vol. 24, no. 1, January 2003), a study of 448 female victims of intimate partner violence. The researchers measured the number of unwelcome calls or visits, threats, threats with weapons, psychological, sexual, or physical abuse, and abuse-related medical care among women who had obtained a civil protection order and those who had not. Holt et al. find that women who obtained a protection order following an abusive incident had a significantly decreased risk of contact by the abuser, threats by weapons, injury, and abuse-related medical care.

Enforcement of Orders of Protection

Robert J. Kane of the American University examines in "Police Responses to Restraining Orders in Domestic Violence Incidents" (*Criminal Justice and Behavior*, vol. 27, no. 5, 2000) arrest patterns of batterers who violate restraining orders. Even though all the violators in his study were required by Massachusetts state law to be immediately arrested, in reality only between 20% and 40% of violators of restraining orders were taken into custody. Kane finds that restraining orders had no significant effect on arrest rate; instead, police perception of imminent danger to the victim was the strongest predictor of arrest. He also finds that as the number of domestic violence calls from one victim to police increased, the rate of arrest decreased, regardless of whether a restraining order was in place. Kane suggests that further studies should be done into variations in arrest rates that include personal characteristics of police officers and the social contexts of the couples involved in domestic violence incidents.

The U.S. Department of Justice observes in *Enforcement of Protective Orders* (January 2002, http://www.ojp.usdoj.gov/ovc/publications/bulletins/legalseries/bulletin4/ncj189190.pdf) that even though all the states have passed some form of legislation to benefit victims of domestic violence, and thirty-two states have integrated these rights at the constitutional level, the scope and enforcement of these rights varies. The Department of Justice calls for law enforcement agencies, prosecutors, and judges to be completely informed about the existence and specific terms and requirements of orders and to act to enforce them. Furthermore, it asserts that "unequivocal standardized enforcement of court orders is imperative if protective orders are to be taken seriously by the offenders they attempt to restrain."

LANDMARK LEGAL DECISIONS

Before the 1962 landmark case *Self v. Self* (58 Cal. 2d 683), when the California Supreme Court ruled that "one spouse may maintain an action against the other for battering," women had no legal recourse against abusive partners. The judicial system had tended to view wife abuse as a matter to be resolved within the family. Maintaining that "a man's home is his castle," the federal government traditionally had been reluctant to violate the sanctity of the home. Furthermore, many legal authorities persisted in "blaming the victim," maintaining that the wife was, to some degree, responsible for her own beating by somehow inciting her husband to lose his temper.

Yet even after *Self v. Self*, turning to the judicial system for help was still unlikely to bring assistance to or result in justice for victims of spousal abuse. Jurisdictions throughout the United States continued to ignore the complaints of battered women until the late 1970s.

Many victims of domestic violence have sought legal protection from their abusive partner. This section summarizes the outcomes of several landmark cases that not only helped define judicial responsibility but also shaped the policies and practices aimed at protecting victimized women.

Baker v. The City of New York

Sandra Baker was estranged from her husband. In 1955 the local domestic relations court issued a protective order directing her husband, who had a history of serious mental illness, "not to strike, molest, threaten, or annoy" his wife. Baker called the police when her husband created a disturbance at the family home. When a police officer arrived, she showed him the court order. The officer told her it was "no good" and "only a piece of paper" and refused to take any action.

Baker went to the domestic relations court and told her story to a probation officer. While making a phone call, she saw her husband in the corridor. She went to the probation officer and told him her husband was in the corridor. She asked if she could wait in his office because she was "afraid to stand in the room with him." The probation officer told her to go to the waiting room. Minutes later, her husband shot and wounded her.

Baker sued the city of New York, claiming that the city owed her more protection than she was given. The New York State Supreme Court Appellate Division, in *Baker v. The City of New York* (1966), agreed that the city of New York failed to fulfill its obligation. The court found that she was "a person recognized by order of protection as one to whom a special duty was owed ... and peace officers had a duty to supply protection to her." Neither the police officer nor the probation officer had fulfilled this duty, and both were found guilty of negligence. Because the officers were representatives of the city of New York, Baker had the right to sue the city.

Equal Protection

Another option desperate women have used in response to unchecked violence and abuse is to sue the police for failing to offer protection, alleging that the police violated their constitutional rights to liberty and equal protection under the law. The Equal Protection Clause of the Fourteenth Amendment provides that no state shall "deny to any person within its jurisdiction the equal protection of the laws." This clause prohibits states from arbitrarily classifying individuals by group membership. If a woman can prove that a police department has a gender-based policy of refusing to arrest men who abuse their wives, she can claim that the policy is based on gender stereotypes and therefore violates the equal protection law.

THURMAN V. CITY OF TORRINGTON. Between October 1982 and June 1983 Tracey Thurman repeatedly called the Torrington, Connecticut, police to report that her estranged husband was threatening her life and that of her child. The police ignored her requests for help no matter how often she called or how serious the situation became. At one point her husband attacked her in view of the police and was arrested. Thurman obtained protection and restraining orders against him after this incident. However, when her husband later came to her home and threatened her again, in violation of his probation and the court orders, police refused to intervene.

On June 10, 1983, Thurman's husband came to her home. She called the police. He then stabbed her repeatedly around the chest, neck, and throat. A police officer arrived twenty-five minutes later but did not arrest her husband, despite the attack. Three more police officers arrived. The husband went into the house and brought out their child and threw him down on his bleeding mother. The officers still did not arrest him. Even though his wife was on the stretcher waiting to be placed in the ambulance, he came at her again. Only at that point did police take him into custody. Thurman later sued the city of Torrington, claiming she was denied equal protection under the law.

In *Thurman v. City of Torrington* (595 F. Supp. 1521 [D. Conn. 1984]), the U.S. District Court for Downstate Connecticut agreed, stating:

> City officials and police officers are under an affirmative duty to preserve law and order, and to protect the personal safety of people in the community. This duty applies equally to women whose personal safety is threatened by individuals with whom they have or have had a domestic relationship as well as to all other people whose personal safety is threatened.... A police officer may not ... automatically decline to make an arrest simply because the assailant and his victim are married to each other. Such inaction on the part of the officer is a denial of the equal protection of the laws.

There could be no question, the court concluded, that the city of Torrington, through its police department, had "condoned a pattern or practice of affording inadequate protection or no protection at all, to women who complained of having been abused by their husbands or others with whom they have had close relations." Therefore, the police had failed in their duty to protect Tracey Thurman and deserved to be sued.

Due Process

The Due Process Clause of the Fourteenth Amendment provides that no state can "deprive any person of life, liberty, or property, without due process of law; nor

deny to any person within its jurisdiction the equal protection of the laws." It does not, however, obligate the state to protect the public from harm or provide services that would protect them. Rather, a state may create special conditions in which that state has constitutional obligations to particular citizens because of a special relationship between the state and the individual. Abused women have used this argument to claim that being under a protection order puts them in a special relationship.

MACIAS V. HIDE. During the eighteen months before her estranged husband, Avelino Macias, murdered her at her place of work, Maria Teresa Macias had filed twenty-two police complaints. In the months before her death, Avelino Macias sexually abused his wife, broke into her home, terrorized, and stalked her. The victim's family filed a wrongful death lawsuit against the Sonoma County Sheriff's Department in California, accusing the department of failing to provide Macias equal protection under the law and of discriminating against her as a Hispanic and a woman.

The U.S. District Court for the Northern District of California dismissed the case because Judge D. Lowell Jensen (1928–) said there was no connection between Macias's murder and how the sheriff's department had responded to her complaints. In *Macias v. Hide* (No. 99-15662 [2000]), the U.S. Court of Appeals for the Ninth Circuit reversed the earlier decision and ruled that the lawsuit could proceed with the discovery phase and pretrial motions. Judge Arthur L. Alarcon (1935–) of the U.S. Court of Appeals for the Ninth Circuit conveyed the unanimous opinion of the court when he wrote, "It is well established that 'there is no constitutional right to be protected by the state against being murdered by criminals or madmen.' There is a constitutional right, however, to have police services administered in a nondiscriminatory manner—a right that is violated when a state actor denies such protection to disfavored persons."

After this decision the case proceeded to trial. In June 2002 Sonoma County agreed to pay $1 million to the Macias family to settle the case. The settlement agreement did not include an admission of any wrongdoing by the county. Nevertheless, domestic violence activists lauded the result.

TOWN OF CASTLE ROCK V. GONZALES. The U.S. Supreme Court reaffirmed in 2005 that governments are not required to offer citizens protection from violent abusers. According to the case *Town of Castle Rock, Colorado v. Gonzales* (000 U.S. 04-278 [2005]), Jessica Gonzales's three children were taken from her home by her estranged husband in violation of an order of protection. When she alerted the police and repeatedly asked them for assistance, they made no effort to find the children or enforce the state's mandatory arrest law. The children were killed later that night. Gonzales sued the town, arguing that by failing to respond to her calls the police had violated her right to due process of law, and the case eventually reached the U.S. Supreme Court. In its review, the Court found in June 2005 that "Colorado law has not created a personal entitlement to enforcement of restraining orders" and that the state's law did not really require arrest in all cases, but actually left considerable discretion in the hands of the police. So even though the Castle Rock police made a tragically incorrect decision in this case, they did not do so in violation of Gonzales's due process rights. The American Civil Liberties Union subsequently filed the case with the Inter-American Commission on Human Rights, arguing that domestic violence victims have the right to be protected by the state from their abuser. The commission heard the case in March 2007. In October 2007 the commission decided to admit the case. In the next phase, the commission will decide whether the human rights of Gonzales and her children were violated.

KEY DOMESTIC VIOLENCE LEGISLATION

Even though appealing to the judicial system for help will not solve all the problems an abused woman faces, the reception a battered woman can expect from the system—police, prosecutors, and courts—improved markedly in the late twentieth century. The Violence against Women Act, signed into law by President Bill Clinton (1946–) in September 1994, did much to help. The act simultaneously strengthened prevention and prosecution of violent crimes against women and provided law enforcement officials with the tools they needed to prosecute batterers. Even though the system is far from perfect, legal authorities are far more likely to view abuse complaints as legitimate and serious than they had in the past.

The Violence against Women Act

A key provision in the Violence against Women Act, the civil rights provisions of Title III, declares that violent crimes against women motivated by gender violate victims' federal civil rights—giving victims access to federal courts for redress. In 2000 the civil rights section of the act was tested in the U.S. Supreme Court. Christy Brzonkala, an eighteen-year-old freshman at Virginia Polytechnic Institute, was violently attacked and raped by two men, Antonio Morrison and James Crawford, on September 21, 1994. Brzonkala did not immediately report the rape, and no physical evidence of the rape was preserved. Two months later, she filed a complaint with the school; after learning that the college took limited action against the two men, she withdrew from the school and sued her assailants for damages in federal court.

Brzonkala's case reached the Supreme Court in 2000. Briefs in favor of giving victims of gender-based violence access to federal courts were filed by dozens of groups (such as the American Medical Women's Association, the National Association of Human Rights Workers, the National Coalition against Domestic Violence, and the National Women's Health Network) as well as by law scholars and human rights experts. However, in May 2000 five of the Supreme Court justices decided in *United States v. Morrison et al.* (529 U.S. 598) that Congress could not enact a law giving victims of gender-motivated violence access to federal civil rights remedies. The majority opinion emphasized that "the Constitution requires a distinction between what is truly national and what is truly local"—and it ruled that the violent assault of Christy Brzonkala was local.

In October 2000 Congress responded to the Supreme Court decision by passing new legislation, the Victims of Trafficking and Violence Protection Act. The new statute included these titles: Strengthening Law Enforcement to Reduce Violence against Women, Strengthening Services to Victims of Violence, Limiting the Effects of Violence on Children, and Strengthening Education and Training to Combat Violence against Women. The act allocated $3.3 billion over five years to fund traditional support services along with prevention and education about dating violence, rape, and stalking via the Internet, as well as new programs for transitional housing and expanded protection for immigrant women. The new act did not mention women's civil rights. The Violence against Women Act was reauthorized in 2005, providing funding to programs through 2009.

Domestic Violence Gun Ban

Federal law includes batterers convicted of domestic violence crimes or those with domestic violence protection orders filed against them among the people who are prohibited from owning or carrying guns. Since 1994, most people attempting to purchase guns in the United States have had to pass a background check first. In *Background Checks for Firearm Transfers, 2006 Statistical Tables* (March 19, 2008, http://www.ojp.usdoj.gov/bjs/pub/pdf/bcft06st.pdf), the BJS states that between 1994 and 2006, 78.5 million applications for firearm permits or transfers were subjected to background investigations by the Federal Bureau of Investigation (FBI) and state and local agencies. (See Table 9.7.) Of these applications, close to 1.5 million (1.9%) were rejected. A substantial proportion of these rejections were because of previous domestic violence convictions. In 2006, 12.4% of applications rejected by the FBI, 10.4% of applications rejected by the state, and 11.1% of applications rejected by local authorities were rejected because of a domestic violence misdemeanor conviction. (See Table 9.8.) After prior felony convictions and other criminal history, domestic violence was the third-leading reason for rejecting applicants' gun permit requests.

Loopholes in state and federal laws allow batterers to purchase guns despite the federal ban. In many states private gun owners can sell their firearms without background checks. In addition, many states keep incomplete records of domestic violence offenders and orders of protection. Still other evidence suggests that some gun dealers knowingly allow people who are not legally eligible to purchase firearms to buy them through a third party. However, Elizabeth Richardson Vigdor and James A. Mercy report in "Do Laws Restricting Access to Firearms by Domestic Violence Offenders Prevent Intimate Partner Homicide?" (*Evaluation Review*, vol. 30, no. 3, June 2006) that female intimate partner homicide declines by 7% after a state passes a law restricting access to firearms by individuals subject to a restraining order, although they see no decline in homicides resulting from restricting access of those convicted of a misdemeanor to firearms.

DIFFICULTIES IN THE COURT SYSTEM

An appeal to the U.S. judicial system should be an effective method of obtaining justice. For battered women, however, this has not always been the case. In the past ignorance, social prejudices, and uneven attention from the criminal justice system all tended to underestimate the severity and importance of battering crimes against women. Even though society has become significantly less tolerant of domestic violence, and laws in many states criminalize behavior previously considered acceptable, old attitudes and biases continue to plague intimate partner violence and spouse abuse cases in the courts.

Intimate partner abuse cases are often complicated by evidence problems, because domestic violence usually takes place behind closed doors. The volatile and unpredictable emotions and motivations influencing the behav-

TABLE 9.7

Number of applications and estimates of denials for firearm transfers or permits, 1994–2006

	Number of applications		
	Received	Denied	Percent denied
Total	78,522,000	1,495,000	1.9%
Brady interim period[a]			
1994–1998	12,740,000	312,000	2.4
Permanent Brady[b]	65,782,000	1,182,000	1.8
1998[c]	893,000	20,000	2.2
1999	8,621,000	204,000	2.4
2000	7,699,000	153,000	2
2001	7,958,000	151,000	1.9
2002	7,806,000	136,000	1.7
2003	7,831,000	126,000	1.6
2004	8,084,000	126,000	1.6
2005	8,278,000	132,000	1.6
2006	8,612,000	134,000	1.6

Note: Counts are rounded to the nearest 1,000.

[a]From March 1, 1994 to November 29, 1998, background checks on applicants were conducted by state and local agencies, mainly on handgun transfers.

[b]The National Instant Criminal Background Check System (NICS) began operations. Checks on handgun and long gun transfers are conducted by the Federal Bureau of Investigation (FBI) and by state and local agencies. Totals combine Firearm Inquiry Statistics (FIST) estimates for state and local agencies with actual transactions and denials reported by the FBI.

[c]November 30 to December 31, 1998. Counts are from the NICS Operations Report for the period and may include multiple transactions for the same application.

SOURCE: "Table 1. Number of Applications and Estimates of Denials for Firearm Transfers or Permits since the Inception of the Brady Act, 1994–2006," in *Background Checks for Firearm Transfers, 2006—Statistical Tables*, U.S. Department of Justice, Office of Justice Programs, Bureau of Justice Statistics, March 2008, http://www.ojp.usdoj.gov/bjs/pub/html/bcft06st/table/bcft06st01.htm (accessed July 3, 2008)

TABLE 9.8

Reasons for rejection of firearm transfer applications, 1999–2006

Reason for denial	2006			1999–2006		
	FBI	State	Local	FBI	State	Local
Total	100%	100%	100%	100%	100%	100%
Felony indictment/conviction	36.1	44.7	26.2	48	56.7	27.3
Other criminal history[a]	28.5	—	—	19.4	—	—
State law prohibition	—	6.1	1.3	—	6.9	14.2
Domestic violence						
Misdemeanor conviction	9.8	10.8	14.1	12.4	10.4	11.1
Restraining order	4.3	3.7	1.3	4.5	3.4	1.8
Fugitive	6.1	9.3	10	4.1	6.7	1.2
Illegal alien	1.6	0.4	0.6	1.3	0.5	0.5
Mental illness or disability	0.6	5.7	3.5	0.4	1.8	4.1
Drug addiction	8.7	1	9.1	6.9	0.8	7.6
Local law prohibition	—	0	2.7	—	0	5.8
Other prohibitions[b]	4.3	18.4	31.3	3	12.7	26.3

Note: Reasons for denials are based on 18 U.S.C. 922 and state laws.

—Not available or Not applicable.

[a]Includes state prohibitions, multiple DUI's, non-NCIC (National Crime Information Center) warrants, and other unspecified criminal history disqualifiers.

[b]Includes juveniles, persons dishonorably discharged from the Armed Services, persons who have renounced their U.S. citizenship, and other unspecified persons.

SOURCE: "Table 4. Reasons for Denial of Firearm Transfer Applications by Checking Agencies, 1999–2006," in *Background Checks for Firearm Transfers, 2006—Statistical Tables*, U.S. Department of Justice, Office of Justice Programs, Bureau of Justice Statistics, March 2008, http://www.ojp.usdoj.gov/bjs/pub/html/bcft06st/table/bcft06st04.htm (accessed July 3, 2008)

ior of both the abuser and victim may not always fit neatly into the organized and systematic framework of legal case presentation. Finally, the varying training mandates to ensure that prosecutors and judges are better informed about the social and personal costs of domestic violence, along with society's changing attitudes toward abuse, influence the responses of the judicial system.

The victim-offender relationship is an important factor in determining how the offender is treated by the criminal justice system. On the one hand, strangers are treated more harshly because stranger offenses are considered more heinous and the true targets of the justice system. As a result, criminal law is strictly enforced against them. On the other hand, the justice system has traditionally perceived nonstranger offenses as a victim's misuse of the legal system to deal with a strained interpersonal relationship.

Willingness of Victims to Prosecute

One of the most formidable problems in prosecuting abusers is the victim's reluctance to cooperate. Even though many abused women have the courage to initiate legal proceedings against their batterer, some are later reluctant to cooperate with the prosecution because of their emotional attachment to their abuser. Other reasons for their reluctance are fear of retaliation, mistrust or lack of information about the criminal justice system, or fear of the demands of court appearances. These reasons are among the findings by Lisa Goodman, Lauren Bennett, and Mary A. Dutton in "Obstacles to Victims' Cooperation with the Criminal Prosecution of Their Abusers: The Role of Social Support" (*Violence and Victims*, vol. 14, no. 4, winter 1999) and by JoAnn Miller of Purdue University in "An Arresting Experiment: Domestic Violence Victim Experiences and Perceptions" (*Journal of Interpersonal Violence*, vol. 18, no. 7, July 2003). A victim's fear and ambivalence about testifying, and the importance of her behavior as a witness, can undoubtedly discourage some prosecutors from taking action.

However, a victim might choose not to move forward with the prosecution because the violence ceases temporarily following the arrest while the batterer is in custody. In most cases, a woman does not want her husband to go to jail with the attendant loss of income and community standing. She simply wants her husband to stop beating her.

Religious convictions, economic dependency, and family influence to drop the charges place great pressure on victimized women. Consequently, many prosecutors, some of whom believe abuse is a purely personal problem and others who believe winning the case is unlikely, test the victim's resolve to make sure she will not back out. This additional pressure drives many women to drop the charges because after being controlled by their husband, they feel that the judicial system is repeating the pattern by abusing

its power. Hence, the prosecutors' fears contribute to the problem, creating a self-perpetuating cycle.

Goodman, Bennett, and Dutton explore the reasons many domestic violence victims refuse to cooperate in the prosecution of their abuser. Surprisingly, the researchers find that the relationship between the emotional support and the cooperation with prosecutors was not significant. Similarly, institutional support, whether from police or victim advocates, was also unrelated to cooperation. Neither the level of depression nor the degree of emotional attachment to the abuser had an effect. These findings refute the common perception that the battered woman is too depressed, helpless, or attached to the abuser to cooperate in his prosecution. Instead, Goodman, Bennett, and Dutton's findings show that many domestic violence victims persevere in the face of depression and the sometimes complex emotional attachment to their partner.

Consistent with findings from earlier studies, Goodman, Bennett, and Dutton note that the more severe the violence, the more likely the abused women were to cooperate with prosecutors. Participants rearing children with the abuser were also more likely to cooperate, perhaps because these women hoped that the criminal justice system would force the abuser into treatment. In contrast, women with substance abuse problems were less than half as likely as other women to cooperate with the prosecution. Goodman, Bennett, and Dutton conclude that the women who used alcohol or drugs believed that the abuse was partly their fault or that a judge would not take them seriously. Some also feared that their substance abuse might negatively affect the court proceedings and possibly even lead to criminal charges or the loss of their children.

Factors Associated with Prosecutors' Charging Decisions in Domestic Violence Cases

In "Modeling Prosecutors' Charging Decisions in Domestic Violence Cases" (*Crime and Delinquency*, vol. 52, no. 3, 2006), John L. Worrall, Jay W. Ross, and Eric S. McCord investigate what factors influenced the decisions of prosecutors to charge a batterer and what factors influenced the decisions of prosecutors to pursue a misdemeanor or a felony charge. They collected data on 245 domestic violence cases filed by police officers, examined the impact of characteristics of the victim, offender, and the offense, and determined how these characteristics influenced the prosecutors' charging decisions.

Worrall, Ross, and McCord find that prosecutors were more likely to charge offenders if they had been arrested or if they had inflicted serious injuries on the victim. The researchers indicate that criminal charges were more likely to be filed against a male batterer than against a female batterer. They also note that if the victim supported prosecution, felony charges were more likely to be filed against the batterer.

TREATMENT FOR MALE BATTERERS

Rather than serving a prison term, many convicted batterers enter treatment programs. As a requirement of probation, most courts will order a batterer into an intervention program. Regardless of an intervention program's philosophy or methods, program directors and criminal justice professionals generally monitor offenders' behavior closely. Most batterers enter intervention programs after having been charged by the police with a specific incident of abuse.

The criminal justice system categorizes offenders based on their potential danger, history of substance abuse, psychological problems, and risk of dropout and rearrest. Ideally, interventions focus on the specific type of batterer and the approach that will most effectively produce results, such as linking a substance abuse treatment program with a batterer intervention program. Other program approaches focus on specific sociocultural characteristics, such as poverty, race, ethnicity, and age. Shelly Jackson argues in "Analyzing the Studies" (Shelly Jackson et al., *Batterer Intervention Programs: Where Do We Go from Here?* June 2003, http://www.ncjrs.gov/pdffiles1/nij/195079.pdf) that the effectiveness of batterer intervention programs might improve if the programs were seen "as part of a broader criminal justice and community response to domestic violence that includes arrest, restraining orders, intensive monitoring of batterers, and changes to social norms that may inadvertently tolerate partner violence."

Batterers leave the program either because of successful completion or because they are asked to leave. The reasons for termination include failure to cooperate, nonpayment of fees, revocation of parole or probation, failure to attend group sessions regularly, or violation of program rules. Successful completion of a program means that the offender has attended the required sessions and accomplished the program's objectives. With court-mandated clients a final report is also made to probation officials. To be successful, batterer intervention programs must have the support of the criminal justice system, which includes coordinated efforts between police, prosecutors, judges, victim advocates, and probation officers.

Program Dropout Rates

Dropout rates in battering programs are high, even though courts have ordered most clients to attend. Several studies, such as that by Jennifer Rooney and R. Karl Hanson in "Predicting Attrition from Treatment Programs for Abusive Men" (*Journal of Family Violence*, vol. 16, no. 2, 2001), record varying dropout rates, some finding that as many as 90% of the men who begin short-term treatment programs do not complete them.

High dropout rates in batterer intervention programs make it difficult to evaluate their success. Evaluations based on men who complete these programs focus on a select group of highly motivated men who likely do not reflect the composition of the group when it began. Because a follow-up is not conducted with program dropouts—the men most likely to continue their violence—research generally fails to accurately indicate the success or failure of a given treatment program.

Certain characteristics are generally related to dropout rates. Bruce Dalton of the University of South Carolina indicates in "Batterer Characteristics and Treatment Completion" (*Journal of Interpersonal Violence*, vol. 16, no. 12, 2001) that the level of threat that the batterer perceived from the referral source (e.g., the court) was, surprisingly, not related to program completion. Unemployment was the one characteristic most consistently related to dropping out of treatment. Dalton theorizes that these men have both trouble paying for the treatment and a lower investment in the "official social order." Loretta J. Stalans and Magnus Seng of Loyola University find similar results in "Identifying Subgroups at High Risk of Dropping out of Domestic Batterer Treatment: The Buffering Effects of a High School Education" (*International Journal of Offender Therapy and Comparative Criminology*, vol. 51, no. 2, 2007). The following groups had a 60% dropout rate or higher: batterers who were aggressive in general, not only in the family setting; high school dropouts who were also ordered into substance abuse treatment; and unemployed offenders who were also ordered into substance abuse treatment.

Rooney and Hanson explain that factors influencing completion rates of batterer intervention programs include youth, not being legally married, low income and little education, unstable work histories, criminal backgrounds, and excessive drinking or drug abuse. Voluntary clients, especially those with college educations, remain in treatment longer. Some researchers, such as Edward W. Gondolf of Indiana University of Pennsylvania in "A Comparison of Four Batterer Intervention Systems: Do Court Referral, Program Length, and Services Matter?" *Journal of Interpersonal Violence*, vol. 14, no. 1, 1999), find better attendance among college-educated men, regardless of whether their enrollment in a program is court ordered or voluntary.

Recidivism Rates

Recidivism (the tendency to relapse to old ingrained patterns of behavior) is a well-documented problem among people in intimate partner violence treatment programs. In "Predictors of Criminal Recidivism among Male Batterers" (*Psychology Crime and Law*, vol. 10, no. 4, December 2004), R. Karl Hanson and Suzanne Wallace-Capretta examine the risk factors associated with the recidivism of

320 male batterers within a five-year follow-up period. Of those men, 25.6% recidivated with a battering offense. Risk factors included being young, having an unstable lifestyle, being a substance abuser, and having a criminal history. Batterers were not deterred by expectations of social or legal negative consequences. However, maintaining positive relationships with community treatment providers was associated with deterrence of future battering. Rodney Kingsnorth of California State University, Sacramento, notes in "Intimate Partner Violence: Predictors of Recidivism in a Sample of Arrestees" (*Violence against Women*, vol. 12, no. 10, October 2006) that risk factors for recidivism during an eighteen-month period included use of a weapon, prior arrests (for domestic violence or other offenses), and the presence of a protective order.

According to Matthew T. Huss and Anthony Ralston of Creighton University, in "Do Batterer Subtypes Actually Matter? Treatment Completion, Treatment Response, and Recidivism across a Batterer Typology" (*Criminal Justice and Behavior*, vol. 35, no. 6, June 2008), men who only expressed violent behaviors in the context of their families were much more likely to complete batterer intervention programs than men who were generally violent or antisocial or who had personality disorders. Because of the higher treatment completion rates, these men were less likely to batter again. However, all men who completed treatment reported reductions in violence toward their partner.

In "The Effects of Domestic Violence Batterer Treatment on Domestic Violence Recidivism" (*Criminal Justice and Behavior*, vol. 30, no. 1, 2003), Jill A. Gordon and Laura J. Moriarty of Virginia Commonwealth University study the effect of batterer treatment on recidivism. The researchers find that attending treatment had no impact on recidivism when comparing the treatment group as a whole with the experimental group. Christopher I. Eckhardt et al., in "Intervention Programs for Perpetrators of Intimate Partner Violence: Conclusions from a Clinical Research Perspective" (*Public Health Reports*, vol. 121, no. 4, July–August 2006), concur in their review of the literature concerning batterer intervention programs and recidivism rates. However, Gordon and Moriarty also find that among the treatment group, the more sessions a batterer completed, the less likely he was to batter again. Batterers who completed all sessions were less likely to be rearrested for domestic violence than were batterers who had not completed all sessions.

Still, as Huss and Ralston note, "even small reductions in rates of domestic violence can have a substantial impact in tens of thousands of women's lives." Therefore, research continues into how to identify batterers who are most likely to benefit from batterer intervention programs.

IMPORTANT NAMES
AND ADDRESSES

ABA Center on Children and the Law
740 Fifteenth St. NW
Washington, DC 20005
(202) 662-1720
1-800-285-2221
URL: http://www.abanet.org/child/

ACLU Women's Rights Project
125 Broad St., Eighteenth Fl.
New York, NY 10004
URL: http://www.aclu.org/womensrights/
index.html

Center for Effective Discipline
155 W. Main St., Ste. 1603
Columbus, OH 43215
(614) 221-8829
FAX: (614) 221-2110
URL: http://www.stophitting.com/

Center for Women Policy Studies
1776 Massachusetts Ave. NW, Ste. 450
Washington, DC 20036
(202) 872-1770
FAX: (202) 296-8962
E-mail: cwps@centerwomenpolicy.org
URL: http://www.centerwomenpolicy.org/

Child Welfare Information Gateway
1250 Maryland Ave. SW, Eighth Fl.
Washington, DC 20024
(703) 385-7565
1-800-394-3366
E-mail: info@childwelfare.gov
URL: http://www.childwelfare.gov/

Child Welfare League of America
2345 Crystal Drive, Ste. 250
Arlington, VA 22202
(703) 412-2400
FAX: (703) 412-2401
URL: http://www.cwla.org/

Children's Defense Fund
25 E St. NW
Washington, DC 20001
(202) 628-8787

1-800-233-1200
E-mail: cdfinfo@childrensdefense.org
URL: http://www.childrensdefense.org/

Crimes against Children Research Center
University of New Hampshire
20 College Rd.
Durham, NH 03824
(603) 862-1888
FAX: (603) 862-1122
URL: http://www.unh.edu/ccrc/

Institute on Violence, Abuse, and Trauma
10065 Old Grove Rd.
San Diego, CA 92131
(858) 527-1860
FAX: (858) 527-1743
URL: http://ivatcenters.org/

International Society for Prevention of Child Abuse and Neglect
245 W. Roosevelt Rd., Bldg. 6, Ste. 39
West Chicago, IL 60185
(630) 876-6913
FAX: (630) 876-6917
E-mail: ispcan@ispcan.org
URL: http://www.ispcan.org/

National Center for Missing and Exploited Children
Charles B. Wang International Children's Building
699 Prince St.
Alexandria, VA 22314-3175
(703) 274-3900
1-800-843-5678
FAX: (703) 274-2200
URL: http://www.missingkids.com/

National Center for the Prosecution of Child Abuse
American Prosecutors Research Institute
44 Canal Center Plaza, Ste. 110
Alexandria, VA 22314
(703) 549-9222
FAX: (703) 836-3195

URL: http://www.ndaa.org/apri/programs/
ncpca/ncpca_home.html

National Center for Victims of Crime
2000 M St. NW, Ste. 480
Washington, DC 20036
(202) 467-8700
FAX: (202) 467-8701
URL: http://www.ncvc.org/

National Clearinghouse for the Defense of Battered Women
125 S. Ninth St., Ste. 302
Philadelphia, PA 19107
(215) 351-0010
1-800-903-0111
URL: http://www.ncdbw.org/

National Coalition against Domestic Violence
1120 Lincoln St., Ste. 1603
Denver, CO 80203
(303) 839-1852
FAX: (303) 831-9251
E-mail: mainoffice@ncadv.org
URL: http://www.ncadv.org/

National Council on Child Abuse and Family Violence
1025 Connecticut Ave. NW, Ste. 1000
Washington, DC 20036
(202) 429-6695
E-mail: info@nccafv.org
URL: http://www.nccafv.org/

National Domestic Violence Hotline
1-800-799-7233
URL: http://www.ndvh.org/

National Runaway Switchboard
3080 N. Lincoln Ave.
Chicago, IL 60657
(773) 880-9860
FAX: (773) 929-5150
1-800-344-2785
URL: http://www.1800runaway.org/

Prevent Child Abuse America
500 N. Michigan Ave., Ste. 200
Chicago, IL 60611-3703
(312) 663-3520
FAX: (312) 939-8962
E-mail: mailbox@preventchildabuse.org
URL: http://www.preventchildabuse.org/

Rape, Abuse, and Incest National Network
2000 L St. NW, Ste. 406
Washington, DC 20036
(202) 544-3064
FAX: (202) 544-3556
E-mail: info@rainn.org
URL: http://www.rainn.org/

Survivors Network of Those Abused by Priests
PO Box 6416
Chicago, IL 60680-6416
(312) 455-1499
1-877-762-7432
E-mail: SNAPdorris@gmail.com
URL: http://www.snapnetwork.org/

RESOURCES

The National Child Abuse and Neglect Data System (NCANDS) of the U.S. Department of Health and Human Services (HHS) is the primary source of national information on child maltreatment known to state child protective services (CPS) agencies. The latest findings from NCANDS are published in *Child Maltreatment 2006* (2008). The most recent national incidence study, the *Third National Incidence Study of Child Abuse and Neglect* (*NIS-3*; Andrea J. Sedlak and Diane D. Broadhurst, 1993), is the single most comprehensive source of information about the incidence of child maltreatment in the United States. *NIS-3* findings are based on data collected not only from CPS but also from community institutions (e.g., day care centers, schools, and hospitals) and investigating agencies (e.g., public health departments, police, and courts).

Other HHS publications used in discussions of child abuse include *The AFGARS Report: Preliminary FY 2006 Estimates as of January 2008* (January 2008), *Children Living with Substance-Abusing or Substance-Dependent Parents* (June 2003), *Results from the 2006 National Survey on Drug Use and Health: National Findings* (September 2007), *Alcohol Dependence or Abuse among Parents with Children Living in the Home* (February 2004), *How Does the Child Welfare System Work?* (April 2006), *Statutory Rape: A Guide to State Laws and Reporting Requirements* (December 2004), *Monitoring the Future: National Results on Adolescent Drug Use, Overview of Key Findings, 2007* (April 2008), and *Major Federal Legislation Concerned with Child Protection, Child Welfare, and Adoption* (February 2008).

Different offices of the U.S. Department of Justice produce publications relating to child maltreatment and domestic violence. The Bureau of Justice Statistics published *Sexual Assault of Young Children as Reported to Law Enforcement: Victim, Incident, and Offender Characteristics* (Howard N. Snyder, July 2000), *Criminal Vic-*

timization in the United States, 2005 Statistical Tables (December 2006), *The Sexual Victimization of College Women* (Bonnie S. Fisher, Francis T. Cullen, and Michael G. Turner, December 2000), *Homicide Trends in the United States* (James Alan Fox and Marianne W. Zawitz, July 2007), *Criminal Victimization, 2006* (Michael Rand and Shannan Catalano, December 2007), *Intimate Partner Violence in the United States* (Shannan Catalano, December 2007), and *Background Checks for Firearm Transfers, 2006 Statistical Tables* (March 2008). The Office for Victims of Crime published the *Children at Clandestine Methamphetamine Labs: Helping Meth's Youngest Victims* (Karen Swetlow, June 2003).

The Federal Bureau of Investigation published *Crime in the United States, 2006* (September 2007). The Violence against Women Grants Office published *Stalking and Domestic Violence: The Third Annual Report to Congress under the Violence against Women Act* (1998). The *Juvenile Justice Bulletin* published "The Decline of Child Sexual Abuse Cases" (Lisa M. Jones and David Finkelhor, 2001) and "Explanations for the Decline in Child Sexual Abuse Cases" (David Finkelhor and Lisa M. Jones, 2004).

"Childhood Victimization: Early Adversity, Later Psychopathology" (Cathy Spatz Widom, January 2000), "Assessing Risk Factors for Intimate Partner Homicide" (Jacquelyn C. Campbell et al., November 2003), and "Prosecutors, Kids, and Domestic Violence Cases" (Debra Whitcomb, March 2002) were all published in the *National Institute of Justice Journal*. The National Institute of Justice also published *An Update on the "Cycle of Violence"* (Cathy S. Widom and Michael G. Maxfield, February 2001), *Extent, Nature, and Consequences of Rape Victimization: Findings from the National Violence against Women Survey* (Patricia Tjaden and Nancy Thoennes, January 2006), *Extent, Nature, and Consequences of Intimate Partner Violence: Findings from the National Violence against Women Survey* (Patricia Tjaden and Nancy Thoennes, July 2000), and *Research in Brief: Violence against Women: Identifying Risk Factors* (November 2004).

Other federal government publications used for this book include *Educator Sexual Misconduct: A Synthesis of Existing Literature* (Charol S. Shakeshaft, 2004) by the U.S. Department of Education; *Child Welfare: HHS Could Play a Greater Role in Helping Child Welfare Agencies Recruit and Retain Staff* (March 2003) and *African American Children in Foster Care: Additional HHS Assistance Needed to Reduce the Proportion in Care* (July 2007) by the U.S. Government Accountability Office; *The Foreign-Born Population in the United States: 2003* (Luke J. Larsen, August 2004) and *Computer and Internet Use in the United States: 2003* (Jennifer Cheeseman Day, Alex Janus, and Jessica Davis, October 2005) by the U.S. Census Bureau; and *U.S. Legal Permanent Residents: 2007* (Kelly Jefferys and Randall Monger, March 2008) by the U.S. Department of Homeland Security. The *Morbidity and Mortality Weekly Report*, published by the Centers for Disease Control and Prevention, published "Youth Risk Behavior Surveillance—United States, 2007" (June 2008).

The Crimes against Children Research Center's *Online Victimization: A Report on the Nation's Youth* (David Finkelhor, Kimberly J. Mitchell, and Janis Wolak, June 2000) discusses the findings of the first Youth Internet Safety Survey. *Teenage Online Victimization of Youth: Five Years Later* (Janis Wolak, Kimberly Mitchell, and David Finkelhor, 2006) finds that online victimization of children actually declined between 2000 and 2005.

A number of studies were conducted on domestic violence when spouse abuse first became a public issue during the 1970s and 1980s. Since that time, however, there has been little government-funded statistical research on domestic abuse. The pioneering work done at the University of New Hampshire's Family Research Laboratory

(FRL) in Durham, New Hampshire, has become an authoritative source of information and insight about family violence. Murray A. Straus, David Finkelhor, Linda Meyer Williams, Kathleen A. Kendall-Tackett, Lisa Jones, Richard K. Ormrod, and many others associated with the laboratory have done some of the most scientifically rigorous research in the field of abuse. Studies released by the FRL investigate all forms of domestic violence, many based on its two major surveys: the National Family Violence Survey (1975) and the National Family Violence Resurvey (1985). Much of the research from these two surveys has been gathered into *Physical Violence in American Families: Risk Factors and Adaptations to Violence in 8,145 Families* (Murray A. Straus and Richard J. Gelles, 1990). Straus is also widely known for his studies on corporal punishment. Several of his journal articles, his book with Denise A. Donnelly *Beating the Devil out of Them: Corporal Punishment in American Families and Its Effects on Children* (2001), and his papers presented at meetings on domestic violence in various countries were helpful in the preparation of this book. Straus and Glenda Kaufman Kantor published data in "Change in Spouse Assault Rates from 1975 to 1992: A Comparison of Three National Surveys in the United States" (1994).

Many journals published useful articles on child maltreatment and domestic violence that were used in the preparation of this book. They include the *Archives of Pediatrics and Adolescent Medicine, Child Abuse and Neglect: The International Journal, Child Maltreatment, Journal of the American Medical Association, Journal of Child Sexual Abuse, Journal of Family Violence, Journal of Interpersonal Violence, Journal of Trauma and Dissociation, Pediatrics, Psychology of Women Quarterly, Violence against Women*, and *Violence and Victims*.

INDEX